Too Little Too Late

Compiled Military Service Records
of the
63rd Alabama Infantry CSA

with

Rosters of Some Companies of
the 89th, 94th and 95th
Alabama Militia CSA

Arthur E. Green

HERITAGE BOOKS
2008

HERITAGE BOOKS
AN IMPRINT OF HERITAGE BOOKS, INC.

Books, CDs, and more—Worldwide

For our listing of thousands of titles see our website
at
www.HeritageBooks.com

Published 2008 by
HERITAGE BOOKS, INC.
Publishing Division
100 Railroad Ave. #104
Westminster, Maryland 21157

Copyright © 2001 Arthur E. Green

Other books by the author:

*Southern Boots and Saddles: The Fifteenth Confederate Cavalry C.S.A.,
First Regiment Alabama and Florida Cavalry, 1863-1865*

Cover illustration courtesy of Paradox Publishing, Inc.
Bay Minette, Alabama

All rights reserved. No part of this book may be reproduced or transmitted in any form or by any means, electronic or mechanical, including photocopying, recording or by any information storage and retrieval system without written permission from the author, except for the inclusion of brief quotations in a review.

International Standard Book Numbers
Paperbound: 978-0-7884-1988-1
Clothbound: 978-0-7884-7224-4

CONTENTS

Introduction 4

History 5

2nd Alabama Reserves/63rd Alabama Infantry Field and Staff 7

Muster Rolls 2nd Alabama Reserves 9

Roster and Service Records Notes 11

Roster and Service Records 2nd Alabama Reserves/
63rd Alabama Infantry Volunteers .... 12—215

89th Alabama Militia 216

94th Alabama Militia, Co. A 222

95th Alabama Militia, Co. D 227

US Hospital Steamer D. A. January 232

Flag of the 2nd Alabama Reserves/63rd Infantry CSA 233

INTRODUCTION

These unsung heros of the War for Southern Independence have largely gone unnoticed and forgotten. They came into the fray late and young but willing. You will find most of these blue-eyed men enlisting at age 17 but some as young as 15 years old. Many could not write their name and signed by a mark "X." Most were from Alabama counties south and east of Jefferson County, led by men such as Captains Charles Martin, John Padgett and Robert Pearson, all age 17. The south had saved the last of their young men and finally in desperation they were to be used up also. They enlisted as Home Guard, Provost Guard and Reserves, and their time "to see the elephant" came at Fort Blakeley, Alabama, in April of 1865. They found themselves in the thick of war - outnumbered, poorly trained, poorly equipped, unpaid, inexperienced; but they mustered to the unrealistic status of regular infantry soldiers. The siege with its thunder of powder and smoke must have first seemed nervously grand then terribly frightening to the young men. They were pitted against the determined and well equipped 13th and 16th United States Army Corps. The enemy came and came and came. The youngsters were captured almost to the man on April 9, 1865, and sent as prisoners to the remote Ship Island near Biloxi, Mississippi. Finally the young men were released to return to their conquered homes and families in May of that final war year. This is their story and their records of participation in the Southern Saga. Too little too late. Oh the stories they could and do tell.

The 2nd Regiment Alabama Reserves was organized in August 1864, and its designation appears to have been changed between March and May 1865 to the 63rd Alabama Infantry. Their records were taken from U.S. National Archives Microfilm Record Group 109, M311, rolls 480, 481, 482 and 483.

The surrender of forces at Citronelle on May 4, 1865, was an official ceremony carried out between C.S.A. Lt. General Richard Taylor and U.S. Major General E. R. S. Canby and their respective staffs. The men of the 63rd Alabama Infantry were not in attendance.

HISTORY

A portion of the history of the Regiment can be learned from the muster rolls; the remainder must come from accounts of the Battle of Fort Blakeley in the Official Register and a few newspaper accounts. The 2nd Alabama Reserve Regiment was created on August 6, 1864, under the strain of war from reserve companies. You will see in the roster that a number of men mustered in at Blakeley, Alabama, in summer and fall of 1864. The regimental designation was changed to the 63rd Alabama Infantry Volunteers in the spring of 1865. The exact date is lost in the turmoil of the war's ending. Most of the men of the 2nd Reserves/63rd Infantry were young and members of home guards, provost guards or exempts. They mustered in at Montgomery, Camp Watts near Notasulga, and other locations, even Blakeley. A few men were stationed near the mouth of Dog River, south of Mobile, while a few others were among troops manning batteries in Mobile. They had been assigned to Fuller's (Thomas's) Brigade, Major General Dabny H. Maury's Corps, Eastern Division, District of the Gulf, CSA Army. Brigadier General St. John R. Liddell was commander of headquarters at Fort Blakeley. Lt. General Richard Taylor was commander of the Department of Alabama, Mississippi and East Louisiana. In March 1865, Maury had only about 9,000 men in his District of the Gulf.

Blakeley is located in hilly country that falls off to the west to the bank of Tensaw River a few miles north of its junction with the Blakeley River. Blakeley is only about 5½ miles north of Mobile Bay, and five miles north of the high bluffs at Spanish Fort, Alabama. The town was incorporated in 1814 and the area was influenced by French, Spanish and British cultures that preceded the coming Americans. In 1820 it was a thriving town that rivaled Mobile in size and development and was, for a time, county seat of Mobile County. It had a newspaper, schools, a courthouse and was a hub of trade on the eastern shore of the bay. The war and the end of riverboat transportation caused Blakeley to wither and die by the early 1900's. The plague of yellow fever did its damage to the population as well. Today Blakeley is one of several ghost towns of the south with only a graveyard, moss-covered oaks, remnants of fortifications and a battlefield park to welcome visitors. Streets are yet marked with modern signs, the courthouse days are attested to by the still-standing oak hanging tree, and the town's river landing is still discernable.

During the war Blakeley, like Spanish Fort, was manned, fortified and entrenched in preparation for the coming inevitable invasion. The threat to Mobile was expected to come from the west or from the Bay and only late was a serious eastern campaign prepared for. Mobile Bay fell to United States Admiral David Farragut and the Naval forces at his command in August of 1864. This strategic move allowed Federal troops to mass unmolested in sufficient numbers to move against central Alabama and Mobile. Military forces, commanded by Major General Edward R. S. Canby, moved about 26,000 men into the area for an attempt from the east. Forces were moved from Pensacola, Dauphin Island, Fort Morgan and others were landed near Weeks Bay on the eastern shore of Mobile Bay, south of Spanish Fort. By the spring of 1865, portions of the US Army 13th and 16th Corps consolidated at Danley's Mills on Fish River in Alabama. They broke camp on March 25, 1865, and proceeded north to Deer Park. A few skirmishes ensued on the 26th as they made their way through Sibley's Mills on Rock Creek and continued north to Spanish Fort. Meanwhile, Major General Frederick Steele's men were moving north and west from Pensacola.

Spanish Fort was fully invested on March 31, as well as the works at Blakeley. Fighting continued until April 8, 1865. After days of bombardment from sea and land, the Confederates abandoned the Spanish Fort works on the night of April 8. Some 700 prisoners and about 46 pieces of artillery are reported having been captured. The U. S. Military Headquarters then moved northward to near Blakeley early on the 9th. At about 5 P.M. a general assault was made, and the Confederate works were carried. Brigadier General John P. Hawkins' 1st Division U. S. Colored Troops was on the extreme right;

Brigadier General Christopher C. Andrews' 2nd Division of the 13th Corps (of Major General Frederick Steele's command) was in the right center; Brigadier General James C. Veach, 1st Division 8th Corps, was in the left center; and Brigadier General Kenner Garrad's 2nd Division, 16th Corps brought up the left. Prisoners taken numbered about 3,700 men and included the Confederate Brigadier Generals St. John R. Liddell and Bryan M. Thomas, Division Commander Brigadier General Francis M. Cockrell and fifty-six pieces of ordnance. The young men of the 63rd Alabama Infantry were in this number. Thus ended the last major confrontation of the war. Federal Major General James H. Wilson's Cavalry raid through central Alabama destroying the Arsenal and Naval facilities at Selma rendered unnecessary the need for Canby to advance farther north.

2nd Alabama Reserves
Filed with 63rd Alabama Infantry
FIELD AND STAFF

2nd Regiment Alabama Reserves, Fuller's Brigade, Maury's Corps, District of the Gulf, CSA Army was organized on August 16, 1864.

Rice, O. F., Colonel
Law, J. A., Lt. Colonel
Echols, John H., Major

Gibbs, J. H., Surgeon
Dobey, J. M., Assistant Surgeon
Zimmerman, Eugene, Ensign
Calhoun, Thomas J., A. Quartermaster
Allen, Lewis D. Adjutant
McSwain, S. T., Assistant Surgeon

Company A
Formerly Echols' Co. Alabama Vols. L.D. & S.S.

Echols, John H., Captain/Major
Armstrong, James, Captain
Zimmerman, W. C., 2nd Lt./Captain Co. B
Kyle, William D., 2nd Lt.
Reid, Boling, 1st Lt.
Owens, Joseph L. P., 2nd Lt.

Company B

Zimmerman, William C., Captain
Calhoun, Thomas, J., 1st Lt./ A.Q.M.
Towndsend, Charles A., 2nd Lt.
Thornton, Allen J., 2nd Lt.
Note 11 men of this Co. transferred to Co. K on October 2, 1864.

Company C

Rogers, Williamson, Captain
Martin, Charles W., Lt./Captain
Lancaster, John M., 2nd Lt.
Chalmers, William E., 2nd Lt.
Alexander, E. S. or S. E., Lt.

Company D

Zorn, D. H., Captain
Pearson, Robert H., 1st Lt.
Johnson, H. P., 2nd Lt.
Bush, A. B., 2nd Lt.
Lane, L. M., 2nd Lt.

Company E

Lee, A. V., Captain
Barton, J. K., Lt.
Turner, L. W., 2nd Lt.
Faulk, M. A., 2nd Lt.
Baetena, Henry C., 2nd Lt.
Jones, W. E., 2nd Lt.

Company F

Brown, J. W., Captain
Edgar, A. A., 1st Lt.
Kennedy, R. J., 2nd Lt.
Donald, William, 2nd Lt.
Simpson, R. T., 1st Corp.

Company G

Padgett, John A. C., Captain
Johnson, Robert S., 1st Lt.
Carter, J. P. 2nd Lt.
Beck, J. J., 2nd Lt.
Garland, S., 1st Corp.
Pruett. S., 2nd Corp.
Robinson, Benjamin, 1st Corp.
McRobinson, B., 1st Corp.

Company H

Suttle, J. N., Captain
Johnston, E. L., 1st Lt.
Killough, R. L., 2nd Lt.
Davis, W. A., 2nd Lt.

Company I

Fulton, William B., Captain
Smith, A. J., 1st. Lt.
Hartley, J. K., 2nd Lt.
Oliver, C. C., 2nd Lt.

"This company was originated September 17, 1864, and is composed principally of men who were transferred from the 3rd Regiment Alabama Reserves in various Companies."

Company K

May, M. H., Captain
Hamner, W. J., 1st Lt.
Skinner, W. A., 2nd Lt.
Battle, R. R., 2nd Lt.

"11 men transferred to this from Co. B - S.O. 15 Regimental Headquarters October 2, 1864, 3 from Co. D September 28, 1864."

MUSTER ROLLS 2ND ALABAMA RESERVES/63rd ALABAMA INFANTRY CSA

Some of the following data cards refer to a muster roll. These microfilm files do not contain the actual Muster Rolls.

Field and Staff 2nd Regiment Reserves, Alabama (63rd Alabama Infantry) for July and August 1864, shows station of Field and Staff at Camp Hood near Blakeley, Alabama.

Field and Staff 2nd Regiment Reserves, Alabama (63rd Alabama Infantry) for September and October 1864, reports station of Field and Staff near Mobile, Alabama.

Company A, 2nd Regiment Alabama Reserves, (63rd Alabama Infantry) formerly Captain Echols' Company of Home Guards, Alabama Volunteers was mustered into service for the war on January 1, 1864, by Major Walter Jones Mustering Officer at Montgomery, Alabama. Muster roll for January and February 1864, at Montgomery, Alabama, States; "This Company is composed from exempts and its organization was approved by the Adjutant and Inspector General." Company A was also known as Captain John H. Echols's Company of Provost Guards before being attached to the 63rd Alabama.

Muster Roll for Company A, 2nd Alabama Regiment Alabama Reserves, (63rd Alabama Infantry) for September and October 1864, reports their location at Mouth of Dog River, Alabama. [on western shore of Mobile Bay south of Mobile, Alabama.]

Company B, 2nd Alabama Regiment Alabama Reserves, (63rd Alabama Infantry) formerly Captain Zimmerman's Company of Alabama Volunteers was mustered into service for the war on January 1, 1864, by Major B. M. Thomas Mustering Officer at Montgomery, Alabama, on March 23, 1864.

Muster Roll for Company B, 2nd Alabama Regiment Alabama Reserves, (63rd Alabama Infantry) for September and October 1864, reports their location at Mouth of Dog River, Alabama, eight miles below Mobile. [on western shore of Mobile Bay south of Mobile, Alabama.]

Company C, 2nd Alabama Regiment Alabama Reserves, (63rd Alabama Infantry) Captain Williamson Rogers Company of Reserves, CSA was organized under General Orders No. 33a, 1864, A. I. G. O. Richmond, Virginia Major and Inspecting and Mustering Officer E. S. Ready, at Camp Watts near Notasulga, Alabama, on June 24, 1864, attest to the fact that each member of the company has satisfactorily proven his age to be between 17 and 18 and no person that has been exempted from Confederate Service has been mustered into service except by special permission from Bureau of Conscription as noted. Company C, 63rd Alabama Infantry was initially known as Captain Rogers Company of Alabama Reserves.

Muster Roll for Company C, 2nd Alabama Regiment Alabama Reserves, (63rd Alabama Infantry) for September and October 1864, reports their location as near Mobile, Alabama.

Company D, 2nd Alabama Regiment Alabama Reserves, (63rd Alabama Infantry) Captain Zorn's Company of Reserves, CSA was organized under General Orders No. 33a, 1864, A. I. G. O. Richmond, Virginia, Major and Inspecting and Mustering Officer E. S. Ready, at Camp Watts near Notasulga, Alabama, on July 30, 1864, attest to the fact that each member of the company has satisfactorily proven his age to be between 17 and 18 and no person that has been exempted from Confederate Service has been mustered into service except by special permission from Bureau of Conscription as noted. Captain Zorn's Company of Alabama Reserves subsequently became Co. D or 2nd Regiment Alabama Reserves.

Muster Roll for Company D, 2nd Alabama Regiment Alabama Reserves, (63rd Alabama Infantry) for August 30 to October 30, 1864, reports their location as near Mobile, Alabama.

Muster Roll for Company E, 2nd Alabama Regiment Alabama Reserves, (63rd Alabama Infantry) for September and October 1864, reports their location as near Mobile, Alabama.

Company F, 2nd Alabama Regiment Alabama Reserves, (63rd Alabama Infantry) formerly Captain Brown's Company of Reserves, CSA was organized under General Orders No. 33a, 1864, A. I. G. O. Richmond, Virginia Major and Inspecting and Mustering Officer John S. Barton at Georgiana, Alabama, on July 25, 1864, attest to the fact that each member of the company has satisfactorily proven his age to be between 17 and 18 and no person that has been exempted from Confederate Service has been mustered into service except by special permission from Bureau of Conscription as noted.

Muster Roll for Company F, 2nd Alabama Regiment Alabama Reserves, (63rd Alabama Infantry) for August 31 to October 31, 1864, reports the Company has changed their station from Blakeley to Battery (H) Mobile, Alabama, on October 10, 1864.

Company G, 2nd Alabama Regiment Alabama Reserves, (63rd Alabama Infantry) Captain Padget's Company of Reserves, CSA was organized under General Orders No. 33a, 1864, A. I. G. O. Richmond, Virginia, Major and Inspecting and Mustering Officer Wm. T. McNeill, 1st Lt. attest to the fact that each member of the company has satisfactorily proven his age to be between 17 and 18 and no person that has been exempted from Confederate Service has been mustered into service except by special permission from Bureau of Conscription as noted.

Muster Roll for Company G, 2nd Alabama Regiment Alabama Reserves, (63rd Alabama Infantry) for September and October 1864, reports their location at Camp near Mobile, Alabama.

Muster Roll for Company H, 2nd Alabama Regiment Alabama Reserves, (63rd Alabama Infantry) for September and October 1864, reports their station near Mobile, Alabama.

Muster Roll for Company I, 2nd Alabama Regiment Alabama Reserves, (63rd Alabama Infantry) for September and October 1864, reports the Company has changed station from Blakeley to Mobile, Alabama, on October 10, 1864.

Muster Roll for Company K, 2nd Alabama Regiment Alabama Reserves, (63rd Alabama Infantry) for September and October, 1864, reports their station near Mobile, Alabama.

ROSTER NOTES

These Military Service Records are abstracted from U.S. National Archives Microfilm Record Group 109, file M311, rolls 480, 481, 482 and 483. While the transcriber has made a serious effort to record all major events in the soldiers service, I do not suggest that all data available from these records are shown here. I highly suggest that individual files be researched for a complete record and to view paperwork that may be in the files. I have only added obvious omissions of the state name and the year where clerks had left them blank. You are urged to check all possible name spellings as the records are hand written and difficult to read. There are instances where company clerks misspelled the names and some soldiers could not write hence their names were spelled phonically. Individual men's service records are available for a copying and handling fee from the Nation Archives in Washington, D. C.

The 2nd Regiment Alabama Reserves was organized in August 1864, and its designation appears to have been changed sometime between March and May 1865, to the 63rd Regiment Alabama Infantry. M. S. 1193517.

Many of these men were shown as having been surrendered by Lt. General Richard Taylor CSA to Major General E. R. S. Canby USA at Citronelle, Alabama, on May 4, 1865. This was a formal surrender by commanders and the men were not present at Citronelle at the time. They probably were not at the parole site listed as Meridian, Mississippi, either. Many of those men reported as Confederate POW's transferred from Ship Island, Mississippi, to Vicksburg, Mississippi, on May 1, 1865, appear on a duplicate partial list or roll of exchanged prisoners at Headquarters of Exchange of Prisoners, Camp Townsend on May 6, 1865. It is signed by H. A. M. Henderson, Lt. Col. & Assistant Commissioner of Exchange CSA.

Surveying the individual records you will note that on September 18, 1864, one day after Company I was created a number of the young men were shown absent without leave. Many of the AWOL were men from Wedowee, Alabama.

It is an interesting puzzle that several men have a reference card in their files to see the personal papers of James M. Alexander - Alabama.

[The transcribers notes are indicated in brackets thus.]

God bless America and God bless these southern boys who fought for southern soil. They only wanted the best as they saw it for their homeland and were willing to give their all to protect it.

ROSTER
and Service Records of
63RD ALABAMA INFANTRY VOLUNTEERS CSA ARMY

Adams, A. B., Pvt. Co. F. (Captain Brown's Co. of Alabama Reserves)
Enlisted on March 9, 1864, at Greenville, Alabama, by Captain Brown for the war. Mustered in at Georgiana, Alabama, on July 25, 1864. Age—17, eyes—dark, hair—dark, complexion—dark, 5 foot 8 ½ inches. Appears on a muster roll for the period August 31 to October 31, 1864. Here his file shows he had never been paid and deserted October 27, 1864. Captured at Blakeley, Alabama, on April 9, 1865. Appears on a roll of POW's received at Ship Island, Mississippi, on April 15, 1865. Appears on a roll of POW's transferred from Ship Island to Vicksburg, Mississippi, on May 1, 1865. Appears on a duplicate roll of POW's of exchanged prisoners received on Parole May 6, 1865 by H. A. M. Henderson, Lt. Colonel CSA. Appears on a roll of POW's of Company F, 63rd Alabama Infantry CSA commanded by Captain R. T. Simpson surrendered at Citronelle, Alabama, by Lt. General R. T. Taylor CSA to Major General E. R. S. Canby USA on May 4, 1865, and paroled at Meridian, Mississippi, on May 11, 1865. File show W. B. Adams of the 63rd Alabama residence—Butler County, Alabama.

Adams, Nurburson (Newton A. Adams), Pvt. Co. C.
Enlisted May 22, 1864, at Coffee County by Captain Payne for the war. Mustered in June 24, 1864, at Camp Watts near Notasulga, Alabama. Residence—Old Town, Alabama. Company muster roll for September and October 1864, shows N. Adams of Company C, deserted while on guard September 1, 1864, at Blakeley, Alabama. N. Adams, Co. A, appears on a roll of POW's who were received at Ship Island, Mississippi, on April 15, 1865, and was transferred to Vicksburg, Mississippi, on May 1, 1865. Newton Adams, Pvt. Co. C, appears on a roll of POW's surrendered by Lt. General Robert Taylor to Major General Canby at Citronelle, Alabama, on May 4, 1865, and paroled at Meridian, Mississippi, on May 11, 1865. In 1914 the Alabama Soldiers Home states that he is not found on any rolls of their organization and no POW record found. N. Adams (also born as Nurburson Adams) Pvt. enlisted May 22, 1864, in Coffee County, Alabama. Age—17, residence—Coffee County, Alabama. Roll last on file shows him deserted while on guard September 1, 1864, at Blakeley, Alabama. POW record shows N. Adams, Co. A, 63rd Regiment Alabama Infantry, captured at Blakeley, Alabama, on April 9, 1865. Transferred from Ship Island, Mississippi, to Vicksburg, Mississippi on May 1, 1865. Newton Adams, Pvt. Co. C, 63rd Regiment Alabama Infantry CSA surrendered at Citronelle, Alabama, by Lt. General Taylor on May 4, 1865, and paroled at Meridian, Mississippi, on May 11, 1865. Residence—Chambers County, Alabama. Rolls of C and E Companies indicate that Nurburnson and N. Adams were one and the same but do not appear to refer to Newton Adams. No additional record was found for Newton Adams in Confederate Archive in 1914. Newton Adams residence was shown as Chambers County, Alabama.

Adams, Zachariah, Pvt. Co. B.
Enlisted at Pollard, Alabama, on August 15, 1864 by Lieutenant Townsend for the war. Appears absent on a muster roll for September and October, 1864, with pay due since enlistment. Absent sick since October 17, 1864. Drew clothing September 11, 1864. POW captured at Blakeley, Alabama, on April 9, 1865, received at Ship Island, Mississippi, on April 15, 1865. Transferred from Ship Island to Vicksburg, Mississippi, on May 1, 1865. Appears on a roll of POWs surrendered at Citronelle, Alabama, by Lt. General Robert Taylor to Major General Canby on May 4, 1865, and paroled at Meridian, Mississippi, on May 11, 1865. Residence—Dale County, Alabama.

Adcock, Anderson E., Pvt. Co. A. (Captain Echols' Co. of Provost Guards, Alabama Volunteers)
Enlisted at Tallapoosa County, Alabama, on January 1, 1865. Mustered in at Montgomery, Alabama, on January 1, 1864, by John H. Echols for the war. Appears present on a muster roll for January and February 1864, with pay due from time of enlistment. Drew clothing in 2nd quarter of 1864. Appears present sick in quarters on a muster roll for September and October 1864. Here he is shown as have been last paid February 29, 1864. Appears on a record of POW's at headquarters of 16th US Army Corps, Montgomery, Alabama, during the month of May 1865. Signed a parole at Montgomery, Alabama, on May 18, 1865. Hair—dark, 5 foot 4 inches, eyes—hazel, complexion—fair. Alabama Pension Commission paper work is in his file dated June 12, 1916.

Adcock, Young F., Pvt. Co. A. (Captain Echols' Company of Provost Guards, Alabama Volunteers)
Enlisted at Coosa, County, Alabama, on January 1, 1864, by Captain J. H. Echols for the war. Mustered in at Montgomery, Alabama, on January 1, 1864. Appears present on a muster roll for January and February 1864, with pay due from time of enlistment. Drew clothing in 2nd Quarter 1864. Appears present on a muster roll for September and October 1864. Here he is shown as having been last paid February 29, 1864. Appears on a roll of POWs commanded by Lieutenant W. D. Kyle, that were surrendered at Citronelle, Alabama, by Lt. General Robert Taylor CSA to Major General Canby USA on May 4, 1865. Paroled at Meridian, Mississippi, on May 11, 1865. Residence—Coosa County, Alabama.

Addesholt. M., Pvt. Co. H.
(Aderholt)
Enlisted March 16, 1864, at Springville, Alabama, by Lieutenant Killough for the war. Appears present on a muster roll for September and October, 1864, Age—17, eyes—dark, hair—dark, complexion—dark. Drew clothing on September 11, 1864. Signed M. Aderholt. POW captured at Blakeley, Alabama, on April 9, 1865. Appears on a roll of POW's received at Ship Island, Mississippi, on April 15, 1865. Transferred to Vicksburg, Mississippi, on May 1, 1865. Appears on a Roll of POW's of Company C and H, 63rd Alabama Infantry CSA commanded by Captain C. W. Martin, surrendered at Citronelle, Alabama, by Lt. General Robert Taylor to Major General Canby USA on May 4, 1865. Paroled at Meridian, Mississippi, on May 11, 1865. Residence—St. Clair County, Alabama.

Addington, W., Pvt. Co. K.
Enlisted July 30, 1864, at Carrolton, Alabama, by Lieutenant Robinson for the war. Appears present on a muster roll for September and October 1864. POW captured at Blakeley, Alabama, on April 9, 1865. Appears on a roll of POWs received at Ship Island, Mississippi, on April 15, 1865. Transferred to Vicksburg, Mississippi, on May 1, 1865. Appears on a Roll of POW's of Cos. I and K 63rd Regiment Alabama Infantry commanded by Lieutenant W. A. Skinner, Co. K, surrendered at Citronelle, Alabama, by Lt. General Robert Taylor CSA to Major General Canby USA on May 4, 1865. Paroled at Meridian, Mississippi, on May 11, 1865. Residence—Pickens County, Alabama.

Adduck, T. F., Pvt. Co. B.
POW captured at Blakeley, Alabama, on April 9, 1865. He appears on a roll of POW's received at Ship Island, Mississippi, on April 15, 1865. Transferred to Vicksburg, Mississippi, on May 1, 1865.

Alexander, Columbus A., Pvt. Co. A. (Captain Echols' Company of Provost Guards, Alabama Volunteers.)
Enlisted January 1, 1864, at Montgomery, Alabama, by Captain John H. Echols

for the war. Mustered in at Montgomery, Alabama, on January 1, 1864, Age—16. Appears present on a muster roll for January and February 1864, with pay due from enlistment. Drew clothing in 2nd quarter of 1864. Appears absent on muster roll for September and October 1864. Absent detached as Orderly from General Withers on July 1, 1864. Here he is shown as having last been paid February 29, 1864. His file contains a card from War Department to Alabama Pension Commission dated February 1, 1922, containing his service data.

Alexander, E. S., 1st Lieutenant Co. C.
Enlisted September 20, 1864, at Baldwin County, Alabama, by Colonel Rice for the war. Appears absent on a company muster roll for September and October, 1864, with pay due from time of enlistment. Absent in hospital in Mobile, October 28, 1864. Elected 1st Lieutenant of Company C, 2nd Regiment Alabama Reserves, Fuller's Brigade, Maury's Corps, District of the Gulf. POW captured at Blakeley, Alabama, on April 9, 1865. Appears on a roll of POW's received at Ship Island, Mississippi on April 16, 1865, transferred to Vicksburg, Miss. on April 28, 1865. Appears on a register of POW's at New Orleans, Louisiana, that were confined April 30, 1865, from Ship Island on April 28, 1865. Exchanged May 1, 1865. Appears on a roll of divers companies and regiments (detached) of the CSA commanded by Lt. Colonel R. H. Lindsay that were surrendered at Citronelle, Alabama, by Lt. General Robert Taylor CSA to Major General Canby USA on May 4, 1865, and paroled at Meridian, Mississippi, on May 12, 1865. Signed a Parole of Honor at Meridian on May 11, 1865.

Alexander, J., Pvt. Co. F.
Enlisted August 4, 1864, at Georgiana, Alabama, by Captain Brown for the war. Appears absent on a muster roll for August 31 to October 31, 1864. Here he is reported absent on 60 days sick furlough from September 23, 1864, with pay due from time of enlistment.

Alexander, William, 2nd Sergeant/Pvt. Co. I.
Appears present on a company muster roll for September and October, 1864. POW captured at Blakeley, Alabama, on April 9, 1865. Appears on a roll of POW's received at Ship Island, Mississippi, on April 15, 1865. Transferred to Vicksburg, Mississippi on May 1, 1865. Appears on a Roll of POW's of Company I and K 63rd Regiment Alabama Infantry commanded by Lieutenant W. A. Skinner, Co. K, that were surrendered at Citronelle, Alabama, by Lt. General Robert Taylor CSA to Major General Canby USA at Citronelle, on May 4, 1865. Paroled at Meridian, Mississippi, on May 13, 1865. Residence—Pickens County, Alabama.

Allen, Green, Pvt. Co. B. (Captain Zimmerman's Co. of Alabama Volunteers)
Enlisted March 23, 1864, at Montgomery, Alabama, by Captain W. C. Zimmerman for the war, Age—17. Mustered in March 23, 1864, at Montgomery. Drew clothing July 8, 1864. Appears absent on a company muster roll for September and October, 1864. Absent sick since September 8, 1864. POW captured at Blakeley, Alabama, on April 9, 1865. Appears on a roll of POW's received at Ship Island, Mississippi, on April 15, 1865, transferred to Vicksburg, Mississippi, on May 1, 1865. Appears on a register of sick and wounded POW's at USA General Hospital No. 2, Vicksburg. Admitted May 3, 1865, from steamer with acute diarrhoea. Age—18. Died May 13, 1865.

Allen, Lewis D., 1st Lieutenant and Adjutant F&S
Appears present on a muster roll for July and August, 1864, near Blakeley, Alabama. Commissioned or appointed August 25, 1864. Appears present on a muster roll for September and October, 1864, near Mobile, Alabama. Appears on a roster of 2nd Regiment Alabama Reserves, Fuller's Brigade, Maury's Corps,

District of the Gulf organized August 16, 1864. Recommended for appointment by Colonel Rice to War Department. Appointment to date from August 24, 1864. Signed a Parole of Honor at Meridian, Mississippi, on May 11, 1865.

Allen, Robert M., Corporal Co. D.
Enlisted June 30, 1864, at Russell County, Alabama, by Lieutenant Carnes for the war. Residence—Seales Station, Alabama, Age—17, eyes—grey, hair—dark, complexion—dark, 5 foot 7 inches. Mustered in on July 30, 1864, at Camp Watts near Notasulga, Alabama. Appears absent on a muster roll for August 30, to October 30, 1864. Absent sick at Mobile, Alabama, hospital since October 26, with pay due from enlistment. Here he is shown as having enlisted at Notasulga, Alabama, by Major Ready on July 10, 1864, for the war. Drew clothing August 7, 1864.

Allen, W. S., Pvt./Sergeant Co. I.
Appears on a roll of POW's received at Ship Island, Mississippi, on April 15, 1865. Captured at Blakeley, Alabama, April 9, 1865. Transferred from Ship Island to Vicksburg, Mississippi, on May 1, 1865. Appears on a roll of POW's of Cos. I and K, 63rd Alabama Regiment commanded by Lieutenant W. A. Skinner of Company K surrendered at Citronelle, Alabama, by Lt. General Robert Taylor CSA to Major General Canby USA at Citronelle, on May 4, 1865. Paroled at Meridian, Mississippi, on May 13, 1865. Drew clothing at Fair Grounds Hospital No. 1 on March 17, 1864. Signed W. S. Allen.

Allender, T. A., Pvt. Co. H.
Enlisted July 23, 1864 at Selma, Alabama, by Captain Suttle for the war. Age—17, eyes—dark, hair—dark, complexion—dark. Appears present on a muster roll for September and October, 1864. Appears on a register of Ross Hospital, Mobile, Alabama, admitted September 16, 1864, with acute diarrhoea and febris intermittes. Returned to duty September 25, 1864. Appears on a roll of POW's of Cos. C and H, 63rd Alabama Regiment commanded by Captain C. W. Martin that were surrendered at Citronelle, Alabama, by Lt. General Robert Taylor CSA to Major General Canby USA on May 4, 1865. Paroled at Meridian, Mississippi, on May 11, 1865. Residence—Jefferson County, Alabama.

Alston, Thomas J., Pvt. Co. D. (Captain Zorn's Co. of Alabama Reserves)
Enlisted July 30, 1864, at Macon County, Alabama, by Major Ready for the war. Residence—Barbour County, Alabama, age—17, eyes—grey, hair—dark, complexion—dark, 5 foot 3 inches, Post Office—Eufaula, Alabama. Appears on a muster-in roll for July 20 to July 30, 1864, at Camp Watts near Notasulga, Alabama. Drew clothing September 12, 1864. Discharge on a Surgeon's Certificate of Disability on October 4, 1864, at Camp Hood near Blakeley, Alabama, due to physical disability. Discharge Certificate is in his file. Occupation reported to be a farmer when he enlisted.

Amerson, N. J., Pvt. Co. I.
Enlisted April 15, 1864, at Wedowee, Alabama, by Captain Robinson, for the war. Appears absent on a company muster roll for September and October, 1864. Absent on 30 day furlough from September 27, 1864.

Ames, B. M., Pvt. Co. C.
Appears on a register of paroled Confederate Soldiers for the month of June, 1865. Paroled by Major Ross Wilkerson A. D. C. and Provost Marshal, 16th US Army Corps. He was reported to have been paroled June 22, 1865. [Individual paroles of the men on this register show them paroled at Montgomery, Alabama.]

Anderson, Charles, S., Pvt. Co. D. (Captain Zorn's Co. of Alabama Reserves)
Enlisted at Macon, County, Alabama, on July 30, 1864, by Major Ready for the war. Residence—Clayton, Barbour County, Alabama, age—17, eyes—dark, hair—light, complexion—fair, 5 foot 5 inches. Appears on a muster roll for July 20 to July 30, 1864, at Camp Watts near Notasulga, Alabama. Drew clothing August 7, 1864. Appears present on a muster roll for August 31 to October 31, 1864, with pay due from time of enlistment. Here he is shown as having enlisted at Clayton, Alabama, by D. M. Seales.

Anderson, C. K., Pvt. Co. E.
Enlisted July 27, 1864, at Montgomery, Alabama, by Captain A. V. Lee for the war. Age—17, eyes—blue, hair—light, complexion—fair. Appears absent on a muster roll for September and October, 1864. Absent furloughed 30 days from October 3, 1864. POW captured at Blakeley, Alabama, on April 9, 1865. Appears on a list of POW's in camp near Spanish Fort, Alabama, requiring hospital treatment. List is dated April 12, 1865, at the headquarters of 23rd Iowa Infantry Volunteers US Army near Spanish Fort, Alabama. Disease—pneumonia. Appears on a roll of POW's received at Ship Island, Mississippi, on April 15, 1865, transferred to Vicksburg, Mississippi, May 1, 1865. Appears on a roll of POW's of Cos. E and G, 63rd, Alabama Regiment commanded by Captain A. V. Lee that were surrendered at Citronelle, Alabama, by Lt. General Robert Taylor CSA to Major General Canby, USA on May 4, 1865, and paroled at Meridian, Mississippi, on May 13, 1865.

Anderson, J. M., Pvt. Co. C.
Appears on a roll of Confederate Soldiers paroled at Headquarters of 16th US Army Corps, Montgomery, Alabama, on May 26, 1665. Signed, by mark "X", a parole of honor at Montgomery, Alabama. Hair—grey, 5 foot 9 inches, eyes—dark, complexion—dark.

Anderson, J., Pvt. Co. F.
POW captured at Blakeley, Alabama, on April 9, 1865. Appears on a roll of POW's received at Ship Island, Mississippi, April 15, 1865. Transferred to Vicksburg, Mississippi on May 1, 1865. Appears on a roll of POW's of Company F, 63rd, Alabama Regiment commanded by Captain R. T. Simpson, that were surrendered at Citronelle, Alabama, by Lt. General Robert Taylor CSA to Major General Canby USA on May 4, 1865, and paroled at Meridian, Mississippi, on May 11, 1865. There is, in his file, a communication to the Commandant of Confederate Soldiers Home at Mountain Creek, Alabama, on October 9, 1915. The communication indicates the J. Anderson was not found on the muster in rolls of Company F, 63rd Alabama Infantry but that he appears on union records of POWs. [see above]

Andrews, John, Pvt. Co. H.
Enlisted March 16, 1864, at Montevallo, Alabama, by Lieutenant Johnston for the war. Age—16, eyes—grey, hair—light, complexion—fair. Appears present on a muster roll for September and October, 1864. Drew clothing on September 11, 1864. Admitted to Ross Hospital, Mobile, Alabama, March 30, 1865, with vulnus sclopeticum (gunshot wound). Sent to General Hospital on April 9, 1865, remarks—Meridian. Appears on a roll of POW stragglers paroled at Selma, Alabama, during the month of June 1865, by William R. Marshall, Colonel 7 Minn. Vols. Commanding Post.

Andrews, Joseph, E., Pvt. Co. A. (Captain Echols' Company of Provost Guards, Alabama Volunteers)
Enrolled January 1, 1864, at Chambers County, Alabama, by Captain John H. Echols, for the war. Appears on a muster roll at Montgomery, Alabama, dated

January 1, 1864, Age—17. Appears present on a muster roll for January and February, 1864, with pay due from time of enlistment. Drew clothing 2nd Quarter of 1864. Appears absent on a muster roll for September and October, 1864. Absent sick in hospital in Mobile, Alabama, since October 8, 1864, last paid February 29, 1864. Admitted to Ross Hospital, Mobile, Alabama, on September 18, 1864, with febris remittens. Reported to have been furloughed for 30 days on October 8, 1864.

Anthony, J. E., Sergeant/Pvt. Co. K.
Enlisted August 6, 1864, at Russell County, Alabama, by Lieutenant Sledge for the war. Appears on a muster roll for September and October, 1864, reported present, reduced to 2nd Sergeant on October 24. Appears on a roll of POW's of Cos. I and K, 63rd, Alabama Regiment commanded by Lieutenant W. A. Skinner, surrendered at Citronelle, Alabama, by Lt. General Robert Taylor CSA to Major General Canby, USA on May 4, 1865, and paroled at Meridian, Mississippi, on May 13, 1865.

Anthony, John, Pvt. Co. A.
Enlisted August 15, 1864, at Tallapoosa, Alabama, by Captain Echols for the war. Appears present sick in quarters on a muster roll for September and October 1864, with pay due from enlistment. Drew clothing on September 11, 1864. Signed by mark "X." Appears on a record of Confederate Solders paroled at headquarters, 16th US Army Corps, Montgomery, Alabama, May 24, 1865. Signed an Oath not to bear arms against the USA, on May 26, 1865. Hair—red, 5 foot 4 inches, eyes—blue, complexion—fair. Signed by his mark "X." This document is in his file.

Appling, J. O., Pvt. Co. E.
Enlisted August 8, 1864, at Pollard, Alabama, by Captain A. V. Lee for the war. Drew clothing on September 11, 1864. Signed by his mark "X." Marked present on a company muster roll for September and October, 1864. Age—17, eyes—dark, hair—dark, complexion—dark. Appears on a roll of Confederate Soldiers paroled at the headquarters of 16th US Army Corps, Montgomery, Alabama, on May 24, 1865. Signed an Oath not to bear Arms against the USA on May 26, 1865. Signed J. O. Appling. This document is in his file.

Arant, J. N., Corporal/Sergeant Co. F.
Enlisted March 9, 1864, at Greenville, Alabama, by Captain Brown for the war. Appears on a company muster-in roll at Georgiana, Alabama, July 25, 1864. Age—17, eyes—dark, hair—dark, complexion—dark, 5 foot 1 inch. Drew clothing on September 14, 1864. Appears present on a company muster roll for August 31 to October 31, 1864, with pay due from time of enlistment. Promoted from Corporal on October 15, 1864. Appears on a roll of Confederate Soldiers paroled at the headquarters of 16th US Army Corps, Montgomery, Alabama, during the month of May 1865. He signed an Oath not to bear Arms against the USA on May 30, 1865. Signed J. N. Arant. This document is in his file.

Archer, C. B., Pvt. Co. F.
Enlisted August 15, 1864, at Georgiana, Alabama by Captain Brown for the war. Appears present on a muster roll from August 31 to October 31, 1864, with pay due from time of enlistment. POW captured at Blakeley, Alabama, on April 9, 1865. Appears on a roll of POW's received at Ship Island, Mississippi, on April 15, 1865. Transferred from Ship Island to Vicksburg, Mississippi, on May 1, 1865. Appears on a register of sick and wounded prisoners at USA General Hospital No. 2, Vicksburg. Admitted on May 3, 1865. Age—16. Admitted from steamer with remittent fever.

Archer, Frederick, C., Pvt. Co. B.

Enlisted March 23, 1864, at Montgomery, Alabama, by Captain Zimmerman for the war. Appears on a muster-in roll at Montgomery, Alabama, on March 23, 1864, Age—47. Drew clothing July 8, 1864. Appears absent on a company muster roll for September and October, 1864. with pay due from enlistment. Absent sick since June 1, 1864. Appears on a record of Confederate Soldiers paroled at the headquarters of 16th US Army Corps, Montgomery, Alabama, during the month of May 1865. Signed an oath not to bear Arms against the USA on May 19, 1865. Signed Fredercik C. Archer. Hair—grey, 5 foot 11 inches, eyes—grey, complexion—dark. His oath document is in his file.

Armstrong, James, 1st Lt./Captain Co. A.

Appears on a company muster roll for January and February, 1864, as present and commanding the company. He drew wood for 10 Barracks of Guard at Montgomery, Alabama, on January 30, 1864. Still at Montgomery, Alabama, he drew seventeen stonewall tents on May 18, 1864. He signed a requisition for fuel for Echols' Company A at Montgomery and signifies that there are 21 subalterns and 110 men present on April 1, 1864. On June 25, 1865, he drew two well buckets and one well rope weighing ten and one half pounds to furnish water for Provost Guards at Montgomery. He appears present on a muster roll for September and October, 1864. Elected 1st Lieutenant on January 1, 1864. Promoted to Captain on August 16, 1864, due to Captain Echols being promoted to Major. On August 11, 1864, he drew 29 pair shoes for company A, and signed as Captain commanding the company. Drew for Company A in 3rd Quarter of 1864; 11 jackets, 11 pants, 17 shirts and 19 shoes. Captured by 2nd Division, 16th US Army Corps on April 9, 1865, at Blakeley, Alabama. His name appears on a roll of POW's received at Ship Island, Mississippi, on April 16, 1865. He was among the men transferred to Vicksburg, Mississippi, on April 28, 1865. Appears on a register of POW's at New Orleans, Louisiana. Confined at New Orleans on April 30, 1865, and exchanged on May 1, 1865. Signed an Oath of Allegiance to the U.S. at Meridian, Mississippi, on May 12, 1865. This document is in his file.

Arnold, Henry, Pvt. Co. D.

Enlisted on August 11, 1864, at Pollard, Alabama, by Captain Zorn for the war. Appears present on a company muster roll for August 30 to October 30, 1864, with pay due from enlistment. Drew clothing on September 12, 1864. He was admitted to 1st Mississippi, CSA Hospital at Jackson, Mississippi, on September 25, 1864, with rubeola. Transferred on October 13, 1864. POW captured at Blakeley, Alabama, on April 9, 1865. His name aAppears on a roll of prisoners received at Ship Island, Mississippi, on April 15, 1865. POW transferred to Vicksburg, Mississippi, on May 1, 1865. Appears on a roll of POW's at Quintard Hospital CSA that were surrendered by Lt. General Richard Taylor on May 4, 1865, at Citronelle, Alabama, and paroled at Meridian, Mississippi, on May 10, 1865.

Arnold, R., Pvt. Co. H.

Enlisted on March 16, 1864, at Montevallo, Alabama, by Captain Suttle for the war. Age—17, eyes—hazel, hair—dark, complexion—dark. Appears present on company muster roll for September and October, 1864. Drew clothing on September 11, 1864.

Ashcraft, W. A., Pvt. Co. I

Enlisted May 18, 1864, at Wedowee, Alabama, by Captain Robinson for the war. He appears absent on a company muster roll for September and October 1864. Absent on 30 day furlough from September 27.

Atkins, Thomas J., Pvt. Co. A/C

Enlisted on July 1, 1864, at Chambers [Chambers County, Alabama?] by Captain Echols for the war. Appears present on a company muster roll for September and October 1864. Here he is shown as having been detailed as regimental teamster. POW captured at Blakeley, Alabama, on April 9, 1865. Appears on a roll of prisoners received at Ship Island, Mississippi, on April 9, 1865. Prisoner transferred to Vicksburg, Mississippi, on May 1, 1865. POW surrendered by Lt. General Richard Taylor at Citronelle, Alabama, on May 4, 1865, and paroled at Meridian, Mississippi, on May 11, 1865.

Atkinson, Samuel, Pvt. Co. D.

Enlisted at Russell County, Alabama, on July 30, 1864, by Lieutenant Carnes for the war. Age—17, eyes—blue, hair—dark, complexion fair, 5 foot 8 inches, residence—Russell County. Appears on a muster-in roll at Camp Watts near Notasulga, Alabama, on July 30, 1864, as a member of Captain Zorn's Company of Alabama Reserves. Appears present on a company muster roll from August 30 to October 30, 1864, with pay due from enlistment. Here the record shows that he enlisted at Notasulga on July 25, 1865, by Captain Ready. Drew clothing on August 7, 1864, he signed the receipt as Saml. Atkinson. POW captured at Blakeley, Alabama, on April 9, 1865. Appears on a roll of prisoners received at Ship Island, Mississippi, on April 15, 1865. POW transferred to Vicksburg, Mississippi, on May 1, 1865. On a roll of POW's at Quintard Hospital CSA that were surrendered by Lt. General Richard Taylor on May 1, 1865, at Citronelle, Alabama, and paroled at Meridian, Mississippi, on May 10, 1865.

Bailey, John, Pvt. Co. B

Enlisted at Montgomery, Alabama, on March 23, 1864, by Captain Zimmerman for the war. Appears present on a company muster roll for September and October 1864, with pay due from enlistment. Drew clothing on July 8 and August 12, 1864, signed John A. Bailey.

Bailey, Julian T., Pvt. Co. A

Joined on January 1, 1864, at Chambers County, Alabama. Enrolled by Captain John Echols for the war into the Provost Guards. Age—16. Present on a company muster roll for January and February, 1864, with pay due from enlistment. He appears absent on a company muster roll for September and October, 1864. He is shown sick in hospital at West Point, Georgia, since July 10, 1864. Drew clothing in 2nd quarter of 1864. Signed as Julian T. Bailey. Admitted to Ross Hospital, Mobile, Alabama, on April 6, 1865, reported to be poisoned. Returned to duty on April 23, 1865.

Bailey, Lucius M., Pvt. Co. D.

Enlisted at Camp Watts near Notasulga, Alabama, on July 30, 1864. Enlisted by Major Ready for the war. Age—17, eyes—dark, hair—dark, complexion—dark, 5 foot 5 inches, residence—Coffee County, Alabama, Post Office—Sylvian Grove.

Baily, J. F., Pvt. Co. F.

Enlisted at Georgiana, Alabama, on May 30, 1864, by Captain Jackson for the war. Age—17, eyes—hazel, hair—dark, complexion—dark, 5 foot 6 inches, residence—Butler County. Reported absent sick on the muster-in roll July 22, 1864. Appears present on a company muster roll for August 31 to October 31, 1864, and never been paid. POW captured at Blakeley, Alabama, on April 9, 1865. Appears on a roll of prisoners received at Ship Island, Mississippi, on April 15, 1865. POW transferred to Vicksburg, Mississippi, on May 1, 1865. His name appears among those men surrendered by Lt. General Richard Taylor at Citronelle, Alabama, and as having been paroled at Meridian, Mississippi, on May 10, 1865.

Baker, Charles J., Pvt. Co. D.
Enlisted on July 30, 1864, in Macon County, Alabama, by Major Ready for the war. Mustered in at Camp Watts near Notasulga, Alabama, on July 30, 1864. Age—17, eyes—dark, hair—dark, complexion—light, 5 foot 0 inches, residence—Barbour County, Alabama, Post Offfice—Texasville. A company muster roll for August 30 to October 30 reports that he was enlisted at Clayton, by D. M. Seales on March 2, 1864, for the war and that he deserted October 1. Pay due from enlistment.

Baker, George, Sgt./Pvt. Co. I.
Enlisted at Columbiana, Alabama, on April 15, 1864, by Lieutenant Bulger for the war. Appears absent sick in Hospital Moore since October 15 on a company muster roll for September and October 1864. Here he is shown as 5th Sergeant. Appears on a roll of prisoners received at Ship Island, Mississippi, on April 15, 1865. Captured at Blakeley, Alabama, on April 9, 1865. POW transferred to Vicksburg, Mississippi, on May 1, 1865. Surrendered by Lt. General Richard Taylor at Citronelle, Alabama, on May 4, 1865, and paroled at Meridian, Mississippi, on May 13, 1865. Here he is listed as Pvt. G. F. Baker of Shelby County, Alabama.

Baker, O. H. P., Pvt. Co. E.
Captured at Blakeley, Alabama, on April 9, 1865. POW received at Ship Island, Mississippi, on April 15, 1865. Surrendered by Lt. General Richard Taylor at Citronelle, Alabama, on May 4, 1865, and paroled at Meridian, Mississippi, on May 13, 1865.

Banks, Robert, Pvt. Co. G.
Enlisted April 19, 1864, at Troy, Alabama, by Captain Wilkerson for the war. Age—17, eyes—blue, hair—dark, complexion—fair, 5 foot 7 inches, residence—Pike County, Alabama. Appears on a company muster-in roll at Blakeley, Alabama, on September 7, 1864. Drew clothing on September 11, 1864, and signed by a mark. Admitted on September 20, 1864, to Ross Hospital, Mobile, Alabama, with rubeola. He was returned to duty on October 3, 1864. Captured at Blakeley, Alabama, on April 9, 1865. Appears on a list of prisoners received at Ship Island, Mississippi, on April 15, 1865. Transferred from Ship Island to Vicksburg, Mississippi, on May 1, 1865. Surrendered by Lt. General Richard Taylor at Citronelle, Alabama, on May 4, 1865, and paroled at Meridian, Mississippi, on May 13, 1865.

Bargianier, M. H., Pvt. Co. F.
Enlisted on March 9, 1864, at Greenville, Alabama, by Captain Brown for the war. Appears on a company muster-in roll at Georgiana, Alabama, July 25, 1864. Age—17, eyes—blue, hair—dark, complexion—dark, 5 foot 7 inches, residence—Lowndes County, Alabama. Show absent in hospital at Mobile, Alabama, on company muster roll for August 31, to October 31, 1864, and never been paid. Drew clothing on September 11, 1864, signed M. H. Bargainier. Admitted October 30, 1864, to Ross Hospital, Mobile, Alabama, with febris intermittes tert. Sent to General Hospital on November 2, 1864. Appears on a register of paroled Confederate Soldiers June 1, 1865, by Major Ross Williamson A. D. C. and Provost Marshal 16th US Army Corps. Signed an Oath of Allegiance to the U.S. at Montgomery, Alabama, on June 1, 1865. This document is in his file.

Barke, D. M., Pvt. Co. F.
Enlisted on May 30, 1862, at Montgomery, Alabama, by Captain Jackson for the war. Mustered in on July 25, 1864, at Georgiana, Alabama. Age—17, eyes—blue, hair—light, complexion— fair, 5 foot. Appears absent on company muster roll for August 31 to October 31, 1864. Absent in hospital at Greenville, Alabama, on

August 30, 1864. Appears on a register of Confederate prisoners paroled at Montgomery, Alabama, in the month of June 1865. Signed an Oath of Allegiance and paroled June 12, 1865. This document is in his file.

Barker, John, Pvt. Co. D.
Enlisted on July 30, 1864, at Macon County, Alabama, by Major Ready for the war. Mustered in at Camp Watts near Notasulga, Alabama, on July 30, 1864. Age—17, eyes—grey, hair—light, complexion—fair, 5 foot 10 inches, Post Office—Blue Springs, Alabama. Appears present on a company muster roll for August 30 to October 30, 1864, with pay due from enlistment. Here he is shown as having enlisted on August 17, 1864, at Barbour County, Alabama, by Lieutenant Johnson. Drew clothing on September 12, 1864.

Barker, John W., Pvt. Co. A. Provost Guards
Enlisted on February 1, 1864, in Chambers County, Alabama, by Captain John H. Echols for the war. Appears present on a company muster roll for January and February 1864, not paid since enlistment. Drew clothing 2nd quarter of 1865. Appears present sick in quarters on a company muster roll for September and October 1864.

Barker, William H., Pvt. Co. A. Provost Guards
Enlisted January 1, 1864, at Tallapoosa County, Alabama, by Captain John H. Echols for the war. Appears on a muster-in roll at Montgomery, Alabama, on January 1, 1864. Age—16. Appears present on a company muster roll for January and February 1865, with pay due from enlistment. Pvt. William F. Barker drew clothing in the 2nd quarter of 1864. Appears present sick in quarters on a company muster roll for September and October 1864.

Barksdale, John M., Pvt. Co. E.
Enlisted at Clayton, Alabama, on March 5, 1864, by Captain A. V. Lee. Discharged due to feeble physical and general bad health on September 14, 1864, at Montgomery, Alabama. He is described as slender and anemic and a unhealthy boy. Born in Barbour County, Alabama, Age—17, 5 foot 2 inches, eyes—dark, complexion—fair, hair—dark, a student. His discharge is in his file.

Barlow, T. R., Pvt. Co. D.
Enlisted August 5, 1864, at Elba, Alabama, by Captain Paine for the war. Appears absent on a company muster roll for August 30 to October 30, 1864. Absent sick at Mobile hospital since October 2, with pay due from enlistment. Signed a parole at Montgomery, Alabama, on June 8, 1865. Signed with a mark "X." Hair—dark, eyes—blue, complexion—fair, 5 foot 8 inches.

Barnes, J., Pvt. Co. H.
Enlisted March 18, 1864, at Montevallo, Alabama, by Captain Suttle for the war. Age—16, eyes—hazel, hair—dark, complexion—dark. Appears absent on a company muster roll for September and October, 1864. Absent with leave since September 29. Drew clothing on September 11, 1864.

Barr, George. W., Pvt. Co. H.
Enlisted August 9, 1864, at Mobile, Alabama, by Lieutenant Johnston for the war. Appears present on a company muster roll for September and October 1865. Age—17, eyes—blue, hair—light, complexion—fair. Drew clothing on September 11, 1864. Admitted to Ross Hospital at Mobile, Alabama, on September 17, 1864, with rubeola. Returned to duty on September 26, 1864. Captured at Blakeley, Alabama, on April 9, 1865. Appears on a roll of POW's received at Ship Island, Mississippi, on April 15, 1865. Transferred to Vicksburg, Mississippi, on May 1, 1865. Surrendered by Lt. General Richard Taylor at

Citronelle, Alabama, on May 4, 1865, and paroled at Meridian, Mississippi, on May 11, 1865.

Barr, John W., Sergeant Co. C.
Enlisted May 11, 1864, at Russell County, Alabama, by Lieutenant Carnes for the war. Mustered in at Camp Watts near Notasulga, Alabama, on June 24, 1864. Age—17, eyes—blue, hair—light, complexion—fair, 5 foot 7 inches, Post Office—Columbus, Georgia. Drew clothing on August 6, 1864. Appears present on a company muster roll for September and October 1864, with pay due from enlistment. Captured at Blakeley, Alabama, on April 9, 1865. Paroled at New Orleans, Louisiana, during May of 1865. Appears with a flesh wound to the leg at U.S. 1st Division, 13th Corps, US Army of the Military Division of West Mississippi, transferred to General Hospital. Wounded at Blakeley on April 9. Released at New Orleans on parole on May 16, 1865. Admitted on April 15, 1865, at St. Louis, USA General Hospital, New Orleans, Louisiana, from Mobile, Alabama, with gunshot wound to the left leg, flesh. Age—19.

Barrow, David G., Pvt. Co. A.
Enlisted on March 29, 1864, at Macon County, Alabama, by Captain Echols for the war. Appears absent on a company muster roll for September and October 1864. Absent sick in hospital at Mobile, Alabama, since October 17, 1864, with pay due from enlistment. Drew clothing 2nd quarter and on September 11, 1864. Signed a parole, D. G. Barrow, at Montgomery, Alabama, on May 18, 1865. Hair—dark, eyes—dark, complexion—fair, 5 foot 9 inches. His parole is in his file.

Barron, James P., Pvt. Co. A.
Enrolled on January 1, 1864 at Tallapoosa County, Alabama, by Captain John H. Echols for the war. Appears present on a company muster roll for January and February 1864, with pay due from time of enlistment. Appears present on a company muster roll for September and October 1864, and last paid February 29. Drew clothing in 2nd quarter of 1864. Captured at Blakeley, Alabama, on April 9, 1865. Appears on a roll of POW's received at Ship Island, Mississippi, on April 15, 1865. Transferred to Vicksburg, Mississippi, on May 1, 1865. Surrendered by Lt. General Richard Taylor at Citronelle, Alabama, on May 4, 1865, and paroled at Meridian, Mississippi, on May 13, 1865.

Barron, John W., Pvt. Co. D.
Appears on a roll of POW's received at Ship Island, Mississippi, on April 15, 1865. Transferred to Vicksburg, Mississippi, on May 1, 1865. Surrendered by Lt. General Richard Taylor at Citronelle, Alabama, on May 4, 1865, and paroled at Meridian, Mississippi, on May 13, 1865.

Barron, Robert, Pvt. Co. A.
Enrolled on January 1, 1864, at Tallapoosa County, Alabama, by Captain John H. Echols for the war. Appears present on a company muster roll for January and February, 1864, reported that he is due pay from time of enlistment. Drew clothing 2nd quarter of 1864. Appears absent on a company muster roll for September and October 1864. Absent sick in hospital at Mobile, Alabama, since October 11, 1864. Admitted to Ross Hospital, Mobile, Alabama, on March 29, 1865, with febris intermittens. Sent to General Hospital on April 2, 1865, with remarks: Meridian. Surrendered by Lt. General Richard Taylor at Citronelle, Alabama, on May 4, 1865, and paroled at Meridian, Mississippi, on May 13, 1865.

Barton, J. K. 1st Lieutenant Co. E.
Enlisted April 15, 1864, at Tuscaloosa, Alabama, by Captain A. V. Lee for the war. Shown present on company muster roll for September and October 1864. Reported to have been a Cadet when elected 1st Lieutenant of the company.

Elected 1st Lieutenant Co. E. on March 25, 1864. Age—17, eyes—dark, hair—dark, complexion—dark. Drew clothing September 12, 1864. Appears on a list of sick and wounded, East Division, District of the Gulf, sent to General Hospital, Vicksburg, Mississippi, via New Orleans, Louisiana, from Spanish Fort, Alabama, on April 8, 1865. His diagnosis was rubeola. He appears on a card as being aboard the US Hospital Steamer Elanore Carrel and transferred to the USA Hospital Steamer D. A. January at New Orleans. He arrived at No. 3 Hospital, Vicksburg upon the Steamer Elanora. Appears on a roll of POW's at USA General Hospital, No. 3 (colored), Vicksburg, Mississippi. Captured at Blakeley, Alabama. Transferred to USA General Hospital, No. 2, at Vicksburg on May 4, 1865. Signed a Parole of Honor at Meridian, Mississippi, on May 11, 1865. His parole is in his file.

Bartz, (Bailey) John A., Pvt. Co. B.

His name appears on a record of Confederate Soldiers paroled at Headquarters of 16th US Army Corps at Montgomery, Alabama, on May 19, 1865. He signed a Parole at Montgomery on May 19, 1865. Signed John A. Bailey, He is described as: 5 foot 11 inches, hair—dark, eyes—dark, complexion—dark. His parole is in his file.

Baskin, Peter B. Pvt. Co. G.

Enlisted on May 16, 1864, at Troy, Alabama, by Captain Wilkerson for the War. Residence—Montgomery County, Alabama, age—17, eyes—blue, hair—dark, complexion—dark, 5 foot 7 inches. Appears absent on a company muster roll for September and October 1864, in hospital, Lauderdale Mississippi, since August 20. Captured Blakeley, Alabama, April 9, 1865. Appears on a roll of POW's at Ship Island, Mississippi, that were transferred to Vicksburg, Mississippi, on May 1, 1865. Appears on a register of sick and wounded Confederate prisoners at USA General Hospital, No. 2, Vicksburg. Admitted on May 3, 1865, with chronic bronchitis. Returned to duty on May 21, 1865. He was admitted to the hospital from steamer.

Baskin, Thomas J., Pvt. Co. G.

Enlisted on May 16, 1864, at Troy, Alabama, by Captain Wilkerson for the war. His name appears on company muster in roll at Blakeley, Alabama, on September 7, 1864. Age—16, eyes—blue, hair—dark, complexion—dark, 5 foot 7 inches. Admitted to Ross Hospital at Mobile, Alabama, September 20, 1864, with rubeola, [furloughed] 30 days. Appears absent on a company muster roll for September and October 1865, in hospital at Greenville, Alabama, since September 25. Drew clothing on September 11, 1864. He signed by his mark "X." Admitted to Ross Hospital at Mobile, Alabama, on March 30, 1865, with vulnus sclopeticum (gunshot wound), sent to General Hospital on April 15, 1865, (Demopolis?). His name appears as a signature on a Parole of POW at Marion, Alabama, on May 16, 1865.

Baspilpin, W. A., Pvt. Co. C.

Appears on a roll of POW's surrendered by Lt. General Richard Taylor at Citronelle, Alabama, in May 1865, and having been paroled at Demopolis, Alabama, on June 6, 1865.

Bass, R. M., Pvt. Co. H.

Enlisted on July 23, 1864, at Selma, Alabama, by Captain Suttle for the war. Age—17, eyes—blue, hair—light, complexion—fair. He appears present on a company muster roll for September and October 1864. Admitted to Ross Hospital at Mobile, Alabama, on September 3, 1864, with dysenteria acuta. Returned to duty on September 28, 1864.

Bass, W., Pvt. Co. I.
Enlisted on April 14, 1864 at Wedowee, Alabama, by Captain Robinson for the war. Appears absent on a company muster roll for September and October 1864, without leave from September 18, 1864.

Bassett, J. A., Pvt./Corp. Co. I/D.
Enlisted on April 15, 1864, at Columbiana, Alabama, by Lieutenant Bulger for the war. Appears absent on a company muster roll for September and October 1864, on detached service. Captured at Blakeley, Alabama, on April 9, 1865. Shown here and here after as a Corporal in Co. D. Appears on a roll of POW's received at Ship Island, Mississippi, on April 15, 1865. Transferred from Ship Island to Vicksburg, Mississippi, on May 1, 1865. Surrendered by Lt. General Richard Taylor at Citronelle, Alabama, on May 4, 1865, and paroled at Meridian, Mississippi, on May 13, 1865.

Batchler, J. B., Pvt. Co. E.
Appears on a record of Confederate Prisoners paroled at the headquarters of 16th US Army Corps at Montgomery, Alabama, on May 19, 1865. Signed a parole at Montgomery on May 19, 1865. Signed J. B. Bachelor, 5 foot 10 inches, hair—dark, eyes—blue, complexion—fair. The parole is in his file.

Battle, R. R., Jr. 2nd Lt./2nd Lt. Co. K.
Enlisted on October 1, 1864, at Blakeley, Alabama, by Captain May for the war. Appears present on a company muster roll for September and October 1864. Elected 2nd Lieutenant on October 1, 1864, of Company K, 2nd Regiment Alabama Reserves, Fuller's Brigade, Maury's Corps, District of the Gulf, CSA. Captured at Blakeley, Alabama, on April 9, 1865. Appears on a roll of Confederate Prisoners received at Ship Island, Mississippi, on April 16, 1865. Transferred from Ship Island to Vicksburg, Mississippi, on April 28, 1865. Appears on a register of POW's confined at New Orleans, Louisiana, on April 30, 1865. Signed a parole of honor at Meridian, Mississippi, on May 11, 1865. His parole is in his file.

Batts, William, Pvt. Co. F.
Enlisted on May 30, 1864, at Montgomery, Alabama, by Captain Jackson for the war. Appears absent without leave on a company muster-in roll on July 25, 1864, at Georgiana, Alabama. Age—17, eyes—dark, hair—dark, complexion—dark, 5 foot 6 inches.

Baxley, John P., Pvt. Co. B.
Enrolled on April 14, 1864, at Montgomery, County, Alabama, by Captain W. C. Zimmerman for the war. Appears on a company muster-in roll at Montgomery, Alabama, on March 23, 1864. Age—17. Drew clothing on July 8, August 12 and September 11, 1864. Signed by his mark. Appears present on a company muster roll for September and October 1864, with pay due from time of enlistment. Captured at Blakeley, Alabama, on April 9, 1865. Appears on a roll of POW's received at Ship Island, Mississippi, on April 15, 1865. Transferred from Ship Island to Vicksburg, Mississippi, on May 1, 1865. Appears on a roll of POW's of Company B, 63rd Regiment, Alabama Infantry commanded by 1st Lieutenant Thomas J. Calhoun, that was surrendered by Lt. General Richard Taylor at Citronelle, Alabama, on May 4, 1865, and paroled at Meridian, Mississippi, on May 11, 1865.

Bean, Bartlett M., Sergeant Co. G.
Enlisted on April 16, 1864, at Troy, Alabama, by Captain Wilkerson for the war. Appears on a company muster-in roll at Blakeley, Alabama, on September 7, 1864. Age—17, eyes—dark, hair—dark, complexion—fair, 5 foot 10 inches. Appears

present on a company muster roll for September and October 1865. Shown here is a 3rd Sgt. Drew clothing on September 11, 1864. Captured at Blakeley, Alabama, on April 9, 1865. Appears on a roll of POW's received at Ship Island, Mississippi, on April 15, 1865. Transferred from Ship Island to Vicksburg, Mississippi, on May 1, 1865. Appears on a roll of POW's of Cos. E and G, 63rd Alabama Regiment Volunteers commanded by Captain A. V. Lee that were surrendered by Lt. General Richard Taylor at Citronelle, Alabama, on May 4, 1865, and paroled at Meridian, Mississippi, on May 13, 1865.

Beard, J. A., Pvt. Co. K.
Enlisted on August 6, 1864, at Russell County, Alabama, by Lieutenant Sledge for the war. Appears present on a company muster roll for September and October 1864. Captured at Blakeley, Alabama, on April 9, 1865. Appears on a roll of POW's received at Ship Island, Mississippi, on April 15, 1865. Transferred from Ship Island to Vicksburg, Mississippi, on May 1, 1865. Appears on a roll of POW's of Cos. I and K, 63rd Alabama Infantry commanded by Lieutenant W. A. Skinner that were surrendered by Lt. General Richard Taylor at Citronelle, Alabama, on May 4, 1865, and paroled at Meridian, Mississippi, on May 13, 1865.

Bearden, R. C., Pvt. Co. H.
Enlisted on March 18, 1864, at Elyton, Alabama, by Lieutenant Killough for the war. Age—17, eyes—blue, hair—light, complexion—fair. Appears absent on a company muster roll for September and October 1864, absent at hospital in Shelby Springs since September 21. Drew clothing on September 11, 1864. Admitted to 1st Mississippi CSA Hospital, Jackson, Mississippi, with rubeola on October 1, 1864. Transferred from hospital on October 13.

Beasley, B., Pvt. Co. F.
Enlisted May 30, 1864, at Montgomery, Alabama, by Captain Jackson for the war. Appears on a company muster-in roll at Georgiana, Alabama, July 23, 1864. Age—17, eyes—blue, hair—light, complexion—fair, 5 foot 6 inches. Appears absent on a company muster roll for August 31 to October 31, 1864, absent in hospital at Mobile on October 13, 1864, and never been paid. Drew clothing September 11, 1864. Appears on a roll of nurses and patients of Moore Hospital of the CSA Army commanded by Surgeon W. C. Cavenaugh, that were surrendered by Lt. General Richard Taylor at Citronelle, Alabama, on May 4, 1865, and paroled at Meridian, Mississippi, on May 14, 1865.

Beasly, Eldridge B., Pvt. Co. B.
Enlisted on August 15, 1864, at Pollard, Alabama, by Lieutenant Townsend for the war. Appears absent on a company muster roll for September and October 1864, absent sick since October 25, 1864, and pay due from time of enlistment. Drew clothing on September 11, 1864.

Beatty, William H., Pvt. Co. D.
Enlisted on July 30, 1864, at Macon County, Alabama, by Major Ready for the war. Appears on a company muster-in roll at Camp Watts near Notasulga, Alabama, on July 30, 1864. Age—17, eyes—grey, hair—auburn, complexion—light, 5 foot 10 inches, residence—Texasville, Barbour County, Alabama. Appears present on a company muster roll for August 30 to October 30, 1864, and pay due from time of enlistment. Here he is shown as having enlisted March 2 at Clayton, Alabama, by D. M. Seals. Drew clothing August 7, 1864. Appears on a list, dated April 8, 1865, of sick and wounded at Spanish Fort, Alabama, to be sent to Vicksburg, Mississippi, or New Orleans, Louisiana, wounded in the thigh. Admitted to 2nd Division, 16th US Army Corps Hospital on April 9, 1865, given chloroform and bullet extracted. Wounded in action in the thigh, flesh.

Appears on a list, dated April 13, 1865, of wounded POW's to be transferred from Blakeley, Alabama, to hospital at New Orleans. Admitted to USA Hospital Steamer D. A. January among wounded rebels and paroled prisoners transferred to Steamer E. Carrel, April 25, 1865. Appears on USA Hospital Steamer Elanora Carrel with Gunshot wound to left knee. He is reported as being transferred from New Orleans to Vicksburg. Appears on a roll of POW's at USA General Hospital No. 3, at Vicksburg that were transferred to USA General Hospital No. 2 on May 4, 1865. Admitted to USA General Hospital No. 2, at Vicksburg on May 4, 1865, with gunshot wound to left leg. Wounded by con. ball on April 9, 1865, at Blakeley, Alabama. Returned to duty on May 8, 1865.

Beck, J. J., Jr. 2nd Lt./2nd Lt. Co. G.
Appears on a company muster-in roll September 7, 1864, at Blakeley, Alabama. Age—17, eyes—grey, hair—dark, complexion—dark, 5 foot 8 inches, residence—Pike County, Alabama. Elected 2nd Lieutenant of Company G on July 1, 1864. He resigned on November 10, 1864. His resignation is in his file with noted endorsements. He wished to join Co. B of the 25, Alabama, which was attached to the Army of Tennessee at Atlanta. His commanders approved his wish.

Beck, Michael, Pvt. Co. G.
Enlisted on August 1, 1864, at Pollard, Alabama, by Captain Padgett for the war. Appears on a company muster-in roll on September 7, 1864, at Blakeley, Alabama. Age—16, hair—dark, eyes—dark, complexion—fair, 5 foot 3 inches. Appears absent on a company muster roll for September and October 1864. Absent on 30 day furlough from the hospital in Mobile, Alabama, from October 25. Drew clothing September 11, 1864. Signed by his mark. Signed a parole at Montgomery, Alabama, on June 20, 1865, at the headquarters of the 16th US Army Corps. The parole is in his file.

Bedell, Taylor, Pvt. Co. A.
Enrolled on January 1, 1864, at Chambers County, Alabama, by Captain John H. Echols for the war. Appears on a company muster roll on January 1, 1864. Age—17. Appears present on a company muster roll of Captain Echols Provost Guards (this company became Co. A of the 63rd Alabama Infantry) for January and February 1864, with pay due from time of enlistment.

Belcher, H., Pvt. Co. I.
Enlisted on May 18, 1864, at Wedowee, Alabama, by Captain Robinson for the war. Appears absent without leave since September 18, 1864, on a company muster roll for September and October 1864.

Belcher, W. E., Pvt. Co. K.
Enlisted on August 15, 1864, at Choctaw County, Alabama, by Lieutenant Everton for the war. Appears absent on a company muster roll for September and October 1864. Absent in hospital at Mobile since October 25, 1864. Captured at Blakeley, Alabama, on April 9, 1865. Appears on a roll of POW's received at Ship Island, Mississippi, on April 15, 1865. Transferred from Ship Island to Vicksburg, Mississippi, on May 1, 1865. Appears on a roll of POW's of Cos. I and K, 63rd Alabama Infantry commanded by Lieutenant W. A. Skinner that were surrendered by Lt. General Richard Taylor at Citronelle, Alabama, on May 4, 1865, and paroled at Meridian, Mississippi, on May 13, 1865.

Belcher, William, Co. I.
He enlisted on April 15, 1864, at Wedowee, Alabama, by Captain Robinson for the war. He appears absent on a company muster roll for September and October 1864. The muster roll reports him absent with a 30 day furlough from September 27.

Bell, J. T., Pvt. Co. F.
Enlisted on July 23, 1864, at Greenville, Alabama, by Lieutenant Barton for the war. Appears present on a company muster roll for August 31 to October 31, 1864, with pay due from enlistment. Captured at Blakeley, Alabama, on April 9, 1865. Appears on a roll of POW's received at Ship Island, Mississippi, on April 15, 1865. Transferred from Ship Island to Vicksburg, Mississippi, on May 1, 1865. He appears on a roll of POW's of Company F, 63rd Alabama Infantry commanded by Lt. R. T. Simpson that were surrendered by Lt. General Richard Taylor at Citronelle, Alabama, on May 4, 1865, and paroled at Meridian, Mississippi, on May 11, 1865.

Bembow, R. M., Pvt. Co. F.
Enlisted on May 30, 1864, at Montgomery, Alabama, by Captain Jackson for the war. Appears on a muster-in roll on July 22, 1864, at Georgiana, Alabama. Age—17, eyes—dark, hair—dark, complexion—dark, 5 foot 6 inches, residence—Pike County, Alabama. Appears absent on a company muster roll for August 31 to October 31, 1864, at Montgomery, Alabama, with pay due from the time of enlistment. Absent sick since August 29, 1864. Captured at Blakeley, Alabama, on April 9, 1865. Appears on a roll of POW's received at Ship Island, Mississippi, on April 15, 1865. Transferred from Ship Island to Vicksburg, Mississippi, on May 1, 1865. Appears on a roll of POW's of Company F, 63rd Alabama Infantry commanded by Lieutenant R. T. Simpson that were surrendered by Lt. General Richard Taylor at Citronelle, Alabama, on May 4, 1865, and paroled at Meridian, Mississippi, on May 11, 1865.

Bennett, Joseph L., Corporal Co. C.
Enlisted on June 14, 1864, at Russell County, Alabama, by Lieutenant Carnes for the war. Appears on a company muster-in roll on June 24, 1864, at Camp Watts near Notasulga, Alabama. Age—17, eyes—blue, hair—light, complexion—dark, 5 foot 5 inches, residence—Crawford, Russell County, Alabama. Drew clothing August 6, 1864. Appears absent on a company muster roll for September and October 1864, with pay from time of enlistment. Absent in hospital at Mobile, Alabama, since October 21, 1864. Appears on a record of Confederate soldiers paroled at headquarters of the 16th US Army Corps at Montgomery, Alabama, on May 13, 1865. His parole is in his file, signed J. L. Bennett.

Bennifield, James A., Pvt. Co. D.
Enlisted July 30, 1864, at Macon County, Alabama, by Major Ready for the war. Appears on a company muster-in roll at Camp Watts near Notasulga, Alabama, on July 30, 1864. Age—17, eyes—blue, hair—light, complexion—fair, 5 foot 4 inches, residence—Henry County, Alabama, Post Office—Clayton, Barbour County. Drew clothing on August 7, 1864. Signed by his mark. Appears absent on a company muster roll for August 30 to October 30, 1864, with pay due from time of enlistment. Absent sick at hospital in Mobile since October 1. Captured at Blakeley, Alabama, on April 9, 1865. Appears on a roll of POW's received at Ship Island, Mississippi, on April 15, 1865. Transferred from Ship Island to Vicksburg, Mississippi, on May 1, 1865. Appears on a roll of POW's of Company D, 63rd Alabama Infantry commanded by Captain Robert H. Pearson that were surrendered by Lt. General Richard Taylor at Citronelle, Alabama, on May 4, 1865, and paroled at Meridian, Mississippi, on May 11, 1865.

Bently, J. W. F., Pvt. Co. C.
Enlisted August 3, 1864, at Tuskegee, Macon County, Alabama, by Captain Rosco for the war. Appears present on a company muster roll for September and October 1864. Admitted to Ross Hospital at Mobile, Alabama, on November 10, 1864, with Febris Remittens, sent to General Hospital on December 7, 1864. On this report under remarks appears Hospital Nidelet. Discharged on December

9, 1864, at Mobile due to deficiency of vision and partial imbecility. Age—18, eyes—grey, hair—light, complexion—fair, 5 foot 8 inches, a farmer by occupation. His discharge is in his file. Appears on a record of Confederate solders paroled at headquarters of the 16th US Army Corps at Montgomery, Alabama, on May 22, 1865. His parole is in his file. He signed by mark "X." Eyes—grey, hair—light, complexion—fair, 5 foot 9 inches.

Berdaux, J. W., Pvt. Co. F.
Enlisted on September 19, 1864, at Hayneville, Alabama, by Captain Buell for the war. Appears present on a company muster roll for August 31 to October 31, 1864. Captured at Blakeley, Alabama, on April 9, 1865. Appears on a roll of POW's received at Ship Island, Mississippi, on April 15, 1865. Transferred from Ship Island to Vicksburg, Mississippi, on May 1, 1865. His name appears on a roll of POW's of Company F, 63rd Alabama Infantry commanded by Lt. R. T. Simpson that were surrendered by Lt. General Richard Taylor at Citronelle, Alabama, on May 4, 1865, and were paroled at Meridian, Mississippi, on May 11, 1865.

Betts, W. H., Pvt. Co. C.
Enlisted on July 3, 1864, at Macon, County, Alabama, by Captain Rogers for the war. Appears present on a company muster roll for September and October 1864. Drew clothing on August 4, 1864. Captured at Blakeley, Alabama, on April 9, 1865. Appears on a roll of POW's received at Ship Island, Mississippi, on April 15, 1865. Transferred from Ship Island to Vicksburg, Mississippi, on May 1, 1865. Appears on a roll of POW's of Cos. C and H, 63rd Alabama Infantry commanded by Captain C. W. Martin that were surrendered by Lt. General Richard Taylor at Citronelle, Alabama, on May 4, 1865, and paroled at Meridian, Mississippi, on May 11, 1865. Residence—Chambers County, Alabama.

Bevins, Andrew, Pvt. Co. G
Appears on a register of POW's received at Military Prison, Louisville, Kentucky, on May 20, 1864. Captured at Resaca, Georgia, on May 16, 1864. Sent to Rock Island Prison, Rock Island, Illinois, on May 30, 1864. Transferred from Louisville to Camp Morton, Indiana, on May 21, 1864, (this entry was canceled). [This entry is probably filed here in error.]

Bilbery, J. D., Pvt. Co. C.
Appears on a register of paroled Confederate soldiers paroled on June 3, 1865, at headquarters of the 16th US Army Corps at Montgomery, Alabama. Hair—light, eyes—blue, complexion—dark, 5 foot 10 inches. Signed J. D. Bilbury. His parole is in his file.

Binns, G. E., Pvt. Co. E.
His name appears on a roll of POW's of divers Confederate companies and regiments commanded by Lt. Colonel R. H. Lindsay that were surrendered by Lt. General Richard Taylor at Citronelle, Alabama, on May 4, 1865, and paroled at Meridian, Mississippi, on May 12, 1865. Residence—Gainesville, Sumpter County, Alabama.

Birchfield, J., Pvt. Co. H.
Enlisted on July 29, 1864, at Selma, Alabama, by Captain Suttle for the war. Appears absent on a company muster roll for September and October 1864. Sick at Mobile Hospital since October 12. Age—17, eyes—grey, hair—light, complexion—fair. Drew clothing on September 11, 1864, signed J. T. Burchfield. Admitted to Ross Hospital in Mobile, Alabama, on October 16, 1864, with febris remittens. Furloughed for 30 days from hospital on October 27.

Bird, Daniel F., Pvt. Co. G.
Enlisted on May 16, 1865, at Troy, Alabama, by Captain Wilkerson for the war. Appears on a company muster-in roll at Blakeley, Alabama, on September 7, 1864. Appears present on a company muster roll for September and October 1864. Drew clothing on September 11, 1864. Signed by his mark.

Bishop, J. A., Corporal/Pvt. Co. K.
Captured at Blakeley, Alabama, on April 9, 1865. Appears on a roll of POW's received at Ship Island, Mississippi, on April 15, 1865. Transferred from Ship Island to Vicksburg, Mississippi, on May 1, 1865. Appears on a roll of POW's of Cos. I and K, 63rd Alabama Infantry commanded by Lieutenant W. A. Skinner that were surrendered by Lt. General Richard Taylor at Citronelle, Alabama, on May 4, 1865, and paroled at Meridian, Mississippi, on May 13, 1865. Residence—Bibb County, Alabama.

Blackman, Theophilus, Pvt. Co. G.
Enlisted on July 1, 1864, at Troy, Alabama, by Captain Wilkerson for the war. Age—17, eyes—dark, hair—dark, complexion—fair, 5 foot 5 inches, residence—Pike County, Alabama. Appears on a company muster-in roll at Blakeley, Alabama, on September 7, 1864. Appears present on a company muster roll for September and October 1864. Captured at Blakeley, Alabama, on April 9, 1865. Appears on a roll of POW's received at Ship Island, Mississippi, on April 15, 1865. Transferred from Ship Island to Vicksburg, Mississippi, on May 1, 1865. Appears on a roll of POW's of Cos. E and G, 63rd Alabama Infantry commanded by Captain A. V. Lee that were surrendered by Lt. General Richard Taylor at Citronelle, Alabama, on May 4, 1865, and paroled at Meridian, Mississippi, on May 13, 1865. Residence—Butler County, Alabama.

Blackshear, W., Pvt. Co. ?.
Appears on a register of enlisted men paroled by Captain George C. Barretson, Provost Marshal, 13th US Army Corps. Surrendered on May 4, 1865, at Citronelle, Alabama, paroled in May 1865 in Selma, Alabama.

Boatwright, E. W., Pvt. Co. E.
Enlisted on August 8, 1864, at Pollard, Alabama, by Captain A. V. Lee for the war. Age—17, eyes—dark, hair—dark, complexion—dark. Appears present on a company muster roll for September and October 1864.

Body, H. B., Pvt. Co. F.
Enlisted on May 30, 1865, at Montgomery, Alabama, by Captain Jackson for the war. Age—17, eyes—dark, hair—dark, complexion—dark, 5 foot 6 inches, residence—Coosa, County, Alabama. Appears absent without leave on a company muster-in roll at Georgiana, Alabama, on July 25, 1865.

Boley, L., Co. K.
Enlisted on September 20, 1864, at Rockford, Alabama, by Captain Hancock for the war. Appears absent on a company muster roll for September and October 1864. Absent in hospital in Mobile since October 25, 1864.

Bolins, A., Pvt. Co. G.
Appears as a signature to a Parole of POW at Marion, Alabama, on May 16, 1865.

Boman, John F., Pvt. Co. C/I.
Enlisted on May 31, 1864, at Montgomery, Alabama, by Captain McDaniel for the war. Appears on a company muster-in roll at Camp Watts near Notasulga, Alabama, on June 24, 1865. Age—17, eyes—grey, hair—light, complexion—light, 5 foot 6 inches, residence—Carnes Cross Roads, Dale County, Alabama. Appears on

a company muster roll for September and October 1864, at Camp Watts. Captured at Blakeley, Alabama, on April 9, 1865. Appears on a roll of POW's received at Ship Island, Mississippi, on April 15, 1865. Transferred from Ship Island to Vicksburg, Mississippi, on May 1, 1865. Appears on a roll of POW's of Cos. C and H, 63rd Alabama Infantry commanded by Captain C. W. Martin that were surrendered by Lt. General Richard Taylor at Citronelle, Alabama, on May 4, 1865, and paroled at Meridian, Mississippi, on May 11, 1865. Residence—Dale County, Alabama.

Bomer, (Boner) H. C., Pvt. Co. D
Paroled at headquarters of the 16th US Army Corps at Montgomery, Alabama, on June 3, 1865. Eyes—blue, Hair—light, complexion—light, 5 foot 5 inches. Signs by his mark "X." His parole is in his file.

Bonds, J. A., Pvt. Co. E.
Captured at Blakeley, Alabama, on April 9, 1865. Appears on a roll of POW's received at Ship Island, Mississippi, on April 15, 1865. Transferred from Ship Island to Vicksburg, Mississippi, on May 1, 1865. Appears on a roll of sick and wounded Confederate prisoners admitted from steamer to USA General Hospital No. 2, Vicksburg, Mississippi, on May 2, 1865, with acute diarrhoea. Age—16. Returned to duty on May 8, 1865. Appears on a roll of POW's of unattached men that were surrendered by Lt. General Richard Taylor at Citronelle, Alabama, on May 4, 1865, and paroled at Jackson, Mississippi, on May 11, 1865. Residence—Monroe County, Alabama.

Bowden, James W., Pvt. Co. G.
Enlisted on May 16, 1864, at Troy, Alabama, by Captain Wilkerson for the war. Appears on a company muster-in roll at Blakeley, Alabama, on September 7, 1864. Eyes—blue, hair—dark, complexion—dark, 5 foot 4 inches, residence—Pike County, Alabama, age—16. Drew clothing on September 11, 1864. Appears absent on a company muster roll for September and October 1864. Absent in hospital at Lauderdale, Mississippi, since Sept. 15, 1865.

Bowling, B., Pvt. Co. H.
Enlisted March 15, 1864, at Centerville, Alabama, by Lieutenant Johnston for the war. Appears absent on a company muster roll for September and October 1864. On detached service since May 1 [by order of] Major General Withers. Age—17, eyes—blue, hair—dark, complexion—dark.

Bowman, Edwin, 4th Corporal/Pvt. Co. B.
Enrolled on March 23, 1864, at Montgomery County, Alabama, by Captain W. C. Zimmerman for the war. Appears on a company muster-in roll at Montgomery, Alabama, on March 23, 1864. Drew clothing on August 12 and July 8, 1864. Appears present on a company muster roll for September and October 1864, with pay due from time of enlistment. Captured at Blakeley, Alabama, on April 9, 1865. Appears on a roll of POW's received at Ship Island, Mississippi, on April 15, 1865. Transferred from Ship Island to Vicksburg, Mississippi, on May 1, 1865. His name appears on a roll of POW's of Company B, 63rd Alabama Infantry under the command of by 1st Lieutenant Thomas J. Calhoun that were surrendered by Lt. General Richard Taylor at Citronelle, Alabama, on May 4, 1865, and were then paroled at Meridian, Mississippi, on May 11, 1865. Residence-Montgomery County, Alabama.

Boyd, J. M., Pvt. Co. E.
Signed a parole at Montgomery, Alabama, at the headquarters of the 16th US. Army Corps on June 5, 1865. Hair—auburn, eyes—grey, complexion—light, 5 foot. Signed by his mark "X." His parole is in his file.

Boyett, R. Pvt. Co. E.
    Enlisted on August 25, 1864, at Camp Hood by Captain A. V. Lee for the war. He appears present on a company muster roll for September and October 1864. Age—17, eyes—blue, hair—light, complexion—fair. Drew clothing on September 11, 1864.

Bradberry, W. H., Pvt. Co. E.
    Enlisted on August 28, 1864, at Montgomery, Alabama, by Major Thompson for the war. Appears absent on a company muster roll for September and October 1864. Absent in hospital since October 12, 1864. Age—17, eyes—blue, hair—light, complexion—fair. Admitted to Ross Hospital at Mobile, Alabama, on October 1, 1864 with febris remittens. Furloughed for 30 days on October 8.

Bradfield, James R., Corporal/Pvt.
    Enlisted on April 30, 1864, at Chambers County, Alabama, by Captain Walker for the war. Appears June 24, 1864, on a company muster-in roll at Camp Watts near Notasulga, Alabama. Age—17, eyes—blue, hair—black, complexion—fair, 5 foot 8 inches, residence—West Point Georgia. Appears present on a company muster roll for September and October 1864. Drew clothing August 6, 1864. Captured March 24, 1864, in Alabama. Appears on a roll of POW's captured by Brigader General T. J. Lucas in command of cavalry forces operating from Pensacola, Florida. Captured at Gravel Hill. Appears on a roll of POW's received at Ship Island, Mississippi, on April 4, 1865. Transferred from Ship Island to Vicksburg, Mississippi, on May 1, 1865.

Bradley, Irwin T. D., Pvt. Co. G.
    Enlisted on May 16, 1864, at Troy, Alabama, by Captain Wilkerson for the war. Appears on a company muster-in roll at Blakeley, Alabama, on September 7, 1864. Age—17, eyes—grey, hair—red, complexion—fair, 5 foot 8 inches. Appears present on a muster roll for September and October 1864. Captured at Blakeley, Alabama, on April 9, 1865. Appears on a roll of POW's received at Ship Island, Mississippi, on April 15, 1865. Transferred from Ship Island to Vicksburg, Mississippi, on May 1, 1865. Appears on a roll of sick and wounded Confederate prisoners admitted from steamer to USA General Hospital No. 2, Vicksburg, Mississippi, on May 2, 1865, with acute diarrhoea. Age—18. Returned to duty on May 10, 1865.

Branch, John, Pvt. Co. D.
    Enlisted on July 30, 1864, at Macon County, Alabama, by Major Ready for the war. Appears on a company muster-in roll at Camp Watts near Notasulga, Alabama, on July 30, 1864, with pay due from time of enlistment. Age—17, eyes—grey, hair—light, complexion—fair, 5 foot 6 inches, residence—Clayton, Barbour County, Alabama. Drew clothing on August 7, 1864. Appears present on a company muster roll for August 30 to October 30, 1864. [Here he is shown as having enlisted at Eufaula on July 15, 1864, by Captain Zorn.] Captured at Blakeley, Alabama, on April 9, 1865. Appears on a roll of POW's received at Ship Island, Mississippi, on April 15, 1865. Transferred from Ship Island to Vicksburg, Mississippi, on May 1, 1865. Appears on a roll of POW's of Company D, 63rd Alabama Infantry commanded by Captain Robert H. Pearson that were surrendered by Lt. General Richard Taylor at Citronelle, Alabama, on May 4, 1865, and paroled at Meridian, Mississippi, on May 13, 1865. Residence—Barbour County, Alabama.

Brand, D., Pvt. Co. I.
    Enlisted on April 15, 1864, at Wedowee by Captain Robinson for the war. Appears absent on a company muster roll for September and October 1864. Furloughed for 30 days from September 27.

Brannin, Seabron R., Pvt. Co. B.
    Enlisted on August 15, 1864, at Pollard, Alabama, by Lieutenant Townsend for the war. Appears present on a company muster roll for September and October 1864, with pay due from time of enlistment. Drew clothing on September 11, 1864. Captured at Blakeley, Alabama, on April 9, 1865. Appears on a roll of POW's received at Ship Island, Mississippi, on April 15, 1865. Transferred from Ship Island to Vicksburg, Mississippi, on May 1, 1865. Appears on a roll of POW's of Company B, 63rd Alabama Infantry commanded by 1st Lieutenant Thomas J. Calhoun that were surrendered by Lt. General Richard Taylor at Citronelle, Alabama, on May 4, 1865, and paroled at Meridian, Mississippi, on May 11, 1865. Residence—Dale County, Alabama.

Brantley, George W., Pvt. Co. C.
    Enlisted on May 31, 1864, at Montgomery, Alabama, by Captain McDaniel for the war. Appears on a company muster-in roll at Camp Watts near Notasulga, Alabama, on June 24, 1864. Age—17, eyes—grey, hair—dark, complexion—dark, 5 foot 5 inches, residence—Elba, Coffee County, Alabama. Drew clothing on August 6, 1864. Signed by his mark. Appears present on a company muster roll for September and October 1864. Captured at Fort Blakeley, Alabama, on April 9, 1865. Appears on a list of wounded Confederates in the hospital of the 1st Division, 13th Corps, Army of Military Division of West Mississippi, at the battle of Blakeley Fort, Alabama, on April 9, 1865. Appears of POW's at New Orleans, Louisiana, confined on May 1, 1865. Died at St. Louis Hospital, New Orleans on May 2. Gunshot fracture of neck of femur. Wounded in hip and arm. Gunshot wounds right forearm and left groin flesh. Minnie ball entering left groin passing through and fracturing neck of left femur emerging posteriorly from left gluteus. Died of Capillary hemorrhage. Buried in grave No. 63, Square 69 Monument Cemetery. No effects.

Brasher, W. J., Pvt. Co. I.
    Enlisted on April 15, 1864, at Columbiana, Alabama, by Lieutenant Bulger for the war. Appears absent on a company muster roll for September and October 1864. Absent without leave from September 18, 1864.

Brewer, Drew M. E., Pvt. Co. A.
    Enrolled on January 1, 1864, at Tallapoosa County, Alabama, by Captain John H. Echols for the war. Appears on a company muster-in roll on January 1, 1864, at Montgomery, Alabama. Appears present on a company muster roll for January and February 1864, with pay due from enlistment. Drew clothing in 2nd Quarter of 1864. Appears present, sick in quarters, on a company muster roll for September and October 1864. Reported on that roll as last paid on February 29, 1864. Captured at Blakeley, Alabama, on April 9, 1865. Appears on a roll of POW's received at Ship Island, Mississippi, on April 15, 1865. Transferred from Ship Island to Vicksburg, Mississippi, on May 1, 1865. Appears on a roll of POW's of Company A, 63rd Alabama Infantry commanded by Lieutenant W. D. Kyle that were surrendered by Lt. General Richard Taylor at Citronelle, Alabama, on May 4, 1865, and paroled at Meridian, Mississippi, on May 13, 1865. Residence—Tallapoosa County, Alabama.

Brewer, Edmond H., Pvt. Co. B.
    Enlisted on August 15, 1864, at Pollard, Alabama, by Lieutenant Townsend for the war. Appears present on a company muster roll for September and October 1864, with pay due from time of enlistment. Drew clothing on September 11, 1864. Captured at Blakeley, Alabama, on April 9, 1865. Appears on a roll of POW's received at Ship Island, Mississippi, on April 15, 1865. Transferred from Ship Island to Vicksburg, Mississippi, on May 1, 1865. Appears on a roll of POW's of Company B, 63rd Alabama Infantry commanded by 1st Lieutenant

Thomas J. Calhoun that were surrendered by Lt. General Richard Taylor at Citronelle, Alabama, on May 4, 1865, and paroled at Meridian, Mississippi, on May 11, 1865. Residence—Dale County, Alabama.

Brewer, H., Pvt. Co. E.
Enlisted on August 8, 1864, at Pollard, Alabama, by Captain A. V. Lee for the war. Appears absent on a company muster roll for September and October 1864. Furloughed indefinitely from August 18, 1864. Age—17, eyes—dark, hair—dark, complexion—dark.

Brewer, J. H., Pvt. I/H
Enlisted on April 15, 1864, at Columbiana, Alabama, by Captain Bulgar for the war. Appears present on a company muster roll for September and October 1864. Appears on a roll of POW's of Cos. C and H, 63rd Alabama Infantry commanded by Captain C. W. Martin that were surrendered by Lt. General Richard Taylor at Citronelle, Alabama, on May 4, 1865, and paroled at Meridian, Mississippi, on May 11, 1865. Residence—Jefferson County, Alabama.

Brewer, Lucius L., Pvt. Co. A.
Enrolled on January 1, 1864, at Tallapoosa County, Alabama, by Captain John H. Echols for the war. Appears on a company muster-in roll of Captain Echols' Provost Guards on January 1, 1864, at Montgomery, Alabama. Age—17. Appears present on a company muster roll for January and February with pay due from time of enlistment. Drew clothing in the 2nd Quarter of 1864. Appears absent on a company muster roll for September and October 1864. Furloughed by Medical Examining Board on October 5, 1864, for 60 days. Captured at Blakeley, Alabama, on April 9, 1865. Appears on a roll of POW's received at Ship Island, Mississippi, on April 15, 1865. Transferred from Ship Island to Vicksburg, Mississippi, on May 1, 1865. Appears on a roll of POW's of Company A, 63rd Alabama Infantry commanded by Lt. W. D. Kyle that were surrendered by Lt. General Richard Taylor at Citronelle, Alabama, on May 4, 1865, and paroled at Meridian, Mississippi, on May 13, 1865. Residence was shown as Tallapoosa County, Alabama.

Brinson, William C., Pvt. Co. C.
Enlisted June 15, 1864, at Macon County, Alabama, by Captain Roscoe for the war. Appears on a company muster-in roll for June 24, 1864, at Camp Watts near Notasulga, Alabama. Age—17, Eyes—hazel, hair—red, complexion—dark, 5 foot 7 inches, Residence—Society Hill, Macon County, Alabama. Drew clothing on August 6, 1864. Appears present on a company muster roll for September and October 1864. Captured at Blakeley, Alabama, on April 9, 1865. Appears on a roll of POW's received at Ship Island, Mississippi, on April 15, 1865. Transferred from Ship Island to Vicksburg, Mississippi, on May 1, 1865. Appears on a roll of POW's of Cos. C and H, 63rd Alabama Infantry commanded by Captain C. W. Martin that were surrendered by Lt. General Richard Taylor at Citronelle, Alabama, on May 4, 1865, and paroled at Meridian, Mississippi, on May 11, 1865. Residence—Macon County, Alabama.

Britten, John R. [W.], Pvt. Co. C.
Enlisted on May 9, 1864, at Tallapoosa County, Alabama, by Captain Brown for the war. Appears on a company muster-in roll on June 24, 1864, at Camp Watts near Notasulga, Alabama. Age—17, eyes—blue, hair—dark, complexion—fair, 6 foot 1 inch, Residence—Dadeville, Tallapoosa County, Alabama. Drew Clothing on August 6, 1864. Signed J. W. Britten. Appears absent on a company muster roll for September and October 1864. In hospital at Mobile since October 28, 1864. Paroled at headquarters of the 16th US Army Corps at Montgomery on May 24, 1865. His parole is in his file. Signed by his mark "X".

Brodgan, John R., Pvt. Co. A.
Enrolled on January 1, 1864, at Tallapoosa County, Alabama, by Captain John H. Echols into his company of Provost Guards. Enrolled for the duration of the war. Appears on a company muster-in roll for January 1, 1864, at Montgomery, Alabama. Appears present on a company muster roll for January and February 1864, with pay due from time of enlistment. Drew clothing in 2nd Quarter of 1864. Appears absent on a company muster roll for September and October 1864, last paid on February 29. Absent sick in hospital in Montgomery, Alabama, since September 25, 1864. Paroled at headquarters of the 16th US Army Corps at Montgomery, on May 20, 1865. His parole is in his file. Hair—light, eyes—blue, complexion—fair, 5 foot 11 inches. Signed by mark "X".

Brooks, G. E., Pvt. Co. F.
Enlisted on August 1, 1864, at Georgiana, Alabama, by Captain Brown for the war. Appears absent on a company muster roll for August 31 to October 31, 1864, with pay due from enlistment. Absent in hospital at Mobile. Drew clothing on September 11, 1864. Captured at Blakeley, Alabama, on April 9, 1865. Appears on a roll of POW's received at Ship Island, Mississippi, on April 15, 1865. Transferred from Ship Island to Vicksburg, Mississippi, on May 1, 1865. Appears on a register of sick and wounded Confederate prisoners at USA General Hospital No. 2, in Vicksburg with measles. Returned to duty on May 22.

Brooks, G. L., Pvt. Co. F.
Enlisted on March 9, 1864, at Greenville, Alabama, by Captain Brown for the war. Appears absent sick on a company muster-in roll on July 25, 1864, at Georgiana, Alabama. Age—17, eyes—blue, hair—light, complexion—fair, 6 foot, residence—Butler County, Alabama. Appears absent on a company muster roll for August 31 to October 31, 1864, with pay due from time of enlistment. Absent in hospital at Mobile since October 13, 1864. Drew clothing on September 11, 1864. Captured at Blakeley, Alabama, on April 9, 1865. Appears on a roll of POW's received at Ship Island, Mississippi, on April 15, 1865. Transferred from Ship Island to Vicksburg, Mississippi, on May 1, 1865. He appears on a roll of POW's of Company F, 63rd Alabama Infantry commanded by Captain R. T. Simpson that were surrendered by Lt. General Richard Taylor at Citronelle, Alabama, on May 4, 1865, and paroled at Meridian, Mississippi, on May 11, 1865. Residence—Butler County, Alabama.

Brooks, William C., Pvt. Co. A.
Enlisted in Captain Echols company of Provost Guards on January 1, 1864, in Tallapoosa County, Alabama, by Captain John H. Echols for the war. Appears on a company muster-in roll for January 1, 1864, at Montgomery, Alabama. Appears present on a company muster roll for January and February 1864, with pay due from enlistment. Appears present on a company muster roll for September and October 1864, last paid on February 29. Captured at Blakeley, Alabama, on April 9, 1865. Appears on a roll of POW's received at Ship Island, Mississippi, on April 15, 1865. Transferred from Ship Island to Vicksburg, Mississippi, on May 1, 1865. Appears on a roll of POW's of Company A, 63rd Alabama Infantry commanded by Lieutenant W. D. Kyle that were surrendered by Lt. General Richard Taylor at Citronelle, Alabama, on May 4, 1865, and paroled at Meridian, Mississippi, on May 13, 1865. His reported residence was Tallapoosa County, Alabama.

Brooks, William L., Pvt./Corporal Co. G.
Enlisted on July 1, 1864, at Troy, Alabama, by Captain Wilkerson for the war. Appears on a company muster-in roll for September 7, 1864, at Blakeley, Alabama. Age—16, eyes—grey, hair—dark, complexion—dark, 5 foot 7 inches, residence—Pike County, Alabama. Appears present on a company muster roll for

September and October 1864. Drew clothing on September 11, 1864. Appointed 1st Corporal on October 19.

Brown, A. J., Pvt. Co. I/H.
Enlisted on May 28, 1864, at Columbiana, Alabama, by Lieutenant Bulgar, for the war. Appears absent on a company muster roll for September and October 1864. Absent without leave from September 18, 1864. Appears on a roll of POW's and deserters from the CSA that entered the military lines of the 16th US Army Corps. Captured on April 19, 1865. Reported voluntarily and took the amnesty oath of allegiance to the US.

Brown, Benjamin S., Pvt. Co. B.
Enlisted on August 15, 1864, at Pollard, Alabama, by Lieutenant Townsend for the war. Appears present on a company muster roll for September and October 1864, with pay due from time of enlistment. Drew clothing on September 11, 1864. Appears on a record of paroled Confederate soldiers at headquarters of the 16th US Army Corps at Montgomery, Alabama, on May 18, 1865. His parole is in his file. Hair—light, eyes—blue, complexion—fair, 5 foot 6 inches. Signed by his mark "X."

Brown, J. M., Pvt./Sergeant Co. K.
Enlisted August 6, 1864 at Russell County, Alabama, by Lieutenant Sledge for the war. Appears present on a company muster roll for September and October 1864. Captured at Blakeley, Alabama, on April 9, 1865. Appears on a roll of POW's received at Ship Island, Mississippi, on April 15, 1865. Transferred from Ship Island to Vicksburg, Mississippi, on May 1, 1865. Appears on a roll of POW's of Cos. I and K, 63rd Alabama Infantry commanded by Lieutenant W. A. Skinner that were surrendered by Lt. General Richard Taylor at Citronelle, Alabama, on May 4, 1865, and paroled at Meridian, Mississippi, on May 13, 1865. Residence—Macon County, Alabama.

Brown, J. W., Captain Co. F.
Enlisted on March 9, 1864 at Butler County, Alabama, for the war. Appears on a company muster-in roll for July 25, 1864, at Georgiana, Alabama. Age—48, eyes—dark, hair—dark, complexion—fair, 5 foot 9 inches. Elected Captain on June 28, 1864, resigned on November 10, 1864. Appears absent on a company muster roll for August 31 to October 31, 1864. Absent in hospital at Greenville, Alabama, since September 10. Captain Brown's resignation is in his file in the form of a telegram sent from Blakeley, Alabama, to General Cooper in Richmond. There is also a letter of resignation with endorsements in the file. Resigned due to feeble health and having been appointed Sutler of the Regiment.

Brown, R., Pvt. Co. G.
Admitted to Ross Hospital at Mobile, Alabama, on August 16, 1864, with scabies. Returned to duty on August 25, 1864.

Brown, W. G., Pvt. Co. F.
Enlisted on July 12, 1864, at Lowndes County, Alabama, by Captain Bud for the war. Appears present on a company muster roll for August 31, to October 31, 1864. Drew clothing on September 11, 1864. Appears on a roll of POW's of nurses and patients at Moore Hospital under the command of Surgeon W. C. Cavenaugh that were surrendered by Lt. General Richard Taylor at Citronelle, Alabama, on May 4, 1865, and paroled at Meridian, Mississippi, on May 16, 1865. Residence—Lowndes County, Alabama.

Brown, William A., Pvt. Co. A.
Enlisted on April 4, 1864, at Macon County, Alabama, by Captain Echols for the

war. Drew clothing in the 2nd quarter of 1864. Appears present on a company muster roll for September and October 1864, with pay due from time of enlistment.

Brown, W. J., Pvt. Co. H.
Enlisted on July 23, 1864, at Selma, Alabama, by Captain Suttle for the war. Appears present on a company muster roll for September and October 1864. Age—17, eyes—blue, hair—light, complexion—fair. Captured at Blakeley, Alabama, on April 9, 1865. Appears on a roll of POW's received at Ship Island, Mississippi, on April 15, 1865. Transferred from Ship Island to Vicksburg, Mississippi, on May 1, 1865.

Browning, S., Pvt. Co. I.
Enlisted at Wedowee, Alabama, on May 18, 1864, by Captain Robinson for the war. Appears absent on a company muster roll for September and October 1864. Absent without leave since September 18, 1864.

Bruner, G. W., Pvt. Co. H.
Enlisted on July 25, 1864, at Selma, Alabama, by Captain Suttle for the war. Admitted to Ross Hospital, Mobile, Alabama, on September 2, 1864, with febris congestia. Died in hospital at Mobile on September 5, 1864. Age—17, eyes—dark, hair—dark, complexion—fair.

Bryant, Francis M., Pvt. Co. A.
Enlisted on January 1, 1864, at Tallapoosa County, Alabama, by Captain John H. Echols for the war. Appears on a company muster-in roll at Montgomery, Alabama, on January 1, 1864. Age—16. Appears present on company muster roll for January and February 1864, with pay due from time of enlistment. Appears present on company muster roll for September and October 1864. Drew clothing in 2nd quarter and on September 11, 1864. Admitted to Ross Hospital in Mobile, Alabama, on November 11, 1864, with febris intermittens. Returned to duty on December 1. Appears on a roll of POW's of Company A, 63rd Alabama Infantry commanded Lieutenant W. D. Kyle, that were surrendered by Lt. General Richard Taylor at Citronelle, Alabama, on May 4, 1865, and paroled at Meridian, Mississippi, on May 13, 1865. Residence—Tallapoosa County, Alabama.

Bryant, Thomas L., Pvt. Co. D.
Enlisted on July 30, 1864, at Macon County, Alabama, by Major Ready for the war. Appears on a company muster-in roll at Camp Watts near Notasulga, Alabama, on July 30, 1864. Age—17, eyes—blue, hair—light, complexion—fair, 5 foot 10 inches, residence—Clayton, Barbour County, Alabama. Appears present on a company muster roll for August 31 to October 30, 1864, with pay due from time of enlistment. Drew clothing on August 7, 1864. Captured and wounded at Blakeley, Alabama, on April 9, 1865. Appears on a list of wounded Confederates in the hospital of US 1st Division, 13th Corps, Military Division of West Mississippi. Wounded in the thigh (flesh). Admitted to St. Louis USA General Hospital on April 15, 1865, from Mobile, with gunshot wound to right thigh (flesh). Transferred to General Hospital on May 16. Marine [Marine Hospital], Age—18. His name appears on a roll of POW's that were paroled at New Orleans, Louisiana, on May 16, 1865.

Buckner, James, Pvt. Co. B.
Enlisted on March 23, 1864, at Montgomery, Alabama, by Captain Zimmerman for the war. Appears on a company muster-in roll at Montgomery for March 23, 1864. Drew clothing on July 8 and September 11, 1864. Appears absent on a company muster roll for September and October 1864, with pay due from time of enlistment. Absent sick since October 28, 1864. Appears on a roll of POW's

of nurses and patients of Moore Hospital of the CSA Army commanded by Surgeon W. C. Cavenaugh that were surrendered by Lt. General Richard Taylor at Citronelle, Alabama, on May 4, 1865, and paroled at Meridian, Mississippi, on May 16, 1865. Residence—Montgomery County, Alabama.

Buckner, Thomas M., Pvt. Co. B.
Enrolled on April 8, 1864, at Montgomery, Alabama, by Captain Zimmerman for the war. Appears on a company muster-in roll for March 23, 1864, at Montgomery.

Budershan, Joseph S., Pvt. Co. B.
Enlisted on August 15, 1864, at Pollard, Alabama, by Lieutenant Townsend for the war. Appears present on a company muster roll for September and October 1864, with pay due from time of enlistment. Drew clothing on September 11, 1864. Captured at Blakeley, Alabama, on April 9, 1865. Appears on a roll of POW's received at Ship Island, Mississippi, on April 15, 1865. Transferred from Ship Island to Vicksburg, Mississippi, on May 1, 1865. Appears on a roll of POW's of Company B, 63rd Alabama Infantry commanded by Lieutenant Thomas J. Calhoun that were surrendered by Lt. General Richard Taylor at Citronelle, Alabama, on May 4, 1865, and paroled at Meridian, Mississippi, on May 11, 1865. Residence—Dale County, Alabama.

Bullard, Alvis W., Pvt. Co. A.
Enlisted on January 1, 1864, at Tallapoosa County, Alabama, by Captain John H. Echols for the war. Appears on a company muster-in roll on January 1, 1864, at Montgomery, Alabama. Appears present on a company muster roll for January and February 1864, with pay due from time of enlistment. Drew clothing in 2nd quarter and on August 12, 1864. Appears absent on a company muster roll for September and October 1864. Absent sick in hospital at Mobile, Alabama, since October 26, 1864. Appears on a record of Confederate soldiers paroled at headquarters of the 16th US Army Corps at Montgomery, Alabama, on May 17, 1864. Hair—light, eyes—blue, complexion—fair, 5 foot 1 inch. His parole is in his file.

Burney, Marshall D., Pvt. Co. G.
Enlisted on August 1, 1864, at Pollard, Alabama, by Captain Padgett for the war. Appears on a company muster-in roll for September 7, 1864, at Blakeley, Alabama. Age—17, eyes—grey, hair—light, complexion—fair, 5 foot 3 inches. Appears present on a company muster roll for September and October 1864. Drew clothing on September 11, 1864. Captured at Blakeley, Alabama, on April 9, 1865. Appears on a roll of POW's received at Ship Island, Mississippi, on April 15, 1865. Transferred from Ship Island to Vicksburg, Mississippi, on May 1, 1865. His name appears on a roll of POW's of Cos. E and G, 63rd Alabama Infantry commanded by Captain A. V. Lee that were surrendered by Lt. General Richard Taylor at Citronelle, Alabama, on May 4, 1865, and then were paroled at Meridian, Mississippi, on May 13, 1865. Residence is shown as Pike County, Alabama.

Bush, Americus B., Jr. 2nd Lt./1st Sergeant Co. D.
Enlisted on July 30, 1864, at Macon County, Alabama, by Major Ready for the war. Appears on a company muster-in roll on July 33, 1864, for Captain Zorn's Alabama Reserves at Camp Watts near Notasulga, Alabama. Age—17, eyes—blue, hair—dark, complexion—fair, 6 foot, residence—Bushville, Barbour County, Alabama. Elected 2nd Lt. on March 2, 1864, resigned on November 11, 1864. Appears present on a company muster roll for August 30 to October 30, 1864, with pay due from time of enlistment. Here he is shown as having enlisted on March 2, 1864, at Clayton by D. W. Seals. Captured at Blakeley, Alabama, on

April 9, 1865. Appears on a roll of POW's received at Ship Island, Mississippi, on April 15, 1865. Transferred from Ship Island to Vicksburg, Mississippi, on May 1, 1865. Appears on a roll of POW's of Company D, 63rd Alabama Infantry commanded by Captain Robert H. Pearson that were surrendered by Lt. General Richard Taylor at Citronelle, Alabama, on May 4, 1865, and paroled at Meridian, Mississippi, on May 13, 1865. Residence—Barbour County, Alabama. His resignation is in his file with endorsements. He resigned due to being totally incompetent and inexperienced. His commander, Colonel O. F. Rice, agreed with Bush's assessment.

Bush, Herbert H., Pvt. Co. D/F.
Enlisted on July 30, 1864, at Macon County, Alabama, by Major Ready for the war. Appears on a company muster-in roll on July 30, 1864, at Camp Watts near Notasulga, Alabama. Age—17, eyes—blue, hair—light, complexion—fair, 5 foot 6 inches, residence—Eufaula, Barbour County, Alabama. Appears present on a muster roll for August 30 to October 30, 1864, with pay due from time of enlistment. Here he is shown as having enlisted at Eufaula, Alabama, on May 5, 1865 by Captain Zorn. Drew clothing on August 7, 1864. Captured at Blakeley, Alabama, on April 9, 1865. Appears on a roll of POW's received at Ship Island, Mississippi, on April 15, 1865. Transferred from Ship Island to Vicksburg, Mississippi, on May 1, 1865. Appears on a roll of POW's of Company D, 63rd Alabama Infantry commanded by Captain Robert H. Pearson that were surrendered by Lt. General Richard Taylor at Citronelle, Alabama, on May 4, 1865, and paroled at Meridian, Mississippi, on May 13, 1865. Residence—Barbour County, Alabama. Appears on a roll of POW's of Quintard Hospital CSA commanded by Surgeon S. V. D. Hill that were surrendered by Lt. General Richard Taylor at Citronelle, Alabama, on May 4, 1865, and paroled at Meridian, Mississippi, on May 13, 1865. Residence—Eufaula, Alabama.

Bush, John E., Pvt./Corporal Co. C.
Enlisted on May 25, 1864, at Russell County, Alabama, by Lieutenant Carnes for the war. Appears on a company muster-in roll at Camp Watts near Notasulga, Alabama, on June 24, 1865. Age—17, eyes—black, hair—black, complexion—dark, 5 foot 10 inches, residence—Sand Fort, Alabama. Appears present on a company muster roll for September and October 1864, with pay due from time of enlistment. Drew clothing August 6, 1864. Captured at Blakeley, Alabama, on April 9, 1865. Appears on a roll of POW's received at Ship Island, Mississippi, on April 15, 1865. Transferred from Ship Island to Vicksburg, Mississippi, on May 1, 1865. His name appears on a roll of POW's of Cos. C and H, 63rd Alabama Infantry commanded by Captain C. W. Martin that were surrendered by Lt. General Richard Taylor at Citronelle, Alabama, on May 4, 1865, and paroled at Meridian, Mississippi, on May 11, 1865. Residence—Russell County, Alabama.

Bush, Ryan O., 1st Sergeant Co. D.
Enlisted on July 30, 1864, at Macon County, Alabama, by Major Ready for the war. Appears on a company muster-in roll at Camp Watts near Notasulga, Alabama, on July 30, 1864. Age—17, eyes—dark, hair—dark, complexion—dark, 5 foot 6 inches, residence—Bushville, Barbour County, Alabama. Appears present on a company muster roll for August 30 to October 30, 1864, with pay due from time of enlistment. Here he is shown as having enlisted at Clayton, Alabama, by D. M. Seals. Drew clothing on August 7, 1864. Captured at Blakeley, Alabama, on April 9, 1865. Appears on a roll of POW's received at Ship Island, Mississippi, on April 15, 1865. Transferred from Ship Island to Vicksburg, Mississippi, on May 1, 1865. Appears on a roll of POW's of Company D, 63rd Alabama Infantry commanded by Captain Robert H. Pearson that were surrendered by Lt. General Richard Taylor at Citronelle, Alabama, on May 4,

1865, and paroled at Meridian, Mississippi, on May 13, 1865. Residence—Barbour County, Alabama.

Butts, Phillips A., Pvt. Co. D.
Enlisted on July 30, 1864, at Macon County, Alabama, by Major Ready for the war. Appears on a company muster-in roll at Camp Watts near Notasulga, Alabama, on July 30, 1864. Age—17, eyes—dark, hair—dark, complexion—dark, 5 foot 5 inches, residence—Texasville, Barbour County, Alabama. Appears present on a company muster roll for August 30 to October 30, 1864, with pay due from time of enlistment. Here he is shown as having enlisted at Eufaula, Alabama, by Captain Zorn. Drew clothing on August 7, 1864. Captured at Blakeley, Alabama, on April 9, 1865. Appears on a roll of POW's received at Ship Island, Mississippi, on April 15, 1865. Transferred from Ship Island to Vicksburg, Mississippi, on May 1, 1865. His name appears on a roll of POW's of Company D, 63rd Alabama Infantry commanded by Captain Robert H. Pearson that were surrendered by Lt. General Richard Taylor at Citronelle, Alabama, on May 4, 1865, and paroled at Meridian, Mississippi, on May 13, 1865. Residence—Barbour County, Alabama.

Cain, J. H., Pvt. Co. E.
Enlisted on March 12, 1864, at Clayton, Alabama, by Captain A. V. Lee for the war. Appears absent on a company muster roll for September and October 1864. Absent without leave since October 25, 1864. Age—17, eyes—dark, hair—dark, complexion—dark.

Caldwell, Hugh M., Pvt./Sergeant Co. C.
Enlisted May 28, 1864, at Russell County, Alabama, by Lieutenant Carnes for the war. Appears on a company muster-in roll at Camp Watts near Notasulga, Alabama, for June 24, 1864. Age—17, eyes—grey, hair—light, complexion—fair, 5 foot 4 inches, residence—Villulah, Russell County, Alabama. Drew clothing on August 6, 1864. Appears present on a company muster roll for September and October 1864, with pay due from time of enlistment.

Caldwell, James, Pvt. Co. I.
Captured at Lebanon, Kentucky, on June 21, 1864. Appears on a roll of POW's at Military Prison, Louisville, Kentucky, that were received on June 23, 1864, and sent to Rock Island, Illinois, on June 24, 1864. Confined at Rock Island Barracks, Rock Island, Illinois, on June 27, 1864. Joined the US Navy on July 6, 1864, and was transferred to US Navy. [These were called Galvanized Yankees. Confederates with at thin coat of Yankee on the outside.]

Caldwell, M. J., 1st Sergeant Co. K.
Enlisted on June 8, 1864, at Macon County, Alabama, by Captain Roscoe for the war. Appears present on a company muster roll for September and October 1864. Captured at Blakeley, Alabama, on April 9, 1865. Appears on a roll of POW's received at Ship Island, Mississippi, on April 15, 1865. Transferred from Ship Island to Vicksburg, Mississippi, on May 1, 1865. Appears on a roll of POW's of Cos. I and K, 63rd Alabama Infantry commanded by Lieutenant W. A. Skinner that were surrendered by Lt. General Richard Taylor at Citronelle, Alabama, on May 4, 1865, and paroled at Meridian, Mississippi, on May 13, 1865. Residence—Macon County, Alabama.

Caldwell, W., Pvt. Co. B.
Captured at Blakeley, Alabama, on April 9, 1865. Appears on a roll of POW's received at Ship Island, Mississippi, on April 15, 1865. Transferred from Ship Island to Vicksburg, Mississippi, on May 1, 1865. Appears on a roll of POW's of Company B, 63rd Alabama Infantry commanded by 1st Lieutenant Thomas J.

Calhoun that were surrendered by Lt. General Richard Taylor at Citronelle, Alabama, on May 4, 1865, and paroled at Meridian, Mississippi, on May 11, 1865. Residence—Pike County, Alabama. Request for information on W. S. Caldwell was processed by Adjutant Generals Office on December 14, 1916. Request was made by an individual from Terrell, Texas.

Calhoun, Thomas J., 1st Lieutenant, AAQM, Co. B/F&S.
His name appears on a company muster-in roll at Montgomery, Alabama, on March 23, 1864. Commissioned near Mobile, Alabama, on March 23, 1864. Requisitioned fuel for Company B, Provost Guard at Montgomery for May 1864, 8 cords of wood for 61 men. Requisitioned to supply Captain Zimmerman's Provost Guards at Montgomery on July 8, 1864; 63 jackets, 63 pair of pants, 63 caps, 67 pair of drawers, 63 pair of shoes, 64 pair of sox and 68 cotton shirts. Appears absent on a company muster roll for September and October, 1864. Detached by Colonel Rice as Regiment Quarter Master since August 10, 1864. Appears present but detached from Company B on a Field and Staff Muster roll for September and October. Captured at Blakeley, Alabama, on April 9, 1865, by the 2nd Division of 16th US Army Corps. Appears on a roll of POW's received at Ship Island, Mississippi, on April 15, 1865. Transferred from Ship Island to Vicksburg, Mississippi, on May 1, 1865. Appears on a register of POW's confined at New Orleans, Louisiana, on April 30, 1865, and exchanged on May 1. His Parole of Honor is in his file, signed at Meridian, Mississippi, on May 11, 1865. Residence shown is Tuskegee, Alabama. There is also in his file a Parole of Honor for Captain Thomas J. Calhoun, Enrolling Officer at Houston, County Texas signed at Houston on July 12, 1865. This is likely another individual.

Callaway, E. J. M., Pvt./Sergeant Co. ?
Appears on a list with the heading "Post Register, Albany, Ga." with the date May 16. Thought to be a list of POW's paroled at Albany, Georgia. Appears on a list of POW's that were surrendered to Brigadier General E. M. McCook USA by Major General Sam Jones CSA at Tallahassee, Florida, on May 10, 1865. Paroled May 12, 1865.

Callaway, Zachary T., Pvt. Co. A.
Enlisted on May 1, 1864, at Chambers County, Alabama, by Captain Echols for the war. Drew clothing in 2nd quarter of 1864. Appears present on a company muster roll for September and October 1864, with pay due from time of enlistment. Captured at Blakeley, Alabama, on April 9, 1865. Appears on a roll of POW's received at Ship Island, Mississippi, on April 15, 1865. Transferred from Ship Island to Vicksburg, Mississippi, on May 1, 1865. Appears on a roll of POW's of Company A, 63rd Alabama Infantry commanded by Lieutenant W. D. Kyle that were surrendered by Lt. General Richard Taylor at Citronelle, Alabama, on May 4, 1865, and paroled at Meridian, Mississippi, on May 13, 1865. Residence—Chambers County, Alabama.

Calloway, David A., Pvt. Co. B.
Enlisted on July 17, 1864, at Montgomery, Alabama, by Lieutenant Calhoun for the war. Drew clothing on September 11, 1864. Appears on a company muster roll for September and October 1864. Reported to have been discharged per order of General Withers on October 10, 1864.

Camp, A. B., Pvt. Co. I.
Enlisted on April 15, 1864, at Wedowee, Alabama, by Captain Robinson for the war. Appears absent on a company muster roll for September and October 1864. Absent without leave from September 18, 1864.

Campbell, John J., Pvt. Co. B.
Enlisted on August 15, 1864, at Pollard, Alabama, by Lieutenant Townsend for the war. Appears present on a company muster roll for September and October 1864.

Canadey, C. C., Pvt. Co. I.
Enlisted on May 18, 1864, at Wedowee, Alabama, by Captain Robinson for the war. Appears present on a company muster roll for September and October 1864.

Cane, S. P., Pvt. Co. F.
Enlisted on August 4, 1864, at Georgiana, Alabama, by Captain Brown for the war. Appears absent on a company muster roll for August 31 to October 31, 1864, with pay due from time of enlistment. Absent in hospital at Mobile, Alabama, since October 21, 1864. Drew clothing on September 11, 1864. Captured at Blakeley, Alabama, on April 9, 1865. Appears on a roll of POW's received at Ship Island, Mississippi, on April 15, 1865. Transferred from Ship Island to Vicksburg, Mississippi, on May 1, 1865. Appears on register of sick and wounded POW's at USA General Hospital No. 2, Vicksburg. Admitted on May 3 from Steamer with acute diarrhoea. Returned to duty on May 8, 1864. Age—16.

Cannan, Stephen, Pvt. Co. B.
Enlisted on June 25, 1864, at Montgomery, Alabama, by Captain Zimmerman for the war. Appears present on a company muster roll for September and October 1864, with pay due from time of enlistment. Drew clothing on September 11, 1864. Captured at Blakeley, Alabama, on April 9, 1865. Appears on a roll of POW's received at Ship Island, Mississippi, on April 15, 1865. Transferred from Ship Island to Vicksburg, Mississippi, on May 1, 1865. Appears on a roll of POW's of Company B, 63rd Alabama Infantry commanded by 1st Lieutenant Thomas J. Calhoun that were surrendered by Lt. General Richard Taylor at Citronelle, Alabama, on May 4, 1865, and paroled at Meridian, Mississippi, on May 11, 1865. Residence—Lowndes County, Alabama.

Capps, D. C., Pvt. Co. E.
Enlisted on September 12, 1864, at Camp Hood by Captain A. V. Lee for the war. Appears absent on a company muster roll for September and October 1864. Absent in hospital since October 7, 1864. Drew clothing on September 11, 1864. Captured at Blakeley, Alabama, on April 9, 1865. Appears on a roll of POW's received at Ship Island, Mississippi, on April 15, 1865. Transferred from Ship Island to Vicksburg, Mississippi, on May 1, 1865. Appears on a roll of POW's of Cos. E and G, 63rd Alabama Infantry commanded by Captain A. V. Lee that were surrendered by Lt. General Richard Taylor at Citronelle, Alabama, on May 4, 1865, and paroled at Meridian, Mississippi, on May 13, 1865. Residence—Monroe County, Alabama.

Card, William D., 2nd Sergeant. Co. A.
Enlisted on January 1, 1864, at Macon County, Alabama, by Captain John H. Echols for the war. Age—17. His name appears on a company muster-in roll at Montgomery, Alabama, on January 1, 1864. Appears present on a company muster roll for January and February 1864, with pay due from time of enlistment. Drew clothing in 2nd quarter of 1864.

Carden, J. L., Pvt. Co. I.
Enlisted on April 15, 1864, at Columbiana, Alabama, by Lieutenant Bulger for the war. Appears absent on a company muster roll for September and October 1864. Furloughed from September 27, 1864, for 30 days.

Carden, Samuel, Pvt. Co. I.
Enlisted on April 15, 1864, at Columbiana, Alabama, by Lieutenant Bulger for the war. Appears absent on a company muster roll for September and October 1864. Absent sick in Hospital Moore since October 25.

Carlisle, Samuel T., Pvt. Co. G.
Enlisted on April 16, 1864, at Troy, Alabama, by Captain Wilkerson for the war. Appears on a company muster-in roll for September 7, 1864, at Blakeley, Alabama. Age—17, eyes—blue, hair—dark, 6 foot 4 inches, residence—Pike County, Alabama. Drew clothing on September 11, 1864. Appears present on a company muster roll for September and October 1864. Appears on a register of paroled Confederate soldiers paroled June 1, 1865, at headquarters of the 16th US Army Corps in Montgomery, Alabama. He signed with a mark "X." His parole is in his file. There is a 1915 request for information in his file from the Oklahoma Board of Pension Commissioners, in Oklahoma City, Oklahoma.

Carlisle, Louis (C. L.), Pvt. Co. H.
Enlisted on August 29, 1864, at Blakeley, Alabama, by Lieutenant Killough for the war. Appears absent on a company muster roll for September and October 1864. Absent sick at hospital in Greenville since September 12. Age—17, eyes—hazel, hair—light, complexion—fair. Drew clothing on September 11, 1864. Admitted to Ross Hospital in Mobile, Alabama, on September 16, 1864, with rubeola. Sent to General Hospital on September 26, 1864. Residence—Greenville. Admitted to Ross Hospital at Mobile on March 29, 1865, with vulnus sclopeticum [gunshot wound]. Sent to General Hospital on April 9, 1865, remarks:Meridian.

Carlos, P. P., Pvt. Co. E.
He signed a parole at headquarters of the 16th US Army Corps in Montgomery, Alabama, on May 8, 1864. He is described as: eyes—dark, hair—dark, complexion—dark, 6 foot 1 inch.

Carmichael, John, Co. B.
Enlisted on August 8, 1864, at Montgomery, Alabama, by Captain Zimmerman for the war. Appears absent on a company muster roll for September and October 1864. Absent sick since September 29, 1864. Appears on a register of wounded prisoners at City Hospital, Mobile, Alabama. Appears on a roll of POW's remaining in hospital in Mobile commanded by Assistant Surgeon Charles O. Helwig captured by Major General E. R. S. Canby USA on April 12, 1865, and paroled at Mobile on May 11, 1865.

Carr, William S., Sergeant Co. B.
Enlisted on March 23, 1864, at Montgomery, Alabama, by Captain W. Zimmerman for the war. Appears on a company muster-in roll on March 23, 1864, at Montgomery. Age—17. Appears present on a company muster roll for September and October 1864. Drew clothing July 8, August 12 and September 11, 1864. Captured at Blakeley, Alabama, on April 9, 1865. Appears on a roll of POW's received at Ship Island, Mississippi, on April 15, 1865. Transferred from Ship Island to Vicksburg, Mississippi, on May 1, 1865. Appears on a roll of POW's of Company B, 63rd Alabama Infantry commanded by 1st Lieutenant Thomas J. Calhoun that were surrendered by Lt. General Richard Taylor at Citronelle, Alabama, on May 4, 1865, and paroled at Meridian, Mississippi, on May 11, 1865. Residence—Macon County, Alabama.

Carroll, Allen, Pvt. Co. G.
Admitted to Ross Hospital, Mobile, Alabama, on September 20, 1864, with rubeola. Sent to General Hospital on September 26, 1864. Remarks:Greenville.

Carroll, F., Pvt. B.
　　Appears on a roll of POW stragglers of CSA Army that were surrendered by Lt. General Richard Taylor at Citronelle, Alabama, on May 4, 1865, and paroled at Selma, Alabama, in May 1865. Residence—Shelby County, Alabama.

Carroll, John A., Pvt. Co. G.
　　Enlisted on May 16, 1864, at Troy, Alabama, by Captain Wilkerson for the war. Age—16, eyes—blue, hair—light, complexion—fair, 5 foot 7 inches, residence—Pike County, Alabama. Appears on a company muster-in roll on September 7, 1864, at Blakeley, Alabama. Appears present on a company muster roll for September and October 1864. Appears on a list of wounded from Thomas's Brigade 2nd Regiment Alabama, sent from Spanish Fort, Alabama, to Vicksburg, Mississippi on April 8, 1865. Admitted to USA Hospital Steamer D. A. January on April 17, 1865. Admitted to USA Hospital Steamer Elanora Carrel at New Orleans, Louisiana, and transferred to General Hospital No. 3, (colored) at Vicksburg. Appears on a roll of POW's at USA General Hospital No. 3, Vicksburg. Transferred to USA General Hospital No. 2 at Vicksburg on May 4, 1865. Captured at Blakeley, Alabama, on April 9, 1865. Admitted to USA General Hospital No. 2 at Vicksburg on May 4, 1865, with gunshot wound to the head (slight). Missile was identified as a conical ball. Age—18. Wounded in action in cranium, left side.

Carter, Charles, W., Pvt. Co. B.
　　Enlisted on June 25, 1864, at Montgomery, Alabama, by Lt. Calhoun for the war. Appears present on a company muster roll for September and October 1864. Drew clothing on July 8, 1864. Signed by his mark. Captured at Blakeley, Alabama, on April 9, 1865. Appears on a roll of POW's received at Ship Island, Mississippi, on April 15, 1865. Transferred from Ship Island to Vicksburg, Mississippi, on May 1, 1865.

Carter, Drewery J., Pvt. Co. B.
　　Enlisted on March 23, 1864, at Montgomery, Alabama, by Captain W. Zimmerman for the war. Age—17. Appears absent on a company muster roll for September and October 1864, with pay due from time of enlistment. Absent sick since 14th. Drew clothing on July 8 and September 11, 1864. Appears on a list of CSA sliders paroled at Montgomery, Alabama, on May 26, 1865. His parole is in his file. Eyes—blue, hair—light, complexion—fair, 5 foot 10 inches.

Carter, J. F., Pvt. Co. F.
　　Enlisted at Greenville, Alabama, by Captain Brown for the war. Appears on a company muster roll of Captain Brown's company of reserves on July 28, 1864, at Georgiana, Alabama. Age—17, eyes—blue, hair—dark, complexion—fair, 5 foot 11 inches, residence—Butler County, Alabama. Appears absent on a company muster roll for August 31 to October 31, 1864, with pay due from time of enlistment. Absent in hospital at Mobile, Alabama, since October 28, 1864. Drew clothing on September 11, 1864. Appears on a roll of Confederate stragglers that were paroled at Selma, Alabama, in June 1865.

Carter, J. P., 2nd Lieutenant, Co. G.
　　Appears on a company muster-in roll for September 7, 1864, at Blakeley, Alabama. He is described as: age—17, eyes—dark, hair—dark, complexion—florid, 5 foot 7 inches, residence—Pike County, Alabama. Elected 2nd Lieutenant on July 1, 1864, resigned on November 11, 1864. His hand written resignation with endorsements is in his file dated August 15, 1864, at Pollard, Alabama. He resigned as he felt incompetent to discharge his duties and prefers to be in the ranks.

Carter, R. G., 3rd Corporal/Pvt. Co. F.
    Enlisted on May 30, 1864, at Montgomery, Alabama, by Captain Moore for the war. Appears on a company muster-in roll for July 25, 1864, at Georgiana, Alabama. Age—17, eyes—blue, hair—dark, complexion—fair, 5 foot 11 ½ inches, residence—Autauga County, Alabama. Appears absent on a company muster roll for August 31 to October 31, 1864. Absent in hospital at Mobile, Alabama. Reduced from Corporal on October 15.

Carter, Thomas W., Pvt. Co. B.
    Enlisted on June 25, 1864, at Montgomery, Alabama, by Lieutenant Calhoun for the war. Appears absent on a company muster roll for September and October 1864, with pay due from time of enlistment. Absent sick since July 20, 1864. Captured at Blakeley, Alabama, on April 9, 1865. Appears on a roll of POW's received at Ship Island, Mississippi, on April 15, 1865. Transferred from Ship Island to Vicksburg, Mississippi, on May 1, 1865. Appears on a roll of POW's at Quintard Hospital, CSA commanded by Surgeon S. V. D. Hill that were surrendered by Lt. General Richard Taylor at Citronelle, Alabama, on May 4, 1865, and paroled at Meridian, Mississippi, on May 10, 1865. Residence—Equality, Alabama. He also show on a roll of POW's of Company B, 63rd Alabama, that were surrendered at Citronelle. Here his residence is reported to be Coosa County, Alabama.

Casey, J., Pvt. Co. I/E.
    Captured at Blakeley, Alabama, on April 9, 1865. Appears on a roll of POW's received at Ship Island, Mississippi, on April 15, 1865. Transferred from Ship Island to Vicksburg, Mississippi, on May 1, 1865. Appears on a roll of POW's of Cos. E and G, 63rd Alabama Infantry commanded by Captain A. V. Lee that were surrendered by Lt. General Richard Taylor at Citronelle, Alabama, on May 4, 1865, and paroled at Meridian, Mississippi, on May 13, 1865. Residence—Barbour County, Alabama.

Cason, Daniel M., Co. B.
    Enlisted on April 23, 1864, at Montgomery, Alabama, by Captain Zimmerman for the war. Appears on a company muster-in roll for March 23, 1864, at Montgomery, Alabama. Appears absent on a company muster roll for September and October 1864, with pay due from time of enlistment. Absent detached per SO [special order] No. 35 dated September 25, 1864, General Liddell. Drew clothing on July 8 and September 11, 1864. Signed by mark. Captured at Blakeley, Alabama, on April 9, 1865. Appears on a roll of POW's received at Ship Island, Mississippi, on April 15, 1865. Transferred from Ship Island to Vicksburg, Mississippi, on May 1, 1865. Appears on a roll of POW's of Company B, 63rd Alabama Infantry commanded by 1st Lieutenant Thomas J. Calhoun that were surrendered by Lt. General Richard Taylor at Citronelle, Alabama, on May 4, 1865, and paroled at Meridian, Mississippi, on May 11, 1865. Residence—Coosa County, Alabama.

Casper, William, Pvt. Co. I.
    Enlisted on May 18, 1864, at Wedowee, Alabama, by Captain Robinson for the war. Appears absent on a company muster roll for September and October 1864. Absent without leave from September 18, 1864.

Caster, C. W., Pvt. Co. B.
    Appears on a roll of POW's of Company B, 63rd Alabama Infantry commanded by 1st Lieutenant Thomas J. Calhoun that were surrendered by Lt. General Richard Taylor at Citronelle, Alabama, on May 4, 1865, and paroled at Meridian, Mississippi, on May 11, 1865. Residence—Coosa County, Alabama.

Castens. H. A., 2nd Lieutenant Co. E.
    Enlisted on September 16, 1864, at Blakeley, Alabama, by Captain A. V. Lee for the war. He is described as: age—19, eyes—blue, hair—light, complexion—fair. Appears absent on a company muster roll for September and October 1864. He was a cadet when elected and was furloughed for 30 days from October 17, 1864. Elected to 2nd Lieutenant on September 16, 1864. His name appears on a report of persons held in confinement by Provost Marshal of 2nd Division, 16th US Army Corps. Captured at Blakeley on April 9, 1865, and confined one day as POW. Appears on a roll of POW's received at Ship Island, Mississippi, on April 16, 1865. Transferred from Ship Island to Vicksburg, Mississippi, on April 28, 1865. Exchanged at New Orleans, Louisiana, on May 1, 1865. Signed a parole of honor at Meridian, Mississippi on May 11, 1865. His parole is in his file.

Catchchart, F. T., Pvt. Co. H.
    Enlisted on March 15, 1864, at Montevallo, Alabama, by Captain Suttle for the war. Eyes—blue, hair—light, complexion—fair. Drew clothing on September 11, 1864. Appears present on a company muster roll for September and October 1864. Appears on a roll of POW Confederate stragglers that were paroled during June 1865, by Colonel William R. Marshall, commander 7th Minn. Vols. at Selma, Alabama.

Caul, Thomas J., Pvt. Co. D.
    Enlisted on July 30, 1864, at Macon County, Alabama, by Major Ready for the war. Appears on a company muster-in roll for July 30, 1864, at Camp Watts near Notasulga, Alabama. Age—17, eyes—blue, hair—dark, complexion—florid, 5 foot 6 inches, residence—Buford, Barbour County, Alabama. Drew clothing on September 11, 1864. Appears absent on a company muster roll for August 30 to October 30, 1864, with pay due from time of enlistment. Absent on sick furlough for 60 days by Medical Examining Board since October 24, 1864. Here he is reported to have been enlisted at Clayton, Alabama, on March 2, 1864, by D. M. Seals for the war. Captured at Blakeley, Alabama, on April 9, 1865. Appears on a roll of POW's received at Ship Island, Mississippi, on April 15, 1865. Transferred from Ship Island to Vicksburg, Mississippi, on May 1, 1865. Appears on a roll of POW's of Company D, 63rd Alabama Infantry commanded by Captain Robert H. Pearson that were surrendered by Lt. General Richard Taylor at Citronelle, Alabama, on May 4, 1865, and paroled at Meridian, Mississippi, on May 13, 1865. Residence—Barbour County, Alabama. Admitted to USA General Hospital No. 2, at Vicksburg on May 3, 1865, from steamer with acute diarrhoea. Returned to duty on May 12, 1864.

Chambers, William E., Jr. 2nd Lieutenant/Brevet 2nd Lieutenant, Co. C.
    Enlisted on June 1, 1864, at Russell County, Alabama, by Lieutenant Carnes for the war. Appears on a company muster-in roll for June 24, 1864, at Camp Watts near Notasulga, Alabama. Age—17, eyes—grey, hair—dark, complexion—fair, 5 foot 2 inches, residence—Columbus, Georgia, (Russell County, Alabama). Appears absent on a company muster roll for September and October 1864, with pay due from time of enlistment. Absent in hospital at Mobile, Alabama, since October 28, 1864. Elected 2nd Lieutenant on June 20, 1864. Captured at Blakeley, Alabama, on April 9, 1865, by 2nd Division, 16th US Army Corps. Appears on a roll of POW's received at Ship Island, Mississippi, on April 15, 1865. Transferred from Ship Island to Vicksburg, Mississippi, on May 1, 1865. Confined at New Orleans, Louisiana, on April 28, 1865, and exchanged on May 1, 1865. Note in his file indicates to see personal paper of James M. Alexander for information relative to Wm. Chambers. Signed a Parole of Honor at Meridian, Mississippi, on May 11, 1865. His parole is in his file.

Chandler, T. S., Sergeant Co. K.
Captured at Blakeley, Alabama, on April 9, 1865. Appears on a roll of POW's received at Ship Island, Mississippi, on April 15, 1865. Transferred from Ship Island to Vicksburg, Mississippi, on May 1, 1865. Appears on a roll of POW's of Cos. I and K, 63rd Alabama Infantry commanded by Lieutenant W. A. Skinner that were surrendered by Lt. General Richard Taylor at Citronelle, Alabama, on May 4, 1865, and paroled at Meridian, Mississippi, on May 13, 1865. Residence—Green County, Alabama.

Chandler, W. S., Pvt. Co. K.
Enlisted on September 3, 1864, at Perry County, Alabama, by Captain Powers for the war. Appears present on a company muster roll for September and October 1864.

Chapman, W. A., Pvt. Co. I.
Enlisted on April 15, 1864, at Columbiana, Alabama, by Lieutenant Bulgar for the war. Appears present on a company muster roll for September and October 1864. Captured at Blakeley, Alabama, on April 9, 1865. Appears on a roll of POW's received at Ship Island, Mississippi, on April 15, 1865. Transferred from Ship Island to Vicksburg, Mississippi, on May 1, 1865. Appears on a roll of POW's of Cos. I and K, 63rd Alabama Infantry commanded by Lieutenant W. A. Skinner that were surrendered by Lt. General Richard Taylor at Citronelle, Alabama, on May 4, 1865, and paroled at Meridian, Mississippi, on May 13, 1865. Residence—Shelby County, Alabama.

Chatham, Thomas J., Pvt. Co. A.
Enlisted on January 1, 1864, at Tallapoosa County, Alabama, by Captain John H. Echols for the war. Appears on a company muster-in roll for January 1, 1864, at Montgomery, Alabama. Appears present on a company muster roll for January and February 1864, with pay due from time of enlistment. Drew clothing in 2nd quarter and August 12, 1864. Signed by his mark. Appears present on a company muster roll for September and October 1864. Captured at Blakeley, Alabama, on April 9, 1865. Appears on a roll of POW's received at Ship Island, Mississippi, on April 15, 1865. Transferred from Ship Island to Vicksburg, Mississippi, on May 1, 1865. Appears on a roll of POW's of Company A, 63rd Alabama Infantry commanded by Lieutenant W. D. Kyle that were surrendered by Lt. General Richard Taylor at Citronelle, Alabama, on May 4, 1865, and paroled at Meridian, Mississippi, on May 13, 1865. Residence—Tallapoosa County, Alabama.

Chatham, Clement, Pvt. Co. B.
Enlisted on March 23, 1864, at Montgomery, Alabama, by Captain W. Zimmerman for the war. Appears on a company muster-in roll for March 23, 1864, at Montgomery. Drew clothing on July 8 and September 11, 1864. He signed by his mark. He appears absent on a company muster roll for September and October 1864, with pay due from the time of enlistment. This muster roll reports him absent sick since October 10, 1864.

Chatten, C. R., Pvt. Co. B.
He signed a parole at the headquarters of the 16th, US Army Corps at Montgomery, Alabama, on May 23, 1865. Signed by mark "X." He is described as: hair—light, eyes—grey, complexion—light, 5 foot 4 inches. His parole is in his file.

Chattwood, E., Pvt, Co. K.
Enlisted on September 22, 1864, at Prattville, Alabama, by Captain Moore for the war. Appears absent on a company muster roll for September and October

1864. Muster roll reports him absent detailed to work in factory on October 25, 1864, by General Withers.

Chestnut, James W., Corporal Co. D.
Enlisted on July 30, 1864, at Macon County, Alabama, by Major Ready for the war. Appears on a company muster-in roll for July 30, 1864, at Camp Watts near Notasulga, Alabama. Age—17, eyes—dark, hair—dark, complexion—dark, 5 foot 10 inches, residence—Kings Post Office, Barbour County, Alabama. Drew clothing on August 7, 1864. Appears present on a company muster roll for August 30 to October 30, 1864, with pay due from time of enlistment. Here he is reported as having enlisted at Clayton, Alabama, on March 2, 1864, by D. M. Seals. Appears on a list of wounded Confederates in the hospital of 1st Division, 16th Corps US Army at the battle of Blakeley Fort, Alabama, on April 9, 1865, with compound fracture of arm. Resection of Humerus by Surgeon O. G. Hunt 11th Illinois Infantry. Appears on a register of POW's at New Orleans, Louisiana, confined on May 1, 1865 and paroled on May 16, 1865. Admitted to St. Louis USA General Hospital, at New Orleans with gunshot fracture of middle third right femur and gunshot fracture of left humerus. Transferred to General Hospital on May 26. Remarks: Marine [Marine Hospital]. Age—18. Died June 20, 1865. Buried in Square 69, Grave 81 of Monument Cemetery. He was reported as single with residence at Eufaula, Alabama, references shown as Michael Chestnut at Eufaula, Alabama.

Childers, Paul A., Pvt. Co. A.
Enlisted on May 1, 1864, at Tallapoosa County, Alabama, by Captain Echols for the war. Drew clothing in the 2nd quarter of 1864. Appears present on a company muster roll for September and October 1864, with pay due from time of enlistment. Captured at Blakeley, Alabama, on April 9, 1865. Appears on a roll of POW's received at Ship Island, Mississippi, on April 15, 1865. Transferred from Ship Island to Vicksburg, Mississippi, on May 1, 1865. Appears on a roll of POW's of Company A, 63rd Alabama Infantry commanded by Lieutenant W. D. Kyle that were surrendered by Lt. General Richard Taylor at Citronelle, Alabama, on May 4, 1865, and paroled at Meridian, Mississippi, on May 13, 1865. Residence—Tallapoosa County, Alabama.

Chivers, James I., Pvt. Co. A.
Enlisted on March 24, 1864, at Macon County, Alabama, by Captain Echols for the war. Drew clothing in the 2nd quarter of 1864. Appears absent on a company muster roll for September and October 1864. Absent sick in hospital at Montgomery, Alabama, since October 10, 1864. Appears present on a hospital muster roll at Ladies' Hospital, Montgomery as a patient on November 15, 1864. Here he is reported to have enlisted on March 1, 1864, at Montgomery. Signed a parole as a POW on May 15, 1865.

Clack, Robert, Pvt. Co. B.
Enlisted on April 14, 1864, at Montgomery, Alabama, by Captain W. Zimmerman for the war. Appears on a company muster-in roll at Montgomery for March 23, 1864. Drew clothing on July 8, 1864. Appears absent on a company muster roll for September and October 1864. Absent sick since October 25, 1864. Admitted to Ross Hospital, Mobile, Alabama, on November 17, 1864, with febris remittens. Returned to duty on December 1, 1864. Shown here as N. Robert Clack.

Clancy, P. D., Pvt. Co. F.
Enlisted on May 30, 1865, at Montgomery, Alabama, by Captain Jackson for the war. Appears on a company muster-in roll at Georgiana, Alabama, for July 25, 1864. Age—17, eyes—blue, hair—dark, complexion—fair, 5 foot 9 inches, residence—Butler County, Alabama. Appears absent on a company muster roll

for August 31 to October 31, 1864, with pay due from time of enlistment. Absent in hospital at Mobile, Alabama, on October 28, 1864. Captured at Blakeley, Alabama, on April 9, 1865. Appears on a roll of POW's received at Ship Island, Mississippi, on April 15, 1865. Transferred from Ship Island to Vicksburg, Mississippi, on May 1, 1865. Appears on a roll of POW's of Company F, 63rd Alabama Infantry commanded by Captain R. T. Simpson that were surrendered by Lt. General Richard Taylor at Citronelle, Alabama, on May 4, 1865, and paroled at Meridian, Mississippi, on May 11, 1865. Residence—Butler County, Alabama.

Clark, C., Pvt. Co. I.
Enlisted on May 15, 1864, at Wedowee, Alabama, by Captain Robinson for the war. Appears absent on a company muster roll for September and October 1864. Absent without leave from September 18, 1864.

Clark, G. W., Pvt. Co. D.
Enlisted on August 4, 1864, at Elba, Alabama, by Captain Paine for the war. Appears absent on a company muster roll for August 30 to October 30, 1864, with pay due from time of enlistment. Absent sick at Mobile hospital since October 27. Admitted to Ross Hospital, Mobile, Alabama, on September 18, 1864, with rubeola. Sent to General Hospital September 26, 1864. Remarks: Greenville.

Clark, J., Pvt. Co. E.
Enlisted on August 8, 1864, at Pollard, Alabama, by Captain A. V. Lee for the war. Age—17, eyes—dark, hair—dark, complexion—dark. Appears present on a company muster roll for September and October 1864. Drew clothing on September 11, 1864. Captured at Blakeley, Alabama, on April 9, 1865. Appears on a roll of POW's received at Ship Island, Mississippi, on April 15, 1865. Transferred from Ship Island to Vicksburg, Mississippi, on May 1, 1865. Appears on a roll of POW's of Cos. E and G, 63rd Alabama Infantry commanded by Captain A. V. Lee that were surrendered by Lt. General Richard Taylor at Citronelle, Alabama, on May 4, 1865, and paroled at Meridian, Mississippi, on May 13, 1865. Residence—Henry County, Alabama.

Clark, Noah R., Pvt. Co. D.
Captured at Fort Blakeley, Alabama, on April 9, 1865. Confined at New Orleans, Louisiana, on May 1, 1865. Released on parole May 16, 1865. Admitted to St. Louis General Hospital, New Orleans with intermitten fever on April 17, 1865. Transferred to General Hospital on May 16, 1865. Remarks: Marine [Marine Hospital].

Cliett, Thomas, Pvt. Co. I.
Enlisted on April 15, 1865, at Wedowee, Alabama, by Captain Robinson for the war. Appears absent on a company muster roll for September and October 1864. Absent on 30 day furlough from September 27.

Cobb, J. N., Corporal, Co. H.
Enlisted on August 4, 1864, at Selma, Alabama, by Captain Suttle for the war. Age—17, eyes—blue, hair—dark, complexion—dark. Appears present on a company muster roll for September and October 1864. Drew clothing on September 11, 1864. Captured at Blakeley, Alabama, on April 9, 1865. Appears on a roll of POW's received at Ship Island, Mississippi, on April 15, 1865. Transferred from Ship Island to Vicksburg, Mississippi, on May 1, 1865. Appears on a roll of sick and wounded Confederate POW's at USA General Hospital No. 2, Vicksburg. Admitted on May 3, 1865, from steamer with acute diarrhoea. Returned to duty on May 23, 1865.

Cockrell, J. A., Pvt. Co. K.
Enlisted on October 3, 1864, at Sumpter County, Alabama, by Lieutenant Kendrick for the war. Appears present on a muster roll for September and October 1864.

Colby, F. M., Pvt. Co. A/B.
Captured at Blakeley, Alabama, on April 9, 1865. Appears on a roll of POW's received at Ship Island, Mississippi, on April 15, 1865. Transferred from Ship Island to Vicksburg, Mississippi, on May 1, 1865. Appears on a roll of POW's of Company B, 63rd Alabama Infantry commanded by 1st Lieutenant Thomas J. Calhoun that were surrendered by Lt. General Richard Taylor at Citronelle, Alabama, on May 4, 1865, and paroled at Meridian, Mississippi, on May 11, 1865. Residence—Coosa County, Alabama.

Coles, C. R., Pvt. Co. A.
Admitted to 2nd Division, 16th US Army Corps Hospital on April 9, 1865. With penetrated abdomen by bullet. Wounded in action.

Coney, R. J., Corporal Co. F.
Enlisted on May 30, 1864, at Montgomery, Alabama, by Captain Moore for the war. Age—17, eyes—blue, hair—brown, complexion—fair, 5 foot 6 ½ inches, residence—Lowndes County, Alabama. Appears on a company muster-in roll for July 25, 1864, at Georgiana, Alabama. Drew clothing on September 11, 1864. Appears on as company muster roll for August 31 to October 31, 1864, with pay due from time of enlistment. Died on October 7, 1864.

Coney, W. C., Pvt. Co. F.
Enlisted on May 30, 1864, at Montgomery, Alabama, by Captain Moore for the war. Age—17, eyes—light, hair—light, complexion—fair, 5 foot 1 inch, residence—Butler County, Alabama. Appears on a company muster-in roll for July 25, 1864, at Georgiana, Alabama. Drew clothing on September 11, 1864. Appears present on as company muster roll for August 31 to October 31, 1864, with pay due from time of enlistment. Captured at Blakeley, Alabama, on April 9, 1865. Appears on a roll of POW's received at Ship Island, Mississippi, on April 15, 1865. Transferred from Ship Island to Vicksburg, Mississippi, on May 1, 1865. Appears on a roll of POW's of Company F, 63rd Alabama Infantry commanded by Captain R. T. Simpson that were surrendered by Lt. General Richard Taylor at Citronelle, Alabama, on May 4, 1865, and paroled at Meridian, Mississippi, on May 11, 1865. Residence—Butler County, Alabama.

Conine, James B., Pvt. Co. A.
Enlisted on January 1, 1864, at Tallapoosa, County, Alabama, by Captain John H. Echols into Echols' company of Provost Guards. Appears on a company muster-in roll on January 1, 1864, at Montgomery, Alabama. Appears present on a company muster roll for January and February 1864, with pay due from time of enlistment. Drew clothing in 2nd quarter 1864. Admitted to Ross Hospital in Mobile, Alabama, on September 2, 1864, with febris remttens. Returned to duty on October 4, 1864. Appears absent on a company muster roll for September and October 1864. Absent on 60 day furlough by the Medical Examining Board from October 31, 1864. Appears on a record of Confederate solders paroled at headquarters of the 16th US Army Corps at Montgomery, Alabama, on May 19, 1865. Eyes—blue, hair—black, complexion—fair, 6 foot 1 inch. His parole is in his file.

Connell, William A., Pvt. Co. B.
Enlisted on June 20, 1864, at Montgomery, Alabama, by Lieutenant Calhoun for the war. Drew clothing on July 8 and September 11, 1864. Appears absent on

a company muster roll for September and October 1864, with pay due from time of enlistment. Absent sick since October 17, 1864.

Conner, Thomas H., Corporal Co. C.
Enlisted on May 4, 1864, at Chambers County, Alabama, by Captain Walker for the war. Appears on a company muster-in roll for June 14, 1864, at Camp Watts near Notasulga, Alabama. Age—17, eyes—black, hair—black, complexion—fair, 5 foot 7 inches, residence—Rough and Ready, Chambers County, Alabama. Drew clothing on August 6, 1864. Appears on a company muster roll for September and October 1864, with pay due from time of enlistment.

Cook, A. M., Pvt. Co. E.
Enlisted on September 6, 1864, at Clayton, Alabama, by Captain Erwin for the war. Age—17, eyes—dark, hair—dark, complexion—dark. Appears absent on a company muster roll for September and October 1864. Admitted to Ross Hospital in Mobile, Alabama, on October 9, 1864, with febris remittens. Returned to duty on November 10. Absent in hospital since October 15, 1864. Appears on a parole of POW's on May 16, 1865, at Marion, Alabama.

Cook, Andrew J., Pvt. Co. B.
Enlisted on August 10, 1864, at West Point, Georgia, by Captain Zimmerman for the war. Drew clothing on September 11, 1864. Signed by his mark. Appears present on a company muster roll for September and October 1864. Appears on a record of Confederate POW's paroled at the headquarters of 16th US Army Corps at Montgomery, Alabama, on May 24, 1865. His parole is in his file. Hair—dark, eyes—grey, complexion—fair, 5 foot 7 inches.

Cook, Charles M., Pvt. Co. B.
Enrolled on April 17, 1864, at Montgomery, Alabama, by Captain Zimmerman for the war. His name appears on a company muster-in roll for March 23, 1864, at Montgomery, Alabama. Appears absent on a company muster roll for September and October 1864, with pay due from time of enlistment. Absent with leave since October 27, 1864. Appears on a register of paroled Confederate soldiers that were paroled on June 1, 1865. He signed a parole at the headquarters of the 16th Corps US Army at Montgomery on June 1, 1865. He signed by mark "X." Hair—light, eyes—grey, complexion—fair, 5 foot. His parole is in his file.

Cook, W., Pvt. Co. F.
Enlisted on May 20, 1864, at Montgomery, Alabama, by Captain Jackson for the war. Appears on a company muster-in roll at Georgiana on July 25, 1864. Age—17, eyes—dark, hair—dark, complexion—dark, 5 foot 4 inches, residence—Autauga County, Alabama. He is reported here to be absent without leave.

Cooper, Wesley, Pvt. Co. B.
Enrolled on April 14, 1865, at Montgomery County, Alabama, by Captain Zimmerman for the war. Appears on a company muster-in roll for March 23, 1864, at Montgomery. Age—17. Drew clothing on July 8 and September 11, 1864. He signed by mark. Appears absent on a company muster roll for September and October 1864, with pay due from time of enlistment. Absent sick since October 3, 1864. POW captured on March 24, 1865, in front of Blakeley, Alabama, by Brigadier General T. J. Lucas in command of Cavalry Forces operating from Pensacola, Florida. Appears on a roll of POW's received at Ship Island, Mississippi, on April 15, 1865. Transferred from Ship Island to Vicksburg, Mississippi, on May 1, 1865.

Copeland, Eugenius W., 4th Corporal Co. G.
Enlisted on May 16, 1864, at Troy, Alabama, by Captain Wilkerson for the war.

Appears on a company muster-in roll at Blakeley, Alabama, on September 7, 1864. Age—17, eyes—grey, hair—dark, complexion—fair, 4 foot 9 inches, residence—Pike County, Alabama. Drew clothing on September 11, 1864. Appears present on a company muster roll for September and October 1864. Captured at Blakeley, Alabama, on April 9, 1865. Appears on a roll of POW's received at Ship Island, Mississippi, on April 15, 1865. Transferred from Ship Island to Vicksburg, Mississippi, on May 1, 1865. Appears on a roll of POW's of Cos. E and G, 63rd Alabama Infantry commanded by Captain A. V. Lee that were surrendered by Lt. General Richard Taylor at Citronelle, Alabama, on May 4, 1865, and paroled at Meridian, Mississippi, on May 13, 1865. Residence—Pike County, Alabama.

Copeland, Hilliard A., Pvt. Co. G.
Enlisted on May 16, 1864, at Troy, Alabama, by Captain Wilkerson for the war. Appears on a company muster-in roll at Blakeley, Alabama, on September 7, 1864. Eyes—grey, hair—dark, complexion—fair, 5 foot 7 inches, age—16. Drew clothing on September 11, 1864. Appears present on a company muster roll for September and October 1864. Captured at Blakeley, Alabama, on April 9, 1865. Appears on a roll of POW's received at Ship Island, Mississippi, on April 15, 1865. Transferred from Ship Island to Vicksburg, Mississippi, on May 1, 1865. Appears on a roll of POW's of Cos. E and G, 63rd Alabama Infantry commanded by Captain A. V. Lee that were surrendered by Lt. General Richard Taylor at Citronelle, Alabama, on May 4, 1865, and paroled at Meridian, Mississippi, on May 13, 1865. Residence—Pike County, Alabama.

Copeland, J. D., Sergeant Co. H. see **Coupland, J. D.**

Corntings, J. D., Pvt. Co. G.
Captured at Blakeley, Alabama, on April 9, 1865. Appears on a roll of POW's received at Ship Island, Mississippi, on April 15, 1865. Transferred from Ship Island to Vicksburg, Mississippi, on May 1, 1865.

Coupland, J. D., Sergeant Co. H.
Enlisted on March 15, 1864, at Springville, Alabama, by Lieutenant Killough for the war. Appears present on a company muster roll for September and October 1864. Age—17, eyes—blue, hair—light, complexion—fair. Drew clothing on September 11, 1864. Captured at Blakeley, Alabama, on April 9, 1865. Appears on a roll of POW's received at Ship Island, Mississippi, on April 15, 1865. Transferred from Ship Island to Vicksburg, Mississippi, on May 1, 1865. Appears on a roll of POW's of Cos. C and H, 63rd Alabama Infantry commanded by Captain C. W. Martin that were surrendered by Lt. General Richard Taylor at Citronelle, Alabama, on May 4, 1865, and paroled at Meridian, Mississippi, on May 11, 1865. Residence—Jefferson County, Alabama.

Cowart, Alfred, J., 4th Sergeant/Pvt. Co. G.
Enlisted on May 16, 1864, at Troy, Alabama, by Captain Wilkerson for the war. Appears on a company muster-in roll at Blakeley, Alabama, on September 7, 1864. Age—17, eyes—dark, hair—dark, complexion—dark, 5 foot 11 inches, residence—Pike County, Alabama. Drew clothing on September 11, 1864. Appears absent on a company muster roll for September and October 1864. Absent in hospital in Mobile, Alabama, since September 25, 1864. Captured at Blakeley, Alabama, on April 9, 1865. Appears on a roll of POW's received at Ship Island, Mississippi, on April 15, 1865. Transferred from Ship Island to Vicksburg, Mississippi, on May 1, 1865. His name appears on a roll of sick and wounded Confederate POW's admitted to USA General Hospital No. 2, Vicksburg, Mississippi, with remittent Fever from steamer. Returned to duty on May 23, 1865.

Cowles, Rodney, Pvt. Co. A.
Enlisted on January 1, 1864, at Macon County, Alabama, by Captain John H. Echols for the war. Appears absent on a company muster roll for January and February 1864, with pay due from time of enlistment. Absent sick in Stonewall Hospital. Drew clothing in 2nd quarter of 1864. Appears absent on a company muster roll for September and October 1864, with pay due from time of enlistment. Absent sick at Montgomery, Alabama, since March 26, 1864.

Cox, James E., Pvt. Co. D.
Enlisted on July 30, 1864, at Macon County, Alabama, by Major Ready for the war. He is described as: age—17, eyes—grey, hair—auburn, complexion—light, 5 foot 6 inches, residence—Eufaula, Barbour County, Alabama. Drew clothing on August 7, 1864. Appears present on a company muster roll for August 30 to October 30, 1864, with pay due from time of enlistment. Captured at Blakeley, Alabama, on April 9, 1865. Appears on a roll of POW's received at Ship Island, Mississippi, on April 15, 1865. Transferred from Ship Island to Vicksburg, Mississippi, on May 1, 1865. Appears on a roll of POW's of Company D, 63rd Alabama Infantry commanded by Captain Robert H. Pearson that were surrendered by Lt. General Richard Taylor at Citronelle, Alabama, on May 4, 1865, and paroled at Meridian, Mississippi, on May 13, 1865. Residence—Barbour County, Alabama.

Cox, J. H., Pvt. Co. E.
Enlisted on July 28, 1864, at Montgomery, Alabama, by Captain A. V. Lee for the war. Age—17, eyes—dark, hair—dark, complexion—dark. Appears present on a company muster roll for September and October 1864. Drew clothing on September 11, 1864.

Cox, Taylor E., Pvt. Co. A/K.
Enlisted on January 1, 1864, at Macon County, Alabama, by Captain John H. Echols for the war. Appears on a company muster-in roll for January 1, 1864. Age—16. Appears present on a company muster roll for January and February 1864, with pay due from time of enlistment. Drew clothing in 2nd quarter 1864. Appears present on a company muster roll for September and October 1864. Here he is shown as having last been paid on February 29, 1864. Captured at Blakeley, Alabama, on April 9, 1865. Appears on a roll of POW's received at Ship Island, Mississippi, on April 15, 1865. Transferred from Ship Island to Vicksburg, Mississippi, on May 1, 1865. Appears on a roll of POW's of Company A, 63rd Alabama Infantry commanded by Lieutenant W. D. Kyle that were surrendered by Lt. General Richard Taylor at Citronelle, Alabama, on May 4, 1865, and paroled at Meridian, Mississippi, on May 13, 1865. Residence is shown as Chambers County, Alabama.

Cozby, N. W., Pvt. Co. H/A.
Enlisted on March 15, 1864, at Springville, Alabama, Lieutenant Killough for the war. Age—17, eyes—dark, hair—dark, complexion—dark. Appears present on a company muster roll for September and October 1864. Captured at Blakeley, Alabama, on April 9, 1865. Appears on a roll of POW's received at Ship Island, Mississippi, on April 15, 1865. Transferred from Ship Island to Vicksburg, Mississippi, on May 1, 1865.

Cozby, Uriah W., Pvt. Co. H.
Drew clothing on September 11, 1864. Appears on a roll of POW's of Cos. C and H, 63rd Alabama Infantry commanded by Captain C. W. Martin that were surrendered by Lt. General Richard Taylor at Citronelle, Alabama, on May 4, 1865, and paroled at Meridian, Mississippi, on May 11, 1865. Residence—Jefferson County, Alabama.

Crawford, George, Pvt. Co. B/K.
Enlisted on April 14, 1864, at Montgomery, Alabama, by Captain Zimmerman for the war. Appears on a company muster-in roll for March 23, 1864, at Montgomery. Age—17. Appears on a company B muster roll for September and October 1864, with pay due from time of enlistment. Roll reports that he was transferred on S. O. No. 15, October 2, 1864, at headquarters of 2nd Regiment Alabama Reserves. Appears present on a company K muster roll for September and October 1864. Appears on a report of furloughs from Ladies', St. Mary's and Stonewall Hospitals in Montgomery, Alabama. Disease reported was intermitten fever and a 60 day furlough was granted on March 28. Drew clothing on July 8, 1864. His Medical Certificate and furlough from Ladies' Hospital is in his file. His residence was reported to be Huntington, Autauga County, Alabama.

Crawford, J. M. D., Pvt. Co. B.
POW paroled at headquarters of the 16th US Army Corps, Office of the Provost Marshal at Montgomery, Alabama, on May 19, 1864. Hair—dark, eyes—blue, complexion—fair, 5 foot 3 inches.

Creech, C., Pvt. Co. F.
Enlisted on March 9, 1864, at Greenville, Alabama, by Captain Brown for the war. Appears on a company muster-in roll for July 23, 1864. Age—17, residence—Butler County, Alabama. Appears present on a company muster roll for September and October 1864, with pay due from time of enlistment. Signed a Parole at the headquarters of the 16th US Army Corps at Montgomery, Alabama, on June 16, 1865. Hair—dark, eyes—blue, complexion—fair, 5 foot 5 inches. His parole is in his file.

Croom, J. M., Pvt. Co. I.
Enlisted on May 28, 1864, at Wedowee, Alabama, by Captain Robinson for the war. Appears absent on a company muster roll for September and October 1864. Absent without leave from September 18, 1864.

Crow, J. B., Pvt. Co. H.
Enlisted on March 15, 1864, at Centerville [?] by Lieutenant Johnson for the war. Age—17, eyes—blue, hair—dark, complexion—dark. Died in hospital at Mobile, Alabama, on September 7, 1864.

Crowson, Z. C.,(Crowson B. C.), Pvt. Co. I.
Enlisted at Columbiana, Alabama, by Lieutenant Bulger for the war. Appears present on a company muster roll for September and October 1864. Captured at Blakeley, Alabama, on April 9, 1865. Appears on a roll of POW's received at Ship Island, Mississippi, on April 15, 1865. Transferred from Ship Island to Vicksburg, Mississippi, on May 1, 1865. Appears on a roll of POW's of Cos. I and K, 63rd Alabama Infantry commanded by Lieutenant W. A. Skinner that were surrendered by Lt. General Richard Taylor at Citronelle, Alabama, on May 4, 1865, and paroled at Meridian, Mississippi, on May 13, 1865. His residence was reported to be Shelby County, Alabama.

Crune, W. J., Pvt. Co. H.
Enlisted on March 15, 1864, at Montevallo, Alabama, by Captain Suttle for the war. Age—17, eyes—dark, hair—dark, complexion—dark. Appears absent on a company muster roll for September and October 1864. Absent in camp of correction since August 14. Captured at Blakeley, Alabama, on April 9, 1865. Appears on a roll of POW's received at Ship Island, Mississippi, on April 15, 1865. Transferred from Ship Island to Vicksburg, Mississippi, on May 1, 1865. Appears on a roll of POW's of Cos. C and H, 63rd Alabama Infantry commanded

by Captain C. W. Martin that were surrendered by Lt. General Richard Taylor at Citronelle, Alabama, on May 4, 1865, and paroled at Meridian, Mississippi, on May 11, 1865. Residence—Jefferson County, Alabama.

Culp, N. N., Pvt. Co. H.
Enlisted on March 15, 1864, at Benson, Alabama, by Lieutenant Johnson for the war. Age—17, eyes—blue, hair—light, complexion—fair. Appears absent on a company muster roll for September and October 1864. Drew clothing on September 11, 1864. Absent sick in hospital in Mobile, Alabama, since October 28. Appears on a list of sick and wounded sent to Vicksburg, Mississippi General Hospital, via New Orleans, Louisiana, on April 8, 1865, from Spanish Fort/Blakeley, Alabama. He is reported to have intermittent fever. Admitted to USA Hospital Steamer D. A. January on April 17, 1865, with sick and diarrhoea. Transferred at New Orleans to Steamer Elanora Carrel on April 24, 1865. Appears as a POW on USA Hospital Steamer Elanora Carrel, transferred from New Orleans to Vicksburg. Appears on a roll of POW's at USA General Hospital No. 3 (colored), Vicksburg, Mississippi. Transferred to USA General Hospital No. 2 at Vicksburg on May 4, 1865. Here he is reported as having been captured on April 9, 1865, at Blakeley, Alabama. Returned to duty on May 12, 1865.

Culpepper, J. B., Pvt. Co. K.
Captured at Blakeley, Alabama, on April 9, 1865. Appears on a roll of POW's received at Ship Island, Mississippi, on April 15, 1865. Transferred from Ship Island to Vicksburg, Mississippi, on May 1, 1865. Appears on a roll of POW's of Cos. I and K, 63rd Alabama Infantry commanded by Lieutenant W. A. Skinner that were surrendered by Lt. General Richard Taylor at Citronelle, Alabama, on May 4, 1865, and paroled at Meridian, Mississippi, on May 13, 1865. His residence was reported to be Choctaw County, Alabama.

Culpepper, J. E., Pvt. Co. K.
Enlisted on September 25, 1864, at Choctaw County, Alabama, by Captain Erinton for the war. Appears absent on a company muster roll for September and October 1864. Absent in hospital in Mobile, Alabama, since October 13.

Cummings, J. B., Pvt. Co. K.
Enlisted on April 19, 1864, at Talladega, Alabama, by Captain Powers for the war. Appears present on a company muster roll for September and October 1864. Appears on a roll of POW's of Cos. I and K, 63rd Alabama Infantry commanded by Lieutenant W. A. Skinner that were surrendered by Lt. General Richard Taylor at Citronelle, Alabama, on May 4, 1865, and paroled at Meridian, Mississippi, on May 13, 1865. Residence—Talladega County, Alabama.

Cunningham, J. W., Pvt. Co. E.
Enlisted on July 28, 1864, at Montgomery, Alabama, by Captain A. V. Lee for the war. Age—17, eyes—dark, hair—dark, complexion—dark. Appears absent on a company muster roll for September and October 1864. Absent in hospital since October 18, 1864. Appears on a muster roll at General Hospital Marion, Alabama, for July and August 1864, with pay due from time of enlistment. Paroled at the headquarters of 16th US Army Corps at Montgomery on May 24, 1865. Hair—black, eyes—blue, complexion—dark, 5 foot 4 inches. His parole is in his file. There is a information request from Oklahoma City on June 15, 1915, in his file also.

Curry, D. C., Pvt. Co. F.
Enlisted on March 9, 1864, at Greenville, Alabama, by Captain Brown for the war. Appears on a company muster-in roll for July 25, 1864, at Georgiana, Alabama. Age—17, eyes—dark, hair—dark, complexion—swarthy, 5 foot,

residence—Butler County, Alabama. Reported to have deserted on October 14, 1864. He was never paid.

Curry, P. R., Pvt. Co. D.
Enlisted on August 6, 1864, at Notasulga, Alabama, by Major Ready for the war. Appears present on a company muster roll for August 30 to October 30, 1864, with pay due from time of enlistment.

Curtis, John R., Corporal/Pvt. Co. G/E.
Enlisted on May 16, 1864, at Troy, Alabama, by Captain Wilkerson for the war. Age—17, eyes—blue, hair—light, complexion—fair, 5 foot 11 inches, residence—Pike County, Alabama. Appears on a company muster-in roll for September 7, 1864, at Blakeley, Alabama. Drew clothing on September 11, 1864. Appears present on a Company G muster roll for September and October 1864. Reduced from 2nd Corporal by order of Regimental Court Marshal October 17, 1864. Captured at Blakeley, Alabama, on April 9, 1865. Appears on a roll of POW's received at Ship Island, Mississippi, on April 15, 1865. Transferred from Ship Island to Vicksburg, Mississippi, on May 1, 1865. Appears on a roll of POW's of Cos. E and G, 63rd Alabama Infantry commanded by Captain A. V. Lee that were surrendered by Lt. General Richard Taylor at Citronelle, Alabama, on May 4, 1865, and paroled at Meridian, Mississippi, on May 13, 1865. Residence—Pike County, Alabama.

Daniel, J. F., Corporal Co. F.
Enlisted on May 30, 1864, at Montgomery, Alabama, by Captain Jackson for the war. Appears on a company muster-in roll for July 25, 1864, at Georgiana, Alabama. Age—17, eyes—blue, hair—light, complexion—fair, 5 foot 10 ½ inches, residence—Butler County, Alabama. Drew clothing on September 11, 1864. Appears present on a company muster roll for August 31 to October 31, 1864, with pay due from time of enlistment. Appears on a roll of POW's of nurses and patients of Moore Hospital CSA commanded by Surgeon W. C. Cavenaugh that were surrendered by Lt. General Richard Taylor at Citronelle, Alabama, on May 4, 1865, and paroled at Meridian, Mississippi, on May 16, 1865. Residence—Butler County, Alabama.

Dansby, A., Pvt. Co. E.
Captured at Blakeley, Alabama, on April 9, 1865. Appears on a roll of POW's received at Ship Island, Mississippi, on April 15, 1865. He was among those men transferred from Ship Island to Vicksburg, Mississippi, on May 1, 1865. His name appears on a roll of POW's of Cos. E and G, 63rd Alabama Infantry that were commanded by Captain A. V. Lee that were surrendered by Lt. General Richard Taylor at Citronelle, Alabama, on May 4, 1865, and then paroled at Meridian, Mississippi, on May 13, 1865. His residence was reported to be Barbour County, Alabama.

Daughety, A., Pvt. Co. E.
Enlisted on August 8, 1864, at Pollard, Alabama, by Captain A. V. Lee for the war. Appears absent on a company muster roll for September and October 1864. Absent in hospital since October 16, 1864. Age—17, eyes—dark, hair—dark, complexion—dark. Drew clothing on September 11, 1864. Admitted to Ross Hospital, Mobile, Alabama, on October 16, 1864, with icterus [jaundice]. Sent to General Hospital on November 30, 1864. Hospital Hustis. Captured at Blakeley, Alabama, on April 9, 1865. Appears on a roll of POW's received at Ship Island, Mississippi, on April 15, 1865. Transferred from Ship Island to Vicksburg, Mississippi, on May 1, 1865. His name appears on a roll of POW's of Cos. E and G, 63rd Alabama Infantry commanded by Captain A. V. Lee that were surrendered by Lt. General Richard Taylor at Citronelle, Alabama, on May 4,

1865, and paroled at Meridian, Mississippi, on May 13, 1865. Residence—Henry County, Alabama.

Davie, M. W., Sergeant Co. E.
Enlisted on March 1, 1864, at Clayton, Alabama, by Captain A. V. Lee for the war. He is described as: age—17, eyes—blue, hair—light, complexion—fair. Appears absent on a company muster roll for September and October 1864. Absent without leave since October 15, 1864. Admitted to Ross Hospital, Mobile, Alabama, on September 26, 1864, with dysenteria acuta. Returned to duty October 6, 1864.

Davis, E. R., Pvt. Co. D.
Enlisted on September 25, 1864, at Elba, Alabama, by Captain Paine for the war. Appears present on a company muster roll for August 30 to October 30, 1864, with pay due from time of enlistment. Admitted to Ross Hospital, Mobile, Alabama, on November 5, 1864, with dysenteria acuta. Returned to duty on November 8, 1864.

Davis, Jefferson, Pvt. Co. E.
Enlisted on August 5, 1864, at Montgomery, Alabama, by Captain A. V. Lee for the war. Drew clothing on September 11, 1864. Appears absent on a company muster roll for September and October 1864. Absent without leave since October 23, 1864. Captured at Blakeley, Alabama, on April 9, 1865. Appears on a roll of POW's received at Ship Island, Mississippi, on April 15, 1865. Transferred from Ship Island to Vicksburg, Mississippi, on May 1, 1865. Appears on a roll of Confederate POW's paroled at New Orleans, Louisiana, during May 1865. Appears on a receipt issued on board US. Transport Belvedere opposite New Orleans on May 3, 1865. "Received from Captain Wm. Gage, Commdg. detachm't of guard, Prisoners on War from Ship Island, by virtue of letter from E. D. Mehaffey, Captain US 1st Infty., A. AAG and Provost Marshal, the following named sick and dead: John H. Gibson, Asst. Surg. 74th US C. I. in charge of Hospital POW, Ship Island, Miss." Confined at New Orleans and paroled on May 16, 1865. Admitted to St. Louis, US General Hospital, New Orleans from Military Prison with chronic diarrhoea. Transferred to General Hospital on May 16, 1865. Remarks: marine [Marine Hospital].

Davis, John, Pvt. Co. A.
Enrolled on January 1, 1864, at Tallapoosa County, Alabama, by Captain John H. Echols for the war. Age—16. Appears on a company muster-in roll for January 1, 1864, at Montgomery, Alabama. Appears absent on a company muster roll for January and February 1864, with pay due from time of enlistment. Absent sick in Stonewall Hospital.

Davis, John E., Pvt. Co. B.
Enrolled on April 16, 1864, at Montgomery, Alabama, by Captain Zimmerman for the war. Appears on a company muster-in roll for March 23, 1864, at Montgomery, Alabama. Age—16. Drew clothing on July 8, August 12 and September 11, 1864. Signed by his mark. Appears present on a company muster roll for September and October 1864, with pay due from time of enlistment. Captured at Blakeley, Alabama, on April 9, 1865. Appears on a roll of POW's received at Ship Island, Mississippi, on April 15, 1865. Transferred from Ship Island to Vicksburg, Mississippi, on May 1, 1865. Appears on a roll of POW's of Company B, 63rd Alabama Infantry commanded by 1st Lieutenant Thomas J. Calhoun that were surrendered by Lt. General Richard Taylor at Citronelle, Alabama, on May 4, 1865, and paroled at Meridian, Mississippi, on May 11, 1865. Residence—Montgomery County, Alabama.

Davis, J. T., Pvt. Co. E.
Enlisted on April 1, 1864, at Clayton, Alabama, by Captain A. V. Lee for the war. Appears present on a company muster roll for September and October 1864. He is described as: age—17, eyes—blue, hair—light, complexion—fair. Drew clothing on September 11, 1864. POW captured at Blakeley, Alabama, on April 9, 1865. His name appears on a roll of POW's received at Ship Island, Mississippi, on April 15, 1865. Transferred from Ship Island to Vicksburg, Mississippi, on May 1, 1865. His name appears on a roll of POW's of Cos. E and G, 63rd, Alabama Regiment commanded by Captain A. V. Lee that were surrendered by Lt. General Richard Taylor at Citronelle, Alabama, on May 4, 1865, and paroled at Meridian, Mississippi, on May 13, 1865. Residence—Barbour County, Alabama.

Davis, J. W., Pvt. Co. K.
Enlisted on September 23, 1864, at Macon County, Alabama, by Major Ready for the war. Appears present on a company muster roll for September and October 1864. Captured at Blakeley, Alabama, on April 9, 1865. Appears on a roll of POW's received at Ship Island, Mississippi, on April 15, 1865. Transferred from Ship Island to Vicksburg, Mississippi, on May 1, 1865. Appears on a roll of POW's of Cos. I and K, 63rd Alabama Infantry commanded by Lieutenant W. A. Skinner that were surrendered by Lt. General Richard Taylor at Citronelle, Alabama, on May 4, 1865, and paroled at Meridian, Mississippi, on May 13, 1865. Residence—Coffee County, Alabama.

Davis, R. M., Pvt. Co. C.
His file contains only a reference envelope with reference to R. M. Dennis, Co. B, 1st Battalion Alabama Cadets.

Davis, W., Pvt. Co. I.
Enlisted on April 15, 1864, at Talladega, Alabama, by Captain Parks for the war. Appears absent on a company muster roll for September and October 1864. Absent without leave since September 18, 1864.

Davis, W. A., Jr. 2nd Lieutenant, Co. H.
Enlisted for the war. Age—19, eyes—dark, hair—dark, complexion—dark. Appears absent on a company muster roll for September and October 1864. Absent sick at Hospital Levert since October 28. Elected 2nd Lieutenant on August 21, 1864. Appears on a list of POW's captured by 2nd Division, 16th US Army Corps and confined for one day on April 9, 1865, near Spanish Fort, Alabama. Captured at Blakeley, Alabama, on April 9, 1865. His name appears on a roll of POW's received at Ship Island, Mississippi, on April 15, 1865. He is reported to have been transferred from Ship Island to Vicksburg, Mississippi, on May 1, 1865. His name also appears on a roll of POW's at New Orleans, Louisiana. Confined on April 30, 1865, at New Orleans and exchanged on May 1, 1865. He signed a Parole of Honor at Meridian Mississippi, on May 10, 1865. His parole is in his file.

Davison, J. W., Pvt. Co. F.
His name appears a signature on a parole of POW's on May 16, 1865, at Marion, Alabama.

Day, James D., Pvt. Co. C.
Enlisted on May 23, 1865, at Covington, County, Alabama, by Lieutenant Kearney for the war. Appears on a company muster-in roll at Camp Watts near Notasulga, Alabama, for June 24, 1864. Age—17 ½, eyes—blue, hair—light, complexion—florid, 5 foot, 5 inches, residence—Andalusia, Covington, Alabama. Appears absent on a company muster roll for September and October 1865.

Absent in hospital at Mobile, Alabama, since October 28, 1864. Drew clothing on August 6, 1864. Signed by his mark.

Dearman, S., Pvt. Co. K.
Enlisted on August 28, 1864, at Sumpter County, Alabama, by Lieutenant Kendrick for the war. Appears absent on a company muster roll for September and October 1864. Absent at hospital in Mobile, Alabama, since October 14. Captured at Blakeley, Alabama, on April 9, 1865. Appears on a roll of POW's received at Ship Island, Mississippi, on April 15, 1865. Transferred from Ship Island to Vicksburg, Mississippi, on May 1, 1865. Appears on a roll of POW's of Cos. I and K, 63rd Alabama Infantry commanded by Lieutenant W. A. Skinner that were surrendered by Lt. General Richard Taylor at Citronelle, Alabama, on May 4, 1865, and paroled at Meridian, Mississippi, on May 13, 1865. Residence—Sumpter County, Alabama.

Deason, Malcolm, G., Pvt. Co. B.
Enlisted on October 2, 1864, at Blakeley, Alabama, by Captain Zimmerman for the war. Appears present on a company muster roll for September and October 1864, with pay due from time of enlistment.

Dennis, A. S., Pvt. Co. F.
Admitted to Ross Hospital, Mobile, Alabama, on August 17, 1864, with debilitas. Returned to duty on August 18, 1864.

Dennis, Patrick C., Pvt. Co. B.
Enlisted on April 14, 1864, at Montgomery, Alabama, by Captain Zimmerman for the war. Appears on a company muster-in roll for March 23, 1864, at Montgomery, Alabama. Age—17. Drew clothing on July 8, 1864. Appears absent on a company muster roll for September and October 1864, with pay due from time of enlistment. Absent sick since October 5, 1864. Captured at Blakeley, Alabama, on April 9, 1865. Appears on a roll of POW's received at Ship Island, Mississippi, on April 15, 1865. Transferred from Ship Island to Vicksburg, Mississippi, on May 1, 1865. Appears on a roll of POW's of Company B, 63rd Alabama Infantry commanded by 1st Lieutenant Thomas J. Calhoun that were surrendered by Lt. General Richard Taylor at Citronelle, Alabama, on May 4, 1865, and paroled at Meridian, Mississippi, on May 11, 1865. Residence—Autauga County, Alabama.

Dent, Richard, H., Pvt. Co. C.
Enlisted on June 22, 1864, at Russell County, Alabama, by Lieutenant Carnes for the war. Appears on a company muster-in roll for June 24, 1864, at Camp Watts near Notasulga, Alabama. Age—17, eyes—grey, hair—dark, complexion—dark, 5 foot 4 inches, residence—Russell County, Alabama, Post Office— Columbus, Georgia. Drew clothing on August 6, 1864. Signed by his mark. Appears present on a company muster roll for September and October 1864. Captured at Blakeley, Alabama, on April 9, 1865. Appears on a roll of POW's received at Ship Island, Mississippi, on April 15, 1865. Transferred from Ship Island to Vicksburg, Mississippi, on May 1, 1865. Appears on a roll of POW's of Cos. C and H, 63rd Alabama Infantry commanded by Captain C. W. Martin that were surrendered by Lt. General Richard Taylor at Citronelle, Alabama, on May 4, 1865, and paroled at Meridian, Mississippi, on May 11, 1865. Residence—Russell County, Alabama.

Deshay, T. L., Pvt. Co. D.
Appears on a list of POW's in camp near Spanish Fort, Alabama, that require hospital treatment. List is from headquarters of 23rd Iowa Infantry Volunteers on April 12, 1864. He had a gunshot wound in arm. Captured at Blakeley,

Alabama, on April 9, 1865. Appears on a roll of POW's received at Ship Island, Mississippi, on April 15, 1865. Transferred from Ship Island to Vicksburg, Mississippi, on May 1, 1865. Appears on a roll of POW's of Company D, 63rd Alabama Infantry commanded by Captain Robert H. Pearson that were surrendered by Lt. General Richard Taylor at Citronelle, Alabama, on May 4, 1865, and paroled at Meridian, Mississippi, on May 13, 1865. Residence—Barbour County, Alabama.

Desmuth, A. B., Pvt. Co. A.
His file contains a reference envelope only. Reference see also A. B. Dismukes, 45th Alabama Infantry.

Dickins, James M., Pvt. Co. D.
Enlisted on July 30, 1864, at Macon County, Alabama, by Major Ready for the war. Appears on a company muster-in roll for July 30, 1864, at Camp Watts near Notasulga, Alabama. Age—17, eyes—dark, hair—light, complexion—fair, 5 foot 5 inches, residence—Texasville, Barbour County, Alabama. Appears absent on a company muster roll for August 30 to October 30, 1864, with pay due from time of enlistment. Absent on 60 day sick furlough by Medical Examining Board since October 8. Here he is shown as having enlisted at Clayton, Alabama, on March 2, 1864. Drew clothing on September 12, 1864.

Dirdin, Erastus, Pvt. Co. F.
POW captured at Greenville, Alabama, on April 25, 1865 by Brigadier General Lucas, commanding 3rd Brigade Cavalry Military Division of West Mississippi, and paroled at Greenville.

Doley, J. M., Assistant Surgeon Co. F/S.
Mustered into service on April 29, 1863. Assigned to duty with Regiment on August 26, 1864, by the Medical Director at Mobile, Alabama. He appears absent on a company muster roll for September and October 1864. This muster roll reports him absent on detached service at the mouth of Dog River with Companies A and B by General Maury.

Dollar, Elisha, Pvt. Co. A.
Enlisted on July 17, 1864, at Macon County, Alabama, by Captain John Echols for the war. Appears present on a company muster roll for September and October 1864, with pay due from time of enlistment. Drew clothing on September 11, 1864. Captured at Blakeley, Alabama, on April 9, 1865. His name appears on a roll of POW's received at Ship Island, Mississippi, on April 15, 1865. He was among those men transferred from Ship Island to Vicksburg, Mississippi, on May 1, 1865. His name appears on a roll of POW's of Company A, 63rd Alabama Infantry commanded by Lieutenant W. D. Kyle that were surrendered by Lt. General Richard Taylor at Citronelle, Alabama, on May 4, 1865, and paroled at Meridian, Mississippi, on May 13, 1865. Residence is shown as Macon County, Alabama.

Dollar, W. A., Co. A.
Drew clothing on August 12, 1864. Signed by his mark.

Donald, William, 2nd Lieutenant, Co. F.
Enlisted on May 30, 1864, at Montgomery, Alabama, by Captain McDaniel for the war. Elected 2nd Lieutenant on June 28, 1864. Appears on a company muster-in roll for July 25, 1864, at Georgiana, Alabama. Age—17, eyes—blue, hair—dark, complexion—fair, 5 foot 8 ½ inches, residence—Richmond, Virginia. Appears present on a company muster roll for August 31 to October 31, 1864. Appears on a list of POW's confined at New Orleans, Louisiana, on April 30, 1865.

Captured at Blakeley, Alabama, on April 9, 1865. Transferred from Ship Island, Mississippi, on April 28, 1865. Exchanged on May 1, 1865.

Dorris, J. E., Pvt. Co. B/A.
Appears on a record of POW's paroled at the headquarters of the 16th US Army Corps at Montgomery, Alabama, on May 17, 1865. *See also file of J. Doss below. His parole in included in this file.

Dorris, John, Pvt. Co. A.
Enlisted on January 1, 1864, at Tallapoosa County, Alabama, by Captain Echols for the war. Drew clothing in the 2nd quarter and September 11, 1864. Appears present on a muster roll for September and October 1864, with pay due from time of enlistment. Admitted to Ross Hospital in Mobile, Alabama, on November 17, 1864, with febris intermittens quot. Deserted on November 30, 1864.

Doss, F., Pvt. Co. F.
Captured at Blakeley, Alabama, on April 9, 1865. Appears on a roll of POW's received at Ship Island, Mississippi, on April 15, 1865. Transferred from Ship Island to Vicksburg, Mississippi, on May 1, 1865. Appears on a roll of POW's of Company F, 63rd Alabama Infantry commanded by Captain R. T. Simpson that were surrendered by Lt. General Richard Taylor at Citronelle, Alabama, on May 4, 1865, and paroled at Meridian, Mississippi, on May 11, 1865. Residence—Dallas County, Alabama.

Doss, J. (Dorris, J. E.), Pvt. Co. K.
Enlisted on September 30, 1864, at Talladega, Alabama, by Captain Ramises for the war. Appears present on a company muster roll for September and October 1864. Appears on a roll of POW's of Cos. I and K, 63rd Alabama Infantry commanded by Lieutenant W. A. Skinner that were surrendered by Lt. General Richard Taylor at Citronelle, Alabama, on May 4, 1865, and paroled at Meridian, Mississippi, on May 11, 1865. Residence—Shelby County, Alabama. Signed a parole as J. E. Dorris at Montgomery, Alabama, at the headquarters of the 16th US Army Corps on May 16, 1865. Hair—light, eyes—blue, complexion—fair, 5 foot 11 inches. The parole is in his file.

Dowling, W. T., Pvt. Co. E.
POW captured at Blakeley, Alabama, on April 9, 1865. Appears on a roll of POW's received at Ship Island, Mississippi, on April 15, 1865. Transferred from Ship Island to Vicksburg, Mississippi, on May 1, 1865. Appears on a roll of sick and wounded POW's at USA General Hospital No. 2, Vicksburg, Mississippi. Admitted there on May 3, 1865 with chronic diarrhoea. Returned to duty on May 12, 1865. Admitted to USA Post Hospital at Jackson, Mississippi, on May 15, 1865, with chronic diarrhoea. Noted that he is a Confederate prisoner.

Downs, Willis, A., Pvt. Co. A.
Enlisted on January 1, 1864, at Tallapoosa County, Alabama, by Captain Echols for the war. Appears on a company muster-in roll for January 1, 1864, at Montgomery, Alabama. Appears present on a company muster roll for January and February 1864, with pay due from time of enlistment. Drew clothing in the 2nd quarter of 1864. Appears absent on a company muster roll for September and October 1865, with pay due from time of enlistment. Absent sick in hospital at Greenville, Alabama, since September 5, 1864. Captured at Blakeley, Alabama, on April 9, 1865. Appears on a roll of POW's received at Ship Island, Mississippi, on April 15, 1865. Transferred from Ship Island to Vicksburg, Mississippi, on May 1, 1865. Appears on a roll of POW's of Company A, 63rd Alabama Infantry commanded by Lieutenant W. D. Kyle that were surrendered by Lt. General Richard Taylor at Citronelle, Alabama, on May 4, 1865, and

paroled at Meridian, Mississippi, on May 13, 1865. His residence is shown as Tallapoosa County, Alabama.

Doy, Benjamin F., Pvt. Co. C.
Enlisted May 9, 1864, at Tallapoosa County, Alabama, by Captain Brown for the war. Appears on a company muster-in roll for June 24, 1864, at Camp Watts near Notasulga, Alabama. Age—17, eyes—blue, hair—dark, complexion—fair, 5 foot 8 inches, residence—DeSoto, Tallapoosa County, Alabama. Drew clothing on August 6, 1864. Appears present on a company muster roll for September and October 1864.

Dozier, Augustus L., Pvt. Co. A.
Enlisted on January 1, 1864, at Chambers County, Alabama, by Captain John Echols for the war. Appears on a company muster-in roll for January 1, 1864, at Montgomery, Alabama. Age—16. Appears present on a company muster roll for January and February 1864, with pay due from time to enlistment. Drew clothing in 2nd quarter on 1864.

Drakeford, Paul, Pvt. Co. D.
Enlisted on July 25, 1864, at Macon County, Alabama, by Major Ready for the war. Age—17, eyes—grey, hair—dark, complexion—dark, 5 foot 0 inches, residence—Tuskegee, Macon County, Alabama. Appears on a company muster-in roll for July 30, 1864, at Camp Watts near Notasulga, Alabama. Drew clothing on August 7, 1864.

Driver, James M., Pvt. Co. B.
Enrolled on April 14, 1864, at Montgomery, Alabama, by Captain Zimmerman for the war. Appears on a company muster-in roll for March 23, 1864. Age—17.

Driver, W. T., Pvt. Co. F.
Enlisted on March 9, 1864, at Greenville, Alabama, by Captain Brown for the war. Appears on a company muster-in roll at Georgiana, Alabama, for July 25, 1864. Age—17, eyes—blue, hair—light, complexion—sallow, 5 foot 7 inches, residence—Butler County, Alabama. Appears absent on a company muster roll for August 31 to October 31, 1864, on March 9, 1864. Absent in hospital since August 12, 1864. Drew clothing on September 11, 1864. Captured at Blakeley, Alabama, on April 9, 1865. Appears on a roll of POW's received at Ship Island, Mississippi, on April 15, 1865. Transferred from Ship Island to Vicksburg, Mississippi, on May 1, 1865. Appears on a roll of POW's of Company F, 63rd Alabama Infantry commanded by Captain R. T. Simpson that were surrendered by Lt. General Richard Taylor at Citronelle, Alabama, on May 4, 1865, and paroled at Meridian, Mississippi, on May 11, 1865. Residence—Butler County, Alabama.

Duberry, Thomas, Pvt. Co. E.
Enlisted on August 5, 1864, at Montgomery, Alabama, by Captain A. V. Lee for the war. Appears present on a company muster roll for September and October 1864. Age—17, eyes—blue, hair—light, complexion—fair. Admitted to Ross Hospital, Mobile, Alabama, on August 26, 1864, with febris intermittens on August 26, 1864. Sent to General Hospital on September 13, 1864. Here is shown remarks: Greenville [Hospital?].

Duett, A., Pvt. Co. F.
Enlisted on October 19, 1864, at Greenville, Alabama, by Captain Elkin for the war. Appears present on a company muster roll for August 31 to October 31, 1864, with pay due from time of enlistment. Captured at Blakeley, Alabama, on April 9, 1865. Appears on a roll of POW's received at Ship Island, Mississippi,

on April 15, 1865. Transferred from Ship Island to Vicksburg, Mississippi, on May 1, 1865. Appears on a roll of POW's of Company F, 63rd Alabama Infantry commanded by Captain R. T. Simpson that were surrendered by Lt. General Richard Taylor at Citronelle, Alabama, on May 4, 1865, and paroled at Meridian, Mississippi, on May 11, 1865. Residence—Butler County, Alabama.

Duke, Edmond H., Pvt. Co. B.
Enlisted on July 11, 1864, at Montgomery, Alabama, by Lieutenant Calhoun for the war. Appears present on a company muster roll for September and October 1864, with pay due from time of enlistment. Appears on a roll of POW's of Company B, 63rd Alabama Infantry commanded by Lieutenant Thomas J. Calhoun that were surrendered by Lt. General Richard Taylor at Citronelle, Alabama, on May 4, 1865, and paroled at Meridian, Mississippi, on May 11, 1865. Residence—Coosa County, Alabama.

Duke, J. H., Pvt. Co. E.
Enlisted on August 25, 1864, at Blakeley, Alabama, by Captain A. V. Lee for the war. Appears absent on a company muster roll for September and October 1864. Absent at hospital since September 25, 1864. Age—17, eyes—dark, hair—dark, complexion—dark. Drew clothing on September 11, 1864. Admitted to Ross Hospital, Mobile, Alabama, on September 26, 1864, with rubeola, diarrhoea acuta, febris remttens. [Furloughed] 30 days. Captured at Blakeley, Alabama, on April 9, 1865. Appears on a roll of POW's received at Ship Island, Mississippi, on April 15, 1865. Transferred from Ship Island to Vicksburg, Mississippi, on May 1, 1865. Appears on a roll of POW's of Cos. E and G, 63rd Alabama Infantry commanded by Captain A. V. Lee that were surrendered by Lt. General Richard Taylor at Citronelle, Alabama, on May 4, 1865, and paroled at Meridian, Mississippi, on May 13, 1865. Residence—Dale County, Alabama.

Duncan, Drury S., Pvt. Co. I.
Enlisted on April 15, 1864, at Wedowee, Alabama, by Captain Robinson for the war. Appears absent on a company muster roll for September and October 1864. Absent on detail since October 4, 1864. Card in his file Subject: Report to Surgeon Potts, SO No. 81, October 4/64.

Duncan, Ithmor (Ithmar) M., Pvt. Co. C.
Enlisted on May 20, 1864, at Macon County, Alabama, by Captain Roscoe for the war. He appears on a company muster-in roll at Camp Watts near Notasulga, Alabama, for June 24, 1864. He is described as: age—17, eyes—grey, hair—light, complexion—fair, 5 foot 8 ¾ inches, residence—Notasulga, Alabama. Appears present on a company muster roll for September and October 1864. Card in file reference: See personal papers of James M. Alexander, Alabama. Drew clothing August 6, 1864.

Duncan, Rhodes, Pvt. Co. B.
Enlisted at Rockford, Alabama, by Captain Hancock for the war. Appears present on a company muster roll for September and October 1864, with pay due from time of enlistment. Captured at Blakeley, Alabama, on April 9, 1865. Appears on a roll of POW's received at Ship Island, Mississippi, on April 15, 1865. Transferred from Ship Island to Vicksburg, Mississippi, on May 1, 1865. Appears on a roll of POW's of Company B, 63rd Alabama Infantry commanded by Lieutenant Thomas J. Calhoun that were surrendered by Lt. General Richard Taylor at Citronelle, Alabama, on May 4, 1865, and paroled at Meridian, Mississippi, on May 11, 1865. Residence—Coosa County, Alabama. There was an enquiry on August 14, 1915, from the State of Texas Commission of Pensions about his file.

Edy, Jefferson H., Pvt. Co. G.
    Enlisted on May 16, 1864, at Troy, Alabama, by Captain Wilkerson for the war. Appears on a company muster-in roll for September 7, 1864. Age—17, eyes—grey, hair—dark, complexion—dark, 5 foot 5 inches, residence—Coffee County, Alabama. Appears as deserted September 1, 1864, from Camp Hood near Blakeley, Alabama, on a company muster roll for September and October 1864.

Eason, W., Pvt. Co. I.
    Enlisted on April 15, 1864, at Talladega, Alabama, by Captain Parks for the war. Appears absent on a company muster roll for September and October 1864. Absent sick in Hospital Moore since October 20, 1864.

Echols, Benson W., Pvt. Co. B.
    Enlisted on August 15, 1864, at Pollard, Alabama, by Lieutenant Townsend for the war. Appears present on a company muster roll for September and October 1864, with pay due from date of enlistment. Drew clothing on September 11, 1864. Captured at Blakeley, Alabama, on April 9, 1865. Appears on a roll of POW's received at Ship Island, Mississippi, on April 15, 1865. Transferred from Ship Island to Vicksburg, Mississippi, on May 1, 1865. Appears on a roll of POW's of Company B, 63rd Alabama Infantry commanded by Lieutenant Thomas J. Calhoun that were surrendered by Lt. General Richard Taylor at Citronelle, Alabama, on May 4, 1865, and paroled at Meridian, Mississippi, on May 11, 1865. Residence—Dale County, Alabama.

Echols, J., Pvt. Co. H.
    Enlisted on July 29, 1864, at Selma, Alabama, by Captain Suttle for the war. Age—17, eyes—blue, hair—auburn, complexion—fair. Appears absent on a company muster roll for September and October 1864. Absent sick at a hospital in Greenville, Alabama, since September 11.

Echols, John H., Captain/Lt. Colonel Co. A., F&S.
    Appears on a company muster-in roll for January 1, 1864, at Montgomery, Alabama. Elected Captain on January 1, 1864. Appears absent on a company muster roll for January and February 1864. Absent Acting Provost Marshal at Montgomery, Alabama, by special Orders No. 262 of December 1, 1863. Appears present with rank of Major at Field and Staff muster roll for July and August 1864, near Blakeley, Alabama. Appointed Major on August 16, 1864, by Major General Withers by order of Secretary of War. Appears absent on a Field and Staff muster roll for September and October 1864. Absent on leave since October 20, 1864, 12 days by General Maury. Captured at Blakeley on April 9, 1865, by 2nd Division of the 16th US Army Corps. Confined as POW for one day near Spanish Fort, Alabama. Appears on a roll of POW's received at Ship Island, Mississippi, on April 15, 1865. His name appears on a register of POW's at New Orleans, Louisiana, reporting that he was confined on April 30, 1865, transferred from hospital on April 28, 1865. He was exchanged on May 1, 1865. His name appears on a Parole of Honor at Meridian, Mississippi, on May 12, 1865. His parole is in his file. His rank is shown as Lt. Colonel, 63rd Alabama Reserves.

Edgar, A. A., 1st Lieutenant Co. F.
    Enlisted on March 9, 1864, at Butler County, Alabama, by Captain Brown for the war. Appears on a company muster-in roll for July 25, 1864, at Georgiana, Alabama. Age—46, eyes—blue, hair—dark, 5 foot 8 inches, residence—Butler County, Alabama. Elected 1st Lieutenant on June 28, 1864. Drew clothing on September 11, 1864. Requisitioned for Company F in the 3rd Quarter of 1864: 1 jacket, 50 pair of pants and 6 pair of shoes. Appears absent on a company muster roll for August 31 to October 31, 1864. Absent in hospital at Greenville,

Alabama, since October 22, 1864. Appears on a report of POW's captured by 2nd Division, 16th US Army Corps on April 9, 1865, and confined near Spanish Fort, Alabama, for one day. Appears on a roll of POW's received at Ship Island, Mississippi, on April 15, 1865. Appears on a register of POW's at New Orleans, Louisiana, confined on April 30, 1865, transferred from Ship Island, Mississippi, on April 28, 1865. Exchanged on May 1, 1865. Signed a Parole of Honor at Meridian, Mississippi, on May 11, 1865. His parole is in his file.

Edwards, Alva C., Pvt. Co. A.
Enlisted on March 1, 1864, at Coosa County, Alabama, by Captain Echols for the war. Drew clothing in 2nd quarter of 1864. Appears absent on a company muster roll for September and October 1864, with pay due from time of enlistment. Absent sick in hospital at Mobile, Alabama, since October 15, 1864. Captured at Blakeley, Alabama, on April 9, 1865. Appears on a roll of POW's received at Ship Island, Mississippi, on April 15, 1865. Transferred from Ship Island to Vicksburg, Mississippi, on May 1, 1865. Appears on a roll of POW's of Company A, 63rd Alabama Infantry commanded by Lieutenant W. D. Kyle that were surrendered by Lt. General Richard Taylor at Citronelle, Alabama, on May 4, 1865, and paroled at Meridian, Mississippi, on May 13, 1865. Residence—Coosa County, Alabama.

Edwards, G., Pvt. Co. K.
Enlisted on October 15, 1864, at Montgomery, Alabama, by Lieutenant Burton for the war. Appears present on September and October 1864.

Edwards, J. T., Corporal Co. K.
Appears on a roll of POW's that were nurses and patient of Moore Hospital CSA, commanded by Surgeon W. C. Cavanaugh that were surrendered by Lt. General Richard Taylor at Citronelle, Alabama, on May 4, 1865, and paroled at Meridian, Mississippi, on May 16, 1865. Residence—Montgomery, Alabama.

Edwards, Robert, Pvt. Co. B.
Enlisted on March 23, 1864, at Montgomery, Alabama, by Captain Zimmerman for the war. Appears on a company muster-in roll for March 23, 1864, at Montgomery, Alabama. Appears absent on a company muster roll for September and October 1864, with pay due from time of enlistment. Absent sick since October 14, 1864. Drew clothing on July 8 and September 11, 1864. Appears on a register of soldiers that were killed in battle or who died of wounds or disease. Died on November 25, 1864, at Mobile, Alabama. Left $12.

Eiland, James A., Pvt. Co. G.
Enlisted on May 16, 1864, at Troy, Alabama, by Captain Wilkerson for the war. Appears on a company muster-in roll for September 7, 1864, at Blakeley, Alabama. Age—16, eyes—grey, hair—dark, complexion—fair, 5 foot 5 inches. Appears present on a company muster roll for September and October 1864. Drew clothing on September 11, 1864. Admitted to 2nd Division 16th US Army Corps hospital on April 9, 1865, with bullet wound in abdomen. Died in hospital.

Eisland (Erland, Eland), G. W., Pvt. Co. E.
Enlisted at Camp Hood [near Blakeley, Alabama] on September 12, 1864, by Captain A. V. Lee for the war. Drew clothing on September 11, 1864. Appears present on a company muster roll for September and October 1864. Age—17, eyes—dark, hair—dark, complexion—dark. Captured at Blakeley, Alabama, on April 9, 1865. Appears on a roll of POW's received at Ship Island, Mississippi, on April 15, 1865. Transferred from Ship Island to Vicksburg, Mississippi, on May 1, 1865. Confined at New Orleans, Louisiana, on May 15, 1865. Appears on a roll of POW's belonging to surrendered commands that were paroled at New Orleans

on May 16, 1865. Admitted to St. Louis USA General Hospital, in New Orleans on May 3, 1865, with chronic diarrhoea. Transferred to General Hospital on May 16, 1865. Remarks: Marine [Marine Hospital].

Elliot, H., Pvt. Co. K.
Enlisted on May 11, 1864, at Prattville, Alabama, by Captain Moore for the war. Appears absent on a company muster roll for September and October 1864. Absent detached to work in factory on October 25, 1864, by General Withers.

Ellis, Benjamin F., Pvt. Co. G.
Enlisted on May 16, 1864, at Troy, Alabama, by Captain Wilkerson for the war. Appears on a company muster roll for September 7, 1864, at Blakeley, Alabama. Age—17, eyes—blue, hair—light, complexion—fair, 5 foot 5 inches, residence—Coffee County, Alabama. Appears present on a company muster roll for September and October 1864. Drew clothing on September 11, 1864. Captured at Blakeley, Alabama, on April 9, 1865. Appears on a roll of POW's received at Ship Island, Mississippi, on April 15, 1865. Transferred from Ship Island to Vicksburg, Mississippi, on May 1, 1865. Appears on a roll of POW's of Cos. E and G, 63rd Alabama Infantry commanded by Captain A. V. Lee that were surrendered by Lt. General Richard Taylor at Citronelle, Alabama, on May 4, 1865, and paroled at Meridian, Mississippi, on May 13, 1865. Residence—Pike County, Alabama.

Ellis, J. T., Corporal Co. H.
Enlisted on March 15, 1864, at Montevallo, Alabama, by Captain Suttle for the war. Appears on a company muster roll for September and October 1865, with the notation that he died in hospital at Greenville, Alabama, on October 10, 1864. Age—17, eyes—blue, hair—dark, complexion—fair.

Ellison, Joseph, Pvt. Co. I.
Enlisted on April 15, 1864, at Columbiana, Alabama, by Lieutenant Bulger for the war. Appears absent on a company muster roll for September and October 1864. Absent with furlough of 30 days from September 27, 1864. Appears on a roll of POW's paroled at Talladega, Alabama, on June 13, 1865.

Ellison, Samuel, Pvt. Co. I.
POW captured at Blakeley, Alabama, on April 9, 1865. His name appears on a roll of POW's received at Ship Island, Mississippi, on April 15, 1865. Transferred from Ship Island to Vicksburg, Mississippi, on May 1, 1865. He appears on a roll of POW's of Cos. I and K, 63rd Alabama Infantry that were commanded by Lieutenant W. A. Skinner that were surrendered by Lt. General Richard Taylor at Citronelle, Alabama, on May 4, 1865, and were paroled at Meridian, Mississippi, on May 13, 1865. His residence is shown as Shelby County, Alabama.

English, Alfred, Pvt. Co. C.
Enlisted on May 11, 1864, at Russell County, Alabama, by Lieutenant Carnes for the war. Appears on a company muster-in roll for June 24, 1864, at Camp Watts near Notasulga, Alabama. Age—17, eyes—hazel, hair—light, complexion—sallow, 5 foot 7 inches, residence—Columbus, Georgia. Drew clothing on August 6, 1864. Appears present on a company muster roll for September and October 1864. Captured at Blakeley, Alabama, on April 9, 1865. Appears on a roll of POW's received at Ship Island, Mississippi, on April 15, 1865. Transferred from Ship Island to Vicksburg, Mississippi, on May 1, 1865. Appears on a roll of POW's of Cos. C and H, 63rd Alabama Infantry commanded by Captain C. W. Martin that were surrendered by Lt. General Richard Taylor at Citronelle, Alabama, on May 4, 1865, and paroled at Meridian, Mississippi, on May 11, 1865.

Residence—Russell County, Alabama. He also appears on a roll of POW's of Quintard Hospital CSA commanded by Surgeon S. V. D. Hill that were surrendered at Citronelle on May 4, 1865, and paroled at Meridian, Mississippi, on May 10, 1865. On both rolls for parole his name is shown as A. L. English.

Enzor, Henry, Pvt. Co. A.
Enlisted on February 1, 1864, at Montgomery, Alabama, by John H. Echols for the war. Appears on a company muster-in roll for January and February, with pay due from time of enlistment. Appears present on a company muster roll for September and October 1864. Drew clothing 2nd quarter and September 11, 1864. Captured at Blakeley, Alabama, on April 9, 1865. Appears on a roll of POW's received at Ship Island, Mississippi, on April 15, 1865. Transferred from Ship Island to Vicksburg, Mississippi, on May 1, 1865. Appears on a roll of POW's of Company A, 63rd Alabama Infantry commanded by Lieutenant W. D. Kyle that were surrendered by Lt. General Richard Taylor at Citronelle, Alabama, on May 4, 1865, and paroled at Meridian, Mississippi, on May 13, 1865. Residence—Montgomery County, Alabama.

Essman, C. E., Sergeant Co. I.
Enlisted on April 15, 1864, at Columbiana, Alabama, by Lieutenant Bulger for the war. Appears present on a company muster roll for September and October 1864. Captured at Blakeley, Alabama, on April 9, 1865. Appears on a roll of POW's received at Ship Island, Mississippi, on April 15, 1865. Transferred from Ship Island to Vicksburg, Mississippi, on May 1, 1865. Appears on a roll of POW's of Cos. I and K, 63rd Alabama Infantry commanded by Lieutenant W. A. Skinner that were surrendered by Lt. General Richard Taylor at Citronelle, Alabama, on May 4, 1865, and paroled at Meridian, Mississippi, on May 13, 1865. Residence—Shelby County, Alabama.

Ethridge, Sanders W., Pvt. Co. C.
Enlisted on June 10, 1864, at Macon County, Alabama, by Major Ready for the war. Appears on a company muster-in roll for June 24, 1864, at Camp Watts near Notasulga, Alabama. Age—17, eyes—grey, hair—black, complexion—fair, 5 foot 10 inches, residence—Society Hill, Alabama. Appears on a company muster roll for September and October 1864. Remarks: Died.

Evans, James, Pvt. Co. B.
Enlisted on March 23, 1864, at Montgomery, Alabama, by Captain Zimmerman for the war. Age—17. His name appears on a company muster-in roll for March 23, 1864. He appears absent on a company muster roll for September and October 1864. This muster roll reports him absent sick since October 28, 1864. He is reported to have drawn clothing on July 8, August 12 and September 11, 1864. He signed by his mark.

Evans, T. J., Corporal/Pvt. Co. I.
Enlisted on April 15, 1864, at Columbiana, Alabama, by Lieutenant Bulger for the war. Appears present on a company muster roll for September and October 1864. Note on this roll says "Co. changed station from Blakeley to Mobile, Alabama, on October 10, 1864." Admitted to Ross Hospital, Mobile, Alabama, on November 11, 1864, with febris intermittens. Returned to duty on November 18. Captured at Blakeley, Alabama, on April 9, 1865. Appears on a roll of POW's received at Ship Island, Mississippi, on April 15, 1865. Transferred from Ship Island to Vicksburg, Mississippi, on May 1, 1865. Appears on a roll of POW's of Cos. I and K, 63rd Alabama Infantry commanded by Lieutenant W. A. Skinner that were surrendered by Lt. General Richard Taylor at Citronelle, Alabama, on May 4, 1865, and paroled at Meridian, Mississippi, on May 13, 1865. Residence—Shelby County, Alabama.

Farber, Phillip, Pvt. Co. B.
>Enlisted on April 23, 1864, at Montgomery County, Alabama, by Captain Zimmerman for the war. Appears on a company muster roll for March 23, 1864. Age—16. Drew clothing on September 11, 1864, and signed by his mark. Appears present on a company muster roll for September and October 1864, with pay due from time of enlistment. Captured at Blakeley, Alabama, on April 9, 1865. Appears on a roll of POW's received at Ship Island, Mississippi, on April 15, 1865. Transferred from Ship Island to Vicksburg, Mississippi, on May 1, 1865. Appears on a roll of POW's of Company B, 63rd Alabama Infantry commanded by Lieutenant Thomas J. Calhoun that were surrendered by Lt. General Richard Taylor at Citronelle, Alabama, on May 4, 1865, and paroled at Meridian, Mississippi, on May 11, 1865. Residence—Montgomery County, Alabama.

Fails, G. B., Pvt. Co. F.
>Enlisted on July 4, 1864, at Lowndes County, Alabama, by Captain Buell for the war. Age—17, eyes—blue, hair—dark, complexion—ruddy, 5 foot 9 inches, residence—Lowndes County, Alabama. Appears on a company muster-in roll for July 25, 1864, at Georgiana, Alabama. Appears present on a company muster roll for August 31 to October 31, 1864. Captured at Blakeley, Alabama, on April 9, 1865. Appears on a roll of POW's received at Ship Island, Mississippi, on April 15, 1865. Transferred from Ship Island to Vicksburg, Mississippi, on May 1, 1865. Appears on a roll of POW's of Company F, 63rd Alabama Infantry commanded by Captain R. T. Simpson that were surrendered by Lt. General Richard Taylor at Citronelle, Alabama, on May 4, 1865, and paroled at Meridian, Mississippi, on May 11, 1865. Residence—Lowndes County, Alabama. He also appears on a roll of POW's of Quintard Hospital CSA commanded by Surgeon S. V. D. Hill that were surrendered at Citronelle on May 4, 1865, and paroled at Meridian, Mississippi, on May 10, 1865.

Falk, P., Pvt. Co. E.
>Admitted to Ross Hospital at Mobile, Alabama, on October 14, 1864, with febris intermittens quot. Returned to duty on October 28, 1864.

Fannell, D. M., Pvt. Co. K.
>Appears on a record of Confederate soldiers paroled the headquarters of the 16th US Army Corps at Montgomery, Alabama, on May 23, 1864.

Fannin, Henry A., Pvt. Co. A.
>Enlisted on January 1, 1864, at Tallapoosa County, Alabama, by Captain Echols for the war. Appears on a company muster-in roll for January 1, 1864, at Montgomery, Alabama. Age—16. Appears present on a company muster roll for January and February 1864, with pay due from time of enlistment. Appears present on a company muster roll for September and October 1864. Here he is shown as last paid by Major J. L. Calhoun on February 29, 1864. Drew clothing in the 2nd quarter of 1864.

Farley, R. J., Pvt. Co. I.
>Captured at Blakeley, Alabama, on April 9, 1865. Appears on a roll of POW's received at Ship Island, Mississippi, on April 15, 1865. Transferred from Ship Island to Vicksburg, Mississippi, on May 1, 1865. Appears on a roll of POW's of Cos. I and K, 63rd Alabama Infantry commanded by Lieutenant W. A. Skinner that were surrendered by Lt. General Richard Taylor at Citronelle, Alabama, on May 4, 1865, and paroled at Meridian, Mississippi, on May 13, 1865. Residence—Shelby County, Alabama.

Farr, James L., Pvt./Corporal Co. B.
>Enlisted on April 14, 1864, at Montgomery County, Alabama, by Captain

Zimmerman for the war. Age—17. Appears on a company muster-in roll at Montgomery, Alabama, for March 23, 1864. Drew clothing on July 8, August 12 and September 11, 1864. Appears present on a company muster roll for September and October 1864, with pay due from time of enlistment. Captured at Blakeley, Alabama, on April 9, 1865. Appears on a roll of POW's received at Ship Island, Mississippi, on April 15, 1865. Transferred from Ship Island to Vicksburg, Mississippi, on May 1, 1865. Appears on a roll of POW's of Company B, 63rd Alabama Infantry commanded by Lieutenant Thomas J. Calhoun that were surrendered by Lt. General Richard Taylor at Citronelle, Alabama, on May 4, 1865, and paroled at Meridian, Mississippi, on May 11, 1865. Residence—Autauga County, Alabama.

Farrior, James, Pvt. Co. B.
Enrolled on March 23, 1864, at Montgomery County, Alabama, by Captain Zimmerman for the war. Age—17. Appears on a company muster-in roll at Montgomery, Alabama, for March 23, 1864. Drew clothing on July 8 and September 11, 1864. Appears absent on a company muster roll for September and October 1864, with pay due from time of enlistment. Absent sick since October 17, 1864. Captured at Blakeley, Alabama, on April 9, 1865. Appears on a roll of POW's received at Ship Island, Mississippi, on April 15, 1865. Transferred from Ship Island to Vicksburg, Mississippi, on May 1, 1865. Appears on a roll of POW's of Company B, 63rd Alabama Infantry commanded by Lieutenant Thomas J. Calhoun that were surrendered by Lt. General Richard Taylor at Citronelle, Alabama, on May 4, 1865, and paroled at Meridian, Mississippi, on May 11, 1865. Residence—Montgomery County, Alabama.

Faulk, James, Pvt. Co. D.
Enlisted on September 30, 1864, at Blakeley, Alabama, by Captain Zorn for the war. Appears present on a company muster roll for August 30 to October 30, 1864, with pay due from time of enlistment. Appears on a list of wounded Confederates in the hospital of 1st Division, 13th US Army Corps at the battle of Blakeley Fort, Alabama, on April 9, 1865, abdomen penetrated. Admitted to St. Louis USA General Hospital, New Orleans, Louisiana, on April 16, 1865, with gunshot fracture of upper third left femur involving trochanter and neck. Age—19. Transferred to General Hospital on May 20, 1865. He was operated on and two inches of shaft of left femur including trochanter was removed. Transferred to Marine General Hospital on May 26. Confined at New Orleans on May 1, 1865. Appears on a roll of POW's paroled and released at New Orleans during May 16, 1865. Died at Marine USA General Hospital at New Orleans on June 5, 1865, from exhaustion consequent on a gunshot wound. Buried at Monument Cemetery. Reported to be a single man and his residence is shown as Louisville, Alabama.

Faulk, J. K., Pvt. Co. E.
Enlisted on August 8, 1864, at Pollard, Alabama, by Captain A. V. Lee for the war. Age—17, eyes—dark, hair—dark, complexion—dark. Appears present on a company muster roll for September and October 1864. Drew clothing on September 11, 1864.

Faulk, J. P., Pvt. Co. E.
Enlisted on March 15, 1864, at Clayton, Alabama, by Captain A. V. Lee for the war. Age—17, eyes—dark, hair—dark, complexion—dark. Appears absent on a company muster roll for September and October 1864. Absent in hospital since October 12, 1864. Captured at Blakeley, Alabama, on April 9, 1865. Appears on a roll of POW's received at Ship Island, Mississippi, on April 15, 1865. Transferred from Ship Island to Vicksburg, Mississippi, on May 1, 1865. Appears on a roll of sick and wounded Confederate POW's at USA General

Hospital No. 2, Vicksburg, Mississippi. Admitted on May 3, 1865, from steamer with acute diarrhoea. Returned to duty on May 8, 1865. Age—17.

Faulk, M. W., Jr. 2nd Lieutenant/2nd Lieutenant Co. E.
Enlisted on March 23, 1864, at Clayton, Alabama, by Captain A. V. Lee for the war. Age—17, eyes—blue, hair—light, complexion—fair. Elected 2nd Lieutenant on March 25, 1864. Appears absent on a company muster roll for September and October 1864. Absent without leave since October 6 & also resigned. Drew clothing on September 11, 1864. Signed for clothing by his mark. Resigned on December 5, 1864.

Faulk, W. R., Pvt. Co. E.
Enlisted on March 13, 1864, at Clayton, Alabama, by Captain A. V. Lee for the war. Age—17, eyes—dark, hair—dark, complexion—dark. Appears present on a company muster roll for September and October 1864. Captured at Blakeley, Alabama, on April 9, 1865. Appears on a roll of POW's received at Ship Island, Mississippi, on April 15, 1865. Transferred from Ship Island to Vicksburg, Mississippi, on May 1, 1865. Appears on a roll of POW's of Cos. E and G, 63rd Alabama Infantry commanded by Captain A. V. Lee that were surrendered by Lt. General Richard Taylor at Citronelle, Alabama, on May 4, 1865, and paroled at Meridian, Mississippi, on May 13, 1865. Residence—Barbour County, Alabama.

Faulkner, L. C., Pvt. Co. I.
Enlisted on April 15, 1864, at Wedowee, Alabama, by Captain Robinson for the war. Appears absent on a company muster roll for September and October 1864. Absent furloughed for 30 days from September 27. Captured at Blakeley, Alabama, on April 9, 1865. Appears on a roll of POW's received at Ship Island, Mississippi, on April 15, 1865. Transferred from Ship Island to Vicksburg, Mississippi, on May 1, 1865. Appears on a roll of POW's of Cos. I and K, 63rd Alabama Infantry commanded by Lieutenant W. A. Skinner that were surrendered by Lt. General Richard Taylor at Citronelle, Alabama, on May 4, 1865, and paroled at Meridian, Mississippi, on May 13, 1865. Residence—Randolph County, Alabama.

Faulkner, R., Pvt. Co. I.
Enlisted on April 15, 1864, at Columbiana, Alabama, by Lieutenant Bulger for the war. Appears absent on a company muster roll for September and October 1864. Absent furloughed for 30 days from September 27.

Faussett, George, Pvt. Co. I.
Enlisted on May 18, 1864, at Wedowee, Alabama, by Captain Robinson for the war. He appears present on a company muster roll for September and October 1864.

Faust, J. R., Pvt. Co. D.
Enlisted on August 21, 1864, at Pollard, Alabama, by Captain Zorn for the war. Appears absent on a company muster roll for September and October 1864, with pay due from time of enlistment. Absent sick at Mobile Hospital since September 15. Drew clothing on September 11, 1864.

Felty, Samuel, T. S., Pvt. Co. H.
Appears on a roll of POW's received at Military Prison, Alton, Illinois. Received on May 25, 1864, discharged on Amnesty Oath May 28, 1864. Captured at Resaca, Georgia on May 16, 1864.

Ferguay, Calvin S., 4th Sergeant Co. D.
Enlisted on July 30, 1864, at Macon County, Alabama, by Major Ready for the

war. Age—17, eyes—blue, hair—light, complexion—fair, 5 foot 6 inches, residence—Bushville, Barbour County, Alabama. Appears on a company muster-in roll for July 30, 1864, at Camp Watts near Notasulga, Alabama. Drew clothing on August 7, 1864. Appears present on a company muster roll for August 30 to October 30, 1864, with pay due from time of enlistment. Here he is shown as having enlisted on March 2, 1864, at Clayton, Alabama, by D. M. Seals. Captured at Blakeley, Alabama, on April 9, 1865. Appears on a roll of POW's received at Ship Island, Mississippi, on April 15, 1865. Transferred from Ship Island to Vicksburg, Mississippi, on May 1, 1865. Appears on a roll of POW's of Company D, 63rd Alabama Infantry commanded by Captain Robert H. Pearson that were surrendered by Lt. General Richard Taylor at Citronelle, Alabama, on May 4, 1865, and paroled at Meridian, Mississippi, on May 13, 1865. Residence—Barbour County, Alabama.

Few, Asberry, Sergeant Co. D.
Enlisted on July 30, 1864, at Macon County, Alabama, by Major Ready for the war. Age—17, eyes—grey, hair—dark, complexion—dark, 5 foot 7 inches, residence—Adkinsons, Barbour County, Alabama. Appears on a company muster-in roll for July 30, 1864, at Camp Watts near Notasulga, Alabama. Drew clothing on August 7, 1864. Appears absent on a company muster roll for August 30 to October 30, 1864. Absent sick at Mobile Hospital since September 8. Here he is shown as having enlisted March 2, 1864, at Clayton, Alabama, by D. M. Seals.

Fikes, C., Pvt. Co. D.
Appears on a list of POW stragglers of the Confederate Army surrendered by Lt. General Richard Taylor in May 1865, and paroled at Selma, Alabama, on May 28, 1865. Residence—Perry County, Alabama.

Fikes, J. (John E. or J. E. Fikes), Pvt. Co. H.
Enlisted on March 15, 1864, at Centerville, Alabama, by Captain Suttle for the war. Age—16, eyes—blue, hair—light, complexion—fair. Drew clothing on September 11, 1864. Appears absent on a company muster roll for September and October 1864. Deserted while in camp near Mobile, Alabama, on October 10, 1864. Appears on an account of clothing etc. of patients at Ross Hospital, Mobile, Alabama, on March 29, 1865, that were delivered on April 8, 1865. Admitted to Ross Hospital, Mobile, Alabama, on March 29, 1864, with vulnus sclopeticum (gunshot wound). Sent to General Hospital on April 9, 1865, remarks: Meridian. John E. Fikes appears on a roll of POW's from Company C, 36th Alabama Regiment, Holtzclaw's Brigade CSA commanded by Captain W. N. Knight that were surrendered at Citronelle, Alabama, by Lt. General Richard Taylor at Citronelle, Alabama, on May 4, 1865, and paroled at Meridian, Mississippi, on May 10, 1865. Residence—Bibb County, Alabama. Card is indexed under 2nd Alabama Reserves.

Fincher, E., Pvt. Captain Hicks Company.
Admitted to Ross Hospital, Mobile, Alabama, on August 3, 1864, with dysenteria acuta. Sent to General Hospital on August 26, 1864, remarks: Selma.

Fleming, Napoleon, B., Pvt. Co. B/D.
Enlisted on May 16, 1864, at Coffee County, Alabama, by Captain Payne for the war. Age—17, eyes—blue, hair—dark, complexion—dark, 5 foot 11 ½ inches, residence—Old Town, Coffee County, Alabama. Appears on a company muster-in roll for July 30, 1864, at Camp Watts near Notasulga, Alabama. Drew clothing on August 7, 1864. Signed by his mark. Appears absent on a company muster roll for August 30 to September 30, 1864. Absent sick at Mobile Hospital since October 24, 1864. Here he is shown as having enlisted at Elba, Alabama, by Captain Payne on May 16. His name appears on a register of POW's paroled at

Montgomery, Alabama, on June 20, 1865. His parole is in his file.

Flowers, Berry, L., Pvt. Co. D.
Enlisted on July 30, 1864, at Macon County, Alabama, by Major Ready for the war. Age—17, eyes—grey, hair—dark, complexion—dark, 5 foot 10 inches, residence—Lawrenceville, Henry County, Alabama. Appears on a company muster-in roll for July 30, 1864, at Camp Watts near Notasulga, Alabama. Drew clothing on August 7, 1864. Appears present on a company muster roll for August 30 to October 30, 1864, with pay due from time of enlistment. Here he is shown as having enlisted on March 2, 1864, at Clayton, Alabama, by D. M. Seals. Appears on a roll of POW's of Company D, 63rd Alabama Infantry commanded by Captain Robert H. Pearson that were surrendered by Lt. General Richard Taylor at Citronelle, Alabama, on May 4, 1865, and paroled at Meridian, Mississippi, on May 13, 1865. Residence—Henry County, Alabama.

Foster, R. W., Pvt. Co. H.
Enlisted on July 29, 1864, at Selma, Alabama, by Captain Suttle for the war. Age—17, eyes—blue, hair—dark, complexion—dark. Appears absent on a company muster roll for September and October 1864. Absent sick at a hospital in Greenville, Alabama, since September 16. Drew clothing on September 11, 1864. Admitted to Ross Hospital, Mobile, Alabama, on September 16, 1864, with rubeola. Sent to General Hospital on September 26, 1864. Remarks: Greenville.

Fowler, Z., Pvt. Co. I
Enlisted on May 18, 1864, at Wedowee, Alabama, by Captain Robinson for the war. Appears absent on a company muster roll for September and October 1864. Absent without leave from September 18, 1864.

Franking, T. G., Pvt. Co. H.
Enlisted on July 29, 1864, at Selma, Alabama, by Captain Suttle for the war. Age—17, eyes—dark, hair—light, complexion—fair. Appears present on a company muster roll for September and October 1864. Drew clothing September 11, 1864.

Frasier, E. P., Pvt. Co. F.
Captured at Blakeley, Alabama, on April 9, 1865. Appears on a roll of POW's received at Ship Island, Mississippi, on April 15, 1865. Transferred from Ship Island to Vicksburg, Mississippi, on May 1, 1865. Appears on a roll of POW's of Company F, 63rd Alabama Infantry commanded by Captain R. T. Simpson that were surrendered by Lt. General Richard Taylor at Citronelle, Alabama, on May 4, 1865, and paroled at Meridian, Mississippi, on May 11, 1865. Residence—Lowndes County, Alabama.

Frazier, L., Pvt. Co. F.
Enlisted on August 4, 1864, at Georgiana, Alabama, by Captain Brown for the war. Appears absent without leave on a company muster roll for August 30, to October 30, 1864, with pay due from time of enlistment.

Freeman, John, Pvt. Co. A.
Enlisted on January 1, 1864, at Tallapoosa County, Alabama, by Captain John Echols for the war. Appears on a company muster-in roll for January 1, 1864. Age—16. Appears present on a company muster roll for January and February 1865, with pay due from time of enlistment. Drew clothing 2nd quarter and on August 12, 1864, signed with his mark. Appears present on a company muster roll for September and October 1864. Captured at Blakeley, Alabama, on April 9, 1865. Appears on a roll of POW's received at Ship Island, Mississippi, on April 15, 1865. Transferred from Ship Island to Vicksburg, Mississippi, on May 1, 1865. Appears on a roll of POW's of Company A, 63rd Alabama Infantry

commanded by Lieutenant W. D. Kyle that were surrendered by Lt. General Richard Taylor at Citronelle, Alabama, on May 4, 1865, and paroled at Meridian, Mississippi, on May 13, 1865. Residence—Tallapoosa County, Alabama.

Freeman, Newton, Pvt. Co. A.
Enlisted at Butler County, Alabama, by Captain Echols for the war. Drew clothing in the 2nd quarter of 1864. Appears present on a company muster roll for September and October 1864, with pay due from time of enlistment. Captured at Blakeley, Alabama, on April 9, 1865. Appears on a roll of POW's received at Ship Island, Mississippi, on April 15, 1865. Transferred from Ship Island to Vicksburg, Mississippi, on May 1, 1865. Appears on a roll of POW's of Company A, 63rd Alabama Infantry commanded by Lieutenant W. D. Kyle that were surrendered by Lt. General Richard Taylor at Citronelle, Alabama, on May 4, 1865, and paroled at Meridian, Mississippi, on May 13, 1865. Residence—Butler County, Alabama.

French, William D., Pvt. Co. G.
Enlisted on May 16, 1864, at Troy, Alabama, by Captain Wilkerson for the war. Age—17, eyes—grey, hair—light, complexion—dark, 5 foot 8 inches, residence—Coffee County, Alabama. Appears on a company muster-in roll for September 7, 1864, at Blakeley, Alabama. Drew clothing on September 11, 1864. Appears present on a company muster roll for September and October 1864. Captured at Blakeley, Alabama, on April 9, 1865. Appears on a roll of POW's received at Ship Island, Mississippi, on April 15, 1865. Transferred from Ship Island to Vicksburg, Mississippi, on May 1, 1865. Appears on a roll of POW's of Cos. E and G, 63rd Alabama Infantry commanded by Captain A. V. Lee that were surrendered by Lt. General Richard Taylor at Citronelle, Alabama, on May 4, 1865, and paroled at Meridian, Mississippi, on May 13, 1865. Residence—Pike County, Alabama.

Fuller, James M., Pvt. Co. A.
Enlisted on January 1, 1864, at Tallapoosa County, Alabama, by Captain John Echols for the war. Age—17. Appears on a company muster-in roll for January 1, 1864. Appears present on a company muster roll for January and February 1864, with pay due from time of enlistment. Here he is shown as having enlisted on January 1 at Montgomery, Alabama. His name appears among those present on a company muster roll for September and October 1864, sick in quarters. Here he is shown as last paid on February 29, 1864. It was reported that he drew clothing in the 2nd quarter of 1864. Admitted to 1st Mississippi CSA Hospital at Jackson, Mississippi, on March 3, 1865, with ascites [accumulation of fluid in abdominal cavity]. Returned to duty on April 4, 1865. Appears on a record of Confederate soldiers paroled at headquarters of the 16th US Army Corps at Montgomery, Alabama, on May 22, 1865. His parole is in his file signed by his mark "X." Hair—dark, eyes—hazel, complexion—fair, 5 foot 10 inches.

Fuller, Thomas, Pvt. Co. I.
Enlisted on April 15, 1864, at Wedowee, Alabama, by Captain Robinson for the war. He is reported to have been admitted to Ross Hospital, Mobile, Alabama, on August 17, 1864, with rubeola. Returned to duty on August 26, 1864. Appears absent on a company muster roll for September and October 1864. Absent on 30 day furlough from September 27, 1864. POW captured at Blakeley, Alabama, on April 9, 1865. Appears on a roll of POW's received at Ship Island, Mississippi, on April 15, 1865. Transferred from Ship Island to Vicksburg, Mississippi, on May 1, 1865. Appears on a roll of POW's of Cos. I and K, 63rd Alabama Infantry commanded by Lieutenant W. A. Skinner that were surrendered by Lt. General Richard Taylor at Citronelle, Alabama, on May 4,

1865, and paroled at Meridian, Mississippi, on May 13, 1865. Residence—Sumpter County, Alabama.

Fuller, W. D., Pvt. Co. F.
Enlisted on May 30, 1864, at Montgomery, Alabama, by Captain Jackson for the war. Age—17, eyes—blue, hair—dark, complexion—fair, 5 foot 8 inches, residence—Butler County, Alabama. Appears on a company muster-in roll for July 25, 1864, at Georgiana, Alabama. Drew clothing on September 11, 1864. Appears present on a company muster roll for August 31 to October 31, 1864, with pay due from time of enlistment. Captured at Blakeley, Alabama, on April 9, 1865. Appears on a roll of POW's received at Ship Island, Mississippi, on April 15, 1865. Transferred from Ship Island to Vicksburg, Mississippi, on May 1, 1865. His name appears on a roll of POW's of Company F, 63rd Alabama Infantry commanded by Captain R. T. Simpson that were surrendered by Lt. General Richard Taylor at Citronelle, Alabama, on May 4, 1865, and paroled at Meridian, Mississippi, on May 11, 1865. His residence is shown as Butler County, Alabama.

Fuller, William C., Pvt./ 2nd M. Sergeant Co. A, F&S.
Enlisted on January 1, 1864, at Montgomery, Alabama, by Captain John Echols for the war. Appears on a company muster-in roll for January 1, 1864, at Montgomery, Alabama. Appears present on a company muster roll for January and February 1864, with pay due from time of enlistment. Here he is shown as having enlisted on January 1, 1864, at Tallapoosa County, Alabama. Drew clothing in 2nd quarter 1864. Appears on a company muster roll for September and October 1864, last paid on February 29, 1864. Promoted or appointed 2nd M. Sergeant per S. O. dated September 4, 1864. Appears on a Field and Staff muster roll for September and October 1864. Captured at Blakeley, Alabama, on April 9, 1865. Appears on a roll of POW's received at Ship Island, Mississippi, on April 15, 1865. Transferred from Ship Island to Vicksburg, Mississippi, on May 1, 1865. Appears on a roll of POW's of Company A, 63rd Alabama Infantry commanded by Lieutenant W. D. Kyle that were surrendered by Lt. General Richard Taylor at Citronelle, Alabama, on May 4, 1865, and paroled at Meridian, Mississippi, on May 13, 1865. Residence—Montgomery, Alabama.

Fulmen, J. R., Corporal Co. F.
Appears on a register of Confederate soldiers paroled on June 19, 1865, at Montgomery, Alabama, by Major Ross Wilkerson A. D. C. and Provost Marshal, 16th US Army Corps. His parole is in his file. Hair—light, eyes—blue, complexion—fair, 5 foot 7 inches. Signed his parole by "X" his mark.

Fulton, William B., Captain Co. I.
Residence was shown as Shelby County, Alabama. Appears absent on a company muster roll for September and October 1864, having never been paid. Furloughed for 20 days from October 22, 1864. Elected Captain on September 17, 1864. Captured at Blakeley, Alabama, on April 9, 1865, by 2nd Division of 16th US. Army Corps. Appears on a roll of POW's received at Ship Island, Mississippi, on April 15, 1865. Transferred from Ship Island to Vicksburg, Mississippi, on May 1, 1865. Confined at New Orleans, Louisiana, on April 30, 1865. Here he is shown as having been transferred from Ship Island on April 28, 1865. Exchanged on May 1, 1865. Appears on a register of sick and wounded Confederate soldiers at USA General Hospital No. 2, Vicksburg, Mississippi. Admitted from steamer on May 3, 1865, with intermential fever. Returned to duty on May 9, 1864. Appears on a roll of POW Officers of CSA that were surrendered by Lt. General Richard Taylor at Citronelle, Alabama, on May 4, 1865, and paroled at Jackson, Mississippi, on May 15, 1865. Signed a Parole of Honor at Jackson. His parole is in his file.

Furgerson, Clairbrone H., Pvt. Co. C.
Enlisted on April 23, 1864, at Tallapoosa County, Alabama, by Captain Brown for the war. Age—17, eyes—dark, hair—dark, complexion—fair, 5 foot 5 inches, residence—Dadeville, Tallapoosa County, Alabama. Appears on a company muster-in roll for June 24, 1864, at Camp Watts near Notasulga, Alabama. Drew clothing on August 5, 1864. Appears present on a company muster roll for September and October 1864. Paroled at headquarters of the 16th US Army Corps at Montgomery, Alabama, on May 26, 1865. His parole is in his file. Here he is shown as 5 foot 1 inch, hair—dark, eyes—dark, complexion—dark. Note in his file is reference to see personal papers of James M. Alexander, Alabama.

Gallespie, Wesley, Pvt. Co. A
Enlisted on January 1, 1864, at Montgomery County, Alabama, by Captain Echols for the war. Age—15. Appears on a company muster-in roll for January 1, 1864, at Montgomery. Appears present on a company muster roll for January and February 1864, with pay due from time of enlistment. Drew clothing in 2nd quarter and August 12, 1864. He signed for clothing by his mark. Appears present on a company muster roll for September and October 1864. He is shown here as being last paid on February 29. Captured at Blakeley, Alabama, on April 9, 1865. Appears on a roll of POW's received at Ship Island, Mississippi, on April 15, 1865. Transferred from Ship Island to Vicksburg, Mississippi, on May 1, 1865. Appears on a roll of POW's of Company A, 63rd Alabama Infantry commanded by Lieutenant W. D. Kyle that were surrendered by Lt. General Richard Taylor at Citronelle, Alabama, on May 4, 1865, and paroled at Meridian, Mississippi, on May 13, 1865. Residence—Montgomery, Alabama.

Galloway, Eli, Pvt. Co. B.
Enlisted on August 15, 1864, at Pollard, Alabama, by Lieutenant Townsend for the war. Appears present on a company muster roll for September and October 1864, with pay due from time of enlistment. Captured at Blakeley, Alabama, on April 9, 1865. Appears on a roll of POW's received at Ship Island, Mississippi, on April 15, 1865. Transferred from Ship Island to Vicksburg, Mississippi, on May 1, 1865. Appears on a roll of POW's of Company B, 63rd Alabama Infantry commanded by Lieutenant Thomas J. Calhoun that were surrendered by Lt. General Richard Taylor at Citronelle, Alabama, on May 4, 1865, and paroled at Meridian, Mississippi, on May 13, 1865. Residence—Dale County, Alabama.

Gammell, John W., Pvt. Co. C.
Enlisted on May 10, 1864, at Tallapoosa County, Alabama, by Captain Brown for the war. Age—17, eyes—blue, hair—light, complexion—fair, 5 foot 4 inches, residence—Tallapoosa County. Appears on a company muster-in roll for June 24, 1864, at Camp Watts near Notasulga, Alabama. Drew clothing on August 6, 1864. Signed by his mark. Appears absent on a company muster roll for September and October 1864. Absent in hospital at Mobile, Alabama, since October 28, 1864. Captured at Blakeley, Alabama, on April 9, 1865. Appears on a roll of POW's received at Ship Island, Mississippi, on April 15, 1865. Transferred from Ship Island to Vicksburg, Mississippi, on May 1, 1865. Appears on a roll of POW's of Cos. C and H, 63rd Alabama Infantry commanded by Captain C. W. Martin that were surrendered by Lt. General Richard Taylor at Citronelle, Alabama, on May 4, 1865, and paroled at Meridian, Mississippi, on May 11, 1865. Residence—Tallapoosa County, Alabama. There is a card in his file with reference to see personal papers of James M. Alexander - Alabama.

Gantt, William L., Pvt. Co. B.
Enrolled on March 23, 1864, at Montgomery County, Alabama, by Captain Zimmerman for the war. Age—17. Appears on a company muster-in roll for March 23, 1864, at Montgomery. Drew clothing on July 8 and September 11,

1864. Signed by his mark. Appears absent on a company muster roll for September and October 1864, with pay due from time of enlistment. Absent sick since October 13.

Gardner, W. J., Pvt. Co. I.
Appears on a roll of POW's that were stragglers of CSA surrendered by Lt. General Richard Taylor in May 1865, and paroled at Selma, Alabama, on May 29, 1865. Residence—Dallas County, Alabama.

Garland, Spotswood, 1st Lieutenant/Captain Co. G.
Residence shown as St. Louis, Missouri. Appears present on a company muster roll for September and October 1864. Elected 1st Lieutenant on September 11, 1864, promoted on September 19. Elected Captain on November 11. There are some discrepancies in the dates of his election and promotion. He requisitioned for Company G, in 3rd quarter of 1864, the following: 61 jackets, 51 pair of pants, 35 pair of shoes, 21 shirts, and 38 pair of drawers. He is reported as a POW from Taylor's Corps, paroled on May 20, 1865, by authority of Major General Canby at Mobile, Alabama. Age—19, eyes—grey, complexion—fair, 5 foot 8 ½ inches. His parole is in his file.

Garner, James L., Pvt. Co. B/K
Enrolled on April 14, 1864, at Montgomery, Alabama, by Captain Zimmerman for the war. Age—17. Appears on a company muster-in roll for March 23, 1864, at Montgomery, Alabama. Drew clothing on July 8, 1864. Appears on a Company B muster roll for September and October 1864, with pay due from time of enlistment. Shown here as having been transferred on S. O. No. 15, October 2, 1864. Appears absent on a Company K muster roll for September and October 1864. Absent with leave since September 26, 1864.

Garrott, Samuel H., Pvt. Co. A.
Enrolled on January 1, 1864, at Tallapoosa County, Alabama, by Captain Echols for the war. Appears on a company muster-in roll for January 1, 1864. Age—16. Appears present on a company muster roll for January and February 1864, with pay due from time of enlistment. Drew clothing in 2nd quarter, August 12 and September 11, 1864. Appears absent on a company muster roll for September and October 1864. Absent detached as a teamster as per S. O. dated September 30, 1864, at headquarters of Left Wing Defense of Mobile, Alabama. Appears on a list of effects of deceased soldiers turned over to Quartermaster CSA. File in 1865. No. 2572.

Gatewood, Charles C., Pvt. Co. C.
Enlisted on May 3, 1864, at Russell County, Alabama, by Lieutenant Carnes for the war. Age—17, eyes—blue, hair—light, complexion—fair, 5 foot 11 ½ inches, residence—Grierville, Russell County, Alabama. Drew clothing on August 6, 1864. Appears present on a company muster roll for September and October 1864. Appears on a roll of POW's of nurses and patients of Moore Hospital CSA that were surrendered by Lt. General Richard Taylor at Citronelle, Alabama, on May 4, 1865, and paroled at Meridian, Mississippi, on May 16, 1865. Residence—Russell County, Alabama.

German, R., Pvt. Co. K.
Enlisted on October 8, 1864, at Coosa County, Alabama, by Captain Hancock for the war. Appears present on a company muster roll for September and October 1864. Admitted on March 3, 1865, to 1st Mississippi CSA Hospital at Jackson, Mississippi, with debilitas. Returned to duty on April 4, 1865. Appears on a roll of POW's paroled on June 3, 1865, at Talladega, Alabama, by Brigadier General M. H. Chrysler, commanding forces at Talladega.

Gibbs, A. W., Pvt. Co. H.
Enlisted on March 15, 1864, at Montevallo, Alabama, by Lieutenant Killough for the war. He is described as: age—17, eyes—dark, hair—light, complexion—fair. Drew clothing on September 11, 1864. Appears present on a company muster roll for September and October 1864. POW captured at Blakeley, Alabama, on April 9, 1865. Appears on a roll of POW's received at Ship Island, Mississippi, on April 15, 1865. Transferred from Ship Island to Vicksburg, Mississippi, on May 1, 1865. His name appears on a roll of sick and wounded Confederate POW's at to USA General Hospital No. 2, Vicksburg, Mississippi. Admitted from steamer on May 3, 1865, with acute bronchitis. Returned to duty on May 12, 1865.

Gibbs, J. H., Surgeon, F & S.
Appears present on a Field and Staff muster roll for September and October 1864, near Mobile, Alabama.

Giddons, W. C., Pvt. Co. B/A.
Captured at Blakeley, Alabama, on April 9, 1865. Appears on a roll of POW's received at Ship Island, Mississippi, on April 15, 1865. Transferred from Ship Island to Vicksburg, Mississippi, on May 1, 1865. Appears on a roll of POW's of Company A, 63rd Alabama Infantry commanded by Lieutenant W. D. Kyle that were surrendered by Lt. General Richard Taylor at Citronelle, Alabama, on May 4, 1865, and paroled at Meridian, Mississippi, on May 13, 1865. Residence—Lowndes County, Alabama.

Gilder, Joseph G., Pvt. Co. A/B.
Enlisted on May 10, 1864, at Chambers County, Alabama, by Captain Echols for the war. Drew clothing in the 2nd quarter of 1864. Appears present on a Company A muster roll for September and October 1864, with pay due from time of enlistment. POW captured at Blakeley, Alabama, on April 9, 1865. His name appears on a roll of POW's received at Ship Island, Mississippi, on April 15, 1865. He was among those men transferred from Ship Island to Vicksburg, Mississippi, on May 1, 1865. Appears on a roll of POW's of Company A, 63rd Alabama Infantry commanded by Lieutenant W. D. Kyle that were surrendered by Lt. General Richard Taylor at Citronelle, Alabama, on May 4, 1865, and paroled at Meridian, Mississippi, on May 13, 1865. Residence is reported as Chambers County, Alabama. He also appears on a roll of POW's at Quintard Hospital CSA commanded by surgeon S. V. D. Hill that were surrendered by Lt. General Richard Taylor at Citronelle, Alabama, on May 4, 1865, and paroled at Meridian, Mississippi, on May 10, 1865. His residence is shown here as LaFayette, Alabama.

Gilmore, J. M., Pvt. Co. E.
Enlisted on August 8, 1864, at Pollard, Alabama, by Captain A. V. Lee for the war. Age—17, eyes—blue, hair—light, complexion—fair. Drew clothing on September 11, 1864. Appears absent on a company muster roll for September and October 1864. Absent in hospital since October 19, 1864. Captured at Blakeley, Alabama, on April 9, 1865. Appears on a roll of POW's received at Ship Island, Mississippi, on April 15, 1865. Transferred from Ship Island to Vicksburg, Mississippi, on May 1, 1865. Appears on a roll of POW's of Cos. E and G, 63rd Alabama Infantry commanded by Captain A. V. Lee that were surrendered by Lt. General Richard Taylor at Citronelle, Alabama, on May 4, 1865, and paroled at Meridian, Mississippi, on May 13, 1865. Residence—Henry County, Alabama. He also appears on a list of Confederate POW's that were paroled at the headquarters of the 16th US Army Corps at Montgomery, Alabama, on May 24, 1865.

Genright, John, Pvt. Co. G.
 Enlisted on May 16, 1864, at Troy, Alabama, by Captain Wilkerson for the war. Appears on a company muster-in roll for September 7, 1864, at Blakeley, Alabama. Drew clothing on September 11, 1864, signed with his mark. Appears present for a company muster roll for September and October 1864. Captured at Blakeley, Alabama, on April 9, 1865. Appears on a roll of POW's received at Ship Island, Mississippi, on April 15, 1865. Transferred from Ship Island to Vicksburg, Mississippi, on May 1, 1865. Appears on a roll of POW's of Cos. E and G, 63rd Alabama Infantry commanded by Captain A. V. Lee that were surrendered by Lt. General Richard Taylor at Citronelle, Alabama, on May 4, 1865, and paroled at Meridian, Mississippi, on May 13, 1865. Residence—Henry County, Alabama.

Gipson, Henry, Pvt. Con D/K.
 Enlisted on August 11, 1864, at Pollard, Alabama, by Captain Zorn for the war. Appears absent on a company D muster roll for August 30 to October 30, 1864. Absent, transferred to Co. K on September 28. Drew clothing on September 12, 1864. Signed by his mark. Appears present on a Company K muster roll for September and October 1864.

Glosson, James M., Pvt. Co. G.
 Enlisted on April 16, 1864, at Troy, Alabama, by Captain Wilkerson for the war. Appears on a company muster-in roll for September 7, 1864, at Blakeley, Alabama. Age—17, eyes—grey, hair—dark, complexion—florid, 5 foot 9 inches, residence—Pike County, Alabama. Drew clothing on September 11, 1864. Signed by his mark. Appears present on a company muster roll for September and October 1864. Captured at Blakeley, Alabama, on April 9, 1865. Appears on a roll of POW's received at Ship Island, Mississippi, on April 15, 1865. Transferred from Ship Island to Vicksburg, Mississippi, on May 1, 1865. Appears on a roll of POW's of Cos. E and G, 63rd Alabama Infantry commanded by Captain A. V. Lee that were surrendered by Lt. General Richard Taylor at Citronelle, Alabama, on May 4, 1865, and paroled at Meridian, Mississippi, on May 13, 1865. Residence—Pike County, Alabama.

Godfrey, William T., Pvt. Co. C.
 Enlisted on May 7, 1864, at Tallapoosa County, Alabama, by Captain Brown for the war. His name appears on a company muster-in roll for June 24, 1864, at Camp Watts near Notasulga, Alabama. He was described as: age—17, eyes—blue, hair—light, complexion—fair, 5 foot 4 inches, residence—Tohopka, Alabama. He appears among those present on a company muster roll for September and October 1865.

Godwin, D. (David), Pvt. Co. F.
 Enlisted on July 14, 1864, at Lowndes County, Alabama, by Captain Buell for the war. Appears on a company muster-in roll for July 25, 1865, at Georgiana, Alabama. Age—17, eyes—hazel, hair—light, complexion—fair, 5 foot 6 inches, residence—Lowndes County, Alabama. Drew clothing September 11, 1864. Appears present on a company muster roll for August 30 to October 30, 1864, with pay due from time of enlistment. Captured at Blakeley, Alabama, on April 9, 1865. Appears on a roll of POW's received at Ship Island, Mississippi, on April 15, 1865. Transferred from Ship Island to Vicksburg, Mississippi, on May 1, 1865. Appears on a roll of POW's of Company F, 63rd Alabama Infantry commanded by Captain R. T. Simpson that were surrendered by Lt. General Richard Taylor at Citronelle, Alabama, on May 4, 1865, and paroled at Meridian, Mississippi, on May 11, 1865. Residence—Lowndes County, Alabama. He is buried at Braggs Cemetery 1846-1926.

Godwin, J. K., Pvt. Co. E.
  Enlisted on July 27, 1864, at Montgomery, Alabama, by Captain A. V. Lee for the war. Age—17, eyes—blue, hair—light, complexion—fair. Appears present on a company muster roll for September and October 1864. Captured at Blakeley, Alabama, on April 9, 1865. Appears on a roll of POW's received at Ship Island, Mississippi, on April 15, 1865. Transferred from Ship Island to Vicksburg, Mississippi, on May 1, 1865. Appears on a roll of POW's of Cos. E and G, 63rd Alabama Infantry commanded by Captain A. V. Lee that were surrendered by Lt. General Richard Taylor at Citronelle, Alabama, on May 4, 1865, and paroled at Meridian, Mississippi, on May 13, 1865. Residence—Wilcox County, Alabama.

Golden, Oliver J., Pvt. Co. G.
  Enlisted on October 1, 1864, at Blakeley, Alabama, by Captain Garland. Appears present on a company muster roll for September and October 1864. Admitted to Yandell Hospital, Meridian, Mississippi, on April 5, 7, 8, 9, 1865, with acute diarrhoea. Appears on a register of paroled POW's that were paroled by Major Ross Wilkerson A. D. C. and Provost Marshal, 16th US Army Corps. Paroled on June 1, 1865, at Montgomery, Alabama. Hair—black, 5 foot, 9 inches, eyes—black, complexion—dark. Signed by "X" his mark. His parole is in his file.

Goldsmith, John C., Pvt. Co. A.
  Enlisted on April 8, 1864, at Butler, Alabama, by Captain Echols for the war. Drew clothing in 2nd quarter and September 11, 1864. Appears absent on a company muster roll for September and October 1864, with pay due from time of enlistment. Absent sick in hospital at Greenville, Alabama, since October 21, 1864.

Goldsmith, William A., Pvt. Co. A.
  Enlisted on April 8, 1864, at Lowndes County, Alabama. Drew clothing in 2nd quarter and September 11, 1864. Signed by his mark. Appears present on a company muster roll for September and October 1864, with pay due from time of enlistment.

Goodwin, H. J., Pvt. Co. F.
  Enlisted on May 30, 1864, at Montgomery, Alabama, by Captain Jackson for the war. Appears on a company muster-in roll for July 25, 1864, at Georgiana, Alabama. Age—17, eyes—dark, hair—dark, complexion—dark, 5 foot 6 inches, residence—Lowndes County, Alabama. Drew clothing on September 11, 1864. Appears absent on a company muster roll for August 31 to October 31, 1864, with pay due from time of enlistment. Absent in hospital at Mobile since October 15, 1864. Captured at Blakeley, Alabama, on April 9, 1865. Appears on a roll of POW's received at Ship Island, Mississippi, on April 15, 1865. Transferred from Ship Island to Vicksburg, Mississippi, on May 1, 1865. Appears on a roll of POW's of Company F, 63rd Alabama Infantry commanded by Captain R. T. Simpson that were surrendered by Lt. General Richard Taylor at Citronelle, Alabama, on May 4, 1865, and paroled at Meridian, Mississippi, on May 11, 1865. Residence—Lowndes County, Alabama.

Goodwin, James, Pvt./Corporal Co. B.
  Enrolled at Montgomery County, Alabama, by Captain Zimmerman for the war. Appears on a company muster-in roll for March 23, 1864. Drew clothing on July 8 and September 11, 1864. Appears as 4th Corporal and present on a company muster roll for September and October 1864, with pay due from time of enlistment. Captured at Blakeley, Alabama, on April 9, 1865. Appears on a roll of POW's received at Ship Island, Mississippi, on April 15, 1865. Transferred from Ship Island to Vicksburg, Mississippi, on May 1, 1865. Appears as 2nd Corporal on a roll of POW's of Company B, 63rd Alabama Infantry commanded

by 1st Lieutenant Thomas J. Calhoun that were surrendered by Lt. General Richard Taylor at Citronelle, Alabama, on May 4, 1865, and paroled at Meridian, Mississippi, on May 11, 1865. Residence—Montgomery County, Alabama.

Gorlick, Eugene B., Pvt. Co. C.
Enlisted on May 31, 1864, at Russell County, Alabama, by Lieutenant Morton for the war. Appears on a company muster-in roll for June 24, 1864, at Camp Watts near Notasulga, Alabama. Age—17, eyes—grey, hair—red, complexion—fair, 6 foot 0 inches, residence—Salem, Russell County, Alabama. Drew clothing on August 6, 1864. Appears present on a company muster roll for September and October 1864.

Grace, Thomas, Pvt. Co. B.
Enlisted on June 18, 1864, at Montgomery, Alabama, by Captain Zimmerman for the war. Drew clothing on July 8, August 12 and September 11, 1864. Signed by his mark. Appears absent on a company muster roll for September and October 1864, with pay due from time of enlistment. Absent sick since October 28, 1864. Captured at Blakeley, Alabama, on April 9, 1865. Appears on a roll of POW's received at Ship Island, Mississippi, on April 15, 1865. Transferred from Ship Island to Vicksburg, Mississippi, on May 1, 1865. Appears as 2nd Corporal on a roll of POW's of Company B, 63rd Alabama Infantry commanded by 1st Lieutenant Thomas J. Calhoun that were surrendered by Lt. General Richard Taylor at Citronelle, Alabama, on May 4, 1865, and paroled at Meridian, Mississippi, on May 11, 1865. Residence—Montgomery County, Alabama.

Gragg, M., Pvt. Co. I.
Enlisted on May 18, 1864, at Wedowee, Alabama, by Captain Robinson for the war. Appears absent on a company muster roll for September and October 1864. Absent without leave from September 18, 1864.

Graham, J. T., Pvt. Co. K.
Enlisted on May 12, 1864, at Carrollton, Alabama, by Captain Hughes for the war. Appears present on a muster roll for September and October 1864.

Graham, William T., Pvt. Co. G.
Enlisted on May 16, 1864, at Troy, Alabama, by Captain Wilkerson for the war. Appears on a company muster-in roll for September 7, 1864, at Blakeley, Alabama. Age—17, eyes—grey, hair—light, complexion—dark, 5 foot 10 inches, residence—Pike County, Alabama. Drew clothing on September 11, 1864. Signed by his mark. Appears present on a company muster roll for September and October 1864. Appears on a roll of POW's of Cos. E and G, 63rd Alabama Infantry commanded by Captain A. V. Lee that were surrendered by Lt. General Richard Taylor at Citronelle, Alabama, on May 4, 1865, and paroled at Meridian, Mississippi, on May 13, 1865. Residence—Pike County, Alabama.

Grant, J. B., Pvt. Co. E.
Enlisted on March 2, 1864, at Clayton, Alabama, by Captain A. V. Lee for the war. Age—17, eyes—dark, hair—dark, complexion—dark. Appears present on a company muster roll for September and October 1864. Captured at Blakeley, Alabama, on April 9, 1865. Appears on a list of wounded Confederates admitted to USA Hospital Steamer D. A. January on April 17, 1865. Transferred to Hospital Steamer Elanora Carrel at New Orleans, Louisiana, on April 25, 1865. Appears on a list of sick and wounded East Division, District of the Gulf that were sent to Vicksburg, Mississippi, via New Orleans, Louisiana, from Spanish Fort, (Blakeley) Alabama, on April 8, 1865. Admitted on April 28 to USA General Hospital No. 3, (colored) at Vicksburg. Transferred to USA General Hospital No. 2 at Vicksburg on May 4. Admitted to General Hospital No. 2, Vicksburg on May

4, 1865, with gunshot wound of left forearm. Age—18. Wound caused by conical ball. Returned to duty on May 8, 1864. Appears on a roll of POW's of divers companies and detached regiments of the CSA that were surrendered by Lt. General Richard Taylor at Citronelle, Alabama, on May 4, 1865, and paroled at Meridian, Mississippi, on May 11, 1865. Residence—Barbour County, Alabama.

Grant, John C., Pvt. Co. G.
Enlisted at Troy, Alabama, by Captain Wilkerson for the war. Appears on a company muster-in roll for September 7, 1864, at Blakeley, Alabama. Age—17, eyes—grey, hair—light, complexion—dark, 5 foot seven inches, residence—Coffee County, Alabama. Appears present on a company muster roll for September and October 1864. Captured at Blakeley, Alabama, on April 9, 1865. Appears on a roll of POW's received at Ship Island, Mississippi, on April 15, 1865. Transferred from Ship Island to Vicksburg, Mississippi, on May 1, 1865. Appears on a roll of POW's of Cos. E and G, 63rd Alabama Infantry commanded by Captain A. V. Lee that were surrendered by Lt. General Richard Taylor at Citronelle, Alabama, on May 4, 1865, and paroled at Meridian, Mississippi, on May 13, 1865. Residence—Coffee County, Alabama.

Grantham, A. A., Pvt. Co. G.
Enlisted on May 16, 1864, at Troy, Alabama, by Captain Wilkerson for the war. Appears on a company muster-in roll for September 7, 1864, at Blakeley, Alabama. Age—17, eyes—grey, hair—light, complexion—dark, 5 foot 7 inches. Drew clothing on September 11, 1864. Signed by his mark. Appears absent on a company muster roll for September and October 1864. Absent furloughed for 60 days from [hospital] Lauderdale, Mississippi, on October 20, 1864. Captured at Blakeley, Alabama, on April 9, 1865. Appears on a roll of POW's received at Ship Island, Mississippi, on April 15, 1865. Transferred from Ship Island to Vicksburg, Mississippi, on May 1, 1865. Appears on a roll of POW's of Cos. E and G, 63rd Alabama Infantry commanded by Captain A. V. Lee that were surrendered by Lt. General Richard Taylor at Citronelle, Alabama, on May 4, 1865, and paroled at Meridian, Mississippi, on May 13, 1865. Residence—Pike County, Alabama.

Graves, George W., Pvt. Co. G.
Enlisted on May 16, 1864, at Troy, Alabama, by Captain Wilkerson for the war. Appears on a company muster-in roll for September 7, 1864, at Blakeley, Alabama. Age—17, eyes—dark, hair—dark, complexion—dark, 5 foot 7 inches, residence—Pike County, Alabama. Drew clothing on September 11, 1864. Signed by his mark. Appears on a company muster roll for September and October 1864. Here he is shown as being in a hospital at Mobile since September 25, 1864. He was reported to be admitted to Way Hospital in Meridian, Mississippi on March 23, 1865, with ulcer, furloughed.

Graves, J. T. J., Pvt./Corporal Co. F.
Enlisted on July 14, 1864, at Lowndes County, Alabama, by Captain Buell for the war. He appears on a company muster-in roll for July 25, 1864, at Georgiana, Alabama. His is described as: age—17, eyes—blue, hair—light, complexion—fair, 5 foot, residence, Lowndes County, Alabama. Drew clothing on September 11, 1864. Appears present on a company muster roll for August 31, to October 31, 1864. Promoted from Private to Corporal on October 15, 1864. Captured at Blakeley, Alabama, on April 9, 1865. His name appears on a roll of POW's received at Ship Island, Mississippi, on April 15, 1865. He was among those men transferred from Ship Island to Vicksburg, Mississippi, on May 1, 1865. Appears on a roll of POW's of Company F, 63rd Alabama Infantry commanded by Captain R. T. Simpson that were surrendered by Lt. General Richard Taylor at Citronelle, Alabama, on May 4, 1865, and paroled at Meridian,

Mississippi, on May 11, 1865. His residence is shown as Lowndes County, Alabama.

Graves, W. M., Pvt. Co. E.
Enlisted on September 12, 1864, at Camp Hood by Captain A. V. Lee. Age—17, eyes—blue, hair—light, complexion—fair. Drew clothing on September 11, 1864. Appears absent on a company muster roll for September and October 1864. Absent in hospital since October 17, 1864. Admitted to Ross Hospital, Mobile, Alabama, on October 14, 1864, with rubeola. Furloughed from hospital Ross for 60 days on November 29, 1864.

Graves, Zacheus H., Pvt. Co. G.
Enlisted on May 16, 1864, at Troy, Alabama, by Captain Wilkerson for the war. Appears on a company muster-in roll for September 7, 1864. Age—17, eyes—dark, hair—dark, complexion—dark, 5 foot 8 inches, residence—Pike County, Alabama. Drew clothing on September 11, 1864. Appears present on a company muster roll for September and October 1864. Appears on a roll of POW's of Cos. E and G, 63rd Alabama Infantry commanded by Captain A. V. Lee that were surrendered by Lt. General Richard Taylor at Citronelle, Alabama, on May 4, 1865, and paroled at Meridian, Mississippi, on May 13, 1865. Residence—Pike County, Alabama.

Grimmett, William, Pvt. Co. C.
Enlisted on May 4, 1864, at Macon County, Alabama, by Captain Roscoe for the war. Age—17, eyes—grey, hair—blue, complexion—fair, 5 foot 8 ½ inches, Residence—Warrior Stand, Macon County, Alabama. Appears on a company muster-in roll for January 24, 1865, at Camp Watts near Notasulga, Alabama. Drew clothing on August 6, 1864. Signed by his mark. Appears present on a company muster roll for September and October 1864. Admitted to Ross Hospital, Mobile, Alabama, on November 10, 1864, with dyspepsia. Sent to General Hospital on November 30, 1864. Remarks: Hospital Nidelet. Discharged on Surgeon's Certificate of Disability, this document not on file.

Gray, Samuel, Sergeant/Pvt. Co. A/B.
Enrolled on January 1, 1864, at Tallapoosa County, Alabama, by Captain John Echols, for the war. Appears on a company muster-in roll for January 1864, at Montgomery, Alabama. Age—17. Appears present on a company muster roll for January and February 1864, with pay due from time of enlistment. Drew clothing in the 2nd quarter of 1864. Appears present on a Company A muster roll as 2nd Sergeant for September and October 1864. Admitted to Ross Hospital, Mobile, Alabama, on November 17, 1864, with febris intermittens quot. Returned to duty on November 29, 1864. Appears as a Private in Co. B, captured at Blakeley, Alabama, on April 9, 1865. Appears on a roll of POW's received at Ship Island, Mississippi, on April 15, 1865. Transferred from Ship Island to Vicksburg, Mississippi, on May 1, 1865. Appears on a roll of POW's of Company A, 63rd Alabama Infantry commanded by Lieutenant W. D. Kyle that were surrendered by Lt. General Richard Taylor at Citronelle, Alabama, on May 4, 1865, and paroled at Meridian, Mississippi, on May 13, 1865. Residence—Tallapoosa County, Alabama.

Grear, D. (Daniel) C., Pvt. Co. H.
Enlisted on March 15, 1864, at Randolph County, Alabama, by Lieutenant Johnson for the war. Age—17, eyes—blue, hair—dark, complexion—fair. Drew clothing September 11, 1864. Appears absent on a company muster roll for September and October 1864. Absent sick in hospital at Mobile, Alabama, since October 28, 1864. Admitted to Ross Hospital, Mobile, Alabama, on October 1, 1864, with febris intermittens quot. Sent to General Hospital on October 6, 1864.

Remarks: Lauderdale Springs [Hospital, Mississippi]. Captured at Blakeley, Alabama, on April 9, 1865. Appears on a roll of POW's received at Ship Island, Mississippi, on April 15, 1865. Transferred from Ship Island to Vicksburg, Mississippi, on May 1, 1865. Appears on a roll of POW's of Cos. C and H, 63rd Alabama Infantry commanded by Captain C. W. Martin that were surrendered by Lt. General Richard Taylor at Citronelle, Alabama, on May 4, 1865, and paroled at Meridian, Mississippi, on May 11, 1865. Residence—Bibb County, Alabama. There is a request for information in his file dated June 13, 1921 by Adjutant of Raphael Semmes Camp 11, U. C. V. Mobile, Alabama.

Green, Charles, Pvt. Co. A.
Enlisted on August 1, 1864, at Chambers County, Alabama, by Captain Echols for the war. Appears present on a company muster roll for September and October 1864, with pay due from time of enlistment. Captured at Blakeley, Alabama, on April 9, 1865. Appears on a roll of POW's received at Ship Island, Mississippi, on April 15, 1865. Transferred from Ship Island to Vicksburg, Mississippi, on May 1, 1865. Appears on a roll of POW's of Company A, 63rd Alabama Infantry commanded by Lieutenant W. D. Kyle that were surrendered by Lt. General Richard Taylor at Citronelle, Alabama, on May 4, 1865, and paroled at Meridian, Mississippi, on May 13, 1865. His residence is shown to be Chambers County, Alabama.

Green, Joseph W., Pvt. Co. A.
Enlisted on July 9, 1864, at Coosa County, Alabama, by Captain Echols for the war. He appears absent on a company muster roll for September and October 1864, with pay due from time of enlistment. Absent sick in hospital at Mobile, Alabama, since October 10, 1864. He appears as a patient on a hospital muster roll at Concert Hall Hospital, Montgomery, Alabama, to November 15, 1864. Remarks: D. [died]. Inquiry in his file from Commissioner of Pensions in Texas 1915.

Green, William D., Pvt. Co. A.
Enlisted on January 1, 1864, at Chambers County, Alabama, by Captain John Echols, for the war. Age—17. Appears on a company muster-in roll for January 1, 1864, at Montgomery, Alabama. Appears present on a company muster roll for January and February 1864, with pay due from time of enlistment. Appears present on a company muster roll for September and October 1864. Drew clothing in 2nd quarter and August 12, 1864. Signed for clothing with his mark. Admitted to Ross Hospital, Mobile, Alabama, on November 11, 1864, with febris remittens. Died on November 12, 1864. Appears on a register of soldiers of CSA who were killed in battle, or who died of wounds or disease. Died November 12, 1864, at Mobile, Alabama. Left $4.25. There is also a card in his file which indicates W. B. Green left $13.75.

Green, W. J., Pvt. Co. F.
Enlisted on March 9, 1864, at Greenville, Alabama, by Captain Brown, for the war. Appears on a company muster roll for July 25, 1864, at Georgiana, Alabama. Age—17, eyes—dark, hair—dark, complexion—dark, 5 foot 6 inches, residence—Butler County, Alabama. Drew clothing on September 11, 1864. Appears present on a company muster roll for August 31 to October 31, 1864, with pay due from time of enlistment. Captured at Blakeley, Alabama, on April 9, 1865. Appears on a roll of POW's received at Ship Island, Mississippi, on April 15, 1865. Transferred from Ship Island to Vicksburg, Mississippi, on May 1, 1865. Appears on a roll of POW's of Company F, 63rd Alabama Infantry commanded by Captain R. T. Simpson that were surrendered by Lt. General Richard Taylor at Citronelle, Alabama, on May 4, 1865, and paroled at Meridian, Mississippi, on May 11, 1865. Residence—Butler County, Alabama.

Gregory, W. H., Pvt. Co. F.
    Enlisted on July 12, 1864, at Lowndes County, Alabama, by Captain Buell, for the war. Appears on a company muster-in roll for July 25, 1864, at Georgiana, Alabama. Age—17, eyes—dark, hair—dark, complexion—dark, 5 foot 1 inch, residence—Lowndes County, Alabama. Drew clothing on September 11, 1864. Appears present on a company muster roll for August 31, to October 31, 1864, with pay due from time of enlistment. Captured at Blakeley, Alabama, on April 9, 1865. Appears on a roll of POW's received at Ship Island, Mississippi, on April 15, 1865. Transferred from Ship Island to Vicksburg, Mississippi, on May 1, 1865. Appears on a roll of POW's of Company F, 63rd Alabama Infantry commanded by Captain R. T. Simpson that were surrendered by Lt. General Richard Taylor at Citronelle, Alabama, on May 4, 1865, and paroled at Meridian, Mississippi, on May 11, 1865. Residence—Lowndes County, Alabama.

Griffin, W. G., Pvt. Co. I.
    Enlisted on May 18, 1864, at Wedowee, Alabama, by Captain Robinson for the war. Appears on a company muster roll for September and October 1864. Absent furloughed for 30 days from September 27, 1864.

Grissett, James G., Pvt. Co. D.
    Enlisted on July 30, 1864, at Macon County, Alabama, by Major Ready for the war. Appears on a company muster-in roll for July 30, 1864, at Camp Watts near Notasulga, Alabama. Age—17, eyes—blue, hair—red, complexion—Florid, 6 foot, residence—Clayton, Barbour County, Alabama. Appears absent on a company muster roll for September and October 1864, with pay due from time of enlistment. Absent at Clayton on sick furlough. He was wounded at Cheraw on July 18, [1864] and absent since then. Here he is shown as having enlisted at Eufaula, Alabama, by Captain Zorn on July 15. Appears on a list of wounded Confederate POW's in the hospital of the 1st Division of 13th US Army Corps. Wounded in thigh and foot (flesh) at the Battle of Blakeley Fort on April 9, 1865. Admitted to USA General Hospital, New Orleans, Louisiana, on April 15, 1865, with a flesh wound by gunshot of the left thigh. Died on April 21, 1865. Remarks: Pyaemia. Age—18, a single man. Buried in Monument Cemetery, Square 69, grave 58. There are hospital and death forms in his file.

Grissett, William C., Pvt. Co. G.
    Enlisted on May 16, 1864, at Troy, Alabama, by Captain Wilkerson for the war. Appears on a company muster-in roll for September 7, 1864, at Blakeley, Alabama. Age—17, eyes—grey, hair—light, complexion—dark, 5 foot 8 inches, residence—Pike County, Alabama. Drew clothing on September 11, 1864. Appears present on a company muster roll for September and October 1864. Captured at Blakeley, Alabama, on April 9, 1865. Appears on a roll of POW's received at Ship Island, Mississippi, on April 15, 1865. Transferred from Ship Island to Vicksburg, Mississippi, on May 1, 1865. Appears on a roll of POW's of Cos. E and G, 63rd Alabama Infantry commanded by Captain A. V. Lee that were surrendered by Lt. General Richard Taylor at Citronelle, Alabama, on May 4, 1865, and paroled at Meridian, Mississippi, on May 13, 1865. Residence—Pike County, Alabama.

Grissom, John W., Pvt. Co. D.
    Enlisted on July 30, 1864, at Macon County, Alabama, by Captain Ready for the war. Age—17, eyes—dark, hair—dark, complexion—dark, 5 foot 5 inches, residence—Adkinsons, Barbour County, Alabama. Drew clothing on August 7, 1864. Appears absent on a company muster roll for August 30 to October 30, 1864. Absent at Clayton, Alabama, on 60 day sick furlough by Medical Examining Board since October 5, 1864.

Grubbs, Ebenezer, Pvt. Co. A.
Enrolled on January 1, 1864, at Tallapoosa County, Alabama, by Captain John Echols for the war. Appears on a company muster-in roll for January 1, 1864, at Montgomery, Alabama. Age—16. Appears present on a company muster roll for January and February 1864, with pay due from time of enlistment. Drew clothing in the 3rd quarter of 1864. Appears absent on a company muster roll for September and October 1864. Absent furloughed on September 30, 1864, for 60 days by Medical Examining Board.

Gunn, George W., Corporal, Co. A/B.
Enrolled on January 1, 1864, at Macon County, Alabama, by Captain John Echols for the war. Appears as 4th Corporal on a company muster-in roll for January 1, 1864, at Montgomery, Alabama. Appears present on a company muster roll for January and February 1864, with pay due from time of enlistment. Drew clothing in 2nd quarter of 1864. Appears present, sick in quarters, on a Company A muster roll for September and October 1864. Appears on a roll of POW's captured at Blakeley, Alabama, on April 9, 1865. Here he is shown a member of Company B. Transferred from Ship Island to Vicksburg, Mississippi, on May 1, 1865. Appears on a roll of POW's of Company A, 63rd Alabama Infantry commanded by Lieutenant W. D. Kyle that were surrendered by Lt. General Richard Taylor at Citronelle, Alabama, on May 4, 1865, and paroled at Meridian, Mississippi, on May 13, 1865. Residence—Macon County, Alabama.

Guthrie, Benjamin J., Pvt. Co. A/B.
Enlisted on January 1, 1864, at Tallapoosa County, Alabama, by Captain John Echols for the war. Appears on a company muster-in roll for January 1, 1864, at Montgomery, Alabama. Age—17. Drew clothing in 2nd quarter of 1864. Signed by his mark. Appears on a company muster roll for January and February 1864, with pay due from time of enlistment. Appears present on a company muster roll for September and October 1864. Appears on a roll of POW's captured at Blakeley, Alabama, on April 9, 1865. Here he is shown a member of Company B. Transferred from Ship Island to Vicksburg, Mississippi, on May 1, 1865. Appears on a roll of POW's of Company A, 63rd Alabama Infantry commanded by Lieutenant W. D. Kyle that were surrendered by Lt. General Richard Taylor at Citronelle, Alabama, on May 4, 1865, and paroled at Meridian, Mississippi, on May 13, 1865. Residence—Tallapoosa County, Alabama.

Guthrie, William T., Pvt. Co. A/B.
Enlisted on January 1, 1864, at Tallapoosa County, Alabama, by Captain John Echols for the war. Appears on a company muster-in roll for January 1, 1864, at Montgomery, Alabama. Age—15. Appears present on a company muster roll for January and February 1864, with pay due from time of enlistment. Drew clothing in 2nd quarter and August 12, 1864. Signed by his mark. Appears present on a company muster roll for September and October 1864. Appears on a roll of POW's captured at Blakeley, Alabama, on April 9, 1865. Here he is shown a member of Company B. Transferred from Ship Island to Vicksburg, Mississippi, on May 1, 1865. Appears on a roll of POW's of Company A, 63rd Alabama Infantry commanded by Lieutenant W. D. Kyle that were surrendered by Lt. General Richard Taylor at Citronelle, Alabama, on May 4, 1865, and paroled at Meridian, Mississippi, on May 13, 1865. His residence is shown as Tallapoosa County, Alabama.

Hadden, John T., Pvt. Co. B.
Enlisted on August 15, 1864, at Pollard, Alabama, by Lieutenant Townsend for the war. Drew clothing on September 11, 1864. Appears present on a company muster roll for September and October 1864, with pay due from time of enlistment. Captured at Blakeley, Alabama, on April 9, 1865. Appears on a roll

of POW's received at Ship Island, Mississippi, on April 15, 1865. Transferred from Ship Island to Vicksburg, Mississippi, on May 1, 1865. Appears on a roll of POW's of Company B, 63rd Alabama Infantry commanded by 1st Lieutenant Thomas J. Calhoun that were surrendered by Lt. General Richard Taylor at Citronelle, Alabama, on May 4, 1865, and paroled at Meridian, Mississippi, on May 11, 1865. Residence—Dale County, Alabama.

Hadley, Thomas, Pvt. Co. B.
Enrolled on March 23, 1864, at Montgomery, Alabama, by Captain Zimmerman for the war. Age—15. Appears on a company muster-in roll for March 23, 1864, at Montgomery. Drew clothing on July 8, August 12 and September 11, 1864. Signed by his mark. Appears present on a company muster roll for September and October 1864, with pay due from time of enlistment. Captured at Blakeley, Alabama, on April 9, 1865. Appears on a roll of POW's received at Ship Island, Mississippi, on April 15, 1865. Transferred from Ship Island to Vicksburg, Mississippi, on May 1, 1865. Appears on a roll of POW's of Company B, 63rd Alabama Infantry commanded by 1st Lieutenant Thomas J. Calhoun that were surrendered by Lt. General Richard Taylor at Citronelle, Alabama, on May 4, 1865, and paroled at Meridian, Mississippi, on May 11, 1865. Residence—Montgomery County, Alabama. He signed a parole at the headquarters of the 16th US Army Corps, office of Provost Marshal on June 23, 1865, in Montgomery. Hair—light, eyes—grey, complexion—fair, 5 foot. His parole is in his file.

Hadly, C., Pvt. Co. E/H.
Enlisted on August 5, at Montgomery, Alabama, by Captain A. V. Lee for the war. Age—17, eyes—blue, hair—light, complexion—fair. Appears absent on a Company E muster roll for September and October 1864. Absent without leave since August 19, 1864. Admitted to Yandell Hospital Meridian, Mississippi, on April 11, 1865, with a wound. Appears on a record of Confederate soldiers paroled at the headquarters of the 16th US Army Corps at Montgomery on May 24, 1865. Here he is shown as being in Company H. Hair—light, eyes—yellow, complexion—fair, 5 foot 9 inches. Signed by his mark "X." His parole is in his file.

Hagood, W. T., Nurse, Pvt. Co. E.
Enlisted on July 19, 1864, at Montgomery, Alabama, by Captain A. V. Lee for the war. Age—17, eyes—blue, hair—light, complexion—fair. Drew clothing on September 11, 1864. Appears present on a company muster roll for September and October 1864. Appears on a list of Surgeons, Hospital Stewards attendants and sick and wounded at Spanish Fort, Alabama, sent to Vicksburg Mississippi, General Hospital via New Orleans, Louisiana, on April 8, 1865. Appears on a list of Hospital Attendants in hospital at Blakeley, Alabama, that were captured at Fort Blakeley, Alabama, on April 9, 1865. He signed a hand written Parole of Honor at Blakeley on April 12, 1865. His parole is in his file. Admitted to the USA Hospital Steamer D. A. January on April 17, 1865, as a Hospital Attendant. Transferred and transported from New Orleans to Vicksburg aboard the USA Hospital Steamer Elanora Carrel. Appears on a roll of POW's at USA General Hospital No. 3, (colored) Vicksburg. Admitted to USA General Hospital No. 3 on April 28, with diarrhoea. Transferred to USA General Hospital No. 2, Vicksburg, on May 4, 1865, (Nurse). Admitted to USA General Hospital No. 2, Vicksburg on May 4, 1865, with acute diarrhoea. Age—16. Returned to duty on May 10.

Hale, James I., Pvt. Co. G.
Enlisted on May 16, 1864, at Troy, Alabama, by Captain Wilkerson, for the war. Appears on a company muster-in roll for September 7, 1864, at Blakeley, Alabama. Age—17, eyes—blue, hair—light, complexion—fair, 5 foot 6 inches.

Appears present on a company muster roll for September and October 1864. Signed a parole as POW at Marion, Alabama, on May 16, 1865.

Hall, A., Pvt. Co. I.
Enlisted on May 18, 1864, at Wedowee, Alabama, by Captain Robinson for the war. Appears absent on a company muster roll for September and October 1864. Absent without leave from September 18, 1864.

Hall, Joiner. D., Pvt. Co. B/K.
Enlisted on March 23, 1864, at Montgomery, Alabama, by Captain Zimmerman for the war. Appears on a company muster-in roll for March 23, 1864, at Montgomery, Alabama. Age—17. His name appears on a Company B muster roll for September and October 1864, with pay due from time of enlistment. Transferred per Special Order No. 15, on October 2, 1864. Appears absent on a Company K muster roll for September and October 1864. Absent without leave since September 11, 1864. Admitted to Way Hospital, Meridian, Mississippi, on January 11 & 12, 1864, with wound. On January 12 complaint was diarrhoea. Furloughed.

Hall, J. W., Pvt. Co. E.
Enlisted on March 25, 1864, at Clayton, Alabama, by Captain A. V. Lee for the war. Age—17, eyes—blue, hair—light, complexion—fair. Appears absent on a company muster roll for September and October 1864. Absent without leave since August 9, 1864.

Hall, Malcomb, Pvt. Co. A.
Enlisted on January 1, 1864, at Tallapoosa County, Alabama, by Captain John Echols for the war. Age—16, Appears on a company muster-in roll for January 1, 1864, at Montgomery, Alabama. Appears present on a company muster roll for January and February 1864, with pay due from time of enlistment. Drew clothing in 2nd quarter of 1864. Appears present on a company muster roll for September and October 1864. Here he is shown as having been last paid on February 29, 1864, by Major J. L. Calhoun. Signed by his mark "X" a parole at the headquarters of the 16th US Army Corps at Montgomery, Alabama, on May 18, 1864. Hair—dark, eyes—grey, complexion—fair, 5 foot 6 inches. His parole is in his file.

Hall, M. W., Sergeant Co. E.
Enlisted on March 3, 1864, at Clayton, Alabama, by Captain A. V. Lee for the war. Age—17, eyes—blue, hair—light, complexion—fair. Drew clothing on September 11, 1864. Signed by his mark. Appears absent on company muster roll for September and October 1864. Absent without leave since October 9, 1864. Captured at Blakeley, Alabama, on April 9, 1865. Appears on a roll of POW's received at Ship Island, Mississippi, on April 15, 1865. Transferred from Ship Island to Vicksburg, Mississippi, on May 1, 1865. Appears on a register of sick and wounded Confederate POW's at USA General Hospital No. 2, Vicksburg. Admitted on May 3,1865, from steamer with acute bronchitis. Returned to duty on May 12, 1865. Age—18. Appears on a roll of stragglers of CSA surrendered by Lt. General Richard Taylor on May 4, 1865, and paroled at Selma, Alabama, in June 1865. Here his residence is shown as Barber [Barbour] County, Alabama.

Halmes, William, Pvt. Co. I.
Enlisted on April 15, 1864, at Wedowee, Alabama, by Captain Robinson for the war. Appears absent on a company muster roll for September and October 1864. Absent without leave from September 18, 1864.

Halstead, Alex. M., Pvt. Co. B.
    Enlisted on August 15, 1864, at Pollard, Alabama, by Captain Zimmerman for the war. Appears absent on a company muster roll for September and October 1864. Absent sick since October 19, 1864.

Hamilton, H. C., Pvt. Co. I.
    Enlisted on April 15, 1864, at Columbiana, Alabama, by Lieutenant Bulger for the war. Appears present on furlough on a company muster roll for September and October 1864. Captured at Blakeley, Alabama, on April 9, 1865. Appears on a roll of POW's received at Ship Island, Mississippi, on April 15, 1865. Transferred from Ship Island to Vicksburg, Mississippi, on May 1, 1865. Appears on a roll of POW's of Cos. I and K, 63rd Alabama Infantry commanded by Lieutenant W. A. Skinner that were surrendered by Lt. General Richard Taylor at Citronelle, Alabama, on May 4, 1865, and paroled at Meridian, Mississippi, on May 13, 1865. Residence—Shelby County, Alabama.

Hamilton, J. C., Pvt. Co. I.
    Enlisted on April 15, 1864, at Wedowee, Alabama, by Captain Robinson for the war. Appears absent on a company muster roll for September and October 1864. Absent furloughed for 30 days from September 27, 1864. Captured at Blakeley, Alabama, on April 9, 1865. Appears on a roll of POW's received at Ship Island, Mississippi, on April 15, 1865. Transferred from Ship Island to Vicksburg, Mississippi, on May 1, 1865.

Hamner, W. J., 1st Lieutenant Co. K.
    Enlisted on October 1, 1864, at Blakeley, Alabama, by Captain May for the war. Elected 1st Lieutenant on October 1, 1864. POW captured at Blakeley, Alabama, on April 9, 1865, by 2nd Division, 16th US Army Corps. Appears on a roll of POW's received at Ship Island, Mississippi, on April 16, 1865. Transferred from Ship Island to Vicksburg, Mississippi, on April 28, 1865. Confined at New Orleans, Louisiana, on April 30, 1865. Exchanged on May 1, 1865. Signed a Parole of Honor on May 12, 1865. His parole is in his file.

Harden, John G., Private Co. B.
    Enlisted on March 23, 1864, at Montgomery, Alabama, by Captain Zimmerman for the war. Age—17. Appears on a company muster-in roll for March 23, 1864, at Montgomery. Drew clothing on July 8, August 12 and September 11, 1864. Signed with his mark. Appears present on a company muster roll for September and October 1864, with pay due from time of enlistment. Captured by Brigadier General T. J. Lucas commanding Cavalry Forces operating from Pensacola, Florida, at Gravel Hill, Alabama, on March 24, 1865. Appears on a roll of POW's received at Ship Island, Mississippi, on April 4, 1865 from Lt. E. M. Burdick, Provost Marshal of Excelsior Brigade. Transferred from Ship Island to Vicksburg, Mississippi, on May 1, 1865. Appears on a roll of POW's of Company B, 63rd Alabama Infantry commanded by 1st Lieutenant Thomas J. Calhoun that were surrendered by Lt. General Richard Taylor at Citronelle, Alabama, on May 4, 1865, and paroled at Meridian, Mississippi, on May 11, 1865. Residence—Coosa County, Alabama.

Hardwick, George S., Pvt. Co. D.
    Enlisted on July 30, 1864, at Macon County, Alabama, by Major Ready for the war. Age—17, eyes—grey, hair—light, complexion—fair, 5 foot 10 inches, residence—Kings, Barbour, Alabama. Appears on a company muster-in roll for July 30, 1864, at Camp Watts near Notasulga, Alabama. Drew clothing on August 7, 1864. Admitted to Ross Hospital, Mobile, Alabama, on September 20, 1864, with dysenteria acuta. Appears on a company muster roll for August 30 to October 30, 1864, with pay due from time of enlistment. Here it is reported that he died

at a Mobile hospital on October 4. He left $15. This muster roll also shows him as having enlisted on March 2, at Clayton, Alabama, by D. M. Seals for the war.

Harper, Joseph, Pvt. Co. E.
Enlisted on August 8, 1864, at Pollard, Alabama, by Captain A. V. Lee for the war. Age—17, eyes—dark, hair—dark, complexion—dark. Drew clothing on September 11, 1864. Appears absent on a company muster roll for September and October 1864. Absent in hospital since September 28, 1864. Admitted to Ross Hospital, Mobile, Alabama, on September 26, 1864, with rubeola. He is reported remaining in the hospital on November 1, 1864. Appears on a roll of POW's of Cos. E and G, 63rd Alabama Infantry commanded by Captain A. V. Lee that were surrendered by Lt. General Richard Taylor at Citronelle, Alabama, on May 4, 1865, and paroled at Meridian, Mississippi, on May 13, 1865. Residence—Henry County, Alabama.

Harper, Madison, Pvt. Co. A.
Enlisted on January 1, 1864, at Tallapoosa, County, Alabama, by Captain John Echols for the war. Age—17. Appears on a company muster-in roll for January 1, 1864, at Montgomery, Alabama. Appears absent on a company muster roll for January and February 1864, with pay due from time of enlistment. Absent on furlough for five days per Special Orders from Headquarters at Montgomery, Alabama. Left company on February 27, 1864. Appears as a patient on a hospital muster roll at General Hospital, Marion, Alabama, for July and August 1864. Drew clothing on August 12, 1864. Appears present sick in quarters on a company muster roll for September and October 1864, with pay due from time of enlistment. Admitted to Ross Hospital, Mobile, Alabama, on November 5, 1864, with febris intermittens. Returned to duty on December 2, 1864. Appears on a list of hospital attendants in hospital at Blakeley, Alabama, captured at Fort Blakeley on April 9, 1865. Appears on a list of surgeons, hospital stewards attendants and sick and wounded POW's sent to Vicksburg, Mississippi, via New Orleans, Louisiana, from Spanish Fort, Alabama, on April 8, 1865. He is reported as an attendant of Thomas' command. Admitted on April 17, 1865, to the US Hospital Steamer D. A. January as an attendant. Transferred to the Hospital Steamer Elanora Carrel on April 24, 1865, at New Orleans, and transported to Vicksburg. Appears on a roll of POW's at USA General Hospital No. 3, Vicksburg, Mississippi, that were transferred to General Hospital No. 2, Vicksburg on May 4, 1865 (nurse). Admitted as an attendant to General Hospital No. 2 on May 4. Returned to duty on May 12. Here he is shown as age 18. Appears on a roll of POW's of unattached men of CSA that were surrendered by Lt. General Richard Taylor at Citronelle, Alabama, on May 4, 1865, and paroled at Jackson, Mississippi, on May 13, 1865. Residence—Tallapoosa County, Alabama. He signed by his mark "X" a hand written parole near Blakeley on April 12, 1865. His parole is in his file.

Harrell, Burrell, W., Pvt. Co. B.
Enlisted on August 10, 1864, at Montgomery, Alabama, by Lieutenant Townsend for the war. Appears present on a company muster roll for September and October 1864, with pay due from time of enlistment. Captured at Blakeley, Alabama, on April 9, 1865. Appears on a roll of POW's received at Ship Island, Mississippi, on April 15, 1865, from Lieutenant E. M. Burdick, Provost Marshal of Excelsior Brigade. Transferred from Ship Island to Vicksburg, Mississippi, on May 1, 1865. Admitted to USA Post Hospital, Jackson, Mississippi, on May 29, 1865, with dysentery. Discharged from hospital on parole May 30, 1865.

Harrington, G., Pvt. Co. A.
Admitted to Ross Hospital, Mobile, Alabama, on September 24, 1864, with febris intermittens quot. Sent to General Hospital at Lauderdale Springs, Mississippi,

on October 6, 1864. This register on page 155 October 64, reports Complt-Syphilis consecutive.

Harris, C. G., Pvt. Co. A.
Admitted to Ross Hospital, Mobile, Alabama, on September 24, 1864, with febris intermittens quot. Returned to duty on September 29, 1864.

Harris, Eli, Pvt. Co. B.
Enrolled on March 23, 1864, at Montgomery, Alabama, by Captain Zimmerman for the war. Appears on a company muster-in roll for March 23, 1864, at Montgomery. Age—17. Drew clothing on July 8, August 12 and September 11, 1864. Signed with his mark. Appears present on a company muster roll for September and October 1864, with pay due from time of enlistment.

Harris, Eli G., Pvt. Co. B.
Enlisted on October 5, 1864, at Blakeley, Alabama, by Captain Zimmerman for the war. Appears absent on a company muster roll for September and October 1864, with pay due from time of enlistment. Absent sick since October 24.

Harris, James T., (#1) Co. C.
Enlisted on May 11, 1864, at Russell County, Alabama, by Lieutenant Carnes for the war. Appears on a company muster-in roll at Camp Watts near Notasulga, Alabama, on June 24, 1864. Age—17, eyes—hazel, hair—dark, complexion—dark, 5 foot 8 ½ inches, residence—Salem, Russell County, Alabama. Drew clothing on August 6 and September 11, 1864. Appears present on a company muster roll for September and October 1864. Captured at Blakeley, Alabama, on April 9, 1865. Appears on a roll of POW's received at Ship Island, Mississippi, on April 15, 1865. Transferred from Ship Island to Vicksburg, Mississippi, on May 1, 1865. Appears on a roll of POW's of Cos. C and H, 63rd Alabama Infantry commanded by Captain C. W. Martin that were surrendered by Lt. General Richard Taylor at Citronelle, Alabama, on May 4, 1865, and paroled at Meridian, Mississippi, on May 11, 1865. Residence—Russell County, Alabama.

Harris, James T., (#2) Co. C.
Enlisted on May 9, 1864, at Macon County, Alabama, by Captain Roscoe for the war. Appears on a company muster-in roll for June 24, 1864, at Camp Watts near Notasulga, Alabama. Age—17, eyes—hazel, hair—dark, complexion—florid, 5 foot 6 inches, residence—Guerryton, Macon County, Alabama. Drew clothing on August 6, 1864. Appears absent on a company muster roll for September and October 1864. Absent in hospital at Mobile, Alabama, since September 11, 1864. Captured at Blakeley, Alabama, on April 9, 1865. Appears on a roll of POW's received at Ship Island, Mississippi, on April 15, 1865. Transferred from Ship Island to Vicksburg, Mississippi, on May 1, 1865. Appears on a roll of POW's of Cos. C and H, 63rd Alabama Infantry commanded by Captain C. W. Martin that were surrendered by Lt. General Richard Taylor at Citronelle, Alabama, on May 4, 1865, and paroled at Meridian, Mississippi, on May 11, 1865. Residence—Macon County, Alabama.

Harris, R., Pvt. Co. H.
Enlisted on March 15, 1864, at Centerville, Alabama, by Lieutenant Johnston for the war. Age—17, eyes—blue, hair—light, complexion—fair. Drew clothing on September 11, 1864. Appears present on a company muster roll for September and October 1864. Appears on a roll of POW's of Cos. C and H, 63rd Alabama Infantry commanded by Captain C. W. Martin that were surrendered by Lt. General Richard Taylor at Citronelle, Alabama, on May 4, 1865, and paroled at Meridian, Mississippi, on May 11, 1865. Residence—Bibb County, Alabama.

Harris, Rob. S., Pvt. Co. H.
   Appears on a undated register of St. Mary's Hospital, West Point, Mississippi, in 1865.

Harris, Simeon, B., Pvt. Co. A.
   Enlisted on January 1, 1864, at Tallapoosa, County, Alabama, by Captain John Echols for the war. Appears on a company muster-in roll for January 1, 1864, at Montgomery, Alabama. Age—17. Appears present on a company muster roll for January and February 1864, with pay due from time of enlistment. Drew clothing in 2nd quarter and August 12, 1864. Appears absent on a company muster roll for September and October 1864. Absent furloughed for sixty days by Medical Examining Board on October 21, 1864. Here he is shown as last paid on February 29, 1864. Captured at Blakeley, Alabama, on April 9, 1865. Appears on a roll of POW's received at Ship Island, Mississippi, on April 15, 1865. Transferred from Ship Island to Vicksburg, Mississippi, on May 1, 1865. Appears on a roll of POW's of Company A, 63rd Alabama Infantry commanded by Lieutenant W. D. Kyle that were surrendered by Lt. General Richard Taylor at Citronelle, Alabama, on May 4, 1865, and paroled at Meridian, Mississippi, on May 13, 1865. Residence—Tallapoosa County, Alabama.

Harris, Wiley, B., Pvt. Co. B.
   Enlisted on October 5, 1864, at Blakeley, Alabama, by Captain Zimmerman for the war. Appears absent on a company muster roll for September and October 1864, with pay due from time of enlistment. Absent sick since October 28, 1864. Signed a parole at headquarters of the 16th US Army Corps at Montgomery, Alabama, on May 23, 1865. Hair—light, eyes—blue, complexion—fair, five foot. Signed by "X" his mark. His parole is in his file.

Harris, William G., Pvt. Co. B.
   Enlisted on March 23, 1864, at Montgomery County, Alabama, by Captain Zimmerman for the war. Age—17. Appears on a company muster-in roll for March 23, 1864, at Montgomery. Drew clothing on July 8, 1864. Appears absent on a company muster roll for September and October 1864. Absent sick since October 13, 1864. Admitted to Ross Hospital, Mobile, Alabama, on December 31, 1864, with anasarca. Returned to duty on January 23, 1865. Captured at Blakeley, Alabama, on April 9, 1865. Appears on a roll of POW's received at Ship Island, Mississippi, on April 15, 1865. Transferred from Ship Island to Vicksburg, Mississippi, on May 1, 1865. Appears on a roll of POW's of Company B, 63rd Alabama Infantry commanded by 1st Lieutenant Thomas J. Calhoun that were surrendered by Lt. General Richard Taylor at Citronelle, Alabama, on May 4, 1865, and paroled at Meridian, Mississippi, on May 11, 1865. Residence—Russell County, Alabama.

Harris, William G., Pvt. Co. B, **1st Alabama Legion**
   This file is improperly filed with the 2nd Alabama Reserves.
   Appears on a roll of privates on extra duty with Major E. Crutchfield, Quartermaster, at Abington, Virginia, by order of Major General Buckner as a teamster for the month of July 1864. Appears on a roll of Privates employed on extra duty by Major E. Cructchfild, Quartermaster at Abington, Virginia, from September 1 to September 30, 1864. Now with his team hauling supplies to Castle Woods and will be sent to his command on his return.

Harris, W. J., Pvt. Co. F.
   Enlisted on May 30, 1864, at Montgomery, Alabama, by Captain Jackson for the war. Appears on a company muster-in roll for July 25, 1864, at Georgiana, Alabama. Age—17, eyes—blue, hair—dark, complexion—dark, 5 foot 8 inches, residence—Autauga County, Alabama. Appears present sick on a company muster

roll for August 31 to October 31, 1864. Captured at Blakeley, Alabama, on April 9, 1865. Appears on a roll of POW's received at Ship Island, Mississippi, on April 15, 1865. Transferred from Ship Island to Vicksburg, Mississippi, on May 1, 1865. Appears on a roll of sick and wounded POW's at USA General Hospital No. 2, Vicksburg, Mississippi. Admitted on May 3, 1865, from steamer with inflammation of the lungs. Returned to duty on May 23. Age—18.

Harrison, J., Pvt. Co. F.
Enlisted on May 30, 1864, at Montgomery, by Captain Jackson for the war. Appears on a company muster-in roll at Georgiana, Alabama, on July 25, 1864. Age—17, eyes—dark, hair—dark, complexion—dark, 5 foot 8 inches, residence—Butler County, Alabama. Appears present on a company muster roll for August 31 to October 31, 1864, with pay due from time of enlistment. Captured at Blakeley, Alabama, on April 9, 1865. Appears on a roll of POW's received at Ship Island, Mississippi, on April 15, 1865. Transferred from Ship Island to Vicksburg, Mississippi, on May 1, 1865. Appears on a roll of POW's of Company F, 63rd Alabama Infantry commanded by Captain R. T. Simpson that were surrendered by Lt. General Richard Taylor at Citronelle, Alabama, on May 4, 1865, and paroled at Meridian, Mississippi, on May 11, 1865. Residence—Butler County, Alabama.

Harrison, Morris, Pvt. Co. G/A.
Enlisted on October 1, 1864, at Blakeley, Alabama, by Captain Garland. Appears present on a company muster roll for September and October 1864. Captured at Blakeley, Alabama, on April 9, 1865. Appears on a roll of POW's received at Ship Island, Mississippi, on April 15, 1865. Transferred from Ship Island to Vicksburg, Mississippi, on May 1, 1865. Appears on a roll of POW's of Cos. E and G, 63rd Alabama Infantry commanded by Captain A. V. Lee that were surrendered by Lt. General Richard Taylor at Citronelle, Alabama, on May 4, 1865, and paroled at Meridian, Mississippi, on May 13, 1865. Residence—Coffee County, Alabama. Here he is shown in Company G.

Harris, J. W., Pvt. Co. K.
Enlisted August 7, 1864, at Uniontown, Alabama, by Captain Daniel for the war. He appears absent on a company muster roll for September and October 1864. This muster roll reports him absent at hospital in Mobile, Alabama. since October 17.

Harrolson, James M., Pvt. Co. C.
Enlisted on May 17, 1864, at Tallapoosa County, Alabama, by Captain Brown for the war. Appears on a company muster-in roll for June 24, 1864, at Camp Watts near Notasulga, Alabama. Age—17, eyes—hazel, hair—dark, complexion—dark, 5 foot 2 ½ inch, residence—Dadeville, Tallapoosa County, Alabama. Drew clothing on August 6, 1864. Signed by his mark. Admitted to Ross Hospital on September 3, 1864, with acute diarrhoea. Sent to General Hospital at Greenville, Alabama, on September 13, 1864. Appears absent on a muster roll for September and October 1864. Absent in hospital in Montgomery from October 28, 1864. Captured at Blakeley, Alabama, on April 9, 1865. Appears on a roll of POW's received at Ship Island, Mississippi, on April 15, 1865. Transferred from Ship Island to Vicksburg, Mississippi, on May 1, 1865. Appears on a roll of POW's of Cos. C and H, 63rd Alabama Infantry commanded by Captain C. W. Martin that were surrendered by Lt. General Richard Taylor at Citronelle, Alabama, on May 4, 1865, and paroled at Meridian, Mississippi, on May 11, 1865. Residence—Tallapoosa County, Alabama.

Hartley, J. K., 2nd Lieutenant Co. I.
Elected 2nd Lieutenant on November 24, 1864. Captured at Blakeley, Alabama,

on April 9, 1865. Appears on a roll of POW's received at Ship Island, Mississippi, on April 16, 1865. Transferred from Ship Island to Vicksburg, Mississippi, on May 1, 1865. Appears on a roll of POW's at New Orleans, Louisiana. Confined at New Orleans on April 30, 1865, from Ship Island, Mississippi. Exchanged on May 1, 1865. Signed a Parole of Honor at Meridian, Mississippi, on May 11, 1865. His parole is in his file.

Harting, J. F., Sergeant Co. K.
Enlisted on June 30, 1864, at Columbus, Georgia, by Lieutenant Hughes for the war. Appears present on a company muster roll for September and October. Reduced to 4th Sergeant on October 24. Captured at Blakeley, Alabama, on April 9, 1865. Appears on a roll of POW's received at Ship Island, Mississippi, on April 15, 1865. Transferred from Ship Island to Vicksburg, Mississippi, on May 1, 1865. Appears on a roll of POW's of Cos. I and K, 63rd Alabama Infantry commanded by Lieutenant W. A. Skinner that were surrendered by Lt. General Richard Taylor at Citronelle, Alabama, on May 4, 1865, and paroled at Meridian, Mississippi, on May 13, 1865. Residence—Barbour County, Alabama.

Harvill, A. G., Pvt. Co. F.
Enlisted on May 30, 1864, at Montgomery, Alabama, by Captain Jackson for the war. Appears on a company muster-in roll at Georgiana, Alabama, on July 25, 1864. Age—17, eyes—blue, hair—dark, complexion—fair, 5 foot 7 inches, residence—Butler County, Alabama. Appears absent on a company muster roll for August 31 to October 31, 1864, with pay due from time of enlistment. Absent in hospital at Greenville, Alabama, from September 9, 1864. Appears on a roll of POW's of divers companies and regiments of CSA Army commanded by Lt. Colonel H. C. Greer that were surrendered by Lt. General Richard Taylor at Citronelle, Alabama, on May 4, 1865, and paroled at Meridian, Mississippi, on May 17, 1865. Residence—Butler County, Alabama.

Haughton, R. H., Hospital Steward, Field and Staff
Appears on a Field and Staff muster roll for September and October 1864. Assigned on September 14, 1864.

Hauners, Jesse M., Sergeant Co. C.
Enlisted on May 11, 1864, at Russell County, Alabama, by Lieutenant Carnes for the war. Age—17, eyes—blue, hair—dark, complexion—fair, 5 foot 10 inches, residence—Russell County, Alabama. His post office is shown as Columbus, Georgia. Drew clothing on August 6, 1864. Appears as 3rd Sergeant on a company muster-in roll for June 24, 1864, at Camp Watts near Notasulga, Alabama. Appears as having died on a company muster roll for September and October 1864.

Hayes, Isaac, Pvt. Co. I.
Enlisted on May 28, 1864, at Wedowee, Alabama, by Lieutenant Scott for the war. Appears absent on a company muster roll for September and October. Absent without leave since September 18, 1864. Captured at Blakeley, Alabama, on April 9, 1865. Appears on a roll of POW's received at Ship Island, Mississippi, on April 15, 1865. Transferred from Ship Island to Vicksburg, Mississippi, on May 1, 1865. Appears on a roll of POW's of Cos. I and K, 63rd Alabama Infantry commanded by Lieutenant W. A. Skinner that were surrendered by Lt. General Richard Taylor at Citronelle, Alabama, on May 4, 1865, and paroled at Meridian, Mississippi, on May 13, 1865. Residence—Randolph County, Alabama.

Hazzard, J., Pvt. Co. F.
Enlisted on October 13, 1864, at Montgomery, Alabama, by Lieutenant Barton for

the war. Appears present on a company muster roll for August 31 to October 31, 1864, with pay due from time of enlistment. Captured at Blakeley, Alabama, on April 9, 1865. Appears on a roll of POW's received at Ship Island, Mississippi, on April 15, 1865. Transferred from Ship Island to Vicksburg, Mississippi, on May 1, 1865. Appears on a roll of POW's of Company F, 63rd Alabama Infantry commanded by Captain R. T. Simpson that were surrendered by Lt. General Richard Taylor at Citronelle, Alabama, on May 4, 1865, and paroled at Meridian, Mississippi, on May 11, 1865. His residence is shown as Lowndes County, Alabama.

Headley, J. T., Pvt. Co. H.
Residence—Autauga County, Alabama. Appears on a roll of POW stragglers at Selma, Alabama, paroled during June 1865.

Hearn, C. C., Pvt. Co. I.
Enlisted on April 15 1864, at Talladega, Alabama, by Captain Parks for the war. Appears absent on a company muster roll for September and October 1864. Absent without leave from September 18, 1864.

Heath, John, Pvt. Co. D.
Enlisted on July 30, 1864 at Macon County, Alabama, by Major Ready for the war. Age—17, eyes—blue, hair—dark, complexion—dark, 5 foot 10 inches, residence—Texasville, Barbour County, Alabama. Appears on a company muster-in roll for July 30, 1864, at Camp Watts near Notasulga, Alabama. Drew clothing on August 7, 1864. Signed by his mark. Appears present on a company muster roll for August 30 to October 30, 1864, with pay due from time of enlistment. Here he is shown as having enlisted at Eufaula, Alabama, by Captain Zorn on April 16, 1864.

Heath, W. H., Pvt. Co. F.
Enlisted on August 24, 1864, at Greenville, Alabama, by Lieutenant Barlow for the war. Appears present but sick on a company muster roll for August 31 to October 31, 1864, with pay due from time of enlistment. Captured at Blakeley, Alabama, on April 9, 1865. Appears on a roll of POW's received at Ship Island, Mississippi, on April 15, 1865. Transferred from Ship Island to Vicksburg, Mississippi, on May 1, 1865. Appears on a roll of POW's of Company F, 63rd Alabama Infantry commanded by Captain R. T. Simpson that were surrendered by Lt. General Richard Taylor at Citronelle, Alabama, on May 4, 1865, and paroled at Meridian, Mississippi, on May 11, 1865. Residence—Butler County, Alabama. Admitted to 1st Mississippi CSA Hospital, Jackson, Mississippi, on March 3, 1865, with anaemia. Returned to duty on April 14, 1865.

Helms, James R., Pvt. Co. D.
Enlisted on July 30, 1864, at Macon County, Alabama, by Major Ready for the war. Age—17, eyes—dark, hair—dark, complexion—dark, 5 foot 5 inches, residence—Clayton, Barbour County, Alabama. Appears on a company muster-in roll for July 30, 1864, at Camp Watts near Notasulga, Alabama. Appears as a patient on a hospital muster roll for General Hospital, Marion, Alabama, for July and August 1864. Drew clothing on August 7, 1864. Signed by his mark. Appears on a company muster roll for August 30, to October 30, 1864, with pay due from time of enlistment. Here he is shown as having enlisted at Clayton by D. M. Seals on March 2, 1864. Died at Mobile Hospital on October 7.

Helton, J. J., Pvt. Co. E.
Enlisted on August 8, 1864, at Pollard, Alabama, by Captain A. V. Lee for the war. Age—17, eyes—blue, hair—light, complexion—fair. Drew clothing on September 11, 1864. Signed by his mark. Appears absent on a company muster

roll for September and October 1864. Muster roll reports him absent in hospital since September 21, 1864.

Henderson, B. S., Pvt. Co. K.
Enlisted on August 31, 1864, at Greene County, Alabama, by Lieutenant Jones for the war. Appears present on a company muster roll for September and October 1864. Captured at Blakeley, Alabama, on April 9, 1865. Appears on a roll of POW's received at Ship Island, Mississippi, on April 15, 1865. Transferred from Ship Island to Vicksburg, Mississippi, on May 1, 1865. Appears on a roll of POW's of Cos. I and K, 63rd Alabama Infantry commanded by Lieutenant W. A. Skinner that were surrendered by Lt. General Richard Taylor at Citronelle, Alabama, on May 4, 1865, and paroled at Meridian, Mississippi, on May 13, 1865. Residence—Greene County, Alabama.

Henderson, S. M., Pvt. Co. K.
Enlisted on August 31, 1864, at Greene County, Alabama, by Captain A. V. Lee for the war. Appears absent on a company muster roll for September and October 1864. Absent in hospital in Mobile, Alabama, since October 14. Captured at Blakeley, Alabama, on April 9, 1865. Appears on a roll of POW's received at Ship Island, Mississippi, on April 15, 1865. Transferred from Ship Island to Vicksburg, Mississippi, on May 1, 1865. Appears on a roll of POW's of Cos. I and K, 63rd Alabama Infantry commanded by Lieutenant W. A. Skinner that were surrendered by Lt. General Richard Taylor at Citronelle, Alabama, on May 4, 1865, and paroled at Meridian, Mississippi, on May 13, 1865. Residence—Greene County, Alabama.

Hendly, J. W., Pvt. Co. H.
Enlisted on March 15, 1864, at Randolph County, Alabama, by Lieutenant Johnson, for the war. He is described as: age—17, eyes—blue, hair—light, complexion—fair. Drew clothing on September 11, 1864. He appears present on a company muster roll for September and October 1864. POW captured at Blakeley, Alabama, on April 9, 1865. His name appears on a roll of POW's received at Ship Island, Mississippi, on April 15, 1865. He was among those men transferred from Ship Island to Vicksburg, Mississippi, on May 1, 1865. His name appears on a roll of POW's of Cos. C and H, 63rd Alabama Infantry commanded by Captain C. W. Martin that were surrendered by Lt. General Richard Taylor at Citronelle, Alabama, on May 4, 1865, and paroled at Meridian, Mississippi, on May 11, 1865. Residence—Bibb County, Alabama.

Henford, Pvt. Co. _.
Captured at Blakeley, Alabama, on April 9, 1865. Appears on a roll of POW's received at Ship Island, Mississippi, on April 15, 1865. Transferred from Ship Island to Vicksburg, Mississippi, on May 1, 1865.

Henley, Hezekiah, Pvt. Co. D/I.
Enlisted on July 30, 1864, at Macon County, Alabama, by Major Ready for the war. Appears on a company muster-in roll for July 30, 1864, at Camp Watts near Notasulga, Alabama. Age—17, eyes—blue, hair—light, complexion—fair, 5 foot 6 inches, residence—Buford, Barbour County, Alabama. Drew clothing on August 7, 1864. Signed by his mark. Appears present on a company muster roll for August 30 to October 30, 1864, with pay due from time of enlistment. Here he is shown as having enlisted in Company D at Eufaula, Alabama, on April 16, 1864, by Captain Zorn. Captured at Blakeley, Alabama, on April 9, 1865. Appears on a roll of POW's [reported as being in Company I] received at Ship Island, Mississippi, on April 15, 1865. Transferred from Ship Island to Vicksburg, Mississippi, on May 1, 1865. Appears on a roll of POW's of Company D, 63rd Alabama Infantry commanded by Captain Robert H. Pearson that were

surrendered by Lt. General Richard Taylor at Citronelle, Alabama, on May 4, 1865, and paroled at Meridian, Mississippi, on May 13, 1865. Residence—Barbour County, Alabama.

Henry, Samuel, B., Pvt. Co. C.
Enlisted on April 14, 1864, at Macon County, Alabama, by Captain Roscoe for the war. Appears on a company muster-in roll for June 24, 1864, at Camp Watts near Notasulga, Alabama. Age—17, eyes—hazel, hair—dark, complexion—dark, 5 foot 2 inches, residence—Tuskegee, Alabama. Drew clothing on August 6, 1864. Signed by his mark. Appears present on a company muster roll for September and October 1864. Captured at Blakeley, Alabama, on April 9, 1865. Appears on a roll of POW's received at Ship Island, Mississippi, on April 15, 1865. Transferred from Ship Island to Vicksburg, Mississippi, on May 1, 1865. Appears on a roll of POW's of Cos. C and H, 63rd Alabama Infantry commanded by Captain C. W. Martin that were surrendered by Lt. General Richard Taylor at Citronelle, Alabama, on May 4, 1865, and paroled at Meridian, Mississippi, on May 11, 1865. Residence—Macon County, Alabama.

Herrin, Stephen W., Pvt. Co. A.
Enlisted on January 1, 1864, at Tallapoosa County, Alabama, by Captain John Echols for the war. Appears on a company muster-in roll for January 1, 1864, at Montgomery, Alabama. Age—17. Appears present on a company muster roll for January and February 1864, with pay due from time of enlistment. Drew clothing in 2nd quarter of 1864, signed Stephen W. Herrin. Appears present, sick in quarters, on a company muster roll for September and October 1864. Captured at Blakeley, Alabama, on April 9, 1865. Appears on a roll of POW's received at Ship Island, Mississippi, on April 15, 1865. Transferred from Ship Island to Vicksburg, Mississippi, on May 1, 1865. Appears on a roll of POW's of Company A, 63rd Alabama Infantry commanded by Lieutenant W. D. Kyle that were surrendered by Lt. General Richard Taylor at Citronelle, Alabama, on May 4, 1865, and paroled at Meridian, Mississippi, on May 13, 1865. Residence—Tallapoosa County, Alabama.

Herrin, S. W., Co. A 1st Alabama Regiment
[This information was filed in error with the 2nd/63rd Alabama.] POW admitted to USA Hospital Steamer Empress on April 23, 1862, with Feb. Typh. Sent to General Hospital at St. Louis, Missouri, on April 26, 1862. 2nd trip from New Madrid and Island No 10.

Herston, (Houston?) James C., Pvt. Co. D.
Enlisted on July 30, 1864, at Macon County, Alabama, by Major Ready for the war. Appears on a company muster-in roll at Camp Watts near Notasulga, Alabama, for July 30, 1864. Age—17, eyes—grey, hair—light, complexion—fair, 5 foot 4 inches, residence—Capton, Dale County, Alabama. Appears absent on a company muster roll for August 30 to October 30, 1864, with pay due from time of enlistment. Absent sick at Greenville Hospital since September 24. Here he is shown as having enlisted at Clayton, Alabama, by D. M. Seals on March 2, 1864. Appears on a list of wounded Confederate POW's in the hospital of the 1st Division, 13th US Army Corps [at Blakeley]. Flesh wound in the face at the Battle of Blakeley Fort on April 9, 1865. Appears on a list of POW's paroled at New Orleans, Louisiana, on May 16, 1865. This list shows that he died at St. Louis Hospital, New Orleans on May 26, 1865, buried on May 27. Admitted to St. Louis Hospital on April 15, 1865. Died of a gunshot wound of the head and buried in Monument Cemetery, Square 69, grave 75. He left no effects. Age—18, Born—Georgia, Residence—Barbour County, Alabama. Reference given Mrs. Lydia Houston, Clapton Post Office, Dale County, Alabama. Minnie ball entered under left ear and escaped through right malar bone. There is a descriptive card on

the wound and procedures taken at St. Louis Hospital along with a copy of his death and interment certificate in his file. *see also Houston, James C., Pvt. Co. D. and Hurton, J. W., Pvt. Co. G.

Hewit, W. G., Pvt. Co. C.
Appears on a roll of POW's unattached men that were surrendered at Citronelle, Alabama, on May 4, 1865, by Lt. General Richard Taylor and paroled at Jackson, Mississippi, on May 19, 1865. Residence—Tallapoosa County, Alabama.

Higgins, William, C., Pvt. Co. A.
Enlisted on March 29, 1864, at Chambers County, Alabama, by Captain John Echols for the war. Drew clothing 2nd quarter and on September 11, 1864. Appears present on a company muster roll for September and October 1864, with pay due from time of enlistment. Here he is shown detailed as a regimental teamster.

Hight, H., Pvt. Co. E.
Enlisted on March 13, 1864, at Clayton, Alabama, by Captain A. V. Lee for the war. Admitted to Post Hospital, Fort Morgan, Alabama, on June 22, 1864, with Iin. Feb. Ter. Returned to duty on July 3, 1864. Drew clothing on September 11, 1864. Signed by his mark. Appears present on a company muster roll for September and October 1864. Age—17, eyes—dark, hair—dark, complexion—dark. Captured at Blakeley, Alabama, on April 9, 1865. Appears on a roll of POW's received at Ship Island, Mississippi, on April 15, 1865. Transferred from Ship Island to Vicksburg, Mississippi, on May 1, 1865. Appears on a roll of POW's of Cos. E and G, 63rd Alabama Infantry commanded by Captain A. V. Lee that were surrendered by Lt. General Richard Taylor at Citronelle, Alabama, on May 4, 1865, and paroled at Meridian, Mississippi, on May 13, 1865. Residence—Barbour County, Alabama.

Hill, William W., Pvt. B/K.
Enlisted on April 14, 1864, at Montgomery, Alabama, by Captain W. C. Zimmerman for the war. Appears on a company muster-in roll at Montgomery, Alabama, for March 23, 1864. Age—17. Appears on a Company B muster roll for September and October 1864, with pay due from time of enlistment. Here he is shown as having been transferred on October 22, 1864. Appears absent on a Company K muster roll for September and October 1864. Absent sick without leave since August 8, 1864. Captured at Blakeley, Alabama, on April 9, 1865. Appears on a roll of POW's received at Ship Island, Mississippi, on April 15, 1865. Transferred from Ship Island to Vicksburg, Mississippi, on May 1, 1865. Appears on a list of sick and wounded Confederate POW's at USA General Hospital, No. 2, Vicksburg, Mississippi. Admitted on May 3, 1865, from steamer with inflammation of the lungs. Returned to duty on May 22, 1865.

Hines, James W., Pvt. Co. G/E.
Enlisted on September 12, 1864, at Blakeley, Alabama, by Captain Garland for the war. Appears present on a company muster roll for September and October 1864. Appears on a register of Confederate POW's that were paroled by the Provost Marshal of the US 16th Army Corps during the month of June 1865. Here he is shown in Company E, 2nd Alabama Reserves. Paroled at Montgomery, Alabama, on June 1, 1864. Eyes—blue, hair—dark, complexion—dark, 5 foot. Signed by his mark "X." His parole is in his file.

Hinkle, George W., Pvt. Co. B.
Enlisted on March 23, 1864, at Montgomery, Alabama, by Captain W. C. Zimmerman for the war. Appears on a company muster-in roll at Montgomery, for March 23. Age—17. Appears absent on a company muster roll for September

and October 1864, with pay due from time of enlistment. Absent detached by order of Colonel Rice from September 1, 1864. Drew clothing on July 8 and September 11, 1864.

Hinson, E. B., Pvt. Co. F.
Enlisted on March 9, 1864, at Greenville, Alabama, by Captain Brown for the war. Appears on a company muster roll for July 25, 1864, at Georgiana, Alabama. Age—17, eyes—grey, hair—light, complexion—fair, 5 foot 9 inches, residence—Butler County, Alabama. Drew clothing on September 11, 1864. Appears present on a company muster roll for August 31 to October 31, 1864, with pay due from time of enlistment. Appears on a roll of POW's of Company F, 63rd Alabama Infantry commanded by Captain R. T. Simpson that were surrendered by Lt. General Richard Taylor at Citronelle, Alabama, on May 4, 1865, and paroled at Meridian, Mississippi, on May 11, 1865. Residence—Butler County, Alabama.

Hinson, J. F., Pvt. Co. F.
Enlisted on March 9, 1864, at Greenville, Alabama, by Captain Brown for the war. Appears on a company muster roll for July 25, 1864, at Georgiana, Alabama. Age—17, eyes—dark, hair—dark, complexion—fair, 5 foot 9 inches, residence—Butler County, Alabama. Appears absent a company muster roll for August 31 to October 31, 1864, with pay due from time of enlistment. Absent in hospital at Greenville since September 27, 1864.

Hinson, W. E., Sergeant. Co. F.
Enlisted as 2nd Sergeant on March 9, 1864, at Greenville, Alabama, by Captain Brown for the war. Appears on a company muster roll for July 25, 1864, at Georgiana, Alabama. Age—17, eyes—blue, hair—brown, complexion—fair, 5 foot 8 inches, residence—Butler County, Alabama. Drew clothing on September 11, 1864. Appears present on a company muster roll for August 31 to October 31, 1864, with pay due from time of enlistment. Reduced to ranks on October 15, 1864. Appears on a roll of POW's of Company F, 63rd Alabama Infantry commanded by Captain R. T. Simpson that were surrendered by Lt. General Richard Taylor at Citronelle, Alabama, on May 4, 1865, and paroled at Meridian, Mississippi, on May 11, 1865. Residence—Butler County, Alabama.

Hinton, J. B., Pvt. Co. I.
Enlisted on May 18, 1864, at Centerville, Alabama, by Captain Grant for the war. Appears absent on a company muster roll for September and October 1864. Absent on 30 day furlough from September 27.

Hixon, Daniel, A., Sergeant Co. G/D.
Enlisted as 2nd Sergeant in Company G on July 1, 1864, at Troy, Alabama, by Captain Wilkerson for the war. Appears on a company muster-in roll for September 7, 1864, at Blakeley, Alabama. He is described as: age—16, eyes—dark, hair—light, complexion—fair, 5 foot 3 inches, residence—Pike County, Alabama. Drew clothing on September 11, 1864. Appears present on a company muster roll for September and October 1864. POW captured at Blakeley, Alabama, on April 9, 1865. Appears on a roll of POW's received at Ship Island, Mississippi, on April 15, 1865. Here he is shown as being in Company D, 63rd Alabama Infantry. Transferred from Ship Island to Vicksburg, Mississippi, on May 1, 1865. His name appears on a roll of POW's of Cos. E and G, 63rd Alabama Infantry commanded by Captain A. V. Lee that were surrendered by Lt. General Richard Taylor at Citronelle, Alabama, on May 4, 1865, and paroled at Meridian, Mississippi, on May 13, 1865. His residence is shown as Pike County, Alabama.

Hobby, E., Pvt. Co. F.
Enlisted on July 12, 1864, at Lowndes County, Alabama, by Captain Buell for the war. Appears on a company muster-in roll for July 25, 1864, at Georgiana, Alabama. Age—17, eyes—dark, hair—dark, complexion—sallow, 5 foot 6 inches, residence—Lowndes County, Alabama. Drew clothing on September 11, 1864. Appears on a company muster roll for September and October 1864, with pay due from time of enlistment. Captured at Blakeley, Alabama, on April 9, 1865. Appears on a roll of POW's received at Ship Island, Mississippi, on April 15, 1865. Transferred from Ship Island to Vicksburg, Mississippi, on May 1, 1865. Appears on a roll of POW's of Company F, 63rd Alabama Infantry commanded by Captain R. T. Simpson that were surrendered by Lt. General Richard Taylor at Citronelle, Alabama, on May 4, 1865, and paroled at Meridian, Mississippi, on May 11, 1865. Residence—Lowndes County, Alabama.

Hodgins, Loemma H., Pvt. Co. A.
Enlisted on January 1, 1864, at Macon County, Alabama, by Captain John Echols for the war. Appears on a company muster-in roll for January 1, 1864, at Montgomery, Alabama. Age—17. Appears present on a company muster roll for January and February 1864, with pay due from time of enlistment. Drew clothing in 2nd quarter of 1864. Signed by his mark. Appears present sick in quarters on a company muster roll for September and October 1864, with pay still due from time of enlistment. Died on November 3, 1864, at Mobile, Alabama. Left $20.

Holbrook, W. H., Pvt. Co. _.
Admitted to Yandell Hospital, Meridian, Mississippi on April 1, 1865. Appears on a roll of POW's and deserters from CSA that entered the military lines of the 16th US Army Corps during the month of April 1865. Captured April 21, 1865, at Montgomery, Alabama, and turned over to the Provost Marshal on May 5, 1865.

Holly, J., Pvt. Co. K.
Enlisted on August 22, 1864, at Coosa County, Alabama, by Captain Hancock for the war. He appears present on a company muster roll for September and October 1864.

Hollingsworth, _., Pvt. Co. H.
Enlisted on August 9, 1864, at Mobile, Alabama, by Captain Killough for the war. Age—17, eyes—blue, hair—light, complexion—fair. Appears absent on a company muster roll for September and October 1864. Absent sick at hospital in Mobile since August 11, 1864.

Hollingsworth, George, Pvt. Co. A.
Enlisted on January 1, 1864, at Tallapoosa County, Alabama, by Captain John Echols for the war. Appears present on a company muster roll for January and February 1864, with pay due from time of enlistment. Drew clothing in 2nd quarter and September 11, 1864. Appears present on a company muster roll for September and October 1864. Captured at Blakeley, Alabama, on April 9, 1865. Appears on a roll of POW's received at Ship Island, Mississippi, on April 15, 1865. Transferred from Ship Island to Vicksburg, Mississippi, on May 1, 1865. Appears on a roll of POW's of Company A, 63rd Alabama Infantry commanded by Lieutenant W. D. Kyle that were surrendered by Lt. General Richard Taylor at Citronelle, Alabama, on May 4, 1865, and paroled at Meridian, Mississippi, on May 13, 1865. Residence—Tallapoosa County, Alabama.

Hollingsworth, John W., Pvt. Co. A.
Enlisted on January 1, 1864, at Tallapoosa County, Alabama.

Hollingsworth, M. C., Pvt. Co. I.
> Enlisted on May 12, 1864, at Pickens County, Alabama, by Captain Hudgens for the war. Appears present on a company muster roll of the 3rd Regiment Alabama Reserves for May 18 to September 1, 1864, with pay due from time of enlistment. Here after he is shown in the 63rd Alabama Infantry. Captured at Blakeley, Alabama, on April 9, 1865. Appears on a roll of POW's received at Ship Island, Mississippi, on April 15, 1865. Transferred from Ship Island to Vicksburg, Mississippi, on May 1, 1865. Appears on a roll of POW's at Quintard Hospital CSA commanded by Surgeon S. V. D. Hill that were surrendered by Lt. General Richard Taylor at Citronelle, Alabama, on May 4, 1865, and paroled at Meridian, Mississippi, on May 10, 1865. Residence—Carrollton, Alabama. His file also contains the following for M. C. Hollingsworth [probably another man]. Appears on a roll of POW's of Cos. I and K, 63rd Alabama Infantry commanded by Lieutenant W. A. Skinner that were surrendered by Lt. General Richard Taylor at Citronelle, Alabama, on May 4, 1865, and paroled at Meridian, Mississippi, on May 13, 1865. Residence—Talladega County, Alabama.

Hollingsworth, William, Pvt. Co. I.
> Enlisted on May 12, at Wedowee, Alabama, by Captain Robinson for the war. Appears absent on a company I muster roll for September and October 1864. Absent sick in Hospital Moore since October 15. Note in file that this may be M. C. Hollingsworth?

Hollon, S. L., Pvt. Co. F.
> Enlisted on May 30, 1864, at Montgomery, Alabama, by Captain Jackson for the war. Appears absent without leave on a company muster-in roll for July 25, 1865, at Georgiana, Alabama. Age—17, eyes—dark, hair—dark, complexion—dark, 5 foot 6 inches, residence—Autauga County, Alabama. Drew clothing on September 11, 1864. Appears as deserted on a company muster roll for August 31 to October 31, 1864, pay due from enlistment. It was reported that he deserted on October 8, 1864.

Hollyfield, Algers, Pvt. Co. B.
> Enlisted on April 24, 1864, at Montgomery, Alabama, by Captain Zimmerman for the war. Appears on a company muster-in roll for March 23, 1864. Age—17.

Hollyfield, Mac, Pvt. Co. B.
> Enlisted on April 24, 1864, at Montgomery, Alabama, by Captain Zimmerman for the war. Appears on a company muster-in roll for March 23, 1864. Age—16.

Holmes, William, Sergeant/Pvt. Co. B.
> Enlisted on March 23, 1864, at Montgomery, Alabama, by Captain Zimmerman for the war. Appears as 3rd Sergeant on a company muster-in roll for March 23, 1864. Age—17. Drew clothing on August 12 and September 11, 1864. Appears absent on a company muster roll for September and October 1864, with pay due from time of enlistment. Absent sick since October 3, 1864. Here he is shown as Private Holmes. Appears on a report of POW's captured by 1st Brigade, 2nd Cavalry during April 1865. Report filed at Headquarters of the 1st Brig. 2nd Cavalry Division at Macon, Georgia, on April 30, 1865.

Holoman, Henry S., Pvt. Co. D.
> Enlisted on July 20, 1864, at Macon County, Alabama, by Major Ready for the war. Age—17, eyes—dark, hair—dark, complexion—dark, 5 foot 10 inches, residence—Clayton, Barbour County, Alabama. Appears on a company muster-in roll for July 30, 1864, at Camp Watts near Notasulga, Alabama. Drew clothing August 7, 1864. Appears present on a company muster roll for August 30 to October 30, 1864, with pay due from time of enlistment.

Hooks, Joseph T., Pvt. Co. G.
Enlisted on May 16, 1864, at Troy, Alabama, by Captain Wilkerson for the war. Appears on a company muster-in roll at Blakeley, Alabama, on September 7, 1864. Age—17, eyes—blue, hair—light, complexion—dark, 5 foot 5 inches, residence—Pike County, Alabama. Appears absent on a company muster roll for September and October 1864. Absent in hospital at Selma, Alabama, since October 1. Appears on a muster roll at General Hospital, Marion, Alabama, for September 1, 1864. Here he is shown as being a patient. Signed, by his mark "X", a parole at headquarters of 16th US Army Corps at Montgomery, Alabama, on June 10, 1865. Hair—black, eyes—blue, complexion—light, 5 foot 5 inches. His parole is in his file.

Hopkins, J. T., Pvt. Co. E.
Enlisted on August 8, 1864, at Pollard, Alabama, by Captain A. V. Lee for the war. Age—17, eyes—dark, hair—dark, complexion—dark. Drew clothing on September 11, 1864. Signed by his mark. Appears present on a company muster roll for September and October 1864. Admitted to Ross Hospital, Mobile, Alabama, on September 29, 1864, with febris intermittens qout. Returned to duty on October 18, 1864. Admitted to Ross Hospital, Mobile, Alabama, on March 29, 1865, with Vulnus Sclopeticum [gunshot wound]. Sent to General Hospital on April 9, 1865. Remarks—Meridian. POW paroled at Marion, Alabama, on May 16, 1865.

Horton, J. B., Pvt. Co. I.
Enlisted on April 15, 1864, at Columbiana, Alabama, by Lieutenant Bulger for the war. Appears absent on a company muster roll for September and October 1864. Absent without leave from September 18, 1864. Captured at Blakeley, Alabama, on April 9, 1865. Appears on a roll of POW's received at Ship Island, Mississippi, on April 15, 1865. Transferred from Ship Island to Vicksburg, Mississippi, on May 1, 1865. Appears on a roll of POW's of Cos. I and K, 63rd Alabama Infantry commanded by Lieutenant W. A. Skinner that were surrendered by Lt. General Richard Taylor at Citronelle, Alabama, on May 4, 1865, and paroled at Meridian, Mississippi, on May 13, 1865. Residence—Shelby County, Alabama.

Houston, James C., Pvt. Co. D. *see Herston, James C., Pvt. Co. D. and Hurton, J. W., Pvt. Co. G.

Howard, James, Pvt. Co. B.
POW captured at Grand [Gravel?] Hill, Alabama, on March 24, 1865, by Cavalry Forces under the command of Brigadier General T. J. Lucas operating from Pensacola, Florida. Appears on a roll of POW's received at Ship Island, Mississippi, on April 4, 1865, from the Provost Marshal of the Excelsior Brigade. Transferred from Ship Island to Vicksburg, Mississippi, on May 1, 1865.

Howard, John W., Pvt. Co. A.
Enlisted on January 1, 1864, at Coosa County, Alabama, by Captain John Echols for the war. Age—16. Appears on a company muster-in roll for January 1, 1864, at Montgomery, Alabama. Appears present on a company muster roll for January and February 1864, with pay due from time of enlistment. He was certified disabled on January 31, 1865, at Montgomery, Alabama, by a Medical Examining Board. This document is in his file. He is described as being born—Russell County, Alabama, age—19, 5 foot 6 inches, eyes—blue, complexion—fair, hair—light, a farmer by profession. "He is unfit for duty due to amputation of his right leg as a result of a gunshot wound received in the line of duty for the Confederate States." He was accidently wounded on duty in Montgomery while serving as a guard.

Huddleston, E., Pvt. Co. H.
Enlisted on March 15, 1864, at Elyton, Alabama, by Lieutenant Killough for the war. Age—17, eyes—dark, hair—light, complexion—dark. Drew clothing on September 11, 1864. Appears present on a company muster roll for September and October 1864. Captured at Blakeley, Alabama, on April 9, 1865. Appears on a roll of POW's received at Ship Island, Mississippi, on April 15, 1865. Transferred from Ship Island to Vicksburg, Mississippi, on May 1, 1865. Appears on a roll of POW's of Cos. C and H, 63rd Alabama Infantry commanded by Captain C. W. Martin that were surrendered by Lt. General Richard Taylor at Citronelle, Alabama, on May 4, 1865, and paroled at Meridian, Mississippi, on May 11, 1865. Residence—Jefferson County, Alabama.

Hudgens, G. W., Pvt. Co. G.
Enlisted on April 29, 1864, at Troy, Alabama, by Captain Wilkerson. Age—17, eyes—blue, hair—dark, complexion—florid, 5 foot 11 inches, residence—Pike County, Alabama. Appears on a company muster-in roll for September 7, 1864, at Blakeley, Alabama. Drew clothing on September 11, 1864. Appears absent on a company muster roll for September and October 1864. Absent on furlough from hospital at Greenville from September 25. Appears on a roll of POW's of Cos. E and G, 63rd Alabama Infantry commanded by Captain A. V. Lee that were surrendered by Lt. General Richard Taylor at Citronelle, Alabama, on May 4, 1865, and paroled at Meridian, Mississippi, on May 13, 1865. Residence—Pike County, Alabama.

Hudgens, Henry, T., Pvt. Co. C.
Enlisted on May 3, 1864, at Macon County, Alabama, by Captain Roscoe for the war. Age—17, eyes—hazel, hair—light, complexion—fair, 5 foot 8 ½ inches, residence—Tuskegee, Macon County, Alabama. Appears on a company muster-in roll for June 24, 1864, at Camp Watts near Notasulga, Alabama. Drew clothing on August 6, 1864. Signed by his mark. Appears present on a company muster roll for September and October 1864.

Hudson, Benjamin, Pvt. Co. D.
Enlisted on August 5, 1864, at Elba, Alabama, by Captain Paine for the war. Appears present on a company muster roll for August 30 to October 30, 1864, with pay due from time of enlistment. Drew clothing on September 12, 1864. Signed a parole with his mark at the headquarters of the 16th US Army Corps at Montgomery, Alabama, on May 16, 1865. Hair—dark, eyes—grey, complexion—fair, 5 foot 9 inches. His parole is in his file.

Hudson, John, Pvt. Co. D.
Enlisted on August 5, 1864, at Elba, Alabama, by Captain Paine for the war. Appears present on a company muster roll for August 30 to October 30, 1864, with pay due from time of enlistment. Captured at Blakeley, Alabama, on April 9, 1865. Appears on a list of wounded Confederates in the hospital of the 1st Division, 13th Corps, US Army of the Military Division of West Mississippi, at the battle of Blakeley Fort, Alabama, on April 9, 1865. Wounded in the leg. Appears on a register of POW's at New Orleans, Louisiana, confined on May 1, 1865. Paroled May 16, 1865. Admitted to St. Louis USA General Hospital on April 15, 1865, with gunshot wound to the right leg (flesh). Transferred to General Hospital (Marine Hospital) on May 16. Age—17.

Huett, William, I., Pvt. Co. C.
Enlisted on May 7, 1864, at Macon County, Alabama, by Major Ready for the war. Appears on a muster-in roll for June 24, 1864, at Camp Watts near Notasulga, Alabama. Age—17, eyes—hazel, hair—light, complexion—fair, 5 foot 10 inches, residence—Society Hill, Macon County, Alabama. Drew clothing on August

6, 1864. Signed by his mark. Appears absent on a company muster roll for September and October 1864. Absent detached on August 28, 1864, by order of General Liddell at Blakeley, Alabama.

Huffman, I., Pvt. Co. F.
Enlisted on July 12, 1864, at Lowndes County, Alabama, by Captain Buell for the war. Appears on a muster-in roll for July 25, 1864, at Georgiana, Alabama. Age—17, eyes—blue, hair—light, complexion—fair, 6 foot, residence—Lowndes County, Alabama. Drew clothing on September 11, 1864. Appears absent on a company muster roll for August 31 to October 31, 1864, with pay due from time of enlistment. Absent in hospital at Mobile, Alabama, since October 28, 1864. Captured at Blakeley, Alabama, on April 9, 1865. Appears on a roll of POW's received at Ship Island, Mississippi, on April 15, 1865. Transferred from Ship Island to Vicksburg, Mississippi, on May 1, 1865. Appears on a roll of POW's of Company F, 63rd Alabama Infantry commanded by Captain R. T. Simpson that were surrendered by Lt. General Richard Taylor at Citronelle, Alabama, on May 4, 1865, and paroled at Meridian, Mississippi, on May 11, 1865. Residence—Lowndes County, Alabama.

Hunt, Daniel, J., Pvt. Co. D.
Enlisted on July 30, 1864, at Macon County, Alabama, by Major Ready for the war. Appears on a company muster-in roll for July 30, 1864, at Camp Watts near Notasulga, Alabama. Age—17, eyes—blue, hair—dark, complexion—fair, 5 foot 6 inches, residence—Eufaula, Barbour County, Alabama. Drew clothing on August 7, 1864. Appears present on a company muster roll for August 30 to October 30, 1864, with pay due from time of enlistment. Here he is shown as having enlisted at Eufaula on June 26, 1864, by Lieutenant Walker.

Hurst, Joe, Pvt. Co. D.
Enlisted on August 31, 1864, at Blakeley, Alabama, by Captain Zorn for the war. Drew clothing on September 12, 1864. Appears present on a company muster roll for September and October 1864, with pay due from time of enlistment. Captured at Blakeley, Alabama, on April 9, 1865. Appears on a roll of POW's received at Ship Island, Mississippi, on April 15, 1865. Transferred from Ship Island to Vicksburg, Mississippi, on May 1, 1865. Appears on a roll of POW's of Company D, 63rd Alabama Infantry commanded by Captain Robert H. Pearson that were surrendered by Lt. General Richard Taylor at Citronelle, Alabama, on May 4, 1865, and paroled at Meridian, Mississippi, on May 13, 1865. Residence—Barbour County, Alabama.

Hurst, John, Pvt. Co. D.
Captured at Blakeley, Alabama, on April 9, 1865. Appears on a roll of POW's received at Ship Island, Mississippi, on April 15, 1865. Transferred from Ship Island to Vicksburg, Mississippi, on May 1, 1865. Appears on a roll of POW's of Company D, 63rd Alabama Infantry commanded by Captain Robert H. Pearson that were surrendered by Lt. General Richard Taylor at Citronelle, Alabama, on May 4, 1865, and paroled at Meridian, Mississippi, on May 13, 1865. Residence—Barbour County, Alabama.

Hurton, J. W., Pvt.
Admitted to Ross Hospital, Mobile, Alabama, on August 16, 1864, with malingering. Returned to duty on August 18, 1864. Drew clothing on September 12, 1864. Here his name appears as J. Huiston. *see also Herston, James C., Pvt. Co. D. and Hurton, J. W., Pvt. Co. G.

Hyde, A. P., Pvt. Co. E.
Enlisted on August 4, 1864, at Montgomery, Alabama, by Captain A. V. Lee for

the war. Age—17, eyes—dark, hair—dark, complexion—dark. Appears absent on a company muster roll for September and October 1864. Absent without leave since August 8, 1864. Appears on a POW roll of Hospital Attendants and Patients at Hinkley, Hospital, Demopolis, Alabama, CSA Army commanded by Surgeon H. Hinkley, that were surrendered by Lt. General Richard Taylor at Citronelle, Alabama, on May 4, 1865, and paroled at Meridian, Mississippi, on May 14, 1865. Residence—Evergreen, Conecuh County, Alabama.

Ingram, John R., Pvt. Co. E.
Enlisted on August 5, 1864, at Montgomery, Alabama, by Captain A. V. Lee for the war. Appears absent on a company muster for September and October 1864. Absent without leave since August 5, 1864. Captured on April 9, 1865, at Blakeley, Alabama, wounded in the hip. Appears on a list of wounded Confederate POW's to be transferred from Blakeley, Alabama, to New Orleans, Louisiana, on April 13, 1865. Admitted to the USA Hospital Steamer D. A. January on April 17, 1865. Transferred to USA Hospital Steamer Elanora Carrell at New Orleans on April 24, 1864, for transport to Vicksburg, Mississippi. Appears on a roll of POW's at USA General Hospital No. 3 (colored), Vicksburg. Transferred to USA General Hospital No. 3 on May 4, 1865. Admitted May 4, to USA General Hospital No. 2 at Vicksburg, Mississippi. Wounded at Battle of Blakeley on April 9, 1865, by conical ball to left hip. Age—17. Returned to duty on May 8, 1865.

Jackson, C. J., Pvt. Co. F.
Enlisted on March 9, 1864, at Greenville, Alabama, by Captain Brown for the war. Appears on a company muster-in roll for July 25, 1864, at Georgiana, Alabama. Age—17, eyes—dark, hair—dark, complexion—dark, 6 foot 1 inch, residence—Butler County, Alabama. Appears absent on a company muster roll for August 31 to October 31, 1864. Absent in arrest at Mobile, Alabama, from desertion on October 20. Appears on a roll of POW's of Company F, 63rd Alabama Infantry commanded by Captain R. T. Simpson that were surrendered by Lt. General Richard Taylor at Citronelle, Alabama, on May 4, 1865, and paroled at Meridian, Mississippi, on May 11, 1865. Residence is shown as Butler County, Alabama.

Jackson, Elisha, Pvt. Co. A.
Enrolled on January 1, 1864, at Coosa County, Alabama, by Captain John Echols for the war. Age—16. Appears on a company muster-in roll for January 1, 1864, at Montgomery, Alabama. Appears present on a company muster roll for January and February 1864, with pay due from time of enlistment. Drew clothing in 2nd quarter of 1864.

Jackson, Floyd, H., Pvt. Co. G.
Enlisted on May 16, 1864, at Troy, Alabama, by Captain Wilkerson for the war. Appears on a company muster-in roll for September 7, 1864, at Blakeley, Alabama. Age—17, eyes—grey, hair—light, complexion—dark, 5 foot 3 inches, residence—Montgomery, Alabama. Appears present on a company muster roll for September and October 1864. Appears on a roll of Confederate POW's nurses and patients of Moore Hospital CSA Army commanded by Surgeon W. C. Cavenaugh that were surrendered by Lt. General Richard Taylor at Citronelle, Alabama, on May 4, 1865, and paroled at Meridian, Mississippi, on May 16, 1865. Residence—Montgomery, Alabama.

Jackson, Henry, Pvt. Co. C.
Enlisted on May 31, 1864, at Henry County, Alabama, by Captain Brukett for the war. Appears on a company muster-in roll for June 24, 1864, at Camp Watts near Notasulga, Alabama. Age—17, eyes—black, hair—dark, complexion—sallow, 5

foot 6 inches, residence—Henry County, Alabama. Appears absent on a company muster roll for September and October 1864. Reported to have deserted on July 7, 1864, from Camp Watts.

Jackson, J. M., Pvt. Co. E.
His name appears on a roll of POW's of Lee Hospital, Lauderdale, Mississippi. CSA Army commanded by Surgeon Henry Yandell that were surrendered by Lt. General Richard Taylor at Citronelle, Alabama, on May 4, 1865, and paroled at Meridian, Mississippi, on May 13, 1865. Residence—Louisville, Barbour County, Alabama.

Jackson, Joseph A. T., Pvt. Co. C.
Enlisted on June 4, 1864, at Russell County, Alabama, by Lieutenant Carnes for the war. Age—17, eyes—blue, hair—dark, complexion—dark, 5 foot 7 inches, residence—Russell County, Alabama, Post Office—Columbus, Georgia. Appears on a company muster-in roll for June 24, 1864, at Camp Watts near Notasulga, Alabama. Drew clothing August 6, 1864. Appears present on a company muster roll for September and October 1864. Captured at Blakeley, Alabama, on April 9, 1865. Appears on a roll of POW's received at Ship Island, Mississippi, on April 15, 1865. Transferred from Ship Island to Vicksburg, Mississippi, on May 1, 1865. Appears on a roll of POW's of Cos. C and H, 63rd Alabama Infantry commanded by Captain C. W. Martin that were surrendered by Lt. General Richard Taylor at Citronelle, Alabama, on May 4, 1865, and paroled at Meridian, Mississippi, on May 11, 1865. Residence—Russell County, Alabama. Pvt. J. T. Jackson appears on a roll of POW's at Quintard Hospital CSA commanded by Surgeon S. V. D. Hill that were surrendered by Lt. General Richard Taylor at Citronelle, Alabama, on May 4, 1865, and paroled at Meridian, Mississippi, on May 10, 1865. Residence—Columbus, Georgia.

Jain, W. G., Pvt. Co. C.
His name appears on a roll of POW stragglers of the CSA Army that were surrendered by Lt. General Richard Taylor at an unspecified site and he was paroled at Selma, Alabama, on May 28, 1865. His residence is shown as Dallas County, Alabama.

James, A. J., Pvt. Co. K.
Enlisted on September 22, 1864, at Macon County, Alabama, by Captain Ready for the war. Appears absent without leave since September 23, 1864, on a company muster roll for September and October 1864.

James C. A., Pvt. Co. E.
Enlisted on March 1, 1864, at Clayton, Alabama, by Captain A. V. Lee for the war. Age—17, eyes—dark, hair—dark, complexion—dark. Appears present on a company muster roll for September and October 1864. Drew clothing on September 11, 1864. Signed by his mark. Captured at Blakeley, Alabama, on April 9, 1865. Appears on a roll of POW's received at Ship Island, Mississippi, on April 15, 1865. Transferred from Ship Island to Vicksburg, Mississippi, on May 1, 1865. Appears on a roll of POW's of Cos. E and G, 63rd Alabama Infantry commanded by Captain A. V. Lee that were surrendered by Lt. General Richard Taylor at Citronelle, Alabama, on May 4, 1865, and paroled at Meridian, Mississippi, on May 13, 1865. Residence—Barbour County, Alabama. See also Jones, A.

James, A. K., Pvt. Co. K.
Enlisted on September 22, 1864, at Macon County, Alabama, by Major Ready for the war. Appears absent on a company muster roll for September and October 1864. Absent without leave since September 23, 1864.

Jefferson, H. A., Pvt. Co. F.
POW paroled at the headquarters of the 16th US Army Corps, Office of the Provost Marshal at Montgomery, Alabama, on May 30, 1865. Hair—dark, eyes—blue, complexion—sallow, 5 foot 5 inches. Signed H. T. Jefferson. His parole is in his file.

Jefferson, T., Pvt. Co. F.
Enlisted on August 8, 1864, at Georgiana, Alabama, by Captain Brown for the war. Appears on a company muster roll for August 31 to October 31, 1864, with pay due from time of enlistment.

Jemerson, James M., Pvt. Co. D.
Enlisted on July 30, 1864, at Macon County, Alabama, by Major Ready for the war. Age—17, eyes—grey, hair—dark, complexion—dark, 5 foot 5 inches, residence—Kings, Barbour County, Alabama. Appears on a company muster-in roll for July 30, 1864, at Camp Watts near Notasulga, Alabama. Drew clothing on August 7, 1864. Signed by his mark. Appears present on a company muster roll for August 30 to October 30, 1864, with pay due from time of enlistment. Here he is shown as having enlisted on March 2, 1864, at Clayton, Alabama, by D. M. Seals.

Jennings, H., Pvt. Co. C.
Captured at Blakeley, Alabama, on April 9, 1865. Appears on a roll of POW's received at Ship Island, Mississippi, on April 15, 1865. Transferred from Ship Island to Vicksburg, Mississippi, on May 1, 1865. Appears on a roll of POW's of Cos. C and H, 63rd Alabama Infantry commanded by Captain C. W. Martin that were surrendered by Lt. General Richard Taylor at Citronelle, Alabama, on May 4, 1865, and paroled at Meridian, Mississippi, on May 11, 1865. Residence—Macon County, Alabama.

Johns, E. N., Pvt. Co. G.
Enlisted on May 7, 1864, at Andalusia, Alabama, by Lieutenant Wiley for the war. Appears on a company muster-in roll for September 7, 1864. Age—17, eyes—grey, hair—dark, complexion—florid, 5 foot 5 inches, residence—Covington, County, Alabama. Appears a deserter on a company muster roll for September and October 1864. Deserted from hospital at Greenville, Alabama, on October 28, 1864. Drew clothing on September 11, 1864. POW captured at Blakeley, Alabama, on April 9, 1865. Appears on a roll of POW's received at Ship Island, Mississippi, on April 15, 1865. Transferred from Ship Island to Vicksburg, Mississippi, on May 1, 1865. Appears on a roll of POW's of Cos. E and G, 63rd Alabama Infantry commanded by Captain A. V. Lee that were surrendered by Lt. General Richard Taylor at Citronelle, Alabama, on May 4, 1865, and paroled at Meridian, Mississippi, on May 13, 1865. Residence—Covington County, Alabama.

Johnson, F. W., Pvt. Co. D.
Enlisted on August 30, 1864, at Blakeley, Alabama, by Captain Brown for the war. Appears absent sick on a company muster roll for August 30 to October 30, 1864, with pay due from time of enlistment. Absent sick at Mobile, since October 25. Drew clothing on September 12, 1864.

Johnson, H. T., Pvt. Co. D.
Enlisted on August 12, 1864, at Pollard, Alabama, by Captain Zorn for the war. Appears present on a company muster roll for August 30 to October 30, 1864, with pay due from time of enlistment. Drew clothing on September 11, 1864.

Johnson, Robert T., 1st Lieutenant, Co. G.
Elected on July 1, 1864. Appears on a company muster-in roll for September

7, 1864, at Blakeley, Alabama. Age—16, eyes—grey, hair—light, complexion—fair, 5 foot 7 inches, residence—Pike County, Alabama. Resigned on November 11, 1864. His resignation is accepted by Colonel O. F. Rice as "this officer is totally incompetent to fill the position..." His resignation with endorsements are in his file.

Johnson, David, Sergeant/Sergeant Major, Co. A.

Enrolled on January 1, 1864, at Macon County, Alabama, by Captain John Echols for the war. Appears on a company muster in roll as 4th Sergeant on January 1, 1864. Age—16. Appears present on a company muster roll for January and February 1864, with pay due from time or enlistment. Drew clothing in the 2nd quarter and September 11, 1864. Appears as 3rd Sergeant and present on a company muster roll for September and October 1864. Shown as last paid on February 29, 1864. POW captured at Blakeley, Alabama, on April 9, 1865. Appears on a roll of POW's received at Ship Island, Mississippi, on April 15, 1865. Transferred from Ship Island to Vicksburg, Mississippi, on May 1, 1865. Appears as Sergeant Major on a roll of POW's of Company A, 63rd Alabama Infantry commanded by Lieutenant W. D. Kyle that were surrendered by Lt. General Richard Taylor at Citronelle, Alabama, on May 4, 1865, and paroled at Meridian, Mississippi, on May 13, 1865. Residence—Tuskegee, Alabama.

Johnson, Edwin M., Pvt./Corporal, Co. B.

Enrolled on April 11, 1864, at Montgomery County, Alabama, by Captain Zimmerman for the war. Age—17. Appears on a company muster-in roll for March 23, 1864, at Montgomery, Alabama. Drew clothing on July 8, 1864. Appears as 3rd Corporal and absent on a company muster roll for September and October 1864, with pay due from time of enlistment. Absent sick since October 28, 1864.

Johnson, E. L., 1st Lieutenant Co. H.

Elected 1st Lieutenant on March 15, 1864. Appears absent on a company muster roll for September and October 1864. Age—21, eyes—dark, hair—dark, complexion—dark. Absent sick at Hospital Levert since October 23.

Johnson, Herbert P., 2nd Lieutenant Co. D.

Enlisted on March 2, 1864, at Clayton, Alabama, by D. M. Seales for the war. Elected 2nd Lieutenant on March 2, 1864. Appears on a company muster-in roll for July 30, 1864, at Camp Watts near Notasulga, Alabama. Here he is shown as having enlisted at Macon County, Alabama, on July 30, 1864. Age—17, eyes—black, hair—auburn, complexion—fair, 5 foot 9 inches, residence—Clayton, Barbour County, Alabama. Appears absent on a company muster roll for August 30 to October 30, 1864, with pay due from time of enlistment. Absent on sick furlough by Medical Examining Board for 30 days from October 8. POW captured at Blakeley, Alabama, on April 9, 1865, by the 2nd Division, 16th US Army Corps and held in confinement for one day. Appears on a roll of POW's received at Ship Island, Mississippi, on April 16, 1865. Transferred from Ship Island to Vicksburg, Mississippi, on April 28, 1865. Confined at New Orleans, Louisiana on April 30, 1865, from Ship Island. Exchanged on May 1, 1865. Signed a Parole of Honor at Meridian, Mississippi, on May 11, 1865. This parole is in his file.

Johnson, James P., Pvt./Corporal Co. A.

Enlisted on May 10, 1864 at Tallapoosa County, Alabama, by Captain Echols for the war. Drew clothing in 2nd quarter and September 11, 1864. Appears present sick in quarters on a company muster roll for September and October 1864. POW captured at Blakeley, Alabama, on April 9, 1865. Appears on a roll of POW's received at Ship Island, Mississippi, on April 15, 1865. Transferred from Ship Island to Vicksburg, Mississippi, on May 1, 1865. Appears on a roll of POW's of Company A, 63rd Alabama Infantry commanded by Lieutenant W. D. Kyle that were surrendered by Lt. General Richard Taylor at Citronelle, Alabama, on May 4, 1865, and paroled at Meridian, Mississippi, on May 13, 1865. Residence—Tallapoosa County, Alabama.

Johnson, John W., Pvt. Co. A.
Enlisted on May 23, 1864, at Coosa County, Alabama, by Captain Hancock for the war. Appears on a company muster-in roll at Camp Watts near Notasulga, Alabama, for June 24, 1864. Age—17, eyes—blue, hair—dark, complexion—fair, 5 foot 9 inches, residence—Nixburg, Coosa County, Alabama. Drew clothing on August 6, 1864. Appears present on a company muster roll for September and October 1864. Captured at Blakeley, Alabama, on April 9, 1865. Appears on a roll of POW's received at Ship Island, Mississippi, on April 15, 1865. Transferred from Ship Island to Vicksburg, Mississippi, on May 1, 1865. Appears on a roll of POW's of Cos. C and H, 63rd Alabama Infantry commanded by Captain C. W. Martin that were surrendered by Lt. General Richard Taylor at Citronelle, Alabama, on May 4, 1865, and paroled at Meridian, Mississippi, on May 11, 1865. Residence—Macon County, Alabama.

Johnston, J. W., Pvt. Co. K.
Enlisted on October 10, 1864, at Pickens County, Alabama, by Captain Hudgens for the war. Appears present on a company muster roll for September and October 1864.

Johnston, William, Corporal/Sergeant Co. A.
Enlisted on January 1, 1864, at Macon County, Alabama, by Captain John Echols for the war. Appears on company muster-in roll for January 1, 1864, at Montgomery, Alabama. Age—17. Appears present on a company muster roll for January and February 1864, with pay due from time of enlistment. Drew clothing in 2nd quarter of 1864. Appears present on a company muster roll for September and October 1864. Here he is shown as last paid on February 29, 1864. Captured at Blakeley, Alabama, on April 9, 1865. Appears on a roll of POW's received at Ship Island, Mississippi, on April 15, 1865. Transferred from Ship Island to Vicksburg, Mississippi, on May 1, 1865. Appears on a roll of POW's of Company A, 63rd Alabama Infantry commanded by Lieutenant W. D. Kyle that were surrendered by Lt. General Richard Taylor at Citronelle, Alabama, on May 4, 1865, and paroled at Meridian, Mississippi, on May 13, 1865. Residence—Macon County, Alabama.

Jolly, James P., Pvt. Co. B.
Enlisted on August 15, 1864, at Pollard, Alabama, by Lieutenant Townsend for the war. Appears present on a company muster roll for September and October 1864, with pay due from time of enlistment. Drew clothing on September 11, 1864. Signed by his mark.

Jones, A., Pvt. Co. E.
His record is filed with James, C. A. POW paroled at the headquarters of the 16th US Army Corps, Office of the Provost Marshal at Montgomery, Alabama, on June 2, 1865. He is described as: hair—light, eyes—grey, complexion—tan, 5 foot 7 inches. Signed by "X" his mark. His parole can be found in the file of C. A. James.

Jones. G. W., Pvt. Co. F.
He was admitted to 1st Mississippi CSA Hospital, Jackson, Mississippi, on March 3, 1865, with a fatty tumor. Returned to duty on April 4.

Jones, Henithan, Pvt. Co. D.
    Enlisted on July 30, 1864, at Macon County, Alabama, by Major Ready for the war. Appears on a company muster-in roll for July 30, 1864, at Camp Watts near Notasulga, Alabama. Age—17, eyes—dark, hair—dark, complexion—dark, 5 foot 6 inches, residence— Eufaula, Barbour County, Alabama. Appears on a company muster roll for August 30 to October 30, 1864, with pay due from time of enlistment. Here he is shown as having deserted on April 20, 1864, and he is shown as having enlisted at Eufaula, Alabama, by Lieutenant Walker on May 23.

Jones, J., Pvt. Co. F.
    Enlisted on October 14, 1864, at Montgomery, Alabama, by Major Thompson for the war. Appears present on a company muster roll for September and October 1864, with pay due from time of enlistment.

Jones, John A., Pvt. Co. C.
    Enlisted on May 27, 1864, at Russell County, Alabama, by Lieutenant Morton for the war. Appears on a company muster-in roll for June 24, 1864, at Camp Watts near Notasulga, Alabama. Age—17, eyes—grey, hair—light, complexion—light, 5 foot 7 ½ inches, residence—Chambers County, Post Office—Opelika, Russell County, Alabama. Drew clothing on August 6, 1864. Signed by his mark. Appears present on a company muster roll for September and October 1864. Captured at Blakeley, Alabama, on April 9, 1865. Appears on a roll of POW's received at Ship Island, Mississippi, on April 15, 1865. Transferred from Ship Island to Vicksburg, Mississippi, on May 1, 1865. Appears on a roll of POW's of Cos. C and H, 63rd Alabama Infantry commanded by Captain C. W. Martin that were surrendered by Lt. General Richard Taylor at Citronelle, Alabama, on May 4, 1865, and paroled at Meridian, Mississippi, on May 11, 1865. Residence—Chambers County, Alabama.

Jones, J. W., Pvt. Co. E.
    Enlisted on August 18, 1864, at Sibly's Mills, Alabama, by Captain A. V. Lee for the war. Appears present on a company muster roll for September and October 1864. Furloughed for 60 days from August 30, 1864. Age—17, eyes—blue, hair—light, complexion—fair.

Jones, Robert, Pvt. Co. A.
    Enlisted on July 24, 1864, at Macon, County, Alabama, Captain Echols for the war. Appears present sick in quarters on a company muster roll for September and October 1864. Drew clothing on September 11, 1864.

Jones, S. H., Pvt. Co. K.
    Enlisted on September 10, 1864, at Derry [Perry?] County by Captain Powers for the war. Appears absent on a company muster roll for September and October 1864. Absent in hospital at Mobile since October 15, 1864.

Jones, Thomas, Pvt. Co. B.
    Enrolled on April 14, 1864, at Montgomery, Alabama, by Captain Zimmerman for the war. Appears on a company muster-in roll for March 23, 1864, at Montgomery. Age—17.

Jones W. E., 1st Sergeant/2nd Lieutenant Co. E.
    Enlisted as 1st Sergeant on May 10, 1864, at Clayton, Alabama, by Captain A. V. Lee for the war. Age—17, eyes—dark, hair—dark, complexion—dark. Appears present on a company muster roll for September and October 1864. Drew clothing on September 11, 1864. Admitted to Ross Hospital, Mobile, Alabama, on November 5, 1864, with febris intermittens. Returned to duty on November 29, 1864. Elected 2nd Lieutenant on December 5, 1864. Captured by 2nd Division

of the 16th US Army Corps at Blakeley, Alabama, on April 9, 1865. Appears on a roll of POW's received at Ship Island, Mississippi, on April 16, 1865. Transferred from Ship Island to Vicksburg, Mississippi, on April 28, 1865. Appears on a roll of POW's confined at New Orleans, Louisiana, on April 9, 1865, from Ship Island. Exchanged May 1, 1865. Signed a Parole of Honor at Meridian, Mississippi, on May 11, 1865. His parole is in his file.

Jones, W. J., Pvt./Corporal Co. F.
Enlisted on May 30, 1864, at Montgomery, Alabama, by Captain Jackson for the war. Appears on a company muster-in roll for July 25, 1864, at Georgiana, Alabama. Age—17, eyes—dark, hair—dark, complexion—fair, 5 foot 5 inches, residence—Montgomery, County, Alabama. Appears present on a company muster roll for August 31 to October 31, 1864, with pay due from time of enlistment. Promoted from Private to Corporal on October 5, 1864. Captured at Blakeley, Alabama, on April 9, 1865. Appears on a roll of POW's received at Ship Island, Mississippi, on April 15, 1865. Transferred from Ship Island to Vicksburg, Mississippi, on May 1, 1865. Appears on a roll of sick and wounded POW's at USA General Hospital No. 2, Vicksburg. He was admitted from steamer with acute diarrhoea.

Jones, W. Y., Sergeant Co. I.
Enlisted on April 15, 1864, at Columbiana, Alabama, by Lieutenant Bulger for the war. Appears present on a company muster roll for September and October 1864. Captured at Blakeley, Alabama, on April 9, 1865. Appears on a roll of POW's received at Ship Island, Mississippi, on April 15, 1865. Transferred from Ship Island to Vicksburg, Mississippi, on May 1, 1865. Appears on a roll of POW's of Cos. I and K, 63rd Alabama Infantry commanded by Lieutenant W. A. Skinner that were surrendered by Lt. General Richard Taylor at Citronelle, Alabama, on May 4, 1865, and paroled at Meridian, Mississippi, on May 13, 1865. Residence—Shelby County, Alabama.

Jordan, G. M., Sergeant Co. E.
Enlisted on March 1, 1864, at Clayton, Alabama, by Captain A. V. Lee for the war. Appears on a company muster roll as 5th Sergeant and absent for September and October 1864. Absent in hospital since October 28, 1864. Age—17, eyes—blue, hair—light, complexion—fair. Drew clothing September 11, 1864. Captured at Blakeley, Alabama, on April 9, 1865. Appears on a roll of POW's received at Ship Island, Mississippi, on April 15, 1865. Transferred from Ship Island to Vicksburg, Mississippi, on May 1, 1865. Appears on a roll of POW's of Cos. E and G, 63rd Alabama Infantry commanded by Captain A. V. Lee that were surrendered by Lt. General Richard Taylor at Citronelle, Alabama, on May 4, 1865, and paroled at Meridian, Mississippi, on May 13, 1865. Residence—Clayton, Alabama.

Jordan, M., Pvt. Co. F.
Enlisted on July 12, 1864, at Lowndes County, Alabama, by Captain Buell for the war. Appears on a company muster-in roll for July 25, 1864, at Georgiana, Alabama. Age—17, eyes—dark, hair—dark, 5 foot 7 inches, residence—Lowndes County, Alabama. Drew clothing on September 11, 1864. He is show on a company muster roll for August 31 to October 31, 1864, as having died on October 3, 1864. He had never been paid.

Jordan, William S., Pvt. Co. D.
Enlisted on July 30, 1864, at Macon County, Alabama, by Major Ready for the war. Appears on a company muster-in roll for July 30, 1864, at Camp Watts near Notasulga, Alabama. Age—17, eyes—dark, hair—light, complexion—dark, 5 foot 10 inches, Residence—Adkinson, Barbour County, Alabama. Drew clothing on

August 7, 1864. Signed by his mark. Appears present on a company muster roll for August 30 to October 30, 1864, with pay due from time of enlistment. Here he is shown as having enlisted at Clayton, Alabama, on March 2, 1864, by D. W. Seals. Appears on a roll of POW's of Company A, 63rd Alabama Infantry commanded by Captain Robert H. Pearson that were surrendered by Lt. General Richard Taylor at Citronelle, Alabama, on May 4, 1865, and paroled at Meridian, Mississippi, on May 13, 1865. Residence—Barbour County, Alabama.

Josey, R. G., Pvt. Co. F.
Enlisted on March 9, 1864, at Greenville, Alabama, by Captain Brown for the war. Appears on a company muster-in roll for July 25, 1864, at Georgiana, Alabama. Age—11, eyes—blue, hair—brown, complexion—fair, 5 foot 5 inches, residence—Butler County, Alabama.

Julian, Edward, Pvt. Co. A.
Enrolled on January 1, 1864, at Lowndes County, Alabama, by Captain Echols for the war. Appears on a company muster-in roll for January 1, 1864, at Montgomery, Alabama. Age—16. Appears present on a company muster roll for January and February 1864, with pay due from time of enlistment. Admitted to Ross Hospital, Mobile, Alabama, on September 2, 1864, with febris intermittens qout. Returned to duty on September 7, 1864. Drew clothing on August 12 and September 11, 1864. Appears on a company muster roll for September and October 1864. Here he is shown as last paid on February 29, 1864.

Journdan, W., Pvt. Co. E.
Admitted to Yandell Hospital, Meridian, Mississippi, on April 6, 1865.

Kelly, James A., Pvt. Co. G.
Enlisted on May 16, 1865, at Troy, Alabama, by Captain Wilkerson for the war. Appears on a company muster-in roll for September 7, 1864, at Blakeley, Alabama. Age—17, eyes—blue, hair—light, complexion—fair, 5 foot 11 inches, residence—Pike County, Alabama. Drew clothing on September 11, 1864. Appears absent on a company muster roll for September and October 1864. Absent in hospital at Greenville, Alabama, since September 25, 1864.

Kelly, Levi, Pvt. Co. E.
Enlisted on August 5, 1864, at Montgomery, Alabama, by Captain A. V. Lee for the war. Age—17, eyes—blue, hair—light, complexion—fair. Drew clothing on September 11, 1864. Signed by his mark. Admitted to Ross Hospital, Mobile, Alabama, on September 20, 1864, with febris remittens and febris typhoides. Died September 29, 1864.

Kelly, Reuben, Pvt. Co. C.
Enlisted on May 30, 1864, at Macon County, Alabama, by Major Ready for the war. Appears on a company muster-in roll for June 24, 1864, at Camp Watts near Notasulga, Alabama. Age—17, eyes—blue, hair—dark, complexion—fair, 5 foot 6 inches, residence—Society Hill, Macon County, Alabama. Drew clothing August 6, 1864. Appears present on a company muster roll for September and October 1864.

Kelly, W. R., Pvt. Co. D.
Enlisted on August 5, 1864, at Elba, Alabama, by Captain Prince for the war. Drew clothing on September 11, 1864. Appears present on a company muster roll for August 30 to October 30, 1864, with pay due from time of enlistment. Captured at Blakeley, Alabama, on April 9, 1865. Appears on a roll of POW's received at Ship Island, Mississippi, on April 15, 1865. Transferred from Ship Island to Vicksburg, Mississippi, on May 1, 1865. Appears on a roll of POW's

of Company D, 63rd Alabama Infantry commanded by Captain Robert H. Pearson that were surrendered by Lt. General Richard Taylor at Citronelle, Alabama, on May 4, 1865, and paroled at Meridian, Mississippi, on May 13, 1865. Residence—Coffee County, Alabama.

Kelly, Berry, Pvt. Co. B.
Enlisted on July 15, 1864, at Pollard, Alabama, by Lieutenant Calhoun for the war. Drew clothing on August 12, 1864. Signed by his mark. Appears present on a company muster roll for September and October 1864, with pay due from time of enlistment. Captured at Blakeley, Alabama, on April 9, 1865. Appears on a roll of POW's received at Ship Island, Mississippi, on April 15, 1865. Transferred from Ship Island to Vicksburg, Mississippi, on May 1, 1865. Appears on a roll of POW's of Company B, 63rd Alabama Infantry commanded by 1st Lieutenant Thomas J. Calhoun that were surrendered by Lt. General Richard Taylor at Citronelle, Alabama, on May 4, 1865, and paroled at Meridian, Mississippi, on May 11, 1865. Residence—Coosa County, Alabama.

Kelly, Henry, Pvt. Co. B.
Enlisted on August 2, 1864, at Montgomery, Alabama, by Lieutenant Calhoun for the war. Drew clothing on September 11, 1864. Signed by his mark. Appears present on a company muster roll for September and October 1864, with pay due from time of enlistment. Captured at Blakeley, Alabama, on April 9, 1865. Appears on a roll of POW's received at Ship Island, Mississippi, on April 15, 1865. Transferred from Ship Island to Vicksburg, Mississippi, on May 1, 1865. Appears on a roll of POW's of Company B, 63rd Alabama Infantry commanded by 1st Lieutenant Thomas J. Calhoun that were surrendered by Lt. General Richard Taylor at Citronelle, Alabama, on May 4, 1865, and paroled at Meridian, Mississippi, on May 11, 1865. Residence—Coosa County, Alabama.

Kennedy, George W., Pvt. Co. A.
Enlisted on January 1, 1864, at Macon County, Alabama, by Captain Echols for the war. Appears on a company muster-in roll for January 1, 1864, at Montgomery, Alabama. Age—16. Appears present on a company muster roll for January and February 1864, with pay due from time of enlistment. Drew clothing in 2nd quarter and August 12, 1864. Appears present, sick in quarters, on a company muster roll for September and October 1864. Here he is shown as having been paid once on February 29, 1864. Signed a parole at headquarters of the 16th US Army Corps at Montgomery on May 18, 1865. Hair—dark, eyes—blue, complexion—fair, 5 foot 3 inches. Signed E. W. Kennedy. His parole is in his file.

Kennedy, R. J., 2nd Lieutenant Co. F.
Enlisted as 2nd Lieutenant on March 9, 1864, at Greenville, Alabama, by Captain Brown for the war. Elected as 2nd Lieutenant on June 28, 1864. Appears on a company muster-in roll for July 25, 1864, at Georgiana, Alabama. Age—47, eyes—blue, hair—dark, complexion—fair, 5 foot 9 ½ inches, residence—Butler County, Alabama. Appears present on a company muster roll for August 31 to October 31, 1864. Captured and paroled on April 27, 1865, at Greenville, Alabama, by Brigadier General Lucas commanding the US 3rd Brigade Cavalry, Military Division of West Mississippi.

Kennedy, T. L., Pvt. Co. F.
Enlisted on March 9, 1864, at Greenville, Alabama, by Captain Brown for the war. Appears on a company muster-in roll for July 25, 1864, at Georgiana, Alabama. Age—17, eyes—blue, hair—light, complexion—fair, 5 foot 4 inches, residence—Butler County, Alabama. Appears present on a company muster roll for August 31 to October 31, 1864, with pay due from time of enlistment.

Kennedy, William W., Pvt. Co. D/E.
Enlisted on July 30, 1864, at Macon County, Alabama, by Major Ready for the war. Appears on a company muster-in roll for July 30, 1864, at Camp Watts near Notasulga, Alabama. Age—17, eyes—grey, hair—dark, complexion—fair, 5 foot 10 inches, residence—Clayton, Barbour County, Alabama. Drew clothing on August 7, 1864. Appears present on a company muster roll for August 30 to October 30, 1864, with pay due from time of enlistment. Captured at Blakeley, Alabama, on April 9, 1865. Appears on a roll of POW's received at Ship Island, Mississippi, on April 15, 1865. Transferred from Ship Island to Vicksburg, Mississippi, on May 1, 1865. On the above records of capture and confinement he is show in Company E, 63rd Alabama Infantry. Appears on a roll of POW's of Company D, 63rd Alabama Infantry commanded by Captain Robert H. Pearson that were surrendered by Lt. General Richard Taylor at Citronelle, Alabama, on May 4, 1865, and paroled at Meridian, Mississippi, on May 13, 1865. Residence—Barbour County, Alabama.

Kent, David, Pvt. Co. D.
POW captured at Fort Blakeley, Alabama, on April 9, 1865. Appears on a list of wounded Confederates in the hospital of 1st Division, 13 Corps, US Army on April 9, 1865, with flesh wound of the thigh. Admitted to St. Louis USA General Hospital, New Orleans, Louisiana, from Mobile on April 15, 1865, with gunshot wound to right thigh. Transferred to General Hospital on May 23. Age—17. Admitted to Marine USA General Hospital, New Orleans on May 23, 1865, returned to duty on June 25. Confined at New Orleans on May 1, 1865. Released May 16 on parole.

Kent, W. P., Pvt. Co. D/K.
Enlisted on August 25, 1864, at Blakeley, Alabama, by Lieutenant Pearson for the war. Drew clothing on September 12, 1864. Signed by his mark. Appears on a company muster roll for August 30 to October 30, 1864, with pay due from time of enlistment. Here he is shown as having transferred to Company K on September 28, 1864. Appears present on Company K muster roll for September and October 1864. Here he is shown as having enlisted on August 5, 1864, at Baldwin County, Alabama, by Colonel Rice. Captured at Blakeley, Alabama, on April 9, 1865. Appears on a roll of POW's received at Ship Island, Mississippi, on April 15, 1865. Transferred from Ship Island to Vicksburg, Mississippi, on May 1, 1865. Appears on a roll of POW's of Cos. I and K, 63rd Alabama Infantry commanded by Lieutenant W. A. Skinner that were surrendered by Lt. General Richard Taylor at Citronelle, Alabama, on May 4, 1865, and paroled at Meridian, Mississippi, on May 13, 1865. Residence—Chambers County, Alabama.

Kierce, Henry, Pvt./Corporal Co. C/E.
Enlisted May 19, 1864, at Covington County, Alabama, by Lieutenant Kearney for the war. Age—17, eyes—black, hair—dark, complexion—dark, 5 foot 9 inches, residence—Andalusia, Covington County, Alabama. Appears on a company muster-in roll for June 24, 1864, at Camp Watts near Notasulga, Alabama. Appears present on a company muster roll for September and October 1864. Here he is shown as having enlisted at Camp Watts on May 16, 1864, by Captain Ready. Drew clothing on August 6, 1864. Appears on a roll of POW's of Cos. E and G, 63rd Alabama Infantry commanded by Captain A. V. Lee that were surrendered by Lt. General Richard Taylor at Citronelle, Alabama, on May 4, 1865, and paroled at Meridian, Mississippi, on May 13, 1865. Residence—Covington County, Alabama.

Killaugh, Martin, 1st Sergeant/Sergeant Co. B.
Enrolled on March 23, 1864, at Montgomery County, Alabama, by Captain Zimmerman for the war. Appears on a company muster-in roll as 1st Sergeant

on March 23, 1864, at Montgomery, Alabama. Age—17. Drew clothing on July 8 and August 12, 1864. Appears present on a company muster roll for September and October 1864, with pay due from time of enlistment. Captured at Blakeley, Alabama, on April 9, 1865. Appears on a roll of POW's received at Ship Island, Mississippi, on April 15, 1865. Transferred from Ship Island to Vicksburg, Mississippi, on May 1, 1865. Appears as 3rd Sergeant on a roll of POW's of Company B, 63rd Alabama Infantry commanded by 1st Lieutenant Thomas J. Calhoun that were surrendered by Lt. General Richard Taylor at Citronelle, Alabama, on May 4, 1865, and paroled at Meridian, Mississippi, on May 11, 1865. Residence—Montgomery County, Alabama.

Killaugh, R. L., Sr. 2nd Lieutenant Co. H.
Appears present on a company muster roll for September and October 1864. Age—21, eyes—dark, hair—dark, complexion—dark. Elected 2nd Lieutenant on March 15, 1864. POW paroled at Talladega, Alabama, on June 13, 1865, by Brevet Brigadier General M. H. Chrysler commanding US forces at Talladega.

Kilpatrick, Alick, Pvt. Co. E.
Captured at Blakeley, Alabama, on April 9, 1865. Appears on a roll of POW's received at Ship Island, Mississippi, on April 15, 1865. Transferred from Ship Island to Vicksburg, Mississippi, on May 1, 1865. Appears on a register of sick and wounded Confederate POW's at USA General Hospital, No. 2, Vicksburg. Admitted on May 3, 1865, from steamer with measles. Returned to duty on May 10, 1865. Age—18. There was an inquiry in 1919 from Oklahoma City, Board of Pension Commissioners as to Private Kilpatrick's service.

Kilpatrick, James. E., Pvt. Co. A.
Enrolled on January 1, 1864, at Tallapoosa County, Alabama, by Captain John Echols for the war. Appears on a company muster-in roll for January 1, 1864, at Montgomery, Alabama. Age—16. Appears present on a company muster roll for January and February 1864, with pay due from time of enlistment. Drew clothing in 2nd quarter and August 12, 1864. Appears present on a company muster roll for September and October 1864. Captured at Blakeley, Alabama, on April 9, 1865. Appears on a roll of POW's received at Ship Island, Mississippi, on April 15, 1865. Transferred from Ship Island to Vicksburg, Mississippi, on May 1, 1865. Appears on a register of sick and wounded Confederate POW's at USA General Hospital, No. 2, Vicksburg. Admitted on May 3, 1865, from steamer with tertium int. fever. Returned to duty on May 12, 1865. Age—19. Appears on a roll of POW's of divers companies and regiments (detached) commanded by Captain D. H. Todd that were surrendered by Lt. General Richard Taylor at Citronelle, Alabama, on May 4, 1865, and paroled at Meridian, Mississippi, on May 14, 1865. Residence—Tallapoosa County, Alabama.

Kilpatrick, Marion, Pvt. Co. C.
Enlisted on May 31, 1864, at Montgomery, Alabama, by Captain McDaniel for the war. Age—17, eyes—blue, hair—light, complexion—fair, 5 foot 7 inches, residence—Victoria, Coffee County, Alabama. Appears on a company muster-in roll for June 24, 1864, at Camp Watts near Notasulga, Alabama. Drew clothing on August 6, 1864. Appears present on a company muster roll for September and October 1864. Admitted to Ross Hospital, Mobile, Alabama, on November 10, 1864, with febris intermittens tert., febris congestia. Returned to duty on December 5. Signed a parole at Montgomery, Alabama, on June 22, 1865, at the headquarters of the 16th US Army Corps. Signed by his mark "X." His parole is in his file.

Kimble, James E., Pvt. Co. B.
Enlisted on July 17, 1864, at Montgomery, Alabama, by Lieutenant Calhoun for

the war. Appears absent on a company muster roll for September and October 1864. Absent sick since September 29, 1864. There is a note in his file to see personal papers of Amzi J. Blair, Rices Tennessee Battery.

Kimbrough, Henry B., Corporal/Pvt. Co. A.
Enlisted as 1st Corporal on January 1, 1864, at Tallapoosa, County, Alabama, by Captain John H. Echols for the war. Age—17. Appears on a company muster-in roll for January 1, 1864. Appears present on a company muster roll for January and February 1864. Drew clothing 2nd quarter, August 12 and September 11, 1864. Appears present, sick in quarters, on a company muster roll for September and October 1864. Shown here as a Private.

King, George, Pvt. Co. C.
Enlisted on May 11, 1864, at Russell County, Alabama, by Captain Carnes for the war. Age—17, eyes—blue, hair—light, complexion—fair, 5 foot 0 inches, residence—Russell County, Alabama, Post Office—Columbus, Georgia. Drew clothing on August 6, 1864. Appears absent on a company muster roll for September and October 1864. Absent in hospital since October 21, 1864.

King, T., Pvt. Co. H/A.
Enlisted on March 15, 1864, at Springville, Alabama, by Lieutenant Killough for the war. Drew clothing on September 11, 1864. Appears absent on a company muster roll for September and October 1864. Absent sick at hospital in Mobile, Alabama, since September 10. Age—17, eyes—hazel, hair—auburn, complexion—fair. Admitted to Ross Hospital, Mobile, September 16, 1864, with febris intermittens quot. Furloughed on October 15, 1864, for 30 days. Captured at Blakeley, Alabama, on April 9, 1865. Appears on a roll of POW's received at Ship Island, Mississippi, on April 15, 1865. Transferred from Ship Island to Vicksburg, Mississippi, on May 1, 1865. Appears on a roll of POW's of Cos. C and H, 63rd Alabama Infantry commanded by Captain C. W. Martin that were surrendered by Lt. General Richard Taylor at Citronelle, Alabama, May 4, 1865, and paroled at Meridian, Mississippi, on May 11, 1865. Residence—St. Clair County, Alabama.

King, W. L., Pvt. Co. C.
Appears on a list of POW stragglers paroled at Selma, Alabama, in June 1865. Residence—Shelby County, Alabama.

Kirkland, E. A., Pvt. Co. E.
Enlisted on August 8, 1864, at Pollard, Alabama, by Captain A. V. Lee for the war. Age—17, eyes—dark, hair—dark, complexion—dark. Drew clothing on September 11, 1864. Appears present on a company muster roll for September and October 1864. Appears on a roll of POW's of Cos. E and G, 63rd Alabama Infantry commanded by Captain A. V. Lee that were surrendered by Lt. General Richard Taylor at Citronelle, Alabama, on May 4, 1865, and paroled at Meridian, Mississippi, on May 13, 1865. Residence—Henry County, Alabama.

Kirkland, R. K., Pvt. Co. E.
Enlisted on September 12, 1864, at Camp Hood by Captain A. V. Lee for the war. Drew clothing on September 11, 1864. Appears absent on a company muster roll for September and October 1864. Absent in hospital since September 28, 1864. Age—17, eyes—blue, hair—light, complexion—fair. Admitted to Ross Hospital, Mobile, Alabama, on October 1, 1864, with segalae rubeola. Sent to General Hospital on October 6, 1864. (Lauderdale Springs, Mississippi). Discharged at Selma, Alabama, due to disability on December 12, 1864. Stationed at Scott Hospital, Marion, Alabama. Here he is shown as having enlisted on July 29, 1864, at Dallas County, Alabama, by Captain Deskar. Age—17, eyes—grey, complexion—fair, hair—light, 5 foot 11 inches, a farmer by occupation,

residence—Dallas County, Alabama. Discharged due to surditis and consequential defeat of iris (both eyes) rendering vision very imperfect. His discharge is in his file.

Kirkland, W. J., Pvt. Co. E.
Enlisted on August 8, 1864, at Pollard, Alabama, by Captain A. V. Lee for the war. Appears present on a company muster roll for September and October 1864. Age—17, eyes—dark, hair—dark, complexion—dark. Drew clothing September 11, 1864. Signed by his mark. Appears present on a company muster roll for September and October 1864. Admitted to Ross Hospital, Mobile, Alabama, on September 18, 1864, with rubeola. Returned to duty on September 26, 1864. Captured at Blakeley, Alabama, on April 9, 1865. Appears on a roll of POW's received at Ship Island, Mississippi, on April 15, 1865. Transferred from Ship Island to Vicksburg, Mississippi, on May 1, 1865. Appears on a roll of POW's of Cos. E and G, 63rd Alabama Infantry commanded by Captain A. V. Lee that were surrendered by Lt. General Richard Taylor at Citronelle, Alabama, on May 4, 1865, and paroled at Meridian, Mississippi, on May 13, 1865. Residence—Henry County, Alabama.

Kirkpatrick, Sydney C., Pvt. Co. A.
Enlisted on May 15, 1864, at Lowndes County, Alabama, by Captain Echols for the war. Appears present, sick in quarters, on a company muster roll for September and October 1864, with pay due from time of enlistment. Drew clothing in 2nd quarter of 1864. POW paroled at headquarters of 16th US Army Corps at Montgomery, Alabama, on May 30, 1864. Eyes—dark, hair—dark, complexion—dark, 5 foot 8 inches.

Kinve, Frank H., Pvt. Co. B/K.
Enlisted on March 23, 1864, at Montgomery, Alabama, by Captain Zimmerman for the war. Appears on a company muster-in roll for March 23, 1864, at Montgomery. Age—17. Drew clothing on July 8, 1864. Appears on a company B muster roll for September and October 1864, with pay due from time of enlistment. Here he is shown as having transferred as per Special Order No. 15. on October 2, 1864. Appears absent on a Company K muster roll for September and October 1864. This roll reports him absent sick without leave since September 13, 1864.

Knight, James M., Pvt. Co. G.
Enlisted on May 16, 1864, at Troy, Alabama, by Captain Wilkerson for the war. Age—17, eyes—black, hair—dark, complexion—dark, 5 foot 8 inches, residence—Coffee County, Alabama. Appears on a company muster-in roll for September 7, 1864, at Blakeley, Alabama. Drew clothing on September 11, 1864. Appears absent on a company muster roll for September and October 1864. Absent in hospital in Mobile, Alabama, since October 15, 1864. Captured at Blakeley, Alabama, on April 9, 1865. Appears on a roll of POW's received at Ship Island, Mississippi, on April 15, 1865. Transferred from Ship Island to Vicksburg, Mississippi, on May 1, 1865. Appears on a roll of POW's of Cos. E and G, 63rd Alabama Infantry commanded by Captain A. V. Lee that were surrendered by Lt. General Richard Taylor at Citronelle, Alabama, on May 4, 1865, and paroled at Meridian, Mississippi, on May 13, 1865. Residence—Coffee County, Alabama.

Knight, Jasper S., Pvt. Co. A/Sergeant Major F&S
Enrolled on January 1, 1864, at Chambers County, Alabama, by Captain John Echols for the war. Age—16. Appears on a company muster-in roll for January 1, 1864, at Montgomery, Alabama. Appears present on a company muster roll for January and February 1864, with pay due from time of enlistment. Drew

clothing in 2nd quarter and September 11, 1864. Appears on a Company A muster roll for September and October 1864. Here he is shown as having been promoted to Sergeant Major per Special Order dated September 29, 1864. Appears on a Field and Staff muster roll for September and October.

Knight, T. D., Pvt. Co. F.
Enlisted on July 12, 1864, at Lowndes County, Alabama, by Captain Buell for the war. Appears on a company muster-in roll for July 25, 1864, at Georgiana, Alabama. Age—17, eyes—blue, hair—dark, complexion—fair, 5 foot 8 inches, residence—Lowndes County, Alabama. Drew clothing on September 11, 1864. Appears present on a company muster roll for August 31 to October 31, 1864, with pay due from time of enlistment. Signed a parole at headquarters of the 16th US Army Corps at Montgomery, Alabama, on May 23. 1864. Hair—dark, eyes—blue, complexion—fair, 5 foot 9 inches. His parole is in his file.

Knop, L. B., Pvt. Co. I.
Enlisted on April 15, 1864, at Wedowee, Alabama, by Captain Robinson for the war. Appears absent on a company muster roll for September and October 1864. Absent without leave since September 18, 1864.

Knowles, George E., Pvt. Co. B/K
See Nowles, George E.

Kyle, Willie D., 2nd Lieutenant Co. A.
Appears as 2nd Lieutenant on a company muster-in roll for January 1, 1864, at Montgomery, Alabama. Appears present on a company muster roll for January and February 1864. Promoted to Lieutenant on March 23, 1864. Appears absent on a company muster roll for September and October 1864. Furloughed for ten days by General Maury on October 26, 1864. Captured at Blakeley, Alabama, on April 9, 1865. Appears on a roll of POW's received at Ship Island, Mississippi, on April 16, 1865. Transferred from Ship Island to Vicksburg, Mississippi, on April 28, 1865. POW received from Ship Island and confined at New Orleans, Louisiana, on April 30, 1865. Exchanged on May 1, 1865. Signed a Parole of Honor at Meridian, Mississippi, on May 11, 1865. His parole is in his file.

Lacey, Thomas A., Corporal Co. H.
Enlisted on March 15, 1864, at Elyton, Alabama, by Lieutenant Killough for the war. Age—17, eyes—grey, hair—light, complexion—fair. Drew clothing on September 11, 1864. Appears absent on a company muster roll for September and October 1864. Absent sick at hospital in Selma, Alabama, since September 21. Captured at Blakeley, Alabama, on April 9, 1865. Appears on a roll of POW's received at Ship Island, Mississippi, on April 15, 1865. Transferred from Ship Island to Vicksburg, Mississippi, on May 1, 1865. Appears on a roll of sick and wounded Confederate POW's admitted to USA General Hospital No. 2., Vicksburg, Mississippi, on May 3, 1865, from steamer. Diagnosis was acute diarrhoea. Returned to duty on May 8, 1865. Age—18.

Lacey, William M., Pvt. Co. H.
Enlisted on March 15, 1864, at Elyton, Alabama, by Lieutenant Killough for the war. Age—16, eyes—grey, hair—dark, complexion—dark. Appears present on a company muster roll for September and October 1864. Admitted to Ross Hospital, Mobile, Alabama, on October 10, 1864, with dysenteria acuta. Returned to duty on October 26, 1864. Captured at Blakeley, Alabama, on April 9, 1865. Appears on a roll of POW's received at Ship Island, Mississippi, on April 15, 1865. Transferred from Ship Island to Vicksburg, Mississippi, on May 1, 1865. Appears on a roll of POW's of Cos. C and H, 63rd Alabama Infantry commanded

by Captain C. W. Martin that were surrendered by Lt. General Richard Taylor at Citronelle, Alabama, on May 4, 1865, and paroled at Meridian, Mississippi, on May 11, 1865. Residence—Jefferson County, Alabama.

Lambret, E. J., Pvt. Co. I.
Enlisted on April 15, 1864, at Wedowee, Alabama, by Captain Robinson for the war. Appears absent on a company muster roll for September and October 1864. Furloughed from September 24, 1864, for 30 days.

Lambreth, John, Pvt. Co. C.
Enlisted on June 10, 1864, at Tallapoosa County, Alabama, by Captain Brown for the war. Age—17, eyes—hazel, hair—dark, complexion—dark, 5 foot 2 ½ inches, residence—Newsite, Tallapoosa County, Alabama. Appears on a company muster-in roll for June 24, 1864, at Camp Watts, near Notasulga, Alabama. Appears absent on a company muster roll for September and October 1864. Absent in hospital in Montgomery since August 7, 1864.

Lambreth, Z. T., Pvt. Co. E.
Enlisted on July 28, 1864, at Montgomery, Alabama, by Captain A. V. Lee for the war. Drew clothing on September 11, 1864. Admitted to Ross Hospital, Mobile, Alabama, September 29, 1864, with febris intermittens, tert. Returned to duty on October 18, 1864. Appears present on a muster roll for September and October 1864. Age—17, eyes—blue, hair—light, complexion—fair. Captured at Blakeley, Alabama, on April 9, 1865. Appears on a roll of POW's received at Ship Island, Mississippi, on April 15, 1865. Transferred from Ship Island to Vicksburg, Mississippi, on May 1, 1865. Appears on a roll of POW's of Cos. E and G, 63rd Alabama Infantry commanded by Captain A. V. Lee that were surrendered by Lt. General Richard Taylor at Citronelle, Alabama, May 4, 1865. Paroled Meridian, Mississippi, May 13, 1865. Residence—Coosa County, Alabama.

Lancaster, John M., 2nd Lieutenant Co. C.
Enlisted on May 4, 1864, at Chambers County, Alabama, by Captain Walker for the war. Age—17, eyes—blue, hair—light, complexion—fair, 5 foot 8 inches, residence—Cusseta, Chambers County, Alabama. Elected 2nd Lieutenant on June 20, 1864. Appears on a company muster-in roll for June 24, 1864, at Camp Watts near Notasulga, Alabama. Appears absent on a company muster roll for September and October 1864, with pay due from time of enlistment. Absent in hospital at Mobile, Alabama, since October 19, 1864. Captured at Blakeley, Alabama, on April 9, 1865. Appears on a roll of POW's received at Ship Island, Mississippi, on April 16, 1865. Transferred from Ship Island to Vicksburg, Mississippi, on April 28, 1865. Appears on a roll of POW's from Ship Island confined at New Orleans, Louisiana, on April 30, 1865. Exchanged on May 1, 1865. Signed a Parole of Honor at Meridian, Mississippi, on May 11, 1865. His parole is in his file.

Lane, Benjamin F., Pvt. Co. A.
Enlisted on January 1, 1864, at Coosa County, Alabama, by Captain John Echols for the war. Appears on a company muster-in roll for January 1, 1864, at Montgomery, Alabama. Appears present on a company muster roll for January and February 1864, with pay due from time of enlistment. Drew clothing in 2nd quarter and September 11, 1864. Appears present on a company muster roll for September and October 1864. Here he is shown as having been last paid on February 29, 1864. Admitted to Ross Hospital, Mobile, Alabama, on April 6, 1865, with febris intermittens tert. Sent to General Hospital on April 15, 1865. Here the record shows Demopolis. Appears on a list of POW's paroled at the headquarters of the 16th US Army Corps at Montgomery, Alabama, on May 23, 1865. Signed a parole at the headquarters of the 16th US Army Corp at

Montgomery on May 23, 1865. He is described as: hair—light, eyes—blue, complexion—fair, 5 foot 9 inches. His parole is in his file. He is shown as a Private in Taylor's Army.

Lane, John H., Pvt. Co. A.
Enlisted on February 1, 1864, at Chambers County, Alabama, by Captain John Echols for the war. Appears present on a company muster roll for January and February 1864, with pay due from time of enlistment. Drew clothing in 2nd quarter and September 11, 1864. Appears present, sick in quarters, on a company muster roll for September and October 1864. Here he is shown as having been last paid on February 29, 1864.

Lane, John J., Pvt./Sergeant Co. A.
Enlisted on January 1, 1864, at Lowndes County, Alabama, by Captain John Echols for the war. Appears on a company muster-in roll for January 1, 1864. Age—16. Appears present on a company muster roll for January and February 1864, with pay due from time of enlistment. Drew clothing in 2nd quarter and September 11, 1864. Appears present on a company muster roll for September and October 1864. Here he is shown as having been last paid on February 29, 1864. Captured at Blakeley, Alabama, on April 9, 1865. Appears on a roll of POW's received at Ship Island, Mississippi, on April 15, 1865. Transferred from Ship Island to Vicksburg, Mississippi, on May 1, 1865. Appears on a roll of POW's of Company A, 63rd Alabama Infantry commanded by Lieutenant W. D. Kyle that were surrendered by Lt. General Richard Taylor at Citronelle, Alabama, on May 4, 1865, and paroled at Meridian, Mississippi, on May 13, 1865. Residence—Lowndes County, Alabama.

Lane, L. M., 3rd/2nd Lieutenant Co. D.
Enlisted as 3rd Lieutenant on August 30, 1864, at Blakeley, Alabama, by Colonel Rice for the war. Drew clothing on September 12, 1864. Appears present on a company muster roll for September and October 1864, with pay due from time of enlistment. Captured at Blakeley, Alabama, on April 9, 1865. Confined for one day at Spanish Fort, Alabama, by 2nd Division of 16th US Army Corps. Appears on a roll of POW's received at Ship Island, Mississippi, on April 16, 1865. Transferred from Ship Island to Vicksburg, Mississippi, on April 28, 1865. Appears on a roll of POW's from Ship Island confined at New Orleans, Louisiana, on April 30, 1865. Exchanged on May 1, 1865. Signed a Parole of Honor at Meridian, Mississippi, on May 11, 1865. His parole is in his file. He is shown as 2nd Lieutenant on his parole.

Lansdon, J. A., Pvt. Co. F.
Enlisted on August 24, 1864, at Greenville, Alabama, by Lieutenant Barton for the war. Appears present on a company muster roll from August 31 to October 31, 1864, with pay due from time of enlistment. Captured at Blakeley, Alabama, on April 9, 1865. Appears on a roll of POW's received at Ship Island, Mississippi, on April 15, 1865. Transferred from Ship Island to Vicksburg, Mississippi, on May 1, 1865. Appears on a roll of POW's of Company F, 63rd Alabama Infantry commanded by Captain R. T. Simpson that were surrendered by Lt. General Richard Taylor at Citronelle, Alabama, on May 4, 1865, and paroled at Meridian, Mississippi, on May 11, 1865. Residence—Butler County, Alabama.

Lard, F., Pvt. Co. H.
Enlisted on September 1, 1864, at Montevallo, Alabama, by Captain Lemmon for the war. Age—17. Appears absent on a company muster roll for September and October 1864. Absent on detached service since September 1, by Major General Withers.

Lassiter, James, Pvt. Co. G.
   Captured at Blakeley, Alabama, on April 9, 1865. Appears on a roll of POW's received at Ship Island, Mississippi, on April 15, 1865. Transferred from Ship Island to Vicksburg, Mississippi, on May 1, 1865. Appears on a roll of POW's of Cos. E and G, 63rd Alabama Infantry commanded by Captain A. V. Lee that were surrendered by Lt. General Richard Taylor at Citronelle, Alabama, on May 4, 1865, and paroled at Meridian, Mississippi, on May 13, 1865. Residence—Coffee County, Alabama.

Law, J. A., Lt. Colonel F&S
   There is a requisition in his file dated November 11, 1863, signed by him as Post Adjutant at Fort Morgan, Alabama. Requisition was for one blank book to be used by garrison for a morning report. Appears present on a Field and Staff muster roll for July and August 1864, near Blakeley, Alabama. Commissioned Lt. Colonel on August 16, 1864. Appears absent on a Field and Staff muster roll for September and October 1864, near Mobile. Absent on sick leave since September 28, 1864, with a 30 day furlough by General Maury. Appointed Lt. Colonel on August 16, 1864, by Major General Withers by order of Secretary of War. Captured at Blakeley, Alabama, on April 9, 1865. Confined for one day at Spanish Fort, Alabama, by 2nd Division of 16th US Army Corps. Appears on a roll of POW's received at Ship Island, Mississippi, on April 16, 1865. Transferred from Ship Island to Vicksburg, Mississippi, on April 28, 1865. Appears on a roll of POW's from Ship Island confined at New Orleans, Louisiana, on April 30, 1865. Admitted from steamer to USA General Hospital No. 2, Vicksburg, on May 3, 1865. with remittent fever. Returned to duty on May 8, 1865. Exchanged on May 1, 1865. Signed a Parole of Honor at Meridian, Mississippi, on May 11, 1865. His parole is in his file.

Lawson, J. M., 4th Corporal Co. H.
   Enlisted on March 16, 1864, at Montevallo, Alabama, by Captain Suttle for the war. Drew clothing on September 11, 1864. Appears present on a company muster roll for September and October 1864. Age—17, eyes—grey, hair—dark, complexion—dark. Captured at Blakeley, Alabama, on April 9, 1865. Appears on a roll of POW's received at Ship Island, Mississippi, on April 15, 1865. Transferred from Ship Island to Vicksburg, Mississippi, on May 1, 1865. Appears on a roll of POW's of Cos. C and H, 63rd Alabama Infantry commanded by Captain C. W. Martin that were surrendered by Lt. General Richard Taylor at Citronelle, Alabama, on May 4, 1865, and paroled at Meridian, Mississippi, on May 11, 1865. Residence—Jefferson County, Alabama.

Ledlow, J. W., Pvt. Co. K.
   Enlisted on September 20, 1864, at Rockford, Alabama, by Captain Hancock for the war. Appears present on a company muster roll for September and October 1864. Captured at Blakeley, Alabama, on April 9, 1865. Appears on a roll of POW's received at Ship Island, Mississippi, on April 15, 1865. Transferred from Ship Island to Vicksburg, Mississippi, on May 1, 1865. Appears on a roll of POW's of Cos. I and K, 63rd Alabama Infantry commanded by Lieutenant W. A. Skinner that were surrendered by Lt. General Richard Taylor at Citronelle, Alabama, on May 4, 1865, and paroled at Meridian, Mississippi, on May 13, 1865. Residence—Coosa County, Alabama.

Lee, A. V., Captain Co. E.
   Enlisted on March 20, 1864, at Clayton, Alabama, by Captain Ewan for the war. Appears present on a company muster roll for September and October 1864. Age—20, eyes—dark, hair—dark. A Cadet when elected to Captain of the company. Elected Captain on March 25, 1864. Requisitioned for Company E in the 2nd quarter of 1864, the following: 62 jackets, 51 pants, 30 pair of

drawers, 15 shirts, 38 pair of shoes. On September 21, 1864 he requisitioned for his company: 6 camp kettles, 6 ovens and lids, 6 frying pans, 6 buckets, 18 tin cups, 3 camp pans at Ledochie Redoubt No. 9. Captured at Blakeley, Alabama, on April 9, 1865. Confined for one day at Spanish Fort, Alabama, by 2nd Division of 16th US Army Corps. Appears on a roll of POW's received at Ship Island, Mississippi, on April 16, 1865. Transferred from Ship Island to Vicksburg, Mississippi, on April 28, 1865. Appears on a roll of POW's from Ship Island confined at New Orleans, Louisiana, on April 30, 1865. Exchanged on May 1, 1865. Signed a Parole of Honor at Meridian, Mississippi, on May 11, 1865. His parole and his requisition are in his file. His residence is shown as Columbus, Georgia, on his parole.

Lee, General T., Pvt. Co. D/B.
Enlisted on July 30, 1864, at Macon County, Alabama, by Major Ready for the war. Appears on a company muster-in roll for July 30, 1864, at Camp Watts near Notasulga, Alabama. Age—17, eyes—grey, hair—light, complexion—fair, residence—Clayton, Barbour County, Alabama. Drew clothing on August 7, 1864. Appears absent on a company muster roll for September and October 1864, with pay due from time of enlistment. Absent on sick furlough by Medical Examining Board since October 24, 1864, for 30 days. Here he is shown as having enlisted on March 2, 1864, at Clayton, Alabama, by D. M. Seals. Captured at Blakeley, Alabama, on April 9, 1865. Appears on a roll of POW's received at Ship Island, Mississippi, on April 15, 1865. Transferred from Ship Island to Vicksburg, Mississippi, on May 1, 1865. Appears on a roll of POW's of Company D, 63rd Alabama Infantry commanded by Captain Robert H. Pearson that were surrendered by Lt. General Richard Taylor at Citronelle, Alabama, May 4, 1865. Paroled Meridian, Mississippi, May 13, 1865. His residence is shown as Barbour County, Alabama.

Lee, G. W., Pvt. Co. F.
Enlisted on May 30, 1864, at Montgomery, Alabama, by Captain Jackson, for the war. Appears absent without leave on a company muster-in roll for July 25, 1864, at Georgiana, Alabama. Age—17, eyes—hazel, hair—dark, complexion—dark, 5 foot 6 inches, residence—Coosa County, Alabama.

Lee, James E., Pvt. Co. B/K.
Enlisted on August 15, 1864, at Pollard, Alabama, by Lieutenant Townsend for the war. Drew clothing on September 11, 1864. Signed by his mark. Appears on a Company B, muster roll for September and October 1864, as having been transferred on October 2, 1864. Appears absent on a Company K muster roll for September and October 1864. Absent sick without leave since August 9, 1864. There was an inquiry as to his service file from Florida in 1916.

Lee, Lemick S., Pvt. Co. C.
Enlisted on May 23, 1864, at Coosa County, Alabama, by Captain Hancock for the war. His name appears on a company muster-in roll for June 24, 1864, at Camp Watts near Notasulga, Alabama. Age—17, eyes—blue, hair—sandy, complexion—fair, 5 foot 10 inches, residence—Nexburg, Alabama. Drew clothing on August 6, 1864. Signed by his mark. Appears absent on a company muster roll for September and October 1864. Absent in hospital in Mobile, Alabama, since October 26, 1864.

Lenley, E. W., Pvt. Co. A.
Appears on a roll of Confederate POW stragglers that were surrendered by Lt. General Richard Taylor at Citronelle, Alabama, in May 1865, and paroled at Selma, Alabama, on May 28, 1865. His residence is shown as Bibb County, Alabama.

Lervell, W. L., Pvt. Co. B.
    His file is filed in error with Wade L. Sewell. Reference card in file to see personal papers of Amji J. Blair, Rice's Battery.

Lethow, William, Pvt. Co. F.
    Appears on a roll of Confederate soldiers paroled at the headquarters of the 16th US Army Corps at Montgomery, Alabama, on May 12, 1865.

Leverett, Gideon L., Pvt. Co. A.
    Enlisted on March 29, 1864, at Chambers County, Alabama, by Captain Echols for the war. Drew clothing in 2nd quarter and September 11, 1864. Appears present, sick in quarters, on a company muster roll for September and October 1864. Admitted to Ross Hospital, Mobile, Alabama, on September 2, 1864, with febris remittens. Returned to duty on September 7. Admitted to 1st Mississippi CSA Hospital, Jackson, Mississippi, on March 3, 1865, with feb Int. qoutid. Returned to duty on April 4, 1865.

Leverett, John D., Pvt. Co. A.
    Enlisted on February 1, 1864, at Chambers County, Alabama, by Captain John Echols for the war. He appears present on a company muster roll for January and February 1864, with pay due from time of enlistment. Drew clothing in 2nd quarter of 1864. Appears present, sick in quarters, on a company muster roll for September and October 1864. Here he is shown as having been last paid on February 29, 1864. POW captured at Blakeley, Alabama, on April 9, 1865. His name appears on a roll of POW's that were received at Ship Island, Mississippi, on April 15, 1865. He was among those men transferred from Ship Island to Vicksburg, Mississippi, on May 1, 1865. His name appears on a roll of POW's of Company A, 63rd Alabama Infantry commanded by Lieutenant W. D. Kyle that were surrendered by Lt. General Richard Taylor at Citronelle, Alabama, on May 4, 1865, and paroled at Meridian, Mississippi, on May 13, 1865. His residence is shown as Chambers County, Alabama.

Lewis, F. M., Pvt. Co. E.
    Enlisted on April 5, 1864, at Clayton, Alabama, by Captain A. V. Lee for the war. Drew clothing on September 11, 1864. Signed by his mark. Appears absent on a company muster roll for September and October 1864. Absent in hospital since September 15, 1864. Age—17, eyes—blue, hair—light, complexion—fair. Captured at Blakeley, Alabama, on April 9, 1865. Appears on a roll of POW's received at Ship Island, Mississippi, on April 15, 1865. Transferred from Ship Island to Vicksburg, Mississippi, on May 1, 1865. Appears on a roll of POW's of Cos. E and G, 63rd Alabama Infantry commanded by Captain A. V. Lee that were surrendered by Lt. General Richard Taylor at Citronelle, Alabama, on May 4, 1865, and paroled at Meridian, Mississippi, on May 13, 1865. Residence—Barbour County, Alabama. He also appears on a roll of POW's at Quintard Hospital CSA commanded by Surgeon S. V. D. Hill that were surrendered by Lt. General Richard Taylor at Citronelle, Alabama, on May 4, 1865, and paroled at Meridian, Mississippi, on May 10, 1865. His residence is shown here as Louisville, Barbour County, Alabama.

Lewis, Lafayette, Pvt. Co. D.
    Enlisted on July 30, 1864, in Macon County, Alabama, by Major Ready for the war. Appears on a company muster-in roll at Camp Watts near Notasulga, Alabama, for July 30, 1864. Age—17, eyes—dark, hair—dark, complexion—dark, 5 foot 10 inches, residence—Eufaula, Barbour County, Alabama. Drew clothing on August 7, 1864. Appears absent on a company muster roll for August 30 to October 30, 1864, with pay due from time of enlistment. Absent on sick furlough by Medical Examining Board since September 15, 1864. [furloughed]

60 days. Here he is shown as having enlisted on June 18, 1864, at Eufaula, Alabama, by Captain Zorn.

Lightfoot, Allen, Pvt. Co. G.
Enlisted on May 18, 1864, at Troy, Alabama, by Captain Wilkerson for the war. Appears on a company muster-in roll for September 7, 1864, at Blakeley, Alabama. Age—17, eyes—blue, hair—dark, complexion—fair, 5 foot 10 inches, residence—Pike County, Alabama. Drew clothing on September 11, 1864. Appears absent on a company muster roll for September and October 1864. Absent in hospital in Greenville, Alabama, since September 1, 1864. Captured at Blakeley, Alabama, on April 9, 1865. His name appears on a roll of POW's received at Ship Island, Mississippi, on April 15, 1865. Transferred from Ship Island to Vicksburg, Mississippi, on May 1, 1865. Appears on a roll of POW's of Cos. E and G, 63rd Alabama Infantry commanded by Captain A. V. Lee that were surrendered by Lt. General Richard Taylor at Citronelle, Alabama, on May 4, 1865, and paroled at Meridian, Mississippi, on May 13, 1865. Residence—Pike County, Alabama.

Lightfoot, James H., Pvt. Co. G.
Enlisted on May 18, 1864, at Troy, Alabama, by Captain Wilkerson for the war. Appears on a company muster-in roll for September 7, 1864, at Blakeley, Alabama. Age—16, eyes—grey, hair—dark, complexion—fair, 5 foot 8 inches, residence—Pike County, Alabama. Drew clothing on September 11, 1864. Appears present on a company muster roll for September and October 1864. Captured at Blakeley, Alabama, on April 9, 1865. Appears on a roll of POW's received at Ship Island, Mississippi, on April 15, 1865. Transferred from Ship Island to Vicksburg, Mississippi, on May 1, 1865. Appears on a roll of POW's of Cos. E and G, 63rd Alabama Infantry commanded by Captain A. V. Lee that were surrendered by Lt. General Richard Taylor at Citronelle, Alabama, on May 4, 1865, and paroled at Meridian, Mississippi, on May 13, 1865. His residence is shown as Pike County, Alabama.

Lindsey, John P., Pvt. Co. G.
Enlisted on May 9, 1864, at Troy, Alabama, by Captain Wilkerson for the war. Appears on a company muster roll for September 7, 1864. Age—16, eyes—grey, hair—light, complexion—florid, 5 foot 5 inches, residence—Pike County, Alabama. Drew clothing on September 11, 1864. Appears absent on a company muster roll for September and October 1864. Absent in hospital in Mobile, Alabama, since September 30, 1864. He is reported to have died in Mobile, Alabama, on October 28, 1864. Left $33.

Linley, John, Pvt. Co. I.
Enlisted on May 18, 1864, at Wedowee, Alabama, by Captain Robinson for the war. Appears absent on a company muster roll for September and October 1864. Absent without leave from September 18, 1864.

Kipp, J. A., Pvt. Co. K.
Enlisted on August 12, 1864, at Carrolton, Alabama, by Lieutenant Robinson for the war. Appears present on a company muster roll for September and October 1864. Appears on a register of paroles given at Columbus, Mississippi, on May 23, 1865.

Lipscomb, Pvt. Co. I.
Enlisted on May 18, 1864, at Wedowee, Alabama, by Captain Robinson for the war. Appears absent on a company muster roll for September and October 1864. Absent without leave from September 18, 1864.

Lisenby, Anthony L., Pvt. Co. C.
  Enlisted on June 1, 1864, at Russell County, Alabama, by Lieutenant Carnes for the war. Age—17, eyes—grey, hair—light, complexion—fair, 5 foot 9 ¼ inches, residence—Columbus, Georgia. Appears on a company muster-in roll for June 24, 1864, at Camp Watts near Notasulga, Alabama. Appears as deserted on a company muster roll for September and October 1864. Deserted on about September 20, 1864, at Blakeley, Alabama. Captured at Blakeley, Alabama, on April 9, 1865. Appears on a roll of POW's received at Ship Island, Mississippi, on April 15, 1865. Transferred from Ship Island to Vicksburg, Mississippi, on May 1, 1865. Appears on a roll of POW's of Cos. C and H, 63rd Alabama Infantry commanded by Captain C. W. Martin that were surrendered by Lt. General Richard Taylor at Citronelle, Alabama, on May 4, 1865, and paroled at Meridian, Mississippi, on May 11, 1865. Residence—Russell County, Alabama.

Lister, F. M., Pvt. Co. E.
  Enlisted on March 4, 1864, at Clayton, Alabama, by Captain A. V. Lee for the war. Drew clothing on September 11, 1864. Appears present on a company muster roll for September and October 1864. Age—17, eyes—dark, hair—dark, complexion—dark. Captured at Blakeley, Alabama, on April 9, 1865. Appears on a roll of POW's received at Ship Island, Mississippi, on April 15, 1865. Transferred from Ship Island to Vicksburg, Mississippi, on May 1, 1865. Appears on a roll of POW's of Cos. E and G, 63rd Alabama Infantry commanded by Captain A. V. Lee that were surrendered by Lt. General Richard Taylor at Citronelle, Alabama, on May 4, 1865, and paroled at Meridian, Mississippi, on May 13, 1865. Residence—Barbour County, Alabama.

Lock, Marion L., Pvt. Co. C.
  Enlisted on May 14, 1864, at Russell County, Alabama, by Lieutenant Carnes for the war. Appears on a company muster in roll for June 24, 1864, at Camp Watts near Notasulga, Alabama. Age—17, eyes—blue, hair—light, complexion—fair, 5 foot 8 inches, residence—Society Hill, Russell County, Alabama. Drew clothing on August 6, 1864. Signed by his mark. Appears absent on a company muster roll for September and October 1864. Absent in hospital at Mobile, Alabama, since October 18, 1864.

Lockheart, J. T., Sergeant Co. F.
  Enlisted as 3rd Sergeant on March 9, 1864, at Greenville, Alabama, by Captain Brown for the war. Appears on a company muster-in roll for July 25, 1864, at Georgiana, Alabama. Age—17, eyes—blue, hair—light, complexion—fair, 5 foot 9 inches, residence—Butler County, Alabama. Drew clothing on September 11, 1864. Appears as having been discharged on October 18, 1864, on a company muster roll for August 31 to October 31, 1864, and having never been paid.

Loffin, Pvt. Co. I.
  Enlisted on May 18, 1864, at Wedowee, Alabama, by Captain Robinson for the war. Appears absent on a company muster roll for September and October 1864. Absent without leave from September 18, 1864.

Loftin, Thomas G., Pvt. Co. B.
  Enlisted on August 15, 1864, at Pollard, Alabama, by Lieutenant Townsend for the war. Drew clothing on September 11, 1864. Signed by his mark. Admitted to Ross Hospital, Mobile, Alabama, on September 20, 1864, with pneumonia. Furloughed for 30 days on October 6, 1864. Appears absent on a company muster roll for September and October 1864, with pay due from time of enlistment. Absent sick since October 6, 1864. Captured at Blakeley, Alabama, on April 9, 1865. Appears on a roll of POW's received at Ship Island, Mississippi, on April 15, 1865. Transferred from Ship Island to Vicksburg,

Mississippi, on May 1, 1865. Appears on a roll of POW's of Company B, 63rd Alabama Infantry commanded by 1st Lieutenant Thomas J. Calhoun that were surrendered by Lt. General Richard Taylor at Citronelle, Alabama, on May 4, 1865, and paroled at Meridian, Mississippi, on May 11, 1865. Residence—Dale County, Alabama.

Logan, D., Pvt. Co. D.
Appears on a roll of POW's of Company D, 63rd Alabama Volunteers CSA commanded by Captain Robert H. Pearson that were surrendered by Lt. General Richard Taylor at Citronelle, Alabama, on May 4, 1865, and paroled at Meridian, Mississippi, on May 13, 1865. Residence—Greene County, Alabama.

Logan, S., Pvt. Co. H.
Enlisted on March 15, 1864, at Montevallo, Alabama, by Lieutenant Johnston for the war. Appears present on a company muster roll for September and October 1864. Age—17, eyes—blue, hair—light, complexion—fair. Captured at Blakeley, Alabama, on April 9, 1865. His name appears on a list of POW's in camp near Spanish Fort, Alabama, that require hospital treatment. The list came from headquarters of 23rd Iowa Infantry Volunteers on April 12, 1864. He is reported to suffer from dysentery. Appears on a roll of POW's received at Ship Island, Mississippi, on April 15, 1865. Transferred from Ship Island to Vicksburg, Mississippi, on May 1, 1865. Appears on a roll of POW's of Cos. C and H, 63rd Alabama Infantry commanded by Captain C. W. Martin that were surrendered by Lt. General Richard Taylor at Citronelle, Alabama, on May 4, 1865, and paroled at Meridian, Mississippi, on May 11, 1865. Residence—Bibb County, Alabama.

Looter, Crawford J., Pvt. Co. B.
Enlisted on August 22, 1864, at Blakeley, Alabama, by Lieutenant Townsend for the war. Drew clothing on September 11, 1864. Signed by his mark. Appears absent on a company Muster roll for September and October 1864, with pay due from time of enlistment. This muster roll reports him absent sick since October 14, 1864.

Lord, F. B., Pvt. Co. K.
Enlisted on September 2, 1864, at Talladega, Alabama, by Captain Ravases for the war. Appears absent on a company muster roll for September and October 1864. Absent detailed to do government work on September 23, 1864, by General Withers.

Louis, John J., Pvt. Co. H.
Enlisted on August 9, 1864, at Mobile, Alabama, by Lieutenant Johnston for the war. Age—17, eyes—dark, hair—dark, complexion—fair. Drew clothing on September 11, 1864. Appears absent on a company muster roll for September and October 1864. Absent sick at hospital in Mobile, Alabama, since October 30. Captured at Blakeley, Alabama, on April 9, 1865. Appears on a roll of POW's received at Ship Island, Mississippi, on April 15, 1865. Transferred from Ship Island to Vicksburg, Mississippi, on May 1, 1865. Appears on a roll of POW's of Cos. C and H, 63rd Alabama Infantry commanded by Captain C. W. Martin that were surrendered by Lt. General Richard Taylor at Citronelle, Alabama, on May 4, 1865, and paroled at Meridian, Mississippi, on May 11, 1865. Residence—Clarke County, Alabama.

Lovern, W. W., Pvt. Co. I.
Enlisted on May 18, 1864, at Wedowee, Alabama, by Captain Robinson for the war. Appears absent on a company muster roll for September and October 1864. Absent without leave since September 18, 1864.

Lowe, James, Pvt. Co. K.
Enlisted on September 10, 1864, at Perry County, Alabama, by Captain Powers for war. Appears present on a company muster roll for September and October 1864. Signed with his mark a parole at headquarters of the 16th US Army Corps at Montgomery, Alabama, on May 17. His parole is in his file. "I James Lowe Pvt. Co. "K" 2nd Ala Reserves A PRISONER OF WAR DO SOLEMNLY SWEAR, that I will not serve in any Army of the Confederate States of America, or perform any Garrison or Constabulary duty of said Confederate States of America, until duly and properly exchanged. This Parole is accepted of my own free will and accord, knowing that the punishment for violating the same will be to me death".

Lowe, J. E., Pvt. Co. K.
Enlisted on October 7, 1864, at Rockford, Alabama, by Captain Hancock for the war. Appears present on a company muster roll for September and October 1864. Admitted to Ross Hospital, Mobile, Alabama, on November 5, 1864, with rubeola. Returned to duty on November 22.

Luckey, G. A., Pvt. Co. F.
Enlisted on May 30, 1864, at Montgomery, Alabama, by Captain Jackson for the war. Appears absent sick on a company muster-in roll for July 25, 1864, at Georgiana, Alabama. Age—17, eyes—blue, hair—light, complexion—fair, 5 foot 7 inches, residence—Lowndes County, Alabama. Appears present on a company muster roll for August 31 to October 31, 1864, with pay due from time of enlistment.

Mabry, William K., Pvt. Co. D.
He was enlisted on July 4, 1864, at Russell County, Alabama, by Lieutenant Shelby for the war. Appears on a company muster-in roll for July 30, 1864, at Camp Watts near Notasulga, Alabama. Age—17, eyes—grey, hair—dark, complexion—dark, 5 foot 9 ½ inches. His residence is shown as Opelika, Russell County, Alabama.

Mackey, Edwin C., Pvt. Co. A.
Enlisted on March 29, 1864, at Coosa County, Alabama, by Captain Echols for the war. Drew clothing in 2nd quarter and August 12, 1864. Appears absent on a company muster roll for September and October 1864, with pay due from time of enlistment. This roll reports him absent in hospital at Mobile, Alabama, since October 10, 1864.

Maddox, B. S., Pvt. Co. I.
Enlisted on May 18, 1864, at Wedowee, Alabama, by Captain Robinson for the war. Appears present on a company muster roll for September and October 1864.

Maddox, Thomas, Pvt. Co. C.
Appears on a list of Confederate POW's paroled by the 16th US Army Corps on June 5, 1864. He signed a parole by his mark on June 5, 1864, at headquarters of the 16th US Army Corps at Montgomery, Alabama. Hair—light, eyes—blue, complexion—fair, 5 foot 9 inches. His parole is in his file.

Malloy, A. M., Pvt. Co. E.
Enlisted on July 30, 1864, at Montgomery, Alabama, by Captain A. V. Lee for the war. Age—17, eyes—dark, hair—dark, complexion—dark. Drew clothing on September 11, 1864. Appears present on a company muster roll for September and October 1864. Appears on a roll of POW's of Cos. E and G, 63rd Alabama Infantry commanded by Captain A. V. Lee that were surrendered by Lt.

General Richard Taylor at Citronelle, Alabama, on May 4, 1865, and paroled at Meridian, Mississippi, on May 13, 1865. His residence is shown as Covington County, Alabama.

Malloy, E. J., Pvt. Co. E.
Enlisted on June 1, 1864, at Clayton, Alabama, by Captain A. V. Lee for the war. Drew clothing on September 11, 1864. Signed by his mark. Appears present on a company muster roll for September and October 1864. Age—17, eyes—dark, hair—dark, complexion—dark. Admitted to Ross Hospital, Mobile, Alabama, on November 5, 1864, with diarrhoea acuta. Sent to General Hospital Nidelet on November 30, 1864. Captured at Blakeley, Alabama, on April 9, 1865. Appears on a roll of POW's received at Ship Island, Mississippi, on April 15, 1865. Transferred from Ship Island to Vicksburg, Mississippi, on May 1, 1865. Appears on a roll of POW's of Cos. E and G, 63rd Alabama Infantry commanded by Captain A. V. Lee that were surrendered by Lt. General Richard Taylor at Citronelle, Alabama, on May 4, 1865, and paroled at Meridian, Mississippi, on May 13, 1865. Residence—Coffee County, Alabama.

Malloy, J., Pvt. Co. E.
Enlisted on March 10, 1864, at Clayton, Alabama, by Captain A. V. Lee for the war. Age—17, eyes—dark, hair—dark, complexion—dark. Drew clothing on September 11, 1864. Admitted to Ross Hospital, Mobile, Alabama, on September 12, 1864, with febris remittens. Returned to duty on September 21, 1864. Appears on a company muster roll for September and October 1864, as having been discharged on September 24, 1864, to be a Cadet at the University of Alabama.

Malloy, W. B., Pvt. Co. F/E.
Enlisted in Company F on July 20, 1864, at Montgomery, Alabama, by Captain A. V. Lee for the war. Here after he is shown in Company E. Drew clothing on September 11, 1864. Appears present on a company muster roll for September and October 1864. Age—17, eyes—dark, hair—dark, complexion—dark. Admitted to 1st Mississippi CSA Hospital, Jackson, Mississippi, on March 3, 1865, with anaemia. Returned to duty on March 3. Appears on a register of wounded Confederate POW's at City Hospital, Mobile, Alabama. Appears on a roll of POW's remaining in hospital at Mobile and belonging to the CSA Army commanded by Assistant Surgeon Charles O. Helwigh captured at Mobile that were surrendered by Lt. General Richard Taylor at Citronelle, Alabama, on May 4, 1865, and paroled at Mobile on May 11, 1865. Residence—Covington County, Alabama.

Mane, S., Pvt. Co. D.
Error Card filed as S. Name 3rd Alabama Reserves. Index card withdrawn.

Manley, Pvt. Co. I.
Enlisted on May 18, 1864, at Wedowee, Alabama, by Captain Robinson for the war. Appears absent on a company muster roll for September and October 1864. Absent with leave since September 18, 1864.

Manor, J. D., Pvt. Co. E.
Enlisted on August 8,m 1864, at Pollard, Alabama, by Captain A. V. Lee for the war. Age—17, eyes—blue, hair—light, complexion—fair. Drew clothing on September 11, 1864. Appears present on a company muster roll for September and October 1864. Captured at Blakeley, Alabama, on April 9, 1865. Appears on a roll of POW's received at Ship Island, Mississippi, on April 15, 1865. Transferred from Ship Island to Vicksburg, Mississippi, on May 1, 1865. Appears on a roll of POW's of Cos. E and G, 63rd Alabama Infantry commanded by Captain A. V. Lee that were surrendered by Lt. General Richard Taylor at

Citronelle, Alabama, on May 4, 1865, and paroled at Meridian, Mississippi, on May 13, 1865. Residence—Henry County, Alabama.

Martin, Alexander L., Corporal Co. E.
Enlisted on March 13, 1864, at Clayton, Alabama, by Captain A. V. Lee for the war. Age—17, eyes—dark, hair—dark, complexion—dark. Drew clothing on September 11, 1864. Appears present on a company muster roll for September and October 1864. Hospital attendant captured in hospital at Fort Blakeley, Alabama, on April 9, 1865, and paroled to accompany the sick. Signed a hand written Parole of Honor on April 12, 1865, at Blakeley agreeing not to attempt escape and to accompany the wounded men in their charge to Vicksburg. This parole is in his file. Appears on a list of medical officers, steward and nurses belonging to the CSA that were sent to New Orleans, Louisiana, in charge of wounded prisoners from Blakeley on April 13, 1865. Admitted to USA Hospital Steamer D. A. January on April 17, 1865, as a hospital attendant. Transferred to [Hospital] Seamer Elanora Carrell at New Orleans on April 24, 1865. Appears on a roll of POW's at USA General Hospital No. 3 (colored), Vicksburg, Mississippi. Transferred to USA General Hospital No. 2, Vicksburg, on May 4, 1865, (nurse). Age—17. Returned to duty from G H No. 2 on May 8, 1865.

Martin, Charles, W., 1st Lieutenant/Captain Co. C.
Enlisted on June 22, 1864, at Macon County, Alabama, by Major Ready for the war. Age—17, eyes—hazel, hair—dark, complexion—fair, 5 foot 8 ½ inches, residence, Tuskegee, Macon County, Alabama. Elected as 1st Lieutenant on June 20, 1864, promoted on November 10, 1864. Appears on a company muster-in roll for June 24, 1864, at Camp Watts near Notasulga, Alabama. Appears present on a company muster roll for September and October 1864, with pay due from time of enlistment. Here he is shown as Captain of Company C. Captured at Blakeley, Alabama, on April 9, 1865. Confined for one day at Spanish Fort, Alabama, by 2nd Division of 16th US Army Corps. Appears on a roll of POW's received at Ship Island, Mississippi, on April 16, 1865. Transferred from Ship Island to Vicksburg, Mississippi, on April 28, 1865. Appears on a roll of POW's from Ship Island confined at New Orleans, Louisiana, on April 30, 1865. Exchanged on May 1, 1865. Signed a Parole of Honor at Meridian, Mississippi, on May 11, 1865. His parole and his requisition are in his file.

Martin, John, Pvt. Co. B
Enlisted on March 23, 1864, at Montgomery County, Alabama, by Captain Zimmerman for the war. Appears on a muster-in roll for March 23, 1864, at Montgomery, Alabama. Age—17. Drew clothing on July 8, August 12 and September 11, 1864. Signed by his mark. Appears absent on a company muster roll for September and October 1864, with pay due from time of enlistment. Absent sick since October 4, 1864.

Martin, John, T., Pvt./Corporal Co. D.
Enlisted on July 30, 1864, at Macon County, Alabama, by Major Ready for the war. Age—17, eyes—dark, hair—dark, complexion—dark, 5 foot 6 inches, residence—Clayton, Barbour County, Alabama. Appears on a company muster-in roll for July 30, 1864, at Camp Watts near Notasulga, Alabama. Appears present on a company muster roll for August 30 to October 30, 1864, with pay due from time of enlistment. Here he is shown as having enlisted on July 15, 1864, at Clayton, Alabama, by Captain Zorn. Hereafter he is shown with rank of Corporal. Captured and wounded in the side and hips at Blakeley, Alabama, on April 9, 1865. Appears on a list of POW's in the hospital of the 1st Division, 13th US Army Corps, at the battle of Blakeley Fort, Alabama. Admitted to St. Louis USA General Hospital, New Orleans, Louisiana, on April 15, 1865, with gunshot wound of left side. Transferred to (Marine) General Hospital on May

16, 1865. Confined at New Orleans, on May 1, 1865. Paroled and released on May 16, 1865, at St. Louis Hospital, New Orleans.

Martin, M. M., Pvt. Co. D.
Enlisted on August 8, 1864, at Newton, Alabama, by Lieutenant White for the war. Drew clothing on September 12, 1864. Appears absent on a company muster roll for August 30 to September 30, 1864, with pay due from time of enlistment. Absent sick at Mobile Hospital since October 28. Captured at Blakeley, Alabama, on April 9, 1865. Appears on a roll of POW's received at Ship Island, Mississippi, on April 15, 1865. Transferred from Ship Island to Vicksburg, Mississippi, on May 1, 1865. Appears on a roll of POW's of Company D, 63rd Alabama Volunteers CSA commanded by Captain Robert H. Pearson that were surrendered by Lt. General Richard Taylor at Citronelle, Alabama, on May 4, 1865, and paroled at Meridian, Mississippi, on May 13, 1865. Residence—Dale County, Alabama.

Mason, Charles, Co. B.
Enlisted on July 17, 1864, at Montgomery, Alabama, by Lieutenant Calhoun for the war. Appears present on a company muster roll for September and October 1864, with pay due from time of enlistment.

Mason, J. C., Pvt./Corporal Co. F.
Enlisted on March 9, 1864, at Greenville, Alabama, by Captain Brown for the war. Age—17, eyes—blue, hair—dark, complexion—dark, 5 foot 8 inches, residence—Butler County, Alabama. Appears on a company muster-in roll for July 25, 1864, at Georgiana, Alabama. Appears present on a company muster roll for September and October 1864, with pay due from time of enlistment. Promoted to Corporal on October 15, 1864. Captured at Blakeley, Alabama, on April 9, 1865. Appears on a roll of POW's received at Ship Island, Mississippi, on April 15, 1865. Transferred from Ship Island to Vicksburg, Mississippi, on May 1, 1865. Appears on a roll of POW's of Company F, 63rd Alabama Infantry commanded by Captain R. T. Simpson that were surrendered by Lt. General Richard Taylor at Citronelle, Alabama, on May 4, 1865, and paroled at Meridian, Mississippi, on May 11, 1865. Residence—Butler County, Alabama.

Massey, J. B., Pvt. Co. E.
Enlisted on March 18, 1864, at Clayton, Alabama, by Captain A. V. Lee for the war. Age—17, eyes—blue, hair—light, complexion—fair. Appears on a hospital muster roll for July and August 1864, as a patient at General Hospital, Marion, Alabama. Here he is shown as having enlisted on July 1, 1864, at Clayton, Alabama. Appears absent on a company muster roll for September and October 1864. Absent in hospital since August 18, 1864. He is show on five receipt rolls for pay as a courier for the Medical Purveyor's Office at Montgomery. Paid $78 on December 2, 1864, for 13 days service in November 1864. Paid $126 for 21 days service in December 1864. Paid $120 for 20 days service January 186? [5?]. Paid $120 for 20 days service only while traveling with hospital and medical supplies February 186? [5?]. Appears on a roll of POW's of Cos. E and G, 63rd Alabama Infantry commanded by Captain A. V. Lee that were surrendered by Lt. General Richard Taylor at Citronelle, Alabama, on May 4, 1865, and paroled at Meridian, Mississippi, on May 13, 1865. Residence—Barbour County, Alabama.

Masters, J. B., Pvt. Co. K.
Enlisted on October 4, 1864, at Perry County, Alabama, by Captain Powers. for the war. He appears present on a company muster roll for September and October 1864.

Mates, T. W., Pvt. Co. I.
Enlisted on May 18, 1864, at Wedowee, Alabama, by Captain Robinson for the war. Appears absent on a company muster roll for September and October 1864. Absent without leave since September 18, 1864.

Matherson, W. M., Pvt. Co. F.
Enlisted on May 30, 1864, at Montgomery, Alabama, by Captain Jackson, for the war. Appears absent without leave on a company muster-in roll for July 25, 1864, at Georgiana, Alabama. Age—17, eyes—dark, hair—dark, complexion—dark, 5 foot 6 inches, residence—Alabama.

Mathis, J. F., Sergeant Co. K.
Enlisted on August 25, 1864, at Tuscaloosa, Alabama, by Captain Slaughter for the war. Appears present on a company muster roll for September and October 1864. Reduced to 3rd Sergeant on October 24.

May, F. T., Pvt. Co. K.
Enlisted on August 31, 1864, at Greene County, Alabama, by Lieutenant Jones for the war. Appears absent on a company muster roll for September and October 1864. Absent in hospital at Mobile, Alabama, since October 26. Captured at Blakeley, Alabama, on April 9, 1865. Appears on a roll of POW's received at Ship Island, Mississippi, on April 15, 1865. Transferred from Ship Island to Vicksburg, Mississippi, on May 1, 1865. Appears on a roll of POW's of Cos. I and K, 63rd Alabama Infantry commanded by Lieutenant W. A. Skinner that were surrendered by Lt. General Richard Taylor at Citronelle, Alabama, on May 4, 1865, and paroled at Meridian, Mississippi, on May 13, 1865. Residence—Greene County, Alabama.

May, J., Pvt. Co. E.
Enlisted on March 19, 1864, at Clayton, Alabama, by Captain A. V. Lee for the war. Age—17, eyes—dark, hair—dark, complexion—dark. Drew clothing on September 11, 1864. Appears absent on a company muster roll for September and October 1864. Absent in hospital since August 18, 1864.

May, M. H., Captain Co. K.
Enlisted on October 1, 1864, at Blakeley, Alabama, by Colonel Rice for the war. Elected Captain on October 1, 1864. Appears absent on a company muster roll for September and October 1864. Absent in hospital at Mobile, Alabama, since October 26, 1864. Appears on a roll of Confederate POW's captured at Tuscaloosa, Alabama, by 2nd regiment Illinois Cavalry on May 18, 1864.

McCane, John, Pvt. Co. E, **1st Alabama** Regiment
Admitted to Ocmulgee Hospital, Macon, Georgia, on July 7, 1864, with diarrhoea. Transferred on July 8, 1864. Residence—Dale County, Alabama. Enlisted on July 15, at Eufaula, Alabama. This record is incorrectly filed with John McLane of the 2nd Alabama.

McCane, George, Corporal/Sergeant Co. B.
Enrolled as 3rd Corporal on March 23, 1864, at Montgomery, Alabama, by Captain Zimmerman for the war. Appears on company muster-in roll for March 23, 1864. Age—17. Drew clothing on July 8, 1864. Appears as 4th Sergeant and present on a company muster roll for September and October 1864, with pay due from time of enlistment. Captured at Blakeley, Alabama, on April 9, 1865. Appears on a roll of POW's received at Ship Island, Mississippi, on April 15, 1865. Transferred from Ship Island to Vicksburg, Mississippi, on May 1, 1865. Appears on a roll of POW's of Company B, 63rd Alabama Infantry commanded by 1st Lieutenant Thomas J. Calhoun that were surrendered by Lt. General

Richard Taylor at Citronelle, Alabama, on May 4, 1865, and paroled at Meridian, Mississippi, on May 11, 1865. Residence—Coosa County, Alabama.

McCardley, Calvin M., Pvt. Co. A/C.
Enlisted on January 1, 1864, at Coosa County, Alabama, by Captain Echols for the war. Appears on a company muster-in roll for January 1, 1864, at Montgomery, Alabama. Age—16. Appears present on a company muster roll for January and February 1864, with pay due from time of enlistment. Drew clothing on September 11, 1864. Appears present on a company muster roll for September and October 1864. Here he is shown as having been last paid on February 29, 1864. Captured at Blakeley, Alabama, on April 9, 1865. Appears on a roll of POW's received at Ship Island, Mississippi, on April 15, 1865. Transferred from Ship Island to Vicksburg, Mississippi, on May 1, 1865. Appears on a roll of POW's of Company A, 63rd Alabama Infantry commanded by Lieutenant W. D. Kyle that were surrendered by Lt. General Richard Taylor at Citronelle, Alabama, on May 4, 1865, and paroled at Meridian, Mississippi, on May 13, 1865. Residence—Coosa County, Alabama.

McCarley, S. A., Pvt. Co. A.
Captured at Blakeley, Alabama, on April 9, 1865. Appears on a roll of POW's received at Ship Island, Mississippi, on April 15, 1865. Transferred from Ship Island to Vicksburg, Mississippi, on May 1, 1865. Appears on a roll of POW's of Company A, 63rd Alabama Infantry commanded by Lieutenant W. D. Kyle that were surrendered by Lt. General Richard Taylor at Citronelle, Alabama, on May 4, 1865, and paroled at Meridian, Mississippi, on May 13, 1865. Residence—Coosa County, Alabama.

McCarthy, D. A., Pvt. Co. I/A.
Captured at Blakeley, Alabama, on April 9, 1865. Here he is shown in Company I. Appears on a roll of POW's received at Ship Island, Mississippi, on April 15, 1865. Transferred from Ship Island to Vicksburg, Mississippi, on May 1, 1865. Appears on a roll of POW's of Company A, 63rd Alabama Infantry commanded by Lieutenant W. D. Kyle that were surrendered by Lt. General Richard Taylor at Citronelle, Alabama, on May 4, 1865, and paroled at Meridian, Mississippi, on May 13, 1865. Residence—Coosa County, Alabama.

McCarty, E. J., Pvt. Co. F.
Signed by his mark a parole at headquarters of the 16th US Army Corps at Montgomery, Alabama, on June 1, 1865. Hair—dark, eyes—grey, complexion—light, 5 foot 4 inches. His parole is in his file.

McCarty, J. D., Pvt. Co. F.
Enlisted on July 12, 1864, at Lowndes County, Alabama, by Captain Buell for the war. Age—17, eyes—hazel, hair—dark, complexion—sallow, 5 foot 5 inches, residence—Lowndes County, Alabama. Appears on a company muster-in roll for July 23, 1864, at Georgiana, Alabama. Drew clothing on September 11, 1864. Appears on a company muster roll for August 31 to October 31, 1864, with pay due from time of enlistment. Captured at Blakeley, Alabama, on April 9, 1865. Appears on a roll of POW's received at Ship Island, Mississippi, on April 15, 1865. Transferred from Ship Island to Vicksburg, Mississippi, on May 1, 1865. Appears on a roll of sick and wounded Confederate POW's at USA General Hospital No. 2, Vicksburg, Mississippi. Admitted to hospital from steamer on May 3, 1865, with acute diarrhoea. Returned to duty on May 8, 1865.

McCary, S. B., Pvt. Co. H.
Enlisted on March 15, 1864, at Randolph County, Alabama, by Lieutenant Johnson, for the war. Age—17, eyes—hazel, hair—light, complexion—dark. Appears

absent on a company muster roll for September and October 1864. Absent sick at hospital in Greenville, Alabama, since October 10, 1864. Drew clothing on September 11, 1864. Admitted to Ross Hospital, Mobile, Alabama, on October 10, 1864, with febris intermittens quot. Sent to General Hospital, Greenville, Alabama, on October 25, 1864. Captured at Blakeley, Alabama, on April 9, 1865. Appears on a roll of POW's received at Ship Island, Mississippi, on April 15, 1865. Transferred from Ship Island to Vicksburg, Mississippi, on May 1, 1865. Appears on a roll of POW's of Cos. C and H, 63rd Alabama Infantry commanded by Captain C. W. Martin that were surrendered by Lt. General Richard Taylor at Citronelle, Alabama, on May 4, 1865, and paroled at Meridian, Mississippi, on May 11, 1865. Residence—Bibb County, Alabama.

McCaul, Daniel S., Pvt. Co. D.
Enlisted on July 30, 1864, at Macon County, Alabama, by Major Ready for the war. Age—17, eyes—dark, hair—dark, complexion—dark, 5 foot 4 inches, residence—Louisville, Barbour County, Alabama. Appears on a company muster-in roll for July 30, 1864, at Camp Watts near Notasulga, Alabama. Appears present on a company muster roll for September and October 1864, with pay due from time of enlistment. Here he is shown as having enlisted on July 15, 1864, at Clayton, Alabama, by Captain Zorn.

McCaul, James S., Pvt. Co. D.
Enlisted on July 30, 1864, at Macon County, Alabama, by Major Ready for the war. Age—17, eyes—grey, hair—dark, complexion—dark, 5 foot 6 inches, residence—Clayton, Barbour County, Alabama. Appears on a company muster-in roll for July 30, 1864, at Camp Watts near Notasulga, Alabama.

McClendon, K., Pvt. Co. D/K.
Enlisted on August 23, 1864, at Blakeley by Lieutenant Pearson for the war. Drew clothing on September 11, 1864. Appears on a company D muster roll for August 30 to October 30, 1864, with pay due from time of enlistment. This entry was canceled. Transferred to Company K on September 28, 1864. Appears present on a Company K muster roll for September and October 1864. Discharged due to general prostration of general health on December 3, 1864, at Mobile, Alabama. Age—17, eyes—blue, complexion—sallow, hair—light, 4 foot 11 inches, a farmer by occupation. Born in Talfirr [Tallaferro?] County, Georgia. His discharge is in his file.

McCollars, Benjamin B., Pvt. Co. B/F.
Enlisted on May 30, 1864, at Montgomery, Alabama, by Captain Jackson for the war. Age—17, eyes—grey, hair—dark, complexion—fair, 5 foot 7 inches, residence—Coosa County, Alabama. Appears on a company muster roll for September and October 1864, with pay due from time of enlistment. Drew clothing on September 11, 1864. Signed by his mark. Captured at Blakeley, Alabama, on April 9, 1865. Appears on a roll of POW's received at Ship Island, Mississippi, on April 15, 1865. Transferred from Ship Island to Vicksburg, Mississippi, on May 1, 1865. Appears on a roll of POW's of Company B, 63rd Alabama Infantry commanded by 1st Lieutenant Thomas J. Calhoun that were surrendered by Lt. General Richard Taylor at Citronelle, Alabama, on May 4, 1865, and paroled at Meridian, Mississippi, on May 11, 1865. Residence—Coosa County, Alabama.

McCombs, W. J., Pvt. Co. H.
Enlisted on March 15, 1864, at Elyton, Alabama, by Lieutenant Killough for the war. Age—17, eyes—grey, hair—light, complexion—fair. Drew clothing on September 11, 1864. Appears absent on a company muster roll for September and October 1864. Absent sick at hospital in Mobile, Alabama, since September

22. Admitted to Ross Hospital, Mobile, Alabama, on September 22, 1864, with rubeola. Sent to General Hospital in Greenville, Alabama, on September 26, 1864.

McCormick, W. J., Pvt. Co. F.
Enlisted on October 10, 1864, at Greenville, Alabama, by Captain Elkins. Appears present on a company muster roll for September and October 1864, with pay due from time of enlistment. Captured at Blakeley, Alabama, on April 9, 1865. Appears on a roll of POW's received at Ship Island, Mississippi, on April 15, 1865. Transferred from Ship Island to Vicksburg, Mississippi, on May 1, 1865. Appears on a roll of POW's of Company F, 63rd Alabama Infantry commanded by Captain R. T. Simpson that were surrendered by Lt. General Richard Taylor at Citronelle, Alabama, on May 4, 1865, and paroled at Meridian, Mississippi, on May 11, 1865. Residence—Butler County, Alabama.

McCowan, J., Pvt. Co. K.
Enlisted on August 25, 1864, at Tallapoosa County, Alabama, by Lieutenant Walker for the war. Appears present on a company muster roll for September and October 1864. Captured at Blakeley, Alabama, on April 9, 1865. Appears on a roll of POW's received at Ship Island, Mississippi, on April 15, 1865. Transferred from Ship Island to Vicksburg, Mississippi, on May 1, 1865. Appears on a roll of POW's of Cos. I and K, 63rd Alabama Infantry commanded by Lieutenant W. A. Skinner that were surrendered by Lt. General Richard Taylor at Citronelle, Alabama, on May 4, 1865, and paroled at Meridian, Mississippi, on May 13, 1865. Residence—Tallapoosa County, Alabama.

McCraney, Murdock, Pvt. Co. D.
Enlisted on July 30, 1864, at Macon County, Alabama, by Major Ready for the war. Appears on a company muster-in roll for July 30, 1864, at Camp Watts near Notasulga, Alabama. Age—17, eyes—blue, hair—dark, complexion—fair, 5 foot 4 inches, residence—Clayton, Barbour County, Alabama. Drew clothing on August 7, 1864. Appears on a company muster roll for August 30 to October 30, 1864, with pay due from time of enlistment. Here it is noted that he died.

McCrulus, Co. I.
Enlisted on May 18, 1864, at Wedowee, Alabama, by Captain Robinson for the war. Appears absent on a company muster roll for September and October 1864. Absent without leave since September 18, 1864.

McDermond, P., Pvt. Co. H.
Admitted to Ross Hospital, Mobile, Alabama, on August 16, 1864, with dysenteria acuta. Returned to duty on August 29, 1864.

McDonald, B. H., Pvt. Co. I.
Enlisted on April 25, 1864, at Talladega, Alabama, by Captain Parks for the war. Appears absent on a company muster roll for September and October 1864. Absent on 30 day furlough from September 27, 1864. Captured at Blakeley, Alabama, on April 9, 1865. Appears on a roll of POW's received at Ship Island, Mississippi, on April 15, 1865. Transferred from Ship Island to Vicksburg, Mississippi, on May 1, 1865. Appears on a roll of POW's at Ship Island that died of dysentery at Ship Island, Mississippi on April 30, 1865. Buried in grave No. 151.

McElvy, Charlton C., Pvt. Co. C.
Enlisted on March 11, 1864, at Russell County, Alabama, by Lieutenant Carnes for the war. Age—17, eyes—hazel, hair—dark, complexion—fair, 5 foot 9 inches, residence—Columbus, Georgia. Appears on a company muster-in roll for June 24, 1864, at Camp Watts near Notasulga, Alabama. Drew clothing on August 6, 1864.

Appears absent on a company muster roll for September and October 1864. Absent in hospital in Mobile, Alabama, since October 18, 1864. Admitted to Ross Hospital at Mobile on November 8, 1864, with febris congestia. Died on November 16, 1864.

McElvy, Marion T., Pvt. Co. C.
Enlisted on May 7, 1864, at Tallapoosa County, Alabama, by Captain Brown for the war. Age—17, eyes—blue, hair—dark, complexion—fair, 5 foot 8 ¾ inches, residence—Tehopka, Tallapoosa County, Alabama. Appears on a company muster roll for June 24, 1864, at Camp Watts near Notasulga, Alabama. Appears present on a company muster roll for September and October 1864. Present in hospital in Mobile, Alabama, on November 9, 1864.

McGhee, J. A., Pvt. Co. F.
Enlisted on October 10, 1864, at Greenville, Alabama, by Captain Elkins for the war. Appears present on a company muster roll for September and October 1864, with pay due from time of enlistment. Appears on a roll of POW's captured and paroled by Brigadier General Lucas Commanding 3rd Brigade Cavalry at Greenville, Alabama, on April 26, 1865.

McGuinty, James A., 4th Sergeant Co. C.
Enlisted on May 11, 1864, at Chambers County, Alabama, by Captain Walker for the war. Age—17, eyes—blue, hair—light, complexion—fair, 5 foot 9 inches, residence—Cusseta, Chambers County, Alabama. Appears on a company muster-in roll for June 24, 1864, at Camp Watts near Notasulga, Alabama. Drew clothing on August 6, 1864. Appears absent on a company muster roll for September and October 1864, with pay due from time of enlistment. Absent in hospital in Mobile, Alabama, since October 18, 1864. Captured at Blakeley, Alabama, on April 9, 1865. Appears on a roll of POW's received at Ship Island, Mississippi, on April 15, 1865. Transferred from Ship Island to Vicksburg, Mississippi, on May 1, 1865. Appears on a roll of POW's of Cos. C and H, 63rd Alabama Infantry commanded by Captain C. W. Martin that were surrendered by Lt. General Richard Taylor at Citronelle, Alabama, on May 4, 1865, and paroled at Meridian, Mississippi, on May 11, 1865. Residence—Chambers County, Alabama.

McKay, Neil C. Pvt.
Enlisted as a Provost Guard in Captain John Echols Co. A. Drew clothing in 2nd quarter of 1864.

Mckinnon, William R., Pvt. Co. A.
Enlisted on July 16, 1864, at Tallapoosa County, Alabama, by Captain Echols for the war. Drew clothing on August 13 and September 11, 1864. Appears present on a company muster roll for September and October 1864, with pay due from time of enlistment.

McKissick, William, Pvt. Co. B.
Enlisted on March 23, 1864, at Montgomery County, Alabama, by Captain Zimmerman for the war. Appears on a company muster-in roll for March 23, 1864, at Montgomery, Alabama. Age—16. Drew clothing on July 8, 1864. Appears present on a company muster roll for September and October 1864, with pay due from time of enlistment. Captured at Blakeley, Alabama, on April 9, 1865. Appears on a roll of POW's received at Ship Island, Mississippi, on April 15, 1865. Transferred from Ship Island to Vicksburg, Mississippi, on May 1, 1865. Appears on a roll of POW's of Company B, 63rd Alabama Infantry commanded by 1st Lieutenant Thomas J. Calhoun that were surrendered by Lt. General Richard Taylor at Citronelle, Alabama, on May 4, 1865, and paroled at Meridian, Mississippi, on May 11, 1865. Residence—Coosa County, Alabama.

McLain, John, Pvt. Co. A.
Enlisted on January 1, 1864, at Tallapoosa County, Alabama, by Captain Echols for the war. Appears on a company muster-in roll for January 1, 1864, at Montgomery, Alabama. Appears present on a company muster roll for January and February 1864, with pay due from time of enlistment. Drew clothing in the 2nd quarter of 1864. Signed by his mark. Appears present on a company muster roll for September and October 1864. Here he is shown as having been last paid on February 29, 1864. * see John McCane of the 1st Alabama, included here in error in this regiment files.

McClure, Charles, Pvt. Co. C.
Enlisted on May 11, 1864, at Tallapoosa County, Alabama, by Captain Brown for the war. Age—17, eyes—blue, hair—dark, complexion—dark, 5 foot 5 inches, residence—Dudleyville, Tallapoosa County, Alabama. Appears on a company muster-in roll for June 24, 1865, at Camp Watts near Notasulga, Alabama. Appears absent on a company muster roll for September and October 1864. This roll reports him absent in hospital at Mobile, Alabama, since October 13, 1864. *See personal papers of James M. Alexander-Alabama, for information relative to this soldier.

McMath, W., Sergeant Co. H.
Enlisted as 5th Sergeant on August 7, 1864, at Selma, Alabama, by Lieutenant Killough for the war. Age—17, eyes—blue, hair—dark, complexion—fair. Appears absent on a company muster roll for September and October 1864. Absent sick at Hospital in Greenville, Alabama, since September 6. Captured at Blakeley, Alabama, on April 9, 1865. Appears on a roll of POW's received at Ship Island, Mississippi, on April 15, 1865. Transferred from Ship Island to Vicksburg, Mississippi, on May 1, 1865. Appears on a roll of POW's of Cos. C and H, 63rd Alabama Infantry commanded by Captain C. W. Martin that were surrendered by Lt. General Richard Taylor at Citronelle, Alabama, on May 4, 1865, and paroled at Meridian, Mississippi, on May 11, 1865. Residence—Jefferson County, Alabama.

McNair, Charles T., Pvt. Co. D.
Enlisted on July 30, 1864, at Macon County, Alabama, by Major Ready for the war. Age—17, eyes—dark, hair—dark, complexion—dark, 6 foot 0 inches, residence—Clayton, Barbour County, Alabama. Appears on a company muster-in roll for July 30, 1864, at Camp Watts near Notasulga, Alabama. Drew clothing on August 7, 1864. Appears present on a company muster roll for August 30 to October 30, 1864, with pay due from time of enlistment. Here he is shown as having enlisted on March 2, 1864, at Clayton by D. M. Seals. Captured at Blakeley, Alabama, on April 9, 1865. Appears on a roll of POW's received at Ship Island, Mississippi, on April 15, 1865. Transferred from Ship Island to Vicksburg, Mississippi, on May 1, 1865. Appears on a roll of POW's of Company D, 63rd Alabama Volunteers CSA commanded by Captain Robert H. Pearson that were surrendered by Lt. General Richard Taylor at Citronelle, Alabama, on May 4, 1865, and paroled at Meridian, Mississippi, on May 13, 1865. Residence—Barbour County, Alabama.

McNair, J., Pvt. Co. K.
Enlisted on August 5, 1864, at Perry County, Alabama, by Lieutenant Martin for the war. Appears present on a company muster roll for September and October 1864. Captured at Blakeley, Alabama, on April 9, 1865. Appears on a roll of POW's received at Ship Island, Mississippi, on April 15, 1865. Transferred from Ship Island to Vicksburg, Mississippi, on May 1, 1865. Appears on a roll of POW's of Cos. I and K, 63rd Alabama Infantry commanded by Lieutenant W. A. Skinner that were surrendered by Lt. General Richard Taylor at Citronelle,

Alabama, on May 4, 1865, and paroled at Meridian, Mississippi, on May 13, 1865. Residence—Shelby County, Alabama.

McRae, Christopher C., Pvt. Co. D.
Enlisted on July 30, 1864, at Macon County, Alabama, by Major Ready for the war. Age—17, eyes—blue, hair—light, complexion—fair, 5 foot 5 inches, residence—Clayton, Barbour County, Alabama. Appears on a company muster-in roll for July 30, 1864, at Camp Watts near Notasulga, Alabama. Appears present on a company muster roll for August 30 to October 30, 1864, with pay due from time of enlistment. Here he is shown as having enlisted on June 6, 1864, at Eufaula, Alabama, by Captain Zorn. Captured at Blakeley, Alabama, on April 9, 1865. Appears on a roll of POW's received at Ship Island, Mississippi, on April 15, 1865. Transferred from Ship Island to Vicksburg, Mississippi, on May 1, 1865. Appears on a roll of POW's of Company D, 63rd Alabama Volunteers CSA commanded by Captain Robert H. Pearson that were surrendered by Lt. General Richard Taylor at Citronelle, Alabama, on May 4, 1865, and paroled at Meridian, Mississippi, on May 13, 1865. Residence—Barbour County, Alabama.

McRae, Daniel A., Pvt. Co. A.
Enlisted on January 1, 1864, at Tallapoosa County, Alabama, by Captain John Echols for the war. Appears on a company muster-in roll for September and October 1864, at Montgomery, Alabama. Appears present on a company muster roll for January and February 1864, with pay due from time of enlistment. Drew clothing 2nd quarter, August 12 and September 11, 1864. Appears present on a company muster roll for September and October 1864. Here he is shown as having been last paid on February 29, 1864. Captured at Blakeley, Alabama, on April 9, 1865. Appears on a roll of POW's received at Ship Island, Mississippi, on April 15, 1865. Transferred from Ship Island to Vicksburg, Mississippi, on May 1, 1865. Appears on a roll of POW's of Company A, 63rd Alabama Infantry commanded by Lieutenant W. D. Kyle that were surrendered by Lt. General Richard Taylor at Citronelle, Alabama, on May 4, 1865, and paroled at Meridian, Mississippi, on May 13, 1865. Residence—Tallapoosa County, Alabama. There is an inquiry from Oklahoma City, Oklahoma, filed from 1915.

McRae, William, Pvt. Co. B.
Enlisted on April 14, 1864, at Montgomery County, Alabama, by Captain Zimmerman for the war. Age—16. Drew clothing on July 8, and September 11, 1864. Appears present on a company muster roll for September and October 1864, with pay due from time of enlistment. Admitted to Ross Hospital, Mobile, Alabama, on November 17, 1864, with febris intermittens tert. Returned to duty on November 29, 1864. Captured at Blakeley, Alabama, on April 9, 1865. Appears on a roll of POW's received at Ship Island, Mississippi, on April 15, 1865. Transferred from Ship Island to Vicksburg, Mississippi, on May 1, 1865. Appears on a roll of POW's of Company B, 63rd Alabama Infantry commanded by 1st Lieutenant Thomas J. Calhoun that were surrendered by Lt. General Richard Taylor at Citronelle, Alabama, on May 4, 1865, and paroled at Meridian, Mississippi, on May 11, 1865. Residence—Montgomery County, Alabama.

McRae, William N., Pvt. Co. D.
Enlisted on July 30, 1864, at Macon County, Alabama, by Major Ready for the war. Age—17, eyes—grey, hair—light, complexion—florid, 5 foot 7 inches, residence—Clayton, Barbour County, Alabama. Appears on a company muster-in roll for September and October 1864, at Camp Watts near Notasulga, Alabama. Drew clothing on August 7, 1864. Appears present on a company muster roll for August 30 to October 30, 1864, with pay due from time of enlistment. Here he is shown as having enlisted on March 2, 1864, at Clayton, Alabama, by D. M. Seals. Admitted to Ross Hospital, Mobile, Alabama, on November 5, 1864, with

febris intermittens tert. Furloughed for 30 days on November 24, 1864. Captured at Blakeley, Alabama, on April 9, 1865. Appears on a roll of POW's received at Ship Island, Mississippi, on April 15, 1865. Transferred from Ship Island to Vicksburg, Mississippi, on May 1, 1865. Appears on a roll of POW's of Company D, 63rd Alabama Volunteers CSA commanded by Captain Robert H. Pearson that were surrendered by Lt. General Richard Taylor at Citronelle, Alabama, on May 4, 1865, and paroled at Meridian, Mississippi, on May 13, 1865. His residence is shown as Barbour County, Alabama.

McRee, Mark C., Pvt. Co. A.
Enlisted on July 20, 1864, at Lowndes County, Alabama, by Captain Echols for the war. Appears absent on a company muster roll for September and October 1864, with pay due from time of enlistment. Absent sick in hospital at West Point, Georgia, since August 5, 1864. Captured at Blakeley, Alabama, on April 9, 1865. Appears on a roll of POW's received at Ship Island, Mississippi, on April 15, 1865. He was among those men transferred from Ship Island to Vicksburg, Mississippi, on May 1, 1865. Appears on a roll of POW's of Company A, 63rd Alabama Infantry commanded by Lieutenant W. D. Kyle that were surrendered by Lt. General Richard Taylor at Citronelle, Alabama, on May 4, 1865, and paroled at Meridian, Mississippi, on May 13, 1865. Residence—Lowndes County, Alabama.

McShan, F. M., Pvt. Co. K.
Enlisted on May 3, 1864, at Carrolton, Alabama, by Captain Hudgens for the war. He appears present on a company muster roll for September and October 1864.

McSwain, Eldridge T., Assistant Surgeon F&S
Enlisted on October 29, 1862. Born in North Carolina. His date of rank is also October 29, 1862. Paid $108 on April 16, 1863, for commutation of quarters at Gainesville, Georgia, from December 16, 1862, to April 16, 1863. Special Order No. 102 of February 7, 1863, at Headquarters of Camp of Instruction, No. 21, Camp Randolph, Decatur, Georgia, assigns him to the duty of examining conscripts in the 9th Congressional District [of Georgia?]. Appointed Assistant Surgeon, Confederate States Army on April 4, 1863, in South Carolina by the Surgeon General, approved by Secretary of War. Paid $97.50 on October 5, 1863, for commutation of quarters and fuel for August 1 to September 30, 1863, at Decatur, Georgia. Paid $135 on September 17, 1864, for commutation of quarters and fuel from May 4 to June 30, 1864, at Cartersville, Georgia. Reference card in his file for 3rd quarter 1864, see manuscript No. 7037, Andersonville, Georgia Drew two tents on July 23, 1864, at Andersonville being without quarters. He was assigned to duty with the regiment [63rd Alabama] by S. O. 338-IV by General Maury on December 3, 1864. Appears on a list of Surgeons and Hospital Stewards captured at Fort Blakeley, Alabama, on April 9, 1865. Admitted with diarrhoea to USA Hospital Steamer D. A. January on April 17, 1865, among wounded and paroled POW's. Transferred to USA Hospital Steamer Elanora Carrel at New Orleans, Louisiana, on April 24, 1865, in charge of sick and wounded. Admitted to No. 3 Colored USA General Hospital, Vicksburg, Mississippi, on April 28, 1865. Transferred to [General Hospital, Vicksburg] No. 2 on May 4, 1865. Appears on a register of sick and wounded POW's admitted to USA General Hospital No. 2, Vicksburg, on May 4, 1865. Age—30, Returned to duty on May 22, 1865. There are a considerable number of documents in his file including requisitions, assignments and payments for sundry expenses, including travel and postage.

McWhorter, Marion W., Pvt. Co. G.
Enlisted on May 16, 1864, at Troy, Alabama, by Captain Wilkerson for the war.

Age—17, eyes—dark, hair—dark, complexion—dark, 5 foot 4 inches. Appears on a company muster-in roll for September 7, 1864, at Blakeley, Alabama. Drew clothing on September 11, 1864. Appears absent on a company muster roll for September and October 1864. Absent furloughed for 60 days from hospital at Mobile from October 25.

Meadows, Daniel, P., Pvt. Co. C.
Enlisted on June 20, 1864, at Macon County, Alabama, by Major Ready for the war. Age—17, eyes—grey, hair—light, complexion—dark, 5 foot 7 ½ inches, residence—Salem, Russell County, Alabama. Drew clothing on August 6, 1864. Appears present on a company muster roll for September and October 1864. Captured at Blakeley, Alabama, on April 9, 1865. Appears on a roll of POW's received at Ship Island, Mississippi, on April 15, 1865. Transferred from Ship Island to Vicksburg, Mississippi, on May 1, 1865. Appears on a roll of POW's of Cos. C and H, 63rd Alabama Infantry commanded by Captain C. W. Martin that were surrendered by Lt. General Richard Taylor at Citronelle, Alabama, on May 4, 1865, and paroled at Meridian, Mississippi, on May 11, 1865. Residence—Salem, Alabama. He also appears on a roll of POW's of Quintard Hospital CSA commanded by Surgeon S. V. D. Hill that were surrendered by Lt. General Richard Taylor at Citronelle, Alabama, on May 4, 1865, and paroled at Meridian, Mississippi, on May 10, 1865.

Meadows, W. S., Pvt. Co. C.
POW captured at Blakeley, Alabama, on April 9, 1865. His name appears on a roll of POW's received at Ship Island, Mississippi, on April 15, 1865. He was among those men transferred from Ship Island to Vicksburg, Mississippi, on May 1, 1865.

Melton, James H., Pvt. Co. A.
Enlisted on Lowndes County, Alabama, by January 1, 1864, by Captain John Echols for the war. Age—16. Appears on a company muster-in roll for January 1, 1864. Appears present on a company muster roll for January and February 1864, with pay due from time of enlistment. Drew clothing in 2nd quarter of 1864. Appears on a company muster roll for September and October 1864. Here he is shown as having last been paid on February 29, 1864. Captured at Blakeley, Alabama, on April 9, 1865. Appears on a roll of POW's received at Ship Island, Mississippi, on April 15, 1865. Transferred from Ship Island to Vicksburg, Mississippi, on May 1, 1865. Appears on a roll of POW's of Company A, 63rd Alabama Infantry commanded by Lieutenant W. D. Kyle that were surrendered by Lt. General Richard Taylor at Citronelle, Alabama, on May 4, 1865, and paroled at Meridian, Mississippi, on May 13, 1865. Residence—Lowndes County, Alabama.

Merchant, J. A., Pvt. Co. F.
Enlisted on March 9, 1864, at Greenville, Alabama, by Captain Brown for the war. Age—17, eyes—grey, hair—dark, complexion—fair, residence—Covington, County, Alabama. Appears on a company muster-in roll for July 25, 1864, at Georgiana, Alabama. Appears on a company muster roll for August 31 to October 31, 1864, with pay due from time of enlistment. Admitted to Ross Hospital, Mobile, Alabama, on September 2, 1864, with Febris remittens, febris typhoides. Died on September 5, 1864, at Ross Hospital. Left $20 and sundries.

Merrell, B. W., Pvt. Co. I/G.
Enlisted on April 21, 1864, at Columbiana, Alabama, by Lieutenant Bulger for the war. Appears present on a company muster roll for September and October 1864. POW paroled at Talladega, Alabama, on May 26, 1865. Here he is shown as being in Company G.

Messer, Alex, Pvt. Co. E.
Captured at Blakeley, Alabama, on April 9, 1865. Appears on a roll of POW's received at Ship Island, Mississippi, on April 15, 1865. Transferred from Ship Island to Vicksburg, Mississippi, on May 1, 1865. Appears on a roll of POW's of Cos. E and G, 63rd Alabama Infantry commanded by Captain A. V. Lee that were surrendered by Lt. General Richard Taylor at Citronelle, Alabama, on May 4, 1865, and paroled at Meridian, Mississippi, on May 13, 1865. Residence—Barbour County, Alabama.

Middleton, W. E., Co. E.
Enlisted on July 25, 1864, at Montgomery, Alabama, by Captain A. V. Lee for the war. Age—17, eyes—dark, hair—dark, complexion—dark. Appears absent on a company muster roll for September and October 1864. Absent in hospital since August 17, 1864. Captured at Blakeley, Alabama, on April 9, 1865. Appears on a roll of POW's received at Ship Island, Mississippi, on April 15, 1865. Transferred from Ship Island to Vicksburg, Mississippi, on May 1, 1865. Appears on a roll of POW's of Cos. E and G, 63rd Alabama Infantry commanded by Captain A. V. Lee that were surrendered by Lt. General Richard Taylor at Citronelle, Alabama, on May 4, 1865, and paroled at Meridian, Mississippi, on May 13, 1865. Residence—Monroe County, Alabama.

Miller, A. J., Pvt. Co. E.
Enlisted on August 8, 1864, at Pollard, Alabama, by Captain A. V. Lee for the war. Age—17, eyes—blue, hair—light, complexion—fair. Drew clothing on September 11, 1864. Signed by his mark. Appears as deserted on a company muster roll for September and October 1864. Deserted on October 29, 1864.

Miller, J. W., Pvt. Co. I.
Enlisted on May 18, 1864, at Wedowee, Alabama, by Captain Robinson, for the war. Appears absent on a company muster roll for September and October 1864. Absent furloughed from September 27, 1864, for 30 days.

Miller, M. D. L., Pvt. Co. K.
Enlisted on October 5, 1864, at Rockford, Alabama, by Captain Hancock for the war. Appears present on a company muster roll for September and October 1864. Captured at Blakeley, Alabama, on April 9, 1865. Appears on a roll of POW's received at Ship Island, Mississippi, on April 15, 1865. Transferred from Ship Island to Vicksburg, Mississippi, on May 1, 1865. Appears on a roll of POW's of Cos. I and K, 63rd Alabama Infantry commanded by Lieutenant W. A. Skinner that were surrendered by Lt. General Richard Taylor at Citronelle, Alabama, on May 4, 1865, and paroled at Meridian, Mississippi, on May 13, 1865. Residence—Coosa County, Alabama.

Miller, Warren P., Pvt. Co. A.
Enrolled on January 1, 1864, 1864, at Tallapoosa County, Alabama, by Captain John Echols for the war. Appears on a company muster-in roll for January 1, 1864, at Montgomery, Alabama. Appears present on a company muster roll for January and February 1864, with pay due from time of enlistment. Appears present, sick in quarters, on a company muster roll for September and October 1864. Here he is shown as having been last paid on February 24, 1864. Drew clothing in 2nd quarter, August 12 and September 11, 1864. Captured at Blakeley, Alabama, on April 9, 1865. Appears on a roll of POW's received at Ship Island, Mississippi, on April 15, 1865. Transferred from Ship Island to Vicksburg, Mississippi, on May 1, 1865. Appears on a roll of POW's of divers companies and regiments (detached) commanded by Captain D. H. Todd that were surrendered by Lt. General Richard Taylor at Citronelle, Alabama, on May 4, 1865, and paroled at Meridian, Mississippi, on May 14, 1865.

Residence—Tallapoosa County, Alabama. POW admitted to USA General Hospital No. 2, Vicksburg, Mississippi, on May 3, 1865, with acute diarrhoea. Returned to duty on May 12, 1865. Age—18.

Milstead, W. H. C., Pvt. Co. H.
Enlisted on March 15, 1864, at Randolph County, Alabama, by Lieutenant Johnson for the war. Age—17, eyes—dark, hair—dark, complexion—fair. Drew clothing on September 11, 1864. Appears absent on a company muster roll for September and October 1864. Absent sick at hospital in Mobile, Alabama, since October 26. Captured at Blakeley, Alabama, on April 9, 1865. Appears on a roll of POW's received at Ship Island, Mississippi, on April 15, 1865. Transferred from Ship Island to Vicksburg, Mississippi, on May 1, 1865. Appears on a roll of POW's of Cos. C and H, 63rd Alabama Infantry commanded by Captain C. W. Martin that were surrendered by Lt. General Richard Taylor at Citronelle, Alabama, on May 4, 1865, and paroled at Meridian, Mississippi, on May 11, 1865. Residence—Bibb County, Alabama.

Mink, N. C., Pvt. Co. I.
Admitted to 1st Mississippi CSA Hospital, Jackson Mississippi, on November 10, 1864, with febris intermittens tert. Returned to duty on April 24, 1865. Appears on a roll of POW's paroled at Talladega, Alabama, on May 24, 1865. His file is included in the records of Pvt. U. Mink, Co. I, below.

Mink, U., Pvt. Co. I.
Enlisted on May 11, 1864, at Wedowee, Alabama, by Captain Robinson for the war. Appears absent on a muster roll for September and October 1864. Absent sick in Hospital Moore from October 15, 1864. See also Pvt. N. C. Mink, Co. I.

Missildine, J. C., Pvt. Co. E.
Enlisted on September 25, 1864, at Montgomery, Alabama, by Major Thompson for the war. Age—17, eyes—dark, hair—dark, complexion—dark. Appears absent on a company muster roll for September and October 1864. Absent in hospital since October 15, 1864. Admitted to Ross Hospital, Mobile, Alabama, on October 10, 1864. Discharged from service on November 6, 1864, due to chronic ascites. Age—17, 5 foot 1 inch, complexion—light, eyes—grey, hair—light. Born in Montgomery County, Alabama. A farmer by occupation. Stationed at Mobile, Alabama. His discharge is in his file.

Mitchell, Charles, Pvt. Co. K.
Enlisted on June 21, 1864, at Montgomery, Alabama, by Captain Zimmerman for the war. Appears absent on company muster roll for September and October 1864. Absent in Camp of Correction at Mobile, Alabama, since September 7, 1864. Drew clothing on July 8, 1864. Signed by his mark. Signed a parole by his mark "X" at the headquarters of the 16th US Army Corps, at Montgomery, Alabama, on May 15, 1864. Hair—dark, eyes—brown, complexion—fair, 6 foot 3 inches.

Mitchell, Hiram, Pvt. Co. D.
Enlisted on July 30, 1864, at Macon County, Alabama, by Major Ready for the war. Age—17, eyes—blue, hair—light, complexion—fair, 5 foot 5 inches, residence—Clayton, Barbour County, Alabama. Appears on a company muster-in roll for July 30, 1864, at Camp Watts near Notasulga, Alabama. Drew clothing August 7, 1864. Appears present on a company muster roll for August 30 to October 30, 1864, with pay due from time of enlistment. Here he is shown as having enlisted on June 28, 1864, at Clayton, Alabama, by Captain Zorn. Captured at Blakeley, Alabama, on April 9, 1865. Appears on a roll of POW's received at Ship Island, Mississippi, on April 15, 1865. Transferred from Ship

Island to Vicksburg, Mississippi, on May 1, 1865. Appears on a roll of POW's of Company D, 63rd Alabama Volunteers CSA commanded by Captain Robert H. Pearson that were surrendered by Lt. General Richard Taylor at Citronelle, Alabama, on May 4, 1865, and paroled at Meridian, Mississippi, on May 13, 1865. Residence—Barbour County, Alabama.

Mitchell, H. S., Pvt. Co. K.
Enlisted on September 2, 1864, at Bibb County, Alabama, by Captain Hudgens for the war. Appears present on a company muster roll for September and October 1864. Captured at Blakeley, Alabama, on April 9, 1865. Appears on a roll of POW's received at Ship Island, Mississippi, on April 15, 1865. Transferred from Ship Island to Vicksburg, Mississippi, on May 1, 1865. Appears on a roll of POW's of Cos. I and K, 63rd Alabama Infantry commanded by Lieutenant W. A. Skinner that were surrendered by Lt. General Richard Taylor at Citronelle, Alabama, on May 4, 1865, and paroled at Meridian, Mississippi, on May 13, 1865. Residence—Bibb County, Alabama.

Mitchell, James, Pvt. Co. B/K.
Enlisted on June 20, 1864, at Montgomery, Alabama, by Captain Zimmerman for the war. Appears on a company B muster roll for September and October 1864, with pay due from time of enlistment. Transferred per Special Order No. 15, on October 2, 1864.

Mixon, G. W., Pvt. Co. F.
Enlisted on August 10, 1864, at Georgiana, Alabama, by Captain Brown. Appears absent on a company muster roll for August 31 to October 31, 1864, with pay due from time of enlistment. Absent in hospital at Mobile, Alabama, since October 28, 1864. Died at a general hospital in Mobile on November 10, 1864. His effects were taken over by his brother without inventory. Born—Butler County, Alabama, age—17, 4 foot 8 inches, complexion—sallow, eyes—dark, hair—dark. Never paid. There is a certificate in his file.

Mizell, George, Pvt. Co. B.
Enlisted on August 15, 1864, at Pollard, Alabama, by Lieutenant Townsend for the war. He appears present on a company muster roll for September and October 1864, with pay due from time of enlistment. Drew clothing on September 11, 1864. Signed by his mark. G. W. Mizell, Pvt. Company D, 2nd Regiment Alabama Reserves appears on a register of effects of deceased soldiers. No. 7786.

Manchew, J., Pvt. Co. E.
Captured at Blakeley, Alabama, on April 9, 1865. Appears on a roll of POW's received at Ship Island, Mississippi, on April 15, 1865. Transferred from Ship Island to Vicksburg, Mississippi, on May 1, 1865. Appears on a roll of POW's of Cos. E and G, 63rd Alabama Infantry commanded by Captain A. V. Lee that were surrendered by Lt. General Richard Taylor at Citronelle, Alabama, on May 4, 1865, and paroled at Meridian, Mississippi, on May 13, 1865. Residence—Barbour County, Alabama.

Monday, J. F., Pvt. Co. K.
Enlisted on May 24, 1864, at Carrolton, Alabama, by Captain Hudgens for the war. Appears present on a company muster roll for September and October 1864.

Money, James, Pvt. Co. E.
Enlisted on August 8, 1864, at Pollard, Alabama, by Captain A. V. Lee for the war. Age—17, eyes—blue, hair—light, complexion—fair. Appears absent on a

company muster roll for September and October 1864. Absent in hospital since September 8, 1864. Drew clothing on September 11, 1864.

Moon, Martin E., Pvt. Co. B/K.
Enrolled on March 23, 1864, at Montgomery, County, Alabama, by Captain Zimmerman for the war. His name appears on a company muster-in roll for March 23, 1864, at Montgomery. Drew clothing on August 8, 1864. Appears on a Company B muster roll for September and October 1864. Transferred as per Special Order No. 15 on October 2, 1864. Appears absent on a company K muster roll for September and October 1864. Absent sick without leave since October 1.

Moor, James, Pvt. Co. A.
Captured at Blakeley, Alabama, on April 9, 1865. Appears on a roll of POW's received at Ship Island, Mississippi, on April 15, 1865. Transferred from Ship Island to Vicksburg, Mississippi, on May 1, 1865. Appears on a roll of POW's of Company A, 63rd Alabama Infantry commanded by Lieutenant W. D. Kyle that were surrendered by Lt. General Richard Taylor at Citronelle, Alabama, on May 4, 1865, and paroled at Meridian, Mississippi, on May 13, 1865. Residence—Macon County, Alabama.

Moore, Anthony, Pvt. Co. F.
He was enlisted on August 4, 1864, at Georgiana, Alabama, by Captain Brown, for the war. Appears present sick on a company muster roll for August 31 to October 31, 1864, with pay due from the time of enlistment. He was reported to have been paroled on June 19, 1865, at the headquarters of 16th US Army Corps in Montgomery, Alabama. Hair—light, eyes—blue, complexion—fair, 5 foot. Signed his parole by mark "X."

Moore, W., Pvt. Co. E.
Enlisted on September 5, 1864, at Montgomery, Alabama, by Major Thompson for the war. Age—17, eyes—dark, hair—dark, complexion—dark. Appears absent on a company muster roll for September and October 1864. Absent detached in Selma Iron Works.

Moore, William E., Pvt. Co. A.
Enlisted on March 26, 1864, at Macon County, Alabama, by Captain Echols for the war. Drew clothing in 2nd quarter of 1864. Appears present on a company muster roll for September and October 1864, with pay due from time of enlistment. Admitted to Ross Hospital, Mobile, Alabama, on November 11, 1864. Sent to General Hospital Nidelet on November 30, 1864. Paroled on May 22, 1865, at headquarters of the 16th US Army Corps in Montgomery, Alabama. Hair—dark, eyes—blue, complexion—fair, 5 foot 6 inches.

Morefield, Thomas W., Pvt./Sergeant Co. B.
Enlisted on March 23, 1864, at Montgomery County, Alabama. Appears on a company muster-in roll for March 23, 1864, at Montgomery, Alabama. Age—17. Drew clothing on July 8 and September 11, 1864. Appears absent on a company muster roll for September and October 1864, with pay due from time of enlistment. Absent without leave since September 26, 1864. Here he is shown as 3rd Sergeant. POW captured at Blakeley, Alabama, on April 9, 1865. His name appears on a roll of POW's received at Ship Island, Mississippi, on April 15, 1865. Transferred from Ship Island to Vicksburg, Mississippi, on May 1, 1865. Appears on a roll of POW's of Company B, 63rd Alabama Infantry commanded by 1st Lieutenant Thomas J. Calhoun that were surrendered by Lt. General Richard Taylor at Citronelle, Alabama, on May 4, 1865, and paroled at Meridian, Mississippi, on May 11, 1865. Residence—Montgomery County, Alabama.

Morgan, S., Pvt. Co. I.
Enlisted on May 18, 1864, at Wedowee, Alabama, by Captain Robinson for the war. Appears absent on a company muster roll for September and October 1864. Absent on 30 day furlough from September 27, 1864.

Morman, E., Pvt. Co. B.
Residence—Dallas County, Alabama. POW straggler paroled at Selma, Alabama, in May 1865.

Morris, E. J., Pvt. Co. F.
Enlisted on July 12, 1864, at Lowndes County, Alabama, by Captain Buck for the war. Age—17, eyes—dark, hair—dark, complexion—dark, 5 foot 6 ½ inches, residence—Lowndes County, Alabama. Appears on a company muster-in roll for July 25, 1864, at Georgiana, Alabama. Appears absent on a company muster roll for September and October 1864. Absent in hospital at Mobile, Alabama, since September 14, 1864. Captured at Blakeley, Alabama, on April 9, 1865. Appears on a roll of POW's received at Ship Island, Mississippi, on April 15, 1865. Transferred from Ship Island to Vicksburg, Mississippi, on May 1, 1865. Appears on a roll of POW's of Company F, 63rd Alabama Infantry commanded by Captain R. T. Simpson that were surrendered by Lt. General Richard Taylor at Citronelle, Alabama, on May 4, 1865, and paroled at Meridian, Mississippi, on May 11, 1865. Residence—Lowndes County, Alabama.

Morris, Elyah O., Pvt. Co. D.
Enlisted on July 30, 1864, at Macon County, Alabama, by Major Ready for the war. Appears on a company muster-in roll for July 30, 1864, at Camp Watts near Notasulga, Alabama. Age—17, eyes—dark, hair—dark, complexion—dark, 5 foot 8 inches, residence—Texasville, Henry County, Alabama. Drew clothing on August 7, 1864. Signed by his mark. Appears present on a company muster roll for August 30 to October 30, 1864. Here he is shown as having enlisted on March 2, 1864, at Clayton, Alabama, by D. M. Seals.

Morris, I. Z. T., 1st Sergeant Co. F.
Enlisted on May 30, 1864, at Greenville, Alabama, by Captain Jackson for the war. Age—17, eyes—blue, hair—dark, complexion—dark, 5 foot 6 inches, residence—Butler County, Alabama. Appears on a company muster-in roll for July 25, 1864, at Georgiana, Alabama. Appears absent on a company muster roll for August 31 to October 31, 1864, with pay due from time of enlistment. Absent in hospital at Mobile, Alabama, since October 28, 1864. POW on a list of stragglers paroled on May 19, 1864, at Mobile. Residence—Greenville.

Morris, J. R., Pvt. Co. F.
Enlisted on March 9, 1864, at Greenville, Alabama, by Captain Brown for the war. Age—17, eyes—grey, hair—dark, complexion—sallow, 5 foot 8 inches, residence—Butler County, Alabama. Appears absent without leave on a company muster-in roll for July 25, 1864, at Georgiana, Alabama.

Morris, William, Pvt. Co. D.
Enlisted on August 12, 1864, at Pollard, Alabama, by Captain Paine for the war. Appears present on a company muster roll for August 30 to October 30, 1864, with pay due from time of enlistment. Admitted to Ross Hospital, Mobile, Alabama, on November 5, 1864, with febris intermittens tert. Furloughed for 30 days on November 24.

Morrison, Daniel A., Pvt. Co. D.
Enlisted on July 30, 1864, at Macon County, Alabama, by Major Ready for the war. Age—17, eyes—dark, hair—dark, complexion—dark, 5 foot 6 inches,

residence—White Oak Springs, Barbour County, Alabama. Appears on a company muster roll for July 30, 1864, at Camp Watts near Notasulga, Alabama. Drew clothing on August 7, 1864. Appears present on a company muster roll for August 30 to October 30, 1864, with pay due from time of enlistment. Here he is shown as having enlisted on March 2, 1864, at Clayton, Alabama, by D. M. Seals. Captured at Blakeley, Alabama, on April 9, 1865. Appears on a roll of POW's received at Ship Island, Mississippi, on April 15, 1865. Transferred from Ship Island to Vicksburg, Mississippi, on May 1, 1865. His name appears on a roll of POW's of Company D, 63rd Alabama Infantry Volunteers CSA commanded by Captain Robert H. Pearson that were surrendered by Lt. General Richard Taylor at Citronelle, Alabama, on May 4, 1865, and paroled at Meridian, Mississippi, on May 13, 1865. His residence is shown as Barbour County, Alabama.

Morton, D., Pvt. Co. H.
Enlisted on August 7, 1864, at Selma, Alabama, by Lieutenant Killough for the war. He is described as: age—17, eyes—blue, hair—dark, complexion—dark. Drew clothing on September 11, 1864. He appears absent on a company muster roll for September and October 1864. Absent sick at hospital in Mobile, Alabama, since October 8, 1864. Captured at Blakeley, Alabama, on April 9, 1865. Appears on a roll of POW's received at Ship Island, Mississippi, on April 15, 1865. Transferred from Ship Island to Vicksburg, Mississippi, on May 1, 1865. Appears on a roll of POW's of Cos. C and H, 63rd Alabama Infantry commanded by Captain C. W. Martin that were surrendered by Lt. General Richard Taylor at Citronelle, Alabama, on May 4, 1865, and paroled at Meridian, Mississippi, on May 11, 1865. Residence—Blount County, Alabama.

Morton, William T., Pvt. Co. A.
Enlisted on March 29, 1864, at Chambers County, Alabama, by Captain Echols for the war. Drew clothing in 2nd quarter and on August 12, 1864. Appears present on a company muster roll for September and October 1864, with pay due from time of enlistment. Captured at Blakeley, Alabama, on April 9, 1865. Appears on a roll of POW's received at Ship Island, Mississippi, on April 15, 1865. Transferred from Ship Island to Vicksburg, Mississippi, on May 1, 1865. Appears on a roll of POW's of Company A, 63rd Alabama Infantry commanded by Lieutenant W. D. Kyle that were surrendered by Lt. General Richard Taylor at Citronelle, Alabama, on May 4, 1865, and paroled at Meridian, Mississippi, on May 13, 1865. Residence—Chambers County, Alabama.

Moseley, I. W., Pvt. Co. F.
Enlisted on May 30, 1864, at Montgomery, Alabama, by Captain Jackson, for the war. Age—17, eyes—blue, hair—light, complexion—sallow, 5 foot 5 inches, residence—Butler County, Alabama. Appears on a company muster-in roll for July 25, 1864, at Georgiana, Alabama. Appears as J. W. Moseley on a company muster roll for August 31, 1864, to October 31, 1864, with pay due from time of enlistment. Drew clothing on September 11, 1864. Admitted to Ross Hospital, Mobile, Alabama, on January 19, 1865, with anasarca. Sent to General Hospital at Lauderdale Springs, Mississippi, on January 31, 1865. Appears on a roll of POW's, a straggler, belonging to divers commands that were surrendered by Lt. General Richard Taylor at Citronelle, Alabama, in May 1865, and paroled at Mobile, Alabama, on May 19, 1865. Residence—Greenville, Alabama.

Mosley, J. A., Pvt. Co. F.
Enlisted on August 8, 1864, at Georgiana, Alabama, by Captain Brown for the war. Appears present on a company muster roll for August 31 to October 31, 1864, with pay due from time of enlistment. Drew clothing on September 11, 1864. Paroled at headquarters of the 16th US Army Corps, at Montgomery,

Alabama, on May 26, 1865. Hair—light, eyes—grey, complexion—fair, 5 foot 4 inches.

Moyo, Robert, Pvt. Co. C.
Enlisted on May 20, 1864, at Tallapoosa County, Alabama, by Captain Brown for the war. Age—17, eyes—dark, hair—dark, complexion—dark, 5 foot 4 ½ inches, residence—Stowes Ferry, Tallapoosa County, Alabama. Appears on a company muster-in roll for June 24, 1864, at Camp Watts near Notasulga, Alabama. Appears absent on a company muster roll for May 20, 1864. Absent in hospital in Mobile, Alabama, since October 28, 1864. Drew clothing on August 6, 1864. Signed by his mark. Appears on a roll of POW's of nurses and patients of Moore Hospital CSA commanded by Surgeon W. C. Cavenaugh that were surrendered by Lt. General Richard Taylor at Citronelle, Alabama, in May 1865, and paroled at Meridian, Mississippi, on May 16, 1865. Residence—Greenville, Alabama.

Mullins, William S., Pvt. Co. H.
Enlisted on August 16, 1864, at Blakeley, Alabama, by Lieutenant Killough for the war. Age—17, eyes—dark, hair—dark, complexion—dark. Drew clothing on September 11, 1864. Admitted to Ross Hospital, Mobile, Alabama, on September 26, 1864, with rubeola. Returned to duty on October 27, 1864. Appears present on a company muster roll for September and October 1864. Captured at Blakeley, Alabama, on April 9, 1865. Appears on a roll of POW's received at Ship Island, Mississippi, on April 15, 1865. Transferred from Ship Island to Vicksburg, Mississippi, on May 1, 1865. Appears on a roll of POW's of Cos. C and H, 63rd Alabama Infantry commanded by Captain C. W. Martin that were surrendered by Lt. General Richard Taylor at Citronelle, Alabama, on May 4, 1865, and paroled at Meridian, Mississippi, on May 11, 1865. Residence—Bibb County, Alabama.

Murphy, Emanuel M., Pvt. Co. B.
Enlisted on July 11, 1864, at Montgomery, Alabama, by Lieutenant Calhoun for the war. Drew clothing on August 12, 1864. Drew clothing on September 11, 1864. Signed by his mark. Appears present on a company muster roll for September and October 1864, with pay due from time of enlistment. Captured at Blakeley, Alabama, on April 9, 1865. Appears on a roll of POW's received at Ship Island, Mississippi, on April 15, 1865. Transferred from Ship Island to Vicksburg, Mississippi, on May 1, 1865. Appears on a roll of POW's of Company B, 63rd Alabama Infantry commanded by 1st Lieutenant Thomas J. Calhoun that were surrendered by Lt. General Richard Taylor at Citronelle, Alabama, on May 4, 1865, and paroled at Meridian, Mississippi, on May 11, 1865. Residence—Coosa County, Alabama.

Murphy, Zachariah T., Pvt. Co. C.
Enlisted on June 20, 1864, at Macon County, Alabama, by Major Ready for the war. Age—17, eyes—blue, hair—dark, complexion—fair, 5 foot 10 inches, residence—Rough and Ready, Chambers County, Alabama. Appears on a company muster-in roll for June 24, 1864, at Camp Watts near Notasulga, Alabama. Drew clothing on August 6, 1864. Appears present on a company muster roll for September and October 1864.

Murrah, A. T., Pvt.
Appears on a roll of POW's of nurses and patients of Moore Hospital CSA commanded by Surgeon W. C. Cavenaugh that were surrendered by Lt. General Richard Taylor at Citronelle, Alabama, on May 4, 1865, and paroled at Meridian, Mississippi, on May 16, 1865. His residence is shown as Shelby [County], Alabama.

Myers, J. R., Sergeant Co. F.

Enlisted on March 9, 1864, at Greenville, Alabama. Age—17, eyes—dark, hair—dark, complexion—dark, 5 foot 11 inches, residence—Butler County, Alabama. Appears absent sick on a company muster-in roll for July 25, 1864, at Georgiana, Alabama. Appears present on a company muster roll for August 31 to October 31, 1864, with pay due from time of enlistment. Appears on a roll of POW's of General Hospital CSA "Stout" commanded by Surgeon H. M. Clarkson that were surrendered by Lt. General Richard Taylor at Citronelle, Alabama, on May 4, 1865, and paroled at Meridian, Mississippi, on May 16, 1865. His residence is shown as Butler, Alabama. Appears on a register of paroles given at Post of Columbus, Mississippi, on May 23, 1865.

Nash, Abner D., Pvt. Co. G.

Enlisted on May 1, 1864, at Troy, Alabama, by Captain Wilkerson for the war. Age—17, eyes—grey, hair—dark, complexion—fair, 5 foot 6 inches, residence—Pike County, Alabama. Appears on a company muster-in roll for September 7, 1864, at Blakeley, Alabama. Drew clothing on September 11, 1864. Signed by his mark. Appears present on a company muster roll for September and October 1864. Captured at Blakeley, Alabama, on April 9, 1865. Appears on a roll of POW's received at Ship Island, Mississippi, on April 15, 1865. Transferred from Ship Island to Vicksburg, Mississippi, on May 1, 1865. Appears on a roll of POW's of Cos. E and G, 63rd Alabama Infantry commanded by Captain A. V. Lee that were surrendered by Lieutenant General Richard Taylor at Citronelle, Alabama, on May 4, 1865, and paroled at Meridian, Mississippi, on May 13, 1865. Residence—Pike County, Alabama.

Nawls, John, Pvt. Co. F.

Enlisted on March 9, 1864, at Greenville, Alabama, by Captain Brown for the war. Age—17, eyes—blue, hair—light, complexion—sallow, 5 foot 6 inches, residence—Covington County, Alabama. Appears on a company muster-in roll for July 25, 1864, at Georgiana, Alabama. Appears absent on a company muster roll for August 31 to October 31, 1864, with pay due from time of enlistment. Absent in arrest at Mobile, Alabama, from October 27, 1864. Appears on a roll of POW's of nurses and patients of Moore Hospital CSA commanded by Surgeon W. C. Cavenaugh that were surrendered by Lt. General Richard Taylor at Citronelle, Alabama, on May 4, 1865, and paroled at Meridian, Mississippi, on May 16, 1865. Residence—Covington County, Alabama.

Neal, J. D., Pvt. Co. E.

Enlisted on July 23, 1864, at Montgomery, Alabama, by Captain A. V. Lee for the war. Age—17, eyes—blue, hair—light, complexion—fair. Drew clothing on September 11, 1864. Died on September 28, 1864.

Nelms, Charles, D., Pvt. Co. A.

Enlisted on May 18, 1864, at Russell County, Alabama, by Captain Echols for the war. Drew clothing in the 2nd quarter and September 11, 1864. Appears on a company muster roll for September and October 1864, with pay due from time of enlistment. Captured at Blakeley, Alabama, on April 9, 1865. Appears on a roll of POW's received at Ship Island, Mississippi, on April 15, 1865. Transferred from Ship Island to Vicksburg, Mississippi, on May 1, 1865. Appears on a roll of POW's of Company A, 63rd Alabama Infantry commanded by Lieutenant W. D. Kyle that were surrendered by Lt. General Richard Taylor at Citronelle, Alabama, on May 4, 1865, and paroled at Meridian, Mississippi, on May 13, 1865. Residence—Russell County, Alabama.

Nelms, Curtis, Pvt. Co. G.

Enlisted on May 4, 1865, at Troy, Alabama, by Captain Wilkerson for the war.

Age—17, eyes—grey, hair—red, complexion—fair, 5 foot 2 inches, residence—Pike County, Alabama. Appears on a company muster-in roll for September 7, 1864. Drew clothing on September 11, 1864. Appears present on a company muster roll for September and October 1864. Appears on a roll of POW's nurses and patients of Moore Hospital CSA commanded by Surgeon W. C. Cavanaugh that were surrendered by Lt. General Richard Taylor at Citronelle, Alabama, on May 4, 1865, and paroled at Meridian, Mississippi, on May 16, 1865. Residence—Pike County, Alabama.

Nelson, John, 1st Sergeant Co. B.
Enlisted on September 10, 1864, at Blakeley, Alabama, by Captain Zimmerman for the war. Appears on a company muster roll for September and October 1864, with pay due from time of enlistment. Appears on a parole of POW's sworn and subscribed to at Marion, Alabama, on May 16, 1865.

Nelson, J. S., Corporal/Pvt. Co. E.
Enlisted as 4th Corporal on May 14, 1864, at Clayton, Alabama, by Captain A. V. Lee for the war. He is described as: age—17, eyes—blue, hair—light, complexion—fair. He is reported to have drawn clothing on September 11, 1864. He appears present on a company muster roll for September and October 1864. His name appears on a roll of POW's of Cos. E and G, 63rd Alabama Infantry commanded by Captain A. V. Lee that were surrendered by Lt. General Richard Taylor at Citronelle, Alabama, on May 4, 1865, and paroled at Meridian, Mississippi, on May 13, 1865. Here he is shown as a Private with residence in Barbour County, Alabama.

Newson, Thomas, P., Pvt. Co. B.
Enlisted on August 15, 1864, at Pollard, Alabama, by Lieutenant Townsend for the war. Drew clothing on September 11, 1864. Appears present on a company muster roll for September and October 1864, with pay due from time of enlistment. Captured at Blakeley, Alabama, on April 9, 1865. Appears on a roll of POW's received at Ship Island, Mississippi, on April 15, 1865. Transferred from Ship Island to Vicksburg, Mississippi, on May 1, 1865. Appears on a roll of POW's of Company B, 63rd Alabama Infantry commanded by 1st Lieutenant Thomas J. Calhoun that were surrendered by Lt. General Richard Taylor at Citronelle, Alabama, on May 4, 1865, and paroled at Meridian, Mississippi, on May 11, 1865. Residence—Dale County, Alabama.

Nichols, John, Pvt. Co. B.
Enlisted on April 28, 1864, at Montgomery County, Alabama, by Captain Zimmerman for the war. Appears on a company muster-in roll for March 23, 1864, at Montgomery, Alabama. Drew clothing on July 8, 1864. Appears present on a company muster roll for September and October 1864, with pay due from time of enlistment.

Noble, W. A., Pvt. Co. B.
POW captured at Gravel Hill, Alabama, on March 24, 1865, by Brigadier General T. J. Lucas commanding Cavalry Forces operating from Pensacola, Florida. Appears on a roll of POW's received at Ship Island, Mississippi, on April 4, 1865. Transferred from Ship Island to Vicksburg, Mississippi, on May 1, 1865. Appears on a roll of POW's of Company B, 63rd Alabama Infantry commanded by 1st Lieutenant Thomas J. Calhoun that were surrendered by Lt. General Richard Taylor at Citronelle, Alabama, on May 4, 1865, and paroled at Meridian, Mississippi, on May 11, 1865. Residence—Montgomery County, Alabama.

Norton, Thomas C., Pvt. Co. D.
Enlisted on July 30, 1864, at Macon County, Alabama, by Major Ready for the

war. Age—17, eyes—dark, hair—light, complexion—fair, 5 foot 3 inches, residence—Clayton, Barbour County, Alabama. Appears on a company muster-in roll for July 30, 1864, at Camp Watts near Notasulga, Alabama. Drew clothing on August 7, 1864. Appears present on a company muster roll for August 30, to October 30, 1864, with pay due from time of enlistment. Here he is shown as having enlisted on June 20, 1864, at Eufaula, Alabama, by Captain Zorn. Captured at Blakeley, Alabama, on April 9, 1865. Appears on a roll of POW's received at Ship Island, Mississippi, on April 15, 1865. Transferred from Ship Island to Vicksburg, Mississippi, on May 1, 1865. Appears on a roll of POW's of Company D, 63rd Alabama Volunteers CSA commanded by Captain Robert H. Pearson that were surrendered by Lt. General Richard Taylor at Citronelle, Alabama, on May 4, 1865, and paroled at Meridian, Mississippi, on May 13, 1865. Residence—Barbour County, Alabama.

Norwood, F., Pvt. Co. H.
Enlisted on March 15, 1864, at Montevallo, Alabama, by Captain Suttle for the war. Age—17, eyes—dark, hair—dark, complexion—dark. Appears absent on a company muster roll for September and October 1864. Absent in Camp of Correction since August 14. Captured at Blakeley, Alabama, on April 9, 1865. Appears on a roll of POW's received at Ship Island, Mississippi, on April 15, 1865. Transferred from Ship Island to Vicksburg, Mississippi, on May 1, 1865. Appears on a roll of POW's of Cos. C and H, 63rd Alabama Infantry commanded by Captain C. W. Martin that were surrendered by Lt. General Richard Taylor at Citronelle, Alabama, on May 4, 1865, and paroled at Meridian, Mississippi, on May 11, 1865. Residence—Jefferson County, Alabama.

Nowles, George E., Pvt. Co. B/K.
Enlisted on March 23, 1864, at Montgomery County, Alabama, by Captain Zimmerman for the war. Appears on a company muster-in roll for March 23, 1864, at Montgomery, Alabama. Age—16. Drew clothing on July 8, 1864. Appears on a Company B muster roll for September and October 1864. Transferred per special order No. 15 on October 2, 1864. Appears absent on a Company K muster roll for September and October 1864. Absent sick without leave since October 19.

Numm, J. W., Pvt. Co. I.
Enlisted on May 18, 1864, at Wedowee, Alabama, by Captain Robinson for the war. Appears absent on a company muster roll for September and October 1864. Absent on 30 day furlough since September 27.

Odom, J. J. I., Pvt. Co. F.
Enlisted on May 30, 1864, at Montgomery, Alabama, by Captain Jackson for the war. Age—17, eyes—grey, hair—light, complexion—fair, 5 foot 7 inches, residence—Butler County, Alabama. Appears absent without leave on a company muster-in roll for July 25, 1864, at Georgiana, Alabama. Captured at Blakeley, Alabama, on April 9, 1865. Appears on a roll of POW's received at Ship Island, Mississippi, on April 15, 1865. Transferred from Ship Island to Vicksburg, Mississippi, on May 1, 1865. Appears on a roll of POW's of Company F, 63rd Alabama Infantry commanded by Captain R. T. Simpson that were surrendered by Lt. General Richard Taylor at Citronelle, Alabama, on May 4, 1865, and paroled at Meridian, Mississippi, on May 11, 1865. Residence—Butler County, Alabama.

Olive, Abram, Pvt. Co. G.
Enlisted on October 24, 1864, at Mobile, Alabama, by Captain Garland, for the war. Appears present on a company muster roll for September and October 1864.

Olive, George W., Pvt. Co. G.
Enlisted on April 27, 1864, at Troy, Alabama, by Captain Wilkerson for the war. Age—17, eyes—hazel, hair—light, complexion—florid, 5 foot 7 inches, residence—Covington County, Alabama. Appears on a company muster-in roll on September 7, 1864, at Blakeley, Alabama. Drew clothing on September 11, 1864. Appears present on a company muster roll for September and October 1864. Captured at Blakeley, Alabama, on April 9, 1865. Appears on a roll of POW's received at Ship Island, Mississippi, on April 15, 1865. Transferred from Ship Island to Vicksburg, Mississippi, on May 1, 1865. Appears on a roll of sick and wounded Confederate POW's at USA Hospital No. 2, Vicksburg, Mississippi. Admitted to Hospital No. 2 on May 3, 1865, from steamer with remittal fever. Age—18.

Oliver, Charlton, C., Sergeant Major/2nd Lieutenant Co. I/F&S.
Enlisted as Sergeant Major on August 28, 1864, near Blakeley, Alabama, by Colonel Rice for the war. Appears present on a company muster roll for July and August 1864, having never been paid. Appears on a Field and Staff muster roll for September and October 1864, with pay due from time of enlistment. Elected 2nd Lieutenant Company I on September 26, 1864. Captured at Blakeley, Alabama, on April 9, 1865. Confined for one day at Spanish Fort, Alabama, by 2nd Division of 16th US Army Corps. Appears on a roll of POW's received at Ship Island, Mississippi, on April 16, 1865. Transferred from Ship Island to Vicksburg, Mississippi, on April 28, 1865. Appears on a roll of POW's from Ship Island confined at New Orleans, Louisiana, on April 30, 1865. He was exchanged on May 1, 1865. Signed a Parole of Honor at Meridian, Mississippi, on May 11, 1865. His parole is in his file.

Oliver, John, Pvt./Sergeant Co. B.
Enlisted on March 23, 1864, at Montgomery County, Alabama, by Captain Zimmerman for the war. Appears on a company muster-in roll for March 23, 1864, at Montgomery, Alabama. Age—17. Drew clothing on July 8 and September 11, 1864. Appears present on a company muster roll for September and October 1864, with pay due from time of enlistment. Captured at Blakeley, Alabama, on April 9, 1865. Appears on a roll of POW's received at Ship Island, Mississippi, on April 15, 1865. Transferred from Ship Island to Vicksburg, Mississippi, on May 1, 1865. Appears on a roll of POW's of Company B, 63rd Alabama Infantry commanded by 1st Lieutenant Thomas J. Calhoun that were surrendered by Lt. General Richard Taylor at Citronelle, Alabama, on May 4, 1865, and paroled at Meridian, Mississippi, on May 11, 1865. His residence was shown as Tallapoosa County, Alabama.

Owen, Edward, H., 1st Sergeant Co. G.
Enlisted on September 5, 1864, at Blakeley, Alabama, by Lieutenant Johnson. Age—17, eyes—black, hair—black, complexion—dark, 5 foot 4 inches, residence—Tuscaloosa County, Alabama. He is shown as a Cadet at University of Alabama. Appears present on a company muster roll for September and October 1864. Appointed 1st Sergeant on September 5, 1864, from Cadet Corps. Captured at Blakeley, Alabama, on April 9, 1865. Appears on a roll of POW's received at Ship Island, Mississippi, on April 15, 1865. Transferred from Ship Island to Vicksburg, Mississippi, on May 1, 1865. Appears on a roll of POW's of Cos. E and G, 63rd Alabama Infantry commanded by Captain A. V. Lee that were surrendered by Lt. General Richard Taylor at Citronelle, Alabama, on May 4, 1865, and paroled at Meridian, Mississippi, on May 13, 1865. Residence—Tuscaloosa County, Alabama.

Owens, Joseph L. P., Brevet 2nd Lieutenant Co. A.
Elected 2nd Lieutenant on May 17, 1864. Appears present on a company muster

roll for September and October 1864. His name appears on a roster of 2nd Regiment Alabama Reserves, Fuller's Brigade, Maury's Corps, District of the Gulf which was organized on August 16, 1864. The Roster is dated January 1865.

Ozier, J. N., Pvt. Co. E.
Enlisted on July 28, 1864, at Montgomery, Alabama, by Captain A. V. Lee for the war. Age—17, eyes—dark, hair—dark, complexion—dark. Appears absent on a company muster roll for September and October 1864. Absent without leave since September 25, 1864.

Padgett, John A. C., Captain/2nd Lieutenant Co. G.
Elected Captain of Company G on July 1, 1864, resigned on November 10, 1864. Appears on a company muster-in roll for September 7, 1864, at Blakeley, Alabama. Age—17, eyes—blue, hair—light, complexion—fair, 5 foot 4 inches, residence—Pike County, Alabama. Appears present on a company muster roll for September and October 1864. Elected 2nd Lieutenant on September 19, 1864. His resignation with endorsements are in his file.

Padgett, A. C., Pvt. Co. G.
Admitted to Yandell Hospital, Meridian, Mississippi, on April 5, 1865, with chronic diarrhoea.

Paine, G. W., Pvt. Co. I.
Enlisted on April 15, 1864, at Columbiana, Alabama, by Lieutenant Burger for the war. Appears absent on a company muster roll for September and October 1864. Absent without leave from September 18, 1864.

Painter, H. C., Pvt. Co. H.
Enlisted on August 9, 1864, at Mobile, Alabama, by Lieutenant Johnston for the war. Age—17, eyes—blue, hair—dark, complexion—fair. Drew clothing on September 11, 1864. Appears present on a company muster roll for September and October 1864. His name appears on a roll of POW's of Cos. C and H, 63rd Alabama Infantry commanded by Captain C. W. Martin that were surrendered by Lt. General Richard Taylor at Citronelle, Alabama, on May 4, 1865, and paroled at Meridian, Mississippi, on May 11, 1865. Residence—Clarke County, Alabama.

Palmore, J. A., Pvt. Co. H.
Enlisted on July 29, 1864, at Selma, Alabama, by Captain Suttle for the war. Age—17, eyes—blue, hair—dark, complexion—fair. Drew clothing on September 11, 1864. Appears absent on a company muster roll for September and October 1864. Absent sick at hospital in Mobile, Alabama since September 15. Admitted to Ross Hospital, Mobile, Alabama, on September 3, 1864, with dysenteria acuta. Returned to duty on September 8, 1864. Admitted again to Ross Hospital, Mobile on October 10, 1864, with febris intermittens tert. Furloughed for 20 days on October 19, 1864.

Parker, W. H., Pvt. Co. H.
Enlisted on March 15, 1864, at Centerville, Alabama, by Captain Suttle for the war. Age—17, eyes—blue, hair—dark, complexion—dark. Drew clothing on September 11, 1864. Appears present on a company muster roll for September and October 1864. Captured at Blakeley, Alabama, on April 9, 1865. Appears on a roll of POW's received at Ship Island, Mississippi, on April 15, 1865. Transferred from Ship Island to Vicksburg, Mississippi, on May 1, 1865. Appears on a roll of POW's of Cos. C and H, 63rd Alabama Infantry commanded by Captain C. W. Martin that were surrendered by Lt. General Richard Taylor

at Citronelle, Alabama, on May 4, 1865, and paroled at Meridian, Mississippi, on May 11, 1865. Residence—Bibb County, Alabama.

Parker, William N., Pvt. Co. D.
Enlisted on July 30, 1864, at Macon County, Alabama, by Major Ready. Age—17, eyes—dark, hair—dark, complexion—dark, 5 foot 10 inches, residence—Kings, Barbour County, Alabama. Appears present on a company muster-in roll for July 30, 1864, at Camp Watts near Notasulga, Alabama. Drew clothing on September 12, 1864. Appears present on a company muster roll for August 30 to October 30, 1864, with pay due from time of enlistment.

Parker, W. P. L. Q., Pvt. Co. E.
Captured at Blakeley, Alabama, on April 9, 1865. Appears on a roll of POW's received at Ship Island, Mississippi, on April 15, 1865. Transferred from Ship Island to Vicksburg, Mississippi, on May 1, 1865. Appears on a roll of POW's of Cos. E and G, 63rd Alabama Infantry commanded by Captain A. V. Lee that were surrendered by Lt. General Richard Taylor at Citronelle, Alabama, on May 4, 1865, and paroled at Meridian, Mississippi, on May 13, 1865. Residence—Sumpter County, Alabama.

Parks, Z., Pvt. Co. I.
Enlisted on May 18, 1864, at Wedowee, Alabama, by Captain Robinson for the war. Appears absent on a company muster roll for September and October 1864. Absent without leave from September 18, 1864.

Parrish, James L., Pvt./Sergeant Co. G/I.
Enlisted on April 29, 1864, at Troy, Alabama, by Captain Wilkerson for the war. Age—17, eyes—dark, hair—dark, complexion—dark, 6 foot 0 inches. Appears as a Private on a Company G muster-in roll for September 7, 1864, at Blakeley, Alabama. Drew clothing on September 11, 1864. Appears as 4th Sergeant and absent on a Company G muster roll for September and October 1864. Absent furloughed for 30 days from October 24. Appointed 4th Sergeant on September 19. Appears on a list of paroled Confederate soldiers that were paroled on May 20, 1865, at the headquarters of the 16th US Army Corps located in Montgomery, Alabama. His parole is in his file. Here he is shown as being 5 foot 11 inches, hair—light, eyes—light, complexion—fair.

Parrish, J. P., Pvt. Co. F.
Enlisted on May 30, 1864, at Montgomery, Alabama, by Captain Jackson for the war. Age—17, eyes—grey, hair—light, complexion—fair, 5 foot 7 inches, residence—Butler County, Alabama. Appears absent without leave on a company muster-in roll for July 25, 1864, at Georgiana, Alabama. Captured at Blakeley, Alabama, on April 9, 1865. Appears on a roll of POW's received at Ship Island, Mississippi, on April 15, 1865. Transferred from Ship Island to Vicksburg, Mississippi, on May 1, 1865. Appears on a roll of POW's of Company F, 63rd Alabama Infantry commanded by Captain R. T. Simpson that were surrendered by Lt. General Richard Taylor at Citronelle, Alabama, on May 4, 1865, and paroled at Meridian, Mississippi, on May 11, 1865. His residence was shown as Autauga County, Alabama.

Pattersion, (Patterson) Ezekiel, Pvt. Co. G.
Enlisted on May 16, 1864, at Troy, Alabama, by Captain Walker for the war. Age—17, eyes—grey, hair—light, complexion—fair, 5 foot 7 inches, residence—Covington County, Alabama. Appears on a company muster-in roll for September 7, 1864, at Blakeley, Alabama. Appears absent on a company muster roll for September and October 1864. Absent furlough extended from October 19 for 30 days by Examining Board at Greenville, Alabama. Captured at

Blakeley, Alabama, on April 9, 1865. Appears on a roll of POW's received at Ship Island, Mississippi, on April 15, 1865. Transferred from Ship Island to Vicksburg, Mississippi, on May 1, 1865. Appears on a roll of POW's of Cos. E and G, 63rd Alabama Infantry commanded by Captain A. V. Lee that were surrendered by Lt. General Richard Taylor at Citronelle, Alabama, on May 4, 1865, and paroled at Meridian, Mississippi, on May 13, 1865. Residence—Covington County, Alabama.

Peacock, James, Pvt. Co. D.
Enlisted on September 5, 1864, at Blakeley, Alabama, by Captain Zorn for the war. Drew clothing on September 12, 1864. Appears present on a company muster roll for September and October 1864, with pay due from time of enlistment. Admitted to Ross Hospital, Mobile, Alabama, on September 18, 1864, with rubeola. Returned to duty on October 6, 1864. Captured at Blakeley, Alabama, on April 9, 1865. Appears on a roll of POW's received at Ship Island, Mississippi, on April 15, 1865. Transferred from Ship Island to Vicksburg, Mississippi, on May 1, 1865. Appears on a roll of POW's of Company D, 63rd Alabama Volunteers CSA commanded by Captain Robert H. Pearson that were surrendered by Lt. General Richard Taylor at Citronelle, Alabama, on May 4, 1865, and paroled at Meridian, Mississippi, on May 13, 1865. Residence—Coffee County, Alabama.

Peacock, Levi, J., Pvt. Co. B.
Enlisted on March 23, 1864, at Montgomery County, Alabama, by Captain Zimmerman for the war. Appears on a company muster-in roll for March 23, 1864, at Montgomery, Alabama. Age—16. Drew clothing on July 8, 1864. Appears on a list of paroled Confederate soldiers that were paroled on May 27, 1865, at the headquarters of the 16th US Army Corps located in Montgomery, Alabama. His parole is in his file. Here he is shown as being 5 foot 6 inches, hair—dark, eyes—blue, complexion—fair.

Peacock, William B., Pvt. Co. B.
Enlisted on March 23, 1864, at Montgomery County, Alabama, by Captain Zimmerman for the war. Appears on a company muster-in roll for March 23, 1864, at Montgomery, Alabama. Age—17. Appears present on a company muster roll for September and October 1864, with pay due from time of enlistment. Drew clothing on July 8 and September 11, 1864. Signed by his mark. Appears on a roll of POW's of Company B, 63rd Alabama Infantry commanded by 1st Lieutenant Thomas J. Calhoun that were surrendered by Lt. General Richard Taylor at Citronelle, Alabama, on May 4, 1865, and paroled at Meridian, Mississippi, on May 11, 1865. Residence—Montgomery County, Alabama.

Pearce, Cicero P., 1st Sergeant/Ordinance Sergeant Co. A, F&S
Enlisted as 1st Sergeant on January 1, 1864, at Montgomery, County, Alabama, by Captain John Echols for the war. Appears on a company muster-in roll for January 1, 1864, at Montgomery, Alabama. Age—17. Appears as 1st Sergeant and present on a company muster roll for January and February 1864, with pay due from time of enlistment. Drew clothing in 2nd quarter of 1864. Appears as 3rd Sergeant on a Company A muster roll for September and October 1864. Promoted Ordnance Sergeant per Special Order dated September 21, 1864. Appears as a patient on two hospital muster rolls at General Hospital No. 6, Fayetteville, N. C. These rolls are dated February 21 and 28, 1865. He is shown present with pay due of $27 for service since June 9, 1864. Here he is shown as being 1st Sergeant of Company E, 2nd Alabama Reserves.

Pearce, L. M., Pvt. Co. F.
Enlisted on March 9, 1864, at Greenville, Alabama, by Captain Brown for the

war. Age—17, eyes—grey, hair—light, complexion—sallow, 5 foot 9 inches, residence—Butler County, Alabama. Appears on a company muster-in roll for July 25, 1864, at Georgiana, Alabama. Appears present on a company muster roll for August 31 to October 31, 1864, with pay due from time of enlistment. Captured at Blakeley, Alabama, on April 9, 1865. Appears on a roll of POW's received at Ship Island, Mississippi, on April 15, 1865. Transferred from Ship Island to Vicksburg, Mississippi, on May 1, 1865. Appears on a roll of POW's of Company F, 63rd Alabama Infantry commanded by Captain R. T. Simpson that were surrendered by Lt. General Richard Taylor at Citronelle, Alabama, on May 4, 1865, and paroled at Meridian, Mississippi, on May 11, 1865. Residence—Butler County, Alabama.

Pearson, Robert H., 1st Lieutenant/Captain Co. D.
Elected 1st Lieutenant on March 2, 1864. Enlisted as 1st Lieutenant on July 30, 1864, at Macon County, Alabama, by Major Ready for the war. Age—17, eyes—grey, hair—dark, complexion—fair, 5 foot 8 inches, residence—Clayton, Barbour County, Alabama. Appears present on a company muster-in roll for July 30, 1864, at Camp Watts near Notasulga, Alabama. Appears present on a company muster roll for August 30 to October 30, 1864, with pay due from time of enlistment. He signs this roll as commanding Company D. Here he is shown as having enlisted on March 2, 1864, at Clayton, Alabama, by D. M. Seals. In the 3rd quarter of 1864 he requisitioned for Company D.: 20 uniform jackets, 15 pair pants, 14 pair drawers, 20 shirts and 21 pair of shoes. Captured at Blakeley, Alabama, on April 9, 1865. Confined for one day at Spanish Fort, Alabama, by 2nd Division of 16th US Army Corps. Appears on a roll of POW's received at Ship Island, Mississippi, on April 16, 1865. Transferred from Ship Island to Vicksburg, Mississippi, on April 28, 1865. Appears on a roll of POW's from Ship Island confined at New Orleans, Louisiana, on April 30, 1865. Exchanged on May 1, 1865. Signed a Parole of Honor at Meridian, Mississippi, on May 11, 1865. His parole is in his file.

Pearson, W. B., Pvt. Co. F.
Enlisted on March 9, 1864, at Greenville, Alabama, by Captain Brown for the war. Age—17, eyes—hazel, hair—dark, complexion—fair, 5 foot 7 inches, residence—Butler County, Alabama. Appears on a company muster-in roll for July 25 1864, at Georgiana, Alabama. Appears present on a company muster roll for August 31 to October 31, 1864, with pay due from time of enlistment. Captured at Blakeley, Alabama, on April 9, 1865. Appears on a roll of POW's received at Ship Island, Mississippi, on April 15, 1865. Transferred from Ship Island to Vicksburg, Mississippi, on May 1, 1865. Appears on a roll of POW's of Company F, 63rd Alabama Infantry commanded by Captain R. T. Simpson that were surrendered by Lt. General Richard Taylor at Citronelle, Alabama, on May 4, 1865, and paroled at Meridian, Mississippi, on May 11, 1865. Residence—Butler County, Alabama.

Peavy, T. P., Pvt. Co. F.
Enlisted on March 9, 1864, at Greenville, Alabama, by Captain Brown for the war. Age—17, eyes—blue, hair—light, complexion—fair, 5 foot 7 inches, residence—Butler County, Alabama. Drew clothing on September 11, 1864. Appears present on a company muster roll for August 31 to October 31, 1864, with pay due from time of enlistment. Admitted to Yandell Hospital, Meridian, Mississippi, on April 1, 1865. POW paroled at the headquarters of the 16th US Army Corps in Montgomery, Alabama, on May 30, 1865. His parole is in his file.

Penn, Thomas L., Pvt. Co. A.
Enlisted on January 1, 1864, at Macon County, Alabama, by Captain John Echols for the war. Appears on a company muster-in roll for January 1, 1864, at

Montgomery, Alabama. Appears present on a company muster roll for January and February 1864, with pay due from time of enlistment. Drew clothing in 2nd quarter of 1864. Appears present on a company muster roll for September and October 1864. Here he is shown as having been last paid on February 29, 1864. POW paroled at the headquarters of the 16th US Army Corps in Montgomery, Alabama, on May 30, 1865. Hair—dark, eyes—hazel, complexion—fair, 5 foot 6 inches. His parole is in his file. Furloughed for 60 days at West Point, Georgia, on April 7, 1865. He is shown as serving in Fuller's Brigade and having suffered with phthisis inflamantis (consumption) for 8 months. His residence is shown as Loachapoka, Macon County, Alabama. His furlough is in his file.

Perkins, Robert D., Corporal Co. G.
Enlisted on April 27, 1864, at Troy, Alabama, by Captain Wilkerson for the war. Age—17, eyes—blue, hair—dark, complexion—dark, 5 foot 9 inches. Appears on a company muster-in roll for September 7, 1864, at Blakeley, Alabama. Drew clothing on September 11, 1864. Appears absent on a company muster roll for September and October 1864. Absent in hospital at Mobile, Alabama, since October 20. Captured at Blakeley, Alabama, on April 9, 1865. Appears on a roll of POW's received at Ship Island, Mississippi, on April 15, 1865. Transferred from Ship Island to Vicksburg, Mississippi, on May 1, 1865. Appears on a roll of POW's of Cos. E and G, 63rd Alabama Infantry commanded by Captain A. V. Lee that were surrendered by Lt. General Richard Taylor at Citronelle, Alabama, on May 4, 1865, and paroled at Meridian, Mississippi, on May 13, 1865. Residence—Pike County, Alabama.

Perry, B. S., Pvt. Co. I.
Enlisted on April 15, 1864, at Talladega, Alabama, by Captain Parks for the war. Appears present on a company muster roll for September and October 1864. Appears on a roll of POW's that were hospital attendants and patients at Hinkley Hospital, Demopolis, Alabama, commanded by Surgeon H. Hinkley that were surrendered by Lt. General Richard Taylor at Citronelle, Alabama, on May 4, 1865, and paroled at Meridian, Mississippi, on May 14, 1865. Residence—Talladega County, Alabama.

Peters, William J., Pvt. Co. H.
Enlisted on March 15, 1864, at Centerville, Alabama, by Lieutenant Johnson for the war. Age—17, eyes—blue, hair—auburn, complexion—fair. Drew clothing on September 11, 1864. Appears absent on a company muster roll for September and October 1864. Absent on sick furlough since September 13. Admitted to Ross Hospital, Mobile, Alabama, on September 24, 1864, with rubeola. Returned to duty September 29. Furloughed at Selma, Alabama, for 60 days from February 21, 1865, due to hacmoptysis. Residence—Six Miles, Alabama.

Peterson, F. F., Pvt. Co. F.
Enlisted on July 12, 1864, at Greenville, Alabama, by Lieutenant Barton for the war. Appears present on a company muster roll for September and October 1864, with pay due from time of enlistment. Captured at Blakeley, Alabama, on April 9, 1865. Appears on a roll of POW's received at Ship Island, Mississippi, on April 15, 1865. Transferred from Ship Island to Vicksburg, Mississippi, on May 1, 1865. Appears on a roll of POW's of Company F, 63rd Alabama Infantry commanded by Captain R. T. Simpson that were surrendered by Lt. General Richard Taylor at Citronelle, Alabama, on May 4, 1865, and paroled at Meridian, Mississippi, on May 11, 1865. Residence—Butler County, Alabama.

Peterson, M., Pvt. Co. D.
Enlisted on September 5, 1864, at Blakeley, Alabama, by Captain Zorn for the war. Drew clothing on September 11, 1864. Appears present on a company

muster roll for August 30 to October 30, 1864, with pay due from time of enlistment. Captured at Blakeley, Alabama, on April 9, 1865. Appears on a roll of POW's received at Ship Island, Mississippi, on April 15, 1865. Transferred from Ship Island to Vicksburg, Mississippi, on May 1, 1865. Appears on a roll of POW's of Company D, 63rd Alabama Infantry commanded by Captain Robert H. Pearson that were surrendered by Lt. General Richard Taylor at Citronelle, Alabama, on May 4, 1865, and paroled at Meridian, Mississippi, on May 13, 1865. Residence—Barbour County, Alabama.

Peterson, R. S., Pvt. Co. F.
Enlisted on August 1, 1864, at Abbeville, Alabama, by Major Hunt, for the war. Drew clothing on September 11, 1864. Appears present on a company muster roll for August 31 to October 31, 1864, with pay due from time of enlistment. Captured at Blakeley, Alabama, on April 9, 1865. Appears on a roll of POW's received at Ship Island, Mississippi, on April 15, 1865. Transferred from Ship Island to Vicksburg, Mississippi, on May 1, 1865. Appears on a roll of POW's of Company F, 63rd Alabama Infantry commanded by Captain R. T. Simpson that were surrendered by Lt. General Richard Taylor at Citronelle, Alabama, on May 4, 1865, and paroled at Meridian, Mississippi, on May 11, 1865. Residence—Henry County, Alabama.

Petty, James, Pvt. Co. D.
Drew clothing on September 12, 1864. Discharged on October 15, 1864, due anemia condition and consequent imperfect nutrition and physical development at Camp Hood near Blakeley, Alabama. Enlisted on August 3, 1864, at Pollard, Alabama, by Captain Zorn for the war. Born in Henry County, Alabama. Age—17, eyes—grey, hair—dark, complexion—dark, 5 foot 4 inches. A student by occupation. His discharge with endorsements are in his file.

Peugh, W. E., Pvt. Co. F.
Enlisted on August 6, 1864, at Georgiana, Alabama, by Captain Brown for the war. Appears on a muster roll for August 31 to October 31, 1864, as having died and was never paid. Died on September 21, 1864.

Phelphs, Frederick, T., Pvt. Co. C.
Enlisted on May 9, 1864, at Macon County, Alabama, by Captain Roscoe for the war. Appears on a company muster-in roll for June 24, 1864, at Camp Watts near Notasulga, Alabama. Age—17, eyes—grey, hair—light, complexion—fair, 5 foot 6 ½ inches, residence—Cotton Valley, Macon County, Alabama. Appears present on a company muster roll for September and October 1864.

Philips, Charles, H., Pvt. Co. A.
It was reported that he drew clothing in 2nd quarter of 1864.

Philips, Lewis E. J., Pvt. Co. C.
Enlisted on May 24, 1864, at Columbus, Georgia, by Captain Hughes for the war. He is described as: age—17, eyes—grey, hair—light, complexion—fair, 5 foot 10 inches, residence—Dudleyville, Tallapoosa County, Alabama. Appears on a company muster-in roll for June 24, 1864, at Camp Watts near Notasulga, Alabama. He appears present on a company muster roll for September and October 1864. Note in his file to see personal papers of James M. Alexander, Alabama.

Philips, Thomas, Pvt. Co. I.
Enlisted on April 15, 1864, at Wedowee, Alabama, by Captain Robinson for the war. Appears present on a company muster roll for September and October 1864.

Phillips, Eden, Pvt. Co. A.
Enlisted on January 1, 1864, at Chambers County, Alabama, by Captain John Echols for the war. Age—16. Appears on a company muster-in roll for January 1, 1864, at Montgomery, Alabama. Appears present on a company muster roll for January and February 1864, with pay due from time of enlistment. Appears present sick in quarters on a company muster roll for September and October 1864. Drew clothing in 2nd quarter of 1864.

Phillips, Godfrey, Pvt. Co. C.
Admitted to Ross Hospital, Mobile, Alabama, on November 24, 1864, as febris remittens. Sent to General Hospital Nidelet, on November 30, 1864.

Phillips, S. M., Sergeant Co. K.
Appears on a roll of POW's and deserters from the CSA that entered the military lines of the 16th US Army Corps, during April 1865. "Turned over to Capt. H. H. Wheatley Asst. Provost Marshal, Post of Montgomery, Alabama, May 5, 1865."

Pickens, W. A., Pvt. Co. F.
Enlisted on July 12, 1864, at Lowndes County, Alabama, by Captain Buell for the war. Age—17, eyes—dark, hair—dark, complexion—fair, 5 foot 9 ½ inches, residence—Lowndes County, Alabama. Appears on a company muster-in roll for July 25, 1864, at Georgiana, Alabama. Drew clothing on September 11, 1864. Appears present sick on a company muster-in roll for August 31, to October 31, 1864, with pay due from time of enlistment. Signed a parole on June 1, 1865, at the headquarters of the 16th US Army Corps in Montgomery, Alabama. Hair—dark, eyes—dark, complexion—florid, 5 foot 8 inches.

Pickett, Abner, Pvt. Co. D.
Enlisted on July 30, 1864, at Macon County, Alabama, by Major Ready for the war. Age—17, eyes—blue, hair—light, complexion—florid, 5 foot 8 inches, residence—Clayton, Barbour County, Alabama. Appears on a company muster-in roll for July 30, 1864, at Camp Watts near Notasulga, Alabama. Drew clothing on August 7, 1864. Signed by his mark. Appears present on a company muster roll for August 30 to October 30, 1864, with pay due from time of enlistment. Here he is shown as having enlisted on March 2, 1864, at Clayton, Alabama, by D. M. Seals. Captured at Blakeley, Alabama, on April 9, 1865. Appears on a roll of POW's received at Ship Island, Mississippi, on April 15, 1865. Transferred from Ship Island to Vicksburg, Mississippi, on May 1, 1865. Appears on a roll of POW's of Company D, 63rd Alabama Infantry commanded by Captain Robert H. Pearson that were surrendered by Lt. General Richard Taylor at Citronelle, Alabama, on May 4, 1865, and paroled at Meridian, Mississippi, on May 13, 1865. Residence—Barbour County, Alabama.

Pierce, A. C., Pvt. Co. F.
Captured at Blakeley, Alabama, on April 9, 1865. Appears on a roll of POW's received at Ship Island, Mississippi, on April 15, 1865. Transferred from Ship Island to Vicksburg, Mississippi, on May 1, 1865. Appears on a roll of POW's of Company F, 63rd Alabama Infantry commanded by Captain R. T. Simpson that were surrendered by Lt. General Richard Taylor at Citronelle, Alabama, on May 4, 1865, and paroled at Meridian, Mississippi, on May 11, 1865. Residence—Butler County, Alabama.

Pippin, Berry, Pvt. Co. D.
Enlisted on July 30, 1864, at Macon County, Alabama, by Major Ready for the war. Age—17, eyes—grey, hair—light, complexion—fair, 5 foot 10 inches, residence—Eufaula, Barbour County, Alabama. Appears on a company muster-in

roll for July 30, 1864, at Camp Watts near Notasulga, Alabama. Drew clothing on August 7, 1864. Signed by his mark. Appears present on a company muster roll for August 30 to October 30, 1864, with pay due from time of enlistment. Here he is shown as having enlisted on June 1, 1864, at Eufaula, Alabama, by Captain Zorn. Appears on a list of wounded Confederates in the hospital of the 1st Division 13th US Army Corps, Army of the Military Division of West Mississippi at the battle of Blakeley Fort, Alabama, on April 9, 1865. Flesh wound to the leg. Admitted on April 15, 1865, to St. Louis, USA General Hospital, New Orleans, Louisiana, with gunshot wound to right leg (flesh). Transferred to Marine General Hospital on May 16, 1865. Age—19. POW confined on May 1, 1865, at New Orleans. Paroled and released on May 16, 1865.

Pippin, Park, Pvt. Co. D.
Enlisted on July 30, 1864, at Macon County, Alabama, by Major Ready for the war. Age—17, eyes—blue, hair—dark, complexion—dark, 5 foot 6 inches, residence—Henry County, Post Office—Eufaula, Alabama. Appears on a company muster-in roll for July 30, 1864, at Camp Watts near Notasulga, Alabama. Drew clothing on August 7, 1864. Appears present on a company muster roll for August 30 to October 30, 1864, with pay due from time of enlistment. Here he is shown as having enlisted on June 1, 1864, at Eufaula, Alabama, by Captain Zorn. Appears on a list of wounded Confederates in the hospital of the 1st Division 13th US Army Corps, Army of the Military Division of West Mississippi at the battle of Blakeley Fort, Alabama, on April 9, 1865, with fracture of knee. Captured and confined at Fort Blakeley, Alabama, on April 9, 1865. POW confined May 1, 1865, at New Orleans, Louisiana. Admitted on April 15, 1865, to St. Louis, USA General Hospital, New Orleans, Louisiana, with gunshot wound to left knee with fracture. Amputated lower third thigh (flaps) on April 26, 1865. Died on May 11, 1865, at St. Louis Hospital. Buried in Square 69, Grave 71 at Monument Cemetery. No effects. Age—18. His death and burial records are in his file. He is also shown as having been a POW confined on May 1, 1865, at New Orleans and paroled during May 1865. [The kind of thing you might expect in Army record keeping.]

Pistol, C. W., Corporal/Pvt. Co. I.
Enlisted on April 15, 1864, at Talladega, Alabama, by Captain Parks for the war. Appears absent on a company muster roll for September and October 1864. Absent sick in Hospital Moore since October 15. Captured at Blakeley, Alabama, on April 9, 1865. Appears on a roll of POW's received at Ship Island, Mississippi, on April 15, 1865. Transferred from Ship Island to Vicksburg, Mississippi, on May 1, 1865. Appears on a roll of POW's of Quintard Hospital CSA commanded by Surgeon S. V. D. Hill that were surrendered by Lt. General Richard Taylor at Citronelle, Alabama, on May 4, 1865, and paroled at Meridian, Mississippi, on May 10, 1865. He also appears on a roll of POW's of Cos. I and K, 63rd Alabama Infantry commanded by Lieutenant W. A. Skinner that were surrendered by Lt. General Richard Taylor at Citronelle, Alabama, on May 4, 1865, and paroled at Meridian, Mississippi, on May 13, 1865. Residence—Randolph County, Alabama.

Pitchford, William M., Pvt. Co. A.
Enrolled on January 1, 1864, at Tallapoosa County, Alabama, by Captain Echols for the war. Age—16. Appears on a company muster-in roll for January 1, 1864, at Montgomery, Alabama. Appears present on a company muster roll for January and February 1864, with pay due from time of enlistment. Here he is shown as having enlisted at Coosa, Alabama. Drew clothing in 2nd quarter of 1864. Appears present on detailed duty on a company muster roll for September and October 1864. Detailed as a regimental teamster. Appears on a roll of POW's of Company A, 63rd Alabama Infantry commanded by Lieutenant

W. D. Kyle that were surrendered by Lt. General Richard Taylor at Citronelle, Alabama, on May 4, 1865, and paroled at Meridian, Mississippi, on May 13, 1865. Residence—Tallapoosa County, Alabama.

Polk, E. S., Pvt. Co. F.
Enlisted on July 12, 1864, at Lowndes County, Alabama, by Captain Buell for the war. Age—17, eyes—grey, hair—light, complexion—fair, 5 foot 4 inches. Appears on a company muster-in roll for July 25, 1864, at Georgiana, Alabama. Drew clothing on September 11, 1864. Appears absent on a company muster roll for August 31 to October 31, 1864. Absent in hospital at Lauderdale Springs, Mississippi, since October 7, 1864. Appears on a register of POW's paroled on June 2, 1865, at Montgomery, Alabama. Signed parole at headquarters of the 16th US Army Corps at Montgomery. His parole is in his file. Signed by "X".

Pollerd, James M., Pvt. Co. C.
Enlisted on May 10, 1864, at Russell County, Alabama, by Lieutenant Carnes for the war. Age—17, eyes—blue, hair—dark, complexion—fair, 5 foot 4 inches, residence—Hartsville, Russell County, Alabama. Appears on a company muster-in roll for June 24, 1864, at Camp Watts near Notasulga, Alabama. Drew clothing on August 6, 1864. Appears present on a company muster roll for September and October 1864. Captured at Blakeley, Alabama, on April 9, 1865. Appears on a roll of POW's received at Ship Island, Mississippi, on April 15, 1865. Transferred from Ship Island to Vicksburg, Mississippi, on May 1, 1865. Appears on a roll of POW's of Cos. C and H, 63rd Alabama Infantry commanded by Captain C. W. Martin that were surrendered by Lt. General Richard Taylor at Citronelle, Alabama, on May 4, 1865, and paroled at Meridian, Mississippi, on May 11, 1865. Residence—Russell County, Alabama.

Poole, C. F., Sergeant Co. K.
Enlisted on September 3, 1864, at Macon County, Alabama, by Major Ready for the war. Appears present on a company muster roll for September and October 1864. Captured at Blakeley, Alabama, on April 9, 1865. Appears on a roll of POW's received at Ship Island, Mississippi, on April 15, 1865. Transferred from Ship Island to Vicksburg, Mississippi, on May 1, 1865. Appears on a roll of POW's of Quintard Hospital CSA commanded by Surgeon S. V. D. Hill that were surrendered by Lt. General Richard Taylor at Citronelle, Alabama, on May 4, 1865, and paroled at Meridian, Mississippi, on May 10, 1865. Here he is shown as C. Poole Jr. with residence in Milledgeville, Georgia. He also appears on a roll of POW's of Cos. I and K, 63rd Alabama Infantry commanded by Lieutenant W. A. Skinner that were surrendered by Lt. General Richard Taylor at Citronelle, Alabama, on May 4, 1865, and paroled at Meridian, Mississippi, on May 13, 1865. Residence—Butler County, Alabama. Here he is shown as 4th Sergeant Company K. [There may be more than one man represented here.]

Poole, E. H., Pvt. Co. K.
Enlisted on September 16, 1864, at Bibb County, Alabama, by Captain Hudgens for the war. Appears present on a company muster roll for September and October 1864. Captured at Blakeley, Alabama, on April 9, 1865. Appears on a roll of POW's received at Ship Island, Mississippi, on April 15, 1865. Transferred from Ship Island to Vicksburg, Mississippi, on May 1, 1865. Appears on a roll of POW's of Cos. I and K, 63rd Alabama Infantry commanded by Lieutenant W. A. Skinner that were surrendered by Lt. General Richard Taylor at Citronelle, Alabama, on May 4, 1865, and paroled at Meridian, Mississippi, on May 13, 1865. Residence—Bibb County, Alabama.

Poole, T. M., Pvt. Co. F.
Enlisted on May 30, 1864, at Montgomery, Alabama, by Captain Moore for the

war. Age—17, eyes—blue, hair—light, complexion—fair, 5 foot 8 inches, residence—Autauga County, Alabama. Appears on a company muster-in roll for July 25, 1864, at Georgiana, Alabama. Appears absent on a company muster roll for August 31 to October 31, 1864, with pay due from time of enlistment. Absent in hospital at Greenville, Alabama, since July 31, 1864. Captured at Blakeley, Alabama, on April 9, 1865. Appears on a roll of POW's received at Ship Island, Mississippi, on April 15, 1865. Transferred from Ship Island to Vicksburg, Mississippi, on May 1, 1865. Appears on a roll of POW's of Company F, 63rd Alabama Infantry commanded by Captain R. T. Simpson that were surrendered by Lt. General Richard Taylor at Citronelle, Alabama, on May 4, 1865, and paroled at Meridian, Mississippi, on May 11, 1865. Residence—Autauga County, Alabama.

Pope, W. C., Pvt. Co. K.
Enlisted on August 17, 1864, at Talladega, Alabama, by Captain Powers for the war. Appears present on a company muster roll for September and October 1864. "Hospital Mobile since made out October 31" is crossed out on the file card. Captured at Blakeley, Alabama, on April 9, 1865. Appears on a roll of POW's received at Ship Island, Mississippi, on April 15, 1865. Transferred from Ship Island to Vicksburg, Mississippi, on May 1, 1865. Appears on a roll of POW's of Cos. I and K, 63rd Alabama Infantry commanded by Lieutenant W. A. Skinner that were surrendered by Lt. General Richard Taylor at Citronelle, Alabama, on May 4, 1865, and paroled at Meridian, Mississippi, on May 13, 1865. Residence—Talladega County, Alabama.

Potter, W. O., Pvt. Co. F.
Enlisted on May 30, 1864, at Montgomery, Alabama, by Captain Jackson for the war. Age—17, eyes—hazel, hair—brown, complexion—fair, 5 foot 3 inches, residence—Butler County, Alabama. He appears on a company muster-in roll for July 25, 1864, at Georgiana, Alabama. He appears absent on a company muster roll for August 31 to October 31, 1864, with pay due from time of enlistment. Absent in hospital at Mobile, Alabama. His name appears on a roll of POW's captured on April 25, 1865, by Brigadier General Lucas commanding 3rd Brigade Cavalry Military Division West Mississippi, and paroled at Greenville, Alabama.

Powell, W. C., Corporal Co. H.
Enlisted on March 15, 1864, at Centerville, Alabama, by Captain Suttle, for the war. Age—17, eyes—grey, hair—dark, complexion—fair. Drew clothing on September 11, 1864. Appears present on a company muster roll for September and October 1864. Captured at Blakeley, Alabama, on April 9, 1865. Appears on a roll of POW's received at Ship Island, Mississippi, on April 15, 1865. Transferred from Ship Island to Vicksburg, Mississippi, on May 1, 1865. Appears on a roll of POW's of Cos. C and H, 63rd Alabama Infantry commanded by Captain C. W. Martin that were surrendered by Lt. General Richard Taylor at Citronelle, Alabama, on May 4, 1865, and paroled at Meridian, Mississippi, on May 11, 1865. Residence—Bibb County, Alabama.

Powers, James M., Pvt. Co. A.
Enlisted on January 1, 1864, at Tallapoosa County, Alabama, by Captain John Echols for the war. Appears on a company muster-in roll for January 1, 1864, at Montgomery, Alabama. Age—17. Appears present on a company muster roll for January and February 1864, with pay due from time of enlistment. Drew clothing in 2nd quarter, August 12 and September 11, 1864. Appears present on a company muster roll for September and October 1864. Here he is shown as having been last paid on February 29, 1864. Captured at Blakeley, Alabama, on April 9, 1865. Appears on a roll of POW's received at Ship Island,

Mississippi, on April 15, 1865. Transferred from Ship Island to Vicksburg, Mississippi, on May 1, 1865. Appears on a roll of POW's of Company A, 63rd Alabama Infantry commanded by Lieutenant W. D. Kyle that were surrendered by Lt. General Richard Taylor at Citronelle, Alabama, on May 4, 1865, and paroled at Meridian, Mississippi, on May 13, 1865. His residence was shown as Tallapoosa County, Alabama.

Powers, W. L. (M. L.), Pvt. Co. F.
Enlisted on July 12, 1864, at Lowndes County, Alabama, by Captain Buell for the war. Age—17, eyes—grey, hair—dark, complexion—fair, 5 foot 5 inches, residence—Lowndes County, Alabama. Appears on a company muster-in roll for July 25, 1864, at Georgiana, Alabama. Appears present on a company muster roll for August 31 to October 31, 1864, with pay due from time of enlistment. Admitted on November 24, 1864, to Ross Hospital, Mobile, Alabama, with febris remittens. Sent to General Hospital Nidelet on November 30, 1864. Captured at Blakeley, Alabama, on April 9, 1865. Appears on a roll of POW's received at Ship Island, Mississippi, on April 15, 1865. Transferred from Ship Island to Vicksburg, Mississippi, on May 1, 1865. Appears on a roll of POW's of Company F, 63rd Alabama Infantry commanded by Captain R. T. Simpson that were surrendered by Lt. General Richard Taylor at Citronelle, Alabama, on May 4, 1865, and paroled at Meridian, Mississippi, on May 11, 1865. Residence—Lowndes County, Alabama.

Preston, A. G., Pvt. Co. I.
Enlisted on April 15, 1864, at Talladega, Alabama, by Captain Parks for the war. Admitted to Ross Hospital, Mobile, Alabama, on August 12, 1864, with febris intermittens quot. Returned to duty on August 18, 1864. Admitted to Ross Hospital, Mobile, Alabama, on August 23, 1864, with debilitas. Returned to duty on September 2, 1864. Appears absent on a company muster roll for September and October 1864. Absent furloughed for 30 days from September 27, 1864.

Price, Hampton, M., Pvt. Co. A.
Enlisted on January 1, 1864, at Macon County, Alabama, by Captain John Echols for the war. Appears on a company muster-in roll for January 1, 1864, at Montgomery, Alabama. Age—15. Appears present on a company muster roll for January and February 1864, with pay due from time of enlistment. Drew clothing in 2nd quarter of 1864. Appears absent on a company muster roll for September and October 1864. Absent sick in Notasulga, Alabama, since August 7, 1864. Here he is shown as having been paid on February 29, 1864. Signed a parole at the headquarters of the 16th US Army Corps in Montgomery on May 19, 1865. Hair—dark, eyes—dark, complexion—fair, 5 foot 5 inches.

Prince, J. W., Pvt. Co. I.
Enlisted on May 18, 1864, at Wedowee, Alabama, by Captain Robinson for the war. Appears absent on a company muster roll for September and October 1864. Absent without leave from September 18, 1864.

Pritchett, Pascal H., Pvt. Co. G.
Enlisted on May 16, 1864, at Troy, Alabama, by Captain Wilkerson for the war. Age—17, eyes—grey, hair—light, complexion—fair, 5 foot 6 inches, residence—Coffee County, Alabama. Appears on a company muster-in roll for September 7, 1864, at Blakeley, Alabama. Drew clothing on September 11, 1864. Appears present on a company muster roll for September and October 1864.

Pruett, Darling H., Pvt. Co. G.
Enlisted on May 16, 1864, at Troy, Alabama, by Captain Wilkerson for the war. Age—17, eyes—grey, hair—light, complexion—fair, 5 foot 8 inches,

residence—Coffee County, Alabama. Appears on a company muster-in roll for September 7, 1864, at Blakeley, Alabama. Drew clothing on September 11, 1864. Signed by his mark. Appears present on a company muster roll for September and October 1864. Captured at Blakeley, Alabama, on April 9, 1865. Appears on a roll of POW's received at Ship Island, Mississippi, on April 15, 1865. Transferred from Ship Island to Vicksburg, Mississippi, on May 1, 1865. Appears on a roll of POW's of Cos. E and G, 63rd Alabama Infantry commanded by Captain A. V. Lee that were surrendered by Lt. General Richard Taylor at Citronelle, Alabama, on May 4, 1865, and paroled at Meridian, Mississippi, on May 13, 1865. Residence—Pike County, Alabama.

Pruett, I. H., O. S. [Ordnance Sergeant] Co. C.
Enlisted on August 28, 1864, at Baldwin County, Alabama, by Captain Rogers for the war. Appears absent on a company muster roll for September and October 1864. Absent in hospital at Mobile, Alabama, since October 18, 1864.

Pruett, Samuel, T., 2nd Lieutenant Co. G.
Appears present on a company muster roll for September and October 1864. Elected Jr. 2nd Lieutenant on September 11, 1864. Elected 2nd Lieutenant on November 10, 1864. Appears on a roll of POW's captured by Brigadier General Lucas commanding the US 3rd Brigade Cavalry, Military Division West Mississippi. Captured on May 2, 1865, at Midway, Alabama.

Pugh, W. E., Pvt. Co. H.
Enlisted on August 1, 1864, at Butler, Alabama, by Captain Brown for the war. Appears present on a company muster roll for July and August 1864, with pay due from time of enlistment.

Purcell, William A., Pvt. Co. C.
Enlisted on May 18, 1864, at Tallapoosa County, Alabama, by Captain Brown for the war. Age—17, eyes—dark, hair—dark, complexion—dark, 5 foot 3 ½ inches, residence—Dadeville, Tallapoosa County, Alabama. Appears on a company muster-in roll for June 24, 1864, at Camp Watts near Notasulga, Alabama. Appears absent on a company muster roll for September and October 1864. Absent in hospital at Camp Watts since August 1, 1864.

Pylant, William M., Pvt. Co. B.
Enlisted on July 17, 1864, at Montgomery, Alabama, by Lieutenant Calhoun for the war. Appears present on a company muster roll for September and October 1864, with pay due from time of enlistment. Captured at Blakeley, Alabama, on April 9, 1865. Appears on a roll of POW's received at Ship Island, Mississippi, on April 15, 1865. Transferred from Ship Island to Vicksburg, Mississippi, on May 1, 1865. Appears on a roll of POW's of Company B, 63rd Alabama Infantry commanded by 1st Lieutenant Thomas J. Calhoun that were surrendered by Lt. General Richard Taylor at Citronelle, Alabama, on May 4, 1865, and paroled at Meridian, Mississippi, on May 11, 1865. Residence—Coosa County, Alabama.

Pyne, Columbus C., Sergeant Co. D.
Enlisted on July 20, 1864, at Macon County, Alabama, by Major Ready for the war. Age—17, eyes—dark, hair—dark, complexion—dark, 5 foot 6 inches, residence—Clayton, Barbour County, Alabama. Appears on a company muster-in roll for July 20, 1864, at Camp Watts near Notasulga, Alabama. Drew clothing on August 7, 1864. Appears on a company muster roll for August 30 to October 30, 1864, with pay due from time of enlistment. Here he is shown as having enlisted on March 2, 1864, at Clayton by D. M. Seals. Captured at Blakeley, Alabama, on April 9, 1865. Appears on a roll of POW's received at Ship Island, Mississippi, on April 15, 1865. Transferred from Ship Island to Vicksburg,

Mississippi, on May 1, 1865. Appears on a roll of POW's of Company D, 63rd Alabama Infantry commanded by Captain Robert H. Pearson that were surrendered by Lt. General Richard Taylor at Citronelle, Alabama, on May 4, 1865, and paroled at Meridian, Mississippi, on May 13, 1865. Residence—Barbour County, Alabama.

Radford, C. M., Pvt. Co. F.
Enlisted on May 30, 1864, at Montgomery, Alabama, by Captain Jackson for the war. Drew clothing on September 11, 1864. Appears present sick on a company muster roll for September and October 1864, with pay due from time of enlistment.

Radford, J. P., Pvt. Co. F.
Enlisted on May 30, 1864, at Montgomery, Alabama, by Captain Jackson for the war. Eyes—dark, hair—dark, complexion—dark, 5 foot 8 inches, residence—Alabama, age—17. Appears absent without leave on a company muster-in roll for July 25, 1864, at Georgiana, Alabama.

Ray, George M., Pvt. Co. B/K.
Enlisted in Co. B. on August 15, 1864, at Pollard, Alabama, by Lieutenant Townsend for the war. Shown as having been transferred on a Company B muster roll for September and October 1864, with pay due from time of enlistment. Transferred per Special Order on October 2, 1864. Appears absent on a Company K muster roll for September and October 1864. Absent sick without leave since October 19.

Ray, Marion A., Pvt. Co. A.
Enlisted on July 17, 1864, at Butler [County?], Alabama, by Captain Echols for the war. Appears present on a company muster roll for September and October 1864, with pay due from time of enlistment. Captured at Blakeley, Alabama, on April 9, 1865. Appears on a roll of POW's received at Ship Island, Mississippi, on April 15, 1865. Transferred from Ship Island to Vicksburg, Mississippi, on May 1, 1865. Appears on a roll of POW's of Company A, 63rd Alabama Infantry commanded by Lieutenant W. D. Kyle that were surrendered by Lt. General Richard Taylor at Citronelle, Alabama, on May 4, 1865, and paroled at Meridian, Mississippi, on May 13, 1865. Residence—Butler County, Alabama.

Ray, M. E., Pvt.
Appears on a register of paroled Confederate soldiers, paroled by the Provost Marshal of the 16th US Army Corps. Signed a parole on June 3, 1865, at Montgomery, Alabama. Hair—dark, eyes—dark, complexion—dark, 6 foot. Signs by his mark "X." His parole shows W. E. Ray and is in his file.

Rayburn, R., Pvt. Co. F.
Captured at Blakeley, Alabama, on April 9, 1865. Appears on a roll of POW's received at Ship Island, Mississippi, on April 15, 1865. Transferred from Ship Island to Vicksburg, Mississippi, on May 1, 1865. Appears on a roll of POW's of Company F, 63rd Alabama Infantry commanded by Captain R. T. Simpson that were surrendered by Lt. General Richard Taylor at Citronelle, Alabama, on May 4, 1865, and paroled at Meridian, Mississippi, on May 11, 1865. His residence is shown as Lowndes County, Alabama.

Reader, William N., Pvt. Co. D.
Enlisted on July 30, 1864, at Macon County, Alabama, by Major Ready for the war. Age—17, eyes—blue, hair—light, complexion—florid, 5 foot 8 inches, residence—Adkinsons, Barbour County, Alabama. Appears on a company muster-in roll for July 30, 1864, at Camp Watts near Notasulga, Alabama. Appears

absent on a company muster roll for August 30 to October 30, 1864. Absent sick at Mobile hospital since October 26. Here he is shown as having enlisted at Clayton, Alabama, on March 2, 1864, by D. M. Seals. His name appears on a list of wounded Confederates in the hospital of the 1st Division 13th US Army Corps, Army of the Military Division of West Mississippi at the battle of Blakeley Fort, Alabama, on April 9, 1865, with flesh wound of the thigh. Captured and confined at Fort Blakeley, Alabama, on April 9, 1865. POW confined May 1, 1865, at New Orleans, Louisiana. Paroled and release at New Orleans on May 16, 1865.

Reddock, William M., Pvt. Co. G/B.
Enlisted on May 16, 1864, at Troy, Alabama, by Captain Wilkerson for the war. Age—17, eyes—black, hair—dark, complexion—florid, 5 foot 2 inches. Appears on a Company G muster-in roll for September 7, 1864, at Blakeley, Alabama. Drew clothing on August 7 and September 11, 1864. Captured at Blakeley, Alabama, on April 9, 1865. Here he is shown as being in Company B. Appears on a roll of POW's received at Ship Island, Mississippi, on April 15, 1865. Transferred from Ship Island to Vicksburg, Mississippi, on May 1, 1865. Appears on a roll of POW's of Cos. E and G, 63rd Alabama Infantry commanded by Captain A. V. Lee that were surrendered by Lt. General Richard Taylor at Citronelle, Alabama, on May 4, 1865, and paroled at Meridian, Mississippi, on May 13, 1865. Residence—Pike County, Alabama.

Redick, J. P., Pvt. Co. F.
Enlisted on March 9, 1864, at Greenville, Alabama, by Captain Brown for the war. Age—17, eyes—blue, hair—dark, complexion—fair, 6 foot, residence—Butler County, Alabama. Appears on a company muster-in roll for July 25, 1864, at Georgiana, Alabama. Appears as having died on a company muster roll for August 31 to October 31, 1864, with pay due from time of enlistment. Died on September 20, 1864.

Reedy, W. P., Pvt. Co. I.
Appears on a list of POW stragglers paroled at Selma, Alabama, during June 1865. Residence—Perry County, Alabama.

Reese, J. B., Pvt. Co. G.
Enlisted on August 1, 1864, at Pollard, Alabama, by Lieutenant Johnson for the war. Age—17, eyes—grey, hair—black, complexion—dark, 5 foot 4 inches, residence—Pike County, Alabama. Appears on a company muster-in roll for September 7, 1864, at Blakeley, Alabama. Appears as having deserted on a company muster roll for September and October 1864. Deserted on August 5, 1864, from Pollard, Alabama.

Reeves, William M., Pvt. Co. G/B.
Enlisted on May 16, 1864, at Troy, Alabama, by Captain Wilkerson for the war. Age—17, eyes—grey, hair—light, complexion—dark, 5 foot 3 inches, residence—Pike County, Alabama. Appears on a Company G muster-in roll for September 7, 1864, at Blakeley, Alabama. Appears absent on a Company G muster roll for September and October 1864. Absent furloughed home and extended to October 30, 1864, by Ex [Medical Examining Board] at Troy. Captured at Blakeley, Alabama, on April 9, 1865. Here he is shown as being in Company B. Appears on a roll of POW's received at Ship Island, Mississippi, on April 15, 1865. Transferred from Ship Island to Vicksburg, Mississippi, on May 1, 1865. His name appears on a roll of POW's of Cos. E and G, 63rd Alabama Infantry commanded by Captain A. V. Lee that were surrendered by Lt. General Richard Taylor at Citronelle, Alabama, on May 4, 1865, and paroled at Meridian, Mississippi, on May 13, 1865. Residence—Pike County, Alabama.

Reid, Boling, 1st Lieutenant Co. A.
    Appears absent on a company A muster roll for September and October 1864. Absent furloughed for 30 days by Medical Examining Board on October 7, 1864. Appears on a roster of the 2nd Alabama Reserves, Fuller's Brigade, Maury's Corps, District of the Gulf in January 1865. Reported to have been elected 1st Lieutenant on August 27.

Reily, T. J., Pvt. Co. H.
    Enlisted on July 29, 1864, at Selma, Alabama, by Lieutenant Killough for the war. Age—17, eyes—blue, hair—dark, complexion—dark. Appears present on a company muster roll for September and October 1864. Drew clothing on September 11, 1864.

Renfroe, Elisha, D., Pvt. Co. C.
    Enlisted on June 15, 1864, at Russell County, Alabama, by Lieutenant Carnes for the war. Age—17, eyes—grey, hair—dark, complexion—dark, 5 foot 7 inches, residence—Russell County, Alabama, Post Office—Columbus, Georgia. Appears on a company muster-in roll for June 24, 1865, at Camp Watts near Notasulga, Alabama. Appears as having deserted on a company muster roll for September and October 1864. He is reported to have deserted on June 20, 1864, at Camp Watts, Alabama.

Renfroe, W. H., Pvt. Co. F.
    Captured at Blakeley, Alabama, on April 9, 1865. Appears on a roll of POW's received at Ship Island, Mississippi, on April 15, 1865. Transferred from Ship Island to Vicksburg, Mississippi, on May 1, 1865. Appears on a roll of POW's of Company F, 63rd Alabama Infantry commanded by Captain R. T. Simpson that were surrendered by Lt. General Richard Taylor at Citronelle, Alabama, on May 4, 1865, and paroled at Meridian, Mississippi, on May 11, 1865. Residence—Butler County, Alabama. Paroled at the headquarters of the 16th US Army Corps in Montgomery, Alabama, on May 20, 1864. Hair—dark, eyes—blue, complexion—fair, 5 foot 4 inches. Signed by his mark "X." His parole is in his file. The records show some confusion as to where he was paroled.

Rencher, Abe, Pvt. Co. K/H.
    Enlisted on August 23, 1864, at Perry County, Alabama, by Lieutenant Donnell for the war. Appears present on a company muster roll for September and October 1864. Appears on a list of wounded Confederates in the hospital of the 1st Division 13th US Army Corps, Army of the Military Division of West Mississippi at the battle of Blakeley Fort, Alabama, on April 9, 1865, with flesh wound to thigh. Captured and confined at Fort Blakeley, Alabama, on April 9, 1865. POW confined May 1, 1865, at New Orleans, Louisiana. Admitted on April 15, 1865, to St. Louis, USA General Hospital, New Orleans, Louisiana, with gunshot wound to right buttocks. Age—15. He is reported to have been transferred to Marine General Hospital on May 16, 1865. Paroled and released on May 16, 1865.

Reynolds, J. R., Pvt. Co. E.
    Enlisted on August 5, 1864, at Montgomery, Alabama, by Captain A. V. Lee for the war. Age—17, eyes—blue, hair—light, complexion—fair. Appears absent on a company muster roll for September and October 1864. Absent without leave since August 7, 1864.

Rice, J., Pvt. Co. I.
    Enlisted on April 15, 1864, at Wedowee, Alabama, by Captain Robinson for the war. Appears absent on a company muster roll for September and October 1864. Absent without leave from September 18, 1864.

Rice, O. F., Colonel, Field and Staff

Born in Kentucky. Appointed as 2nd Lieutenant CSA Army from Kentucky on June 12, 1861, to take rank from March 16, 1861. Appointment was confirmed on October 14, 1862, acceptance on June 12, 1861. Shown on a US register of 1861 as Cadet 2 class of 44. Original entry into service [US] July 1, 1856. Appears on a register of appointments CSA Army, reported by General S. B. Buckner as appointed Major on February 9, 1863. To take rank from January 26, 1863. Appears as Major on a list of Officers of Adjutant and Inspector General's Department on duty in District of the Gulf, at Mobile, Alabama, on May 25, 1863. Appointed on January 24, 1863. Appears present on a Field and Staff muster roll for July and August 1864, near Blakeley, Alabama. Appointed Colonel of the 2nd Regiment Alabama Reserves, Fuller's Brigade, Maury's Corps, District of the Gulf by Major General Withers by order of Secretary of War on August 16, 1864. Appears present on a Field and Staff muster roll for September and October 1864, near Mobile, Alabama. He signed a requisition for stationary for the month of September 1864, at Camp Hood near Blakeley, Alabama. The requisition is in his file.

Richards, I. M., Pvt. Co. C.

Enlisted on September 15, 1864, at Baldwin County, Alabama, by Captain Martin for the war. Appears absent on a company muster roll for September and October 1864. Absent in hospital at Mobile, Alabama, since October 26, 1864.

Richards, Robert D., Corporal Co. D.

Enlisted as 2nd Corporal on July 30, 1864, at Macon County, Alabama, by Major Ready. Age—17, eyes—dark, hair—dark, complexion—dark, 5 foot 6 inches, residence—Kings, Barbour County, Alabama. Appears on a company muster-in roll for July 30, 1864, at Camp Watts near Notasulga, Alabama. Drew clothing on August 7, 1864. Appears present on a company muster roll for August 30 to October 30, 1864, with pay due from time of enlistment. Here he is shown as having enlisted on March 2, 1864, at Clayton, Alabama, by D. M. Seals. R. D. Richards, Pvt. 2nd Battalion Alabama Infantry appears on a list which bears the following heading "Post Register, Albany Ga." dated May 23, 1865. This last entry my likely be another R. D. Richards.

Richardson, J. M., Pvt. Co. E.

Enlisted on September 5, 1864, at Camp Hood [near Blakeley, Alabama] by Captain A. V. Lee for the war. Age—17, eyes—dark, hair—dark, complexion—dark. Drew clothing on September 11, 1864. Signed by his mark. Appears absent on a company muster roll for September and October 1864. Absent in hospital since October 1, 1864.

Richardson, John D., Pvt. Co. B.

Enlisted on March 23, 1864, at Montgomery, Alabama, by Captain Zimmerman for the war. Age—16. Appears on a company muster-in roll for March 23, 1864, at Montgomery. Drew clothing on July 8, 1864. Appears present on a company muster roll for September and October 1864, with pay due from time of enlistment. Captured and wounded at Blakeley, Alabama, on April 9, 1865. Appears on a list of hospital attendants and sick and wounded that were sent to Vicksburg, Mississippi, via New Orleans, Louisiana, from Spanish Fort, Alabama, on April 8, 1865. Appears on a list of wounded POW's to be transferred to hospital at New Orleans from Blakeley. List is dated April 13, 1865. Admitted to USA Hospital Steamer D. A. January on April 17, 1865. He was transferred to the US Hospital Steamer Elanore Carrel on April 25, 1865 [at New Orleans]. He was transferred to USA General Hospital No. 3, Vicksburg on April 28, 1865. Appears on a roll of POW's at USA General Hospital No. 3, Vicksburg that were transferred to USA General Hospital No. 2 at Vicksburg on May 4. Appears on a list of sick and wounded Confederate POW's at USA General Hospital No. 2, Vicksburg. Admitted on May 4, 1865, with severe gunshot wound right shoulder. Age—18. Wounded by conical ball. Returned to duty on May 8, 1865. There is paper work in his file as to an inquiry from the State of Florida in 1915.

Richardson, Samuel, Pvt. Co. A.
Enlisted on January 1, 1864, at Tallapoosa County, Alabama, by Captain Echols for the war. Age—16. Appears on a company muster-in roll for January 1, 1864, at Montgomery, Alabama. Appears present on a company muster roll for January and February 1864, with pay due from time of enlistment. Drew clothing in 2nd quarter, August 12 and September 11, 1864. Appears present on a company muster roll for September and October 1864. Here he is shown as having been last paid on February 29, 1864. Captured at Blakeley, Alabama, on April 9, 1865. Appears on a roll of POW's received at Ship Island, Mississippi, on April 15, 1865. Transferred from Ship Island to Vicksburg, Mississippi, on May 1, 1865. Appears on a roll of POW's of Company A, 63rd Alabama Infantry commanded by Lieutenant W. D. Kyle that were surrendered by Lt. General Richard Taylor at Citronelle, Alabama, May 4, 1865, and paroled at Meridian, Mississippi, on May 13, 1865. Residence—Tallapoosa County, Alabama.

Richie, G. W., Pvt. Co. E.
Enlisted on August 5, 1864, at Montgomery, Alabama, by Captain A. V. Lee for the war. Age—17, eyes—blue, hair—light, complexion—fair. Drew clothing on September 11, 1864. Admitted to Ross Hospital, Mobile, Alabama, on September 18, 1864, with rubeola parotitis. Returned to duty on October 6, 1864. Appears present on a company muster roll for September and October 1864. Appears on a register of sick and wounded POW's at City Hospital, Mobile, Alabama. Here he is shown as wounded but no date. Appears on a roll of POW's remaining in hospital in Mobile and belonging to the CSA Army commanded by Assistant Surgeon Charles O. Helwig. They were captured at Mobile and paroled by Major General Canby USA on May 11, 1865. His residence was reported to be Conecuh County, Alabama.

Riley, G. H., Pvt. Co. A.
Admitted to Ross Hospital, Mobile, Alabama, with febris intermittens quot. on September 24, 1864. Returned to duty on September 28, 1864.

Riley, J., Pvt. Co. C.
Enlisted on August 2, 1864, at Montgomery, Alabama, by Captain Rogers for the war. Drew clothing on August 6, 1864. Appears present on a company muster roll for September and October 1864. Captured at Blakeley, Alabama, on April 9, 1865. Appears on a roll of POW's received at Ship Island, Mississippi, on April 15, 1865. Transferred from Ship Island to Vicksburg, Mississippi, on May 1, 1865. Appears on a roll of POW's of Cos. C and H, 63rd Alabama Infantry commanded by Captain C. W. Martin that were surrendered by Lt. General Richard Taylor at Citronelle, Alabama, on May 4, 1865, and paroled at Meridian, Mississippi, on May 11, 1865. His residence is shown as Russell County, Alabama.

Riley, J. M., Sergeant Co. E.
Enlisted on August 1, 1864, at Montgomery, Alabama, by Captain A. V. Lee for the war. Age—17, eyes—blue, hair—light, complexion—fair. Appears as 2nd Sergeant and present on a company muster roll for September and October 1864. Appears on a report of POW's captured by the 2nd Brigade Cavalry Division, Macon Georgia. Report is dated April 30, 1865.

Riley, Thomas J., Pvt. Co. H.
Captured at Blakeley, Alabama, on April 9, 1865. Appears on a roll of POW's received at Ship Island, Mississippi, on April 15, 1865. Transferred from Ship Island to Vicksburg, Mississippi, on May 1, 1865. Appears on a roll of POW's of Cos. C and H, 63rd Alabama Infantry commanded by Captain C. W. Martin that were surrendered by Lt. General Richard Taylor at Citronelle, Alabama, on May 4, 1865, and paroled at Meridian, Mississippi, on May 11, 1865. Residence—Jefferson County, Alabama.

Riley, W., Corporal/Pvt. Co. K/G.
Enlisted on May 11, 1864, at Bibb County, Alabama, by Captain Jerk for the war. Appears as 3rd Corporal and present on a company muster roll for September and October 1864. Captured at Blakeley, Alabama, on April 9, 1865. Appears on a roll of POW's received at Ship Island, Mississippi, on April 15, 1865. Here he is shown as a Private in Company G. Transferred from Ship Island to Vicksburg, Mississippi, on May 1, 1865. Appears on a roll of POW's of Cos. I and K, 63rd Alabama Infantry commanded by Lieutenant W. A. Skinner that were surrendered by Lt. General Richard Taylor at Citronelle, Alabama, on May 4, 1865, and paroled at Meridian, Mississippi, May 13, 1865. Residence—Bibb County, Alabama. Here he is shown as Private in Company K.

Ritchie, James, Pvt. Co. B/K.
Enlisted on June 25, 1864, at Montgomery, Alabama, by Captain Zimmerman for the war. Drew clothing on July 8, 1864. Signed by his mark. Appears as having been transferred on a Company B muster roll for September and October 1864, with pay due from time of enlistment. Transferred per. Special Order No. 15 dated October 2, 1864. Appears absent on a Company K muster roll for September and October 1864. Muster roll reports him absent sick without leave since September 1, 1864.

Roberson, Raymond, Pvt. Co. B.
Enlisted on March 23, 1864, at Montgomery, Alabama, by Captain Zimmerman for the war. Age—16. Appears on a company muster-in roll for March 23, 1864. Drew clothing on August 12 and September 11, 1864. Signed by his mark. Appears present on a company muster roll for September and October 1864, with pay due from time of enlistment. Captured at Blakeley, Alabama, on April 9, 1865. Appears on a roll of POW's received at Ship Island, Mississippi, on April 15, 1865. Transferred from Ship Island to Vicksburg, Mississippi, on May 1, 1865. Appears on a roll of sick and wounded POW's at USA General Hospital, No. 2, Vicksburg. Admitted from steamer on May 3, 1865, with acute diarrhoea. Returned to duty on May 8, 1865. Age—16. Paroled on June 23, 1865, at headquarters of the 16th US Army Corps at Montgomery, Alabama. He was described as: hair—light, eyes—blue, complexion—fair, 5 foot. His parole is in his file signed by mark "X."

Roberts, I. W., Pvt./Sergeant Co. E.
Enlisted on August 1, 1864, at Montgomery, Alabama, by Captain A. V. Lee for the war. Age—17, eyes—blue, hair—light, complexion—fair. Appears absent on a company muster roll for September and October 1864. Absent on 30 day furlough from October 20, 1864. Captured at Blakeley, Alabama, on April 9, 1865. Appears on a roll of POW's received at Ship Island, Mississippi, on April 15, 1865. Transferred from Ship Island to Vicksburg, Mississippi, on May 1, 1865. Appears on a roll of POW's of Cos. E and G, 63rd Alabama Infantry commanded by Captain A. V. Lee that were surrendered by Lt. General Richard Taylor at Citronelle, Alabama, on May 4, 1865, and paroled at Meridian, Mississippi, on May 13, 1865. His residence is shown as Montgomery, Alabama.

Roberts, James W., Pvt. Co. I.
Appears on a register of St. Mary's Hospital, West Point, Georgia, in 1865.

Roberts, J. W., Pvt. Co. I.
Enlisted on April 15, 1864, at Wedowee, Alabama, by Captain Robinson for the war. Appears present on company muster roll for September and October 1864.

Robertson, Daniel, S., Sergeant/Pvt. Co. B.
Enlisted as 4th Sergeant on April 8, 1864, at Montgomery County, Alabama, by Captain Zimmerman for the war. Appears on a company muster-in roll for March 23, 1864, at Montgomery. Age—17. Drew clothing on July 8, 1864. Appears present on a company muster roll for September and October 1864, with pay due from time of enlistment. Captured at Blakeley, Alabama, on April 9, 1865. Appears on a roll of POW's received at Ship Island, Mississippi, on April 15, 1865. Transferred from Ship Island to Vicksburg, Mississippi, on May 1, 1865. Appears on a roll of POW's of Company B, 63rd Alabama Infantry commanded by 1st Lieutenant Thomas J. Calhoun that were surrendered by Lt. General Richard Taylor at Citronelle, Alabama, on May 4, 1865, and paroled at Meridian, Mississippi, on May 11, 1865. Residence—Chambers County, Alabama.

Robertson, Leonard, B., Pvt. Co. A.
Enlisted on January 1, 1864, at Macon County, Alabama, by Captain Echols for the war. Appears on a company muster-in roll for January 1, 1864, at Montgomery, Alabama. Age—16. Appears present on a company muster roll for January and February 1864, with pay due from time of enlistment. Drew clothing in 2nd quarter of 1864. Appears present on a company muster-roll for September and October 1864. Captured at Blakeley, Alabama, on April 9, 1865. Appears on a roll of POW's received at Ship Island, Mississippi, on April 15, 1865. Transferred from Ship Island to Vicksburg, Mississippi, on May 1, 1865. Appears on a roll of POW's of Company A, 63rd Alabama Infantry commanded by Lieutenant W. D. Kyle that were surrendered by Lt. General Richard Taylor at Citronelle, Alabama, on May 4, 1865, and paroled at Meridian, Mississippi, on May 13, 1865. Residence—Macon County, Alabama.

Robinson, Benjamin, 1st Lieutenant Co. G.
Appears present on a company muster roll for September and October 1864. Elected 1st Lieutenant on September 25, 1864. Appears on a roster of 2nd Regiment Alabama Reserves, Fuller's Brigade, Maury's Corps, District of the Gulf, CSA for January 1865. Here he is shown as having been elected on November 11, 1864. POW captured and paroled at Tuscaloosa, Alabama, on May 18, 1865, by 2nd Regiment Illinois US Cavalry.

Robinson, E. M., Pvt. Co. F.
Enlisted on May 30, 1864, at Montgomery, Alabama, by Captain Moore for the war. Age—17, eyes—hazel, hair—brown, complexion—fair, 5 foot 5 inches, residence—Autauga County, Alabama. Appears on a company muster-in roll for July 25, 1864, at Georgiana, Alabama.

Robinson, Z. D., Pvt. Co. I.
Captured at Blakeley, Alabama, on April 9, 1865. Appears on a roll of POW's received at Ship Island, Mississippi, on April 15, 1865. Transferred from Ship Island to Vicksburg, Mississippi, on May 1, 1865. Appears on a roll of POW's of Cos. I and K, 63rd Alabama Infantry commanded by Lieutenant W. A. Skinner that were surrendered by Lt. General Richard Taylor at Citronelle, Alabama, on May 4, 1865, and paroled at Meridian, Mississippi, May 13, 1865. Residence—Shelby County, Alabama.

Rode, [Rhode] G., Pvt./Corporal Co. K/G.
Enlisted on September 4, 1864, at Walker County, Alabama, by Captain Goodman for the war. Appears present on a Company K muster roll for September and October 1864. Captured at Blakeley, Alabama, on April 9, 1865. Here he is shown in Company G. Appears on a roll of POW's received at Ship Island, Mississippi, on April 15, 1865. Transferred from Ship Island to Vicksburg, Mississippi, on May 1, 1865. Appears on a roll of POW's of Cos. I and K, 63rd Alabama Infantry commanded by Lieutenant W. A. Skinner that were surrendered by Lt. General Richard Taylor at Citronelle, Alabama, on May 4, 1865, and paroled at Meridian, Mississippi, May 13, 1865. Residence—Walker County, Alabama. Here he is shown as 3rd Corporal.

Rogers, Baize, M., Pvt. Co. G.
Enlisted on May 16, 1864, at Troy, Alabama, by Captain Wilkerson for the war. Age—17, eyes—grey, hair—light, complexion—fair, 5 foot 2 inches, residence—Montgomery, Alabama. Appears on a company muster-in roll for September 7, 1864, at Blakeley, Alabama. Drew clothing on September 11, 1864. Appears present on a company muster roll for September and October 1864. Captured at Blakeley, Alabama, on April 9, 1865. Appears on a roll of POW's received at Ship Island, Mississippi, on April 15, 1865. Transferred from Ship Island to Vicksburg, Mississippi, on May 1, 1865. Appears on a roll of POW's of Cos. E and G, 63rd Alabama Infantry commanded by Captain A. V. Lee that were surrendered by Lt. General Richard Taylor at Citronelle, Alabama, on May 4, 1865, and paroled at Meridian, Mississippi, on May 13, 1865. Residence—Montgomery County, Alabama.

Rogers, Robert L., Corporal/Sergeant Co. G.
Enlisted on July 1, 1864, at Troy, Alabama, by Captain Wilkerson for the war. Age—17, eyes—grey, hair—dark, complexion—fair, 5 foot 6 inches, residence—Pike County, Alabama. Appears on a company muster-in roll for September 7, 1864, at Blakeley, Alabama. Drew clothing on September 11, 1864. Signed by his mark. Appears present on a company muster roll for September and October 1864. Appointed 5th Sergeant on October 19, 1864. Captured at Blakeley, Alabama, on April 9, 1865. Appears on a roll of POW's received at Ship Island, Mississippi, on April 15, 1865. Transferred from Ship Island to Vicksburg, Mississippi, on May 1, 1865. Appears on a roll of POW's of Cos. E and G, 63rd Alabama Infantry commanded by Captain A. V. Lee that were surrendered by Lt. General Richard Taylor at Citronelle, Alabama, on May 4, 1865, and paroled at Meridian, Mississippi, on May 13, 1865. Residence—Pike County, Alabama.

Rogers, M. W., Pvt. Co. G/B.
Enlisted on August 1, 1864, at Pollard, Alabama, by Lieutenant Johnson for the war. Age—17, eyes—grey, hair—light, complexion—fair, 5 foot 5 inches, residence—Covington County, Alabama. Appears on a company muster-in roll for September 7, 1864, at Blakeley, Alabama. Drew clothing on September 11, 1864. Appears absent on a company muster roll for September and October 1864. Absent in hospital at Greenville, Alabama since September 29, 1864. Captured at Blakeley, Alabama, on April 9, 1865. Appears on a roll of POW's received at Ship Island, Mississippi, on April 15, 1865. Transferred from Ship Island to Vicksburg, Mississippi, on May 1, 1865. Appears on a roll of POW's of Cos. E and G, 63rd Alabama Infantry commanded by Captain A. V. Lee that were surrendered by Lt. General Richard Taylor at Citronelle, Alabama, on May 4, 1865, and paroled at Meridian, Mississippi, on May 13, 1865. Residence—Pike County, Alabama.

Rogers, Williamson, Captain Co. C.
Enlisted on May 5, 1864, at Macon County, Alabama, by Major Ready for the

war. Age—46, eyes—blue, hair—light, complexion—fair, 5 foot 7 ½ inches, Residence—Society Hill, Macon County, Alabama. Appears on a company muster in roll for June 24, 1864, at Camp Watts near Notasulga, Alabama. Elected Captain on June 20, 1864. He requisitioned for Company C, on July 30, 1864: 58 jackets, 58 pair pants, 58 drawers, 58 shirts, 58 pair stockings, 58 pair shoes and 58 caps. Captain Rogers submitted his resignation at Sibley's Mills on August 28, 1864. It was accepted and forwarded with his endorsement by Colonel O. Rice. The hand written resignation with endorsements is in his file.

Rollin, John, Pvt. Co. G.
Enlisted on May 16, 1864, at Troy, Alabama, by Captain Wilkerson for the war. Age—17, eyes—grey, hair—light, complexion—dark, 5 foot 6 inches, residence—Pike County, Alabama. Appears on a company muster-in roll for September 7, 1864, at Blakeley, Alabama. Drew clothing on September 11, 1864. Appears absent on a company muster roll for September and October 1864. Absent in hospital at Mobile, Alabama, since October 30, 1864.

Rotten, John P., Pvt. Co. G.
Enlisted on May 3, 1864, at Troy, Alabama, by Captain Wilkerson for the war. Age—17, eyes—blue, hair—light, complexion—fair, 5 foot, residence—Pike County, Alabama. Appears on a company muster-in roll for September 7, 1864, at Blakeley, Alabama. Drew clothing on September 11, 1864. Appears absent on a company muster roll for September and October 1864. Absent in hospital at Mobile, Alabama, since October 20, 1864. Paroled at the headquarters of the 16th US Army Corps in Montgomery, Alabama, on May 20, 1865. His parole is in his file.

Rotton, William T., Pvt. Co. G.
Enlisted on May 3, 1864, at Troy, Alabama, by Captain Wilkerson for the war. Age—17, eyes—blue, hair—light, complexion—fair, 5 foot 6 inches, residence—Pike County, Alabama. Appears on a company muster-in roll for September 7, 1864, at Blakeley, Alabama. Drew clothing on September 11, 1864. Appears absent on a company muster roll for September and October 1864. Absent in hospital at Lauderdale Springs, Mississippi, since October 30, 1864. Admitted to 1st Mississippi CSA Hospital, Jackson, Mississippi on November 10, 1864, with febris intermittens, qout. Returned to duty on April 4, 1865. Paroled at the headquarters of the 16th US Army Corps in Montgomery, Alabama, on May 20, 1865. His parole is in his file.

Rouse, Alonzo D., Pvt. Co. B.
Enlisted on April 11, 1864, at Montgomery, Alabama, by Captain Zimmerman for the war. Appears present on a company muster roll for September and October 1864, with pay due from time of enlistment. Captured at Blakeley, Alabama, on April 9, 1865. Appears on a roll of POW's received at Ship Island, Mississippi, on April 15, 1865. Transferred from Ship Island to Vicksburg, Mississippi, on May 1, 1865. Appears on a roll of POW's of Company B, 63rd Alabama Infantry commanded by 1st Lieutenant Thomas J. Calhoun that were surrendered by Lt. General Richard Taylor at Citronelle, Alabama, on May 4, 1865, and paroled at Meridian, Mississippi, on May 11, 1865. Residence—Montgomery County, Alabama.

Rowell, Robert W., Pvt./Sergeant Co. A.
Enlisted on January 1, 1864, at Macon County, Alabama, by Captain John Echols for the war. Appears on a company muster-in roll for January 1, 1864, at Montgomery, Alabama. Age—16. Appears present on a company muster roll for January and February 1864, with pay due from time of enlistment. Drew clothing in 2nd quarter and September 11, 1864. Appears present sick in quarters on a company muster roll for September and October 1864. Here he

is shown as having been last paid on February 29, 1864. Captured at Blakeley, Alabama, on April 9, 1865. Here he is shown as Sergeant. Appears on a roll of POW's received at Ship Island, Mississippi, on April 15, 1865. Transferred from Ship Island to Vicksburg, Mississippi, on May 1, 1865. Appears on a roll of POW's of Company A, 63rd Alabama Infantry commanded by Lieutenant W. D. Kyle that were surrendered by Lt. General Richard Taylor at Citronelle, Alabama, on May 4, 1865, and paroled at Meridian, Mississippi, on May 13, 1865. Residence—Macon County, Alabama.

Roy, Jacob, Pvt. Co. D/A.
Enlisted on July 25, 1864, at Macon County, Alabama, by Major Ready. Age—17, eyes—grey, hair—light, complexion—fair, 5 foot 3 ½ inches, residence—Tuskegee, Macon County, Alabama. Appears on a company muster-in roll for July 30, 1864, at Camp Watts near Notasulga, Alabama. Drew clothing on August 7, 1864. Appears as having been transferred on a Company D muster roll for August 30 to October 30, 1864. Transferred to Company A on September 20. Appears present sick in quarters on a Company A muster roll for September and October 1864. Appears on a roll of POW's of Company A, 63rd Alabama Infantry commanded by Lieutenant W. D. Kyle that were surrendered by Lt. General Richard Taylor at Citronelle, Alabama, on May 4, 1865, and paroled at Meridian, Mississippi, on May 13, 1865. His residence is shown here as Macon County, Alabama.

Rutherford, Eli, S., 1st Sergeant/Pvt. Co. C.
Enlisted on June 4, 1864, at Russell County, Alabama, by Lieutenant Carnes for the war. Age—17, eyes—grey, hair—light, complexion—fair, 5 foot 5 ½ inch, residence—Dover, Russell County, Alabama. Appears on a company muster-in roll for June 24, 1864, at Camp Watts near Notasulga, Alabama. Drew clothing on August 6, 1864. Appears present on a company muster roll for September and October 1864. Captured at Blakeley, Alabama, on April 9, 1865. Appears on a roll of POW's received at Ship Island, Mississippi, on April 15, 1865. Transferred from Ship Island to Vicksburg, Mississippi, on May 1, 1865. Appears on a roll of POW's of Cos. C and H, 63rd Alabama Infantry commanded by Captain C. W. Martin that were surrendered by Lt. General Richard Taylor at Citronelle, Alabama, on May 4, 1865, and paroled at Meridian, Mississippi, on May 11, 1865. Residence—Russell County, Alabama.

Rutland, Z. T., Pvt. Co. D.
Enlisted on August 28, 1864, at Pollard, Alabama, by Captain Zorn for the war. Drew clothing on September 12, 1864. Appears present on a company muster roll for August 30 to October 30, 1864, with pay due from time of enlistment. Captured at Blakeley, Alabama, on April 9, 1865. Appears on a roll of POW's received at Ship Island, Mississippi, on April 15, 1865. Transferred from Ship Island to Vicksburg, Mississippi, on May 1, 1865. Appears on a roll of POW's of Company D, 63rd Alabama Infantry commanded by Captain Robert H. Pearson that were surrendered by Lt. General Richard Taylor at Citronelle, Alabama, on May 4, 1865, and paroled at Meridian, Mississippi, on May 13, 1865. Residence—Barbour County, Alabama.

Ryals, H., Pvt. Co. F.
Enlisted on July 12, 1864, at Lowndes County, Alabama, by Captain Buell for the war. Age—17, eyes—grey, hair—light, complexion—sallow, 5 foot 7 inches, residence—Lowndes County, Alabama. Appears on a company muster-in roll for July 25, 1864, at Georgiana, Alabama. Drew clothing on September 11, 1864. Appears present on a company muster roll for August 31 to October 31, 1864, with pay due from time of enlistment. Captured at Blakeley, Alabama, on April 9, 1865. Appears on a roll of POW's received at Ship Island, Mississippi, on

April 15, 1865. Transferred from Ship Island to Vicksburg, Mississippi, on May 1, 1865. Appears on a roll of POW's of Company F, 63rd Alabama Infantry commanded by Captain R. T. Simpson that were surrendered by Lt. General Richard Taylor at Citronelle, Alabama, on May 4, 1865, and paroled at Meridian, Mississippi, on May 11, 1865. Residence—Lowndes County, Alabama.

Sadderwhite, R., Pvt. Co. H.
Enlisted on July 29, 1864, at Selma, Alabama, by Captain Suttle for the war. Age—17, eyes—hazel, hair—dark, complexion—fair. Appears absent on a company muster roll for September and October 1864. Absent sick at hospital in Greenville, Alabama, since September 6.

Saddler, T. A., Sergeant Co. H.
Enlisted on March 15, 1864, at Elyton, Alabama, by Lieutenant Killough for the war. Age—17, eyes—blue, hair—dark, complexion—dark. Drew clothing on September 11, 1864. Appears as 3rd Sergeant and absent on a company muster roll for September and October 1864. Absent sick at hospital in Mobile, Alabama, since October 8. Captured at Blakeley, Alabama, on April 9, 1865. Appears on a roll of POW's received at Ship Island, Mississippi, on April 15, 1865. Transferred from Ship Island to Vicksburg, Mississippi, on May 1, 1865. His name appears on a roll of POW's of Cos. C and H, 63rd Alabama Infantry commanded by Captain C. W. Martin that were surrendered by Lt. General Richard Taylor at Citronelle, Alabama, on May 4, 1865, and paroled at Meridian, Mississippi, on May 11, 1865. His residence is reported to be Jefferson County, Alabama.

Salter, J. W., Pvt. Co. F.
Enlisted on May 30, 1864, at Montgomery, Alabama, by Captain Jackson for the war. Age—17, eyes—dark, hair—dark, complexion—dark, 5 foot 9 inches, residence—Coosa County, Alabama. Appears absent without leave on a company muster-in roll for August 25, 1864, at Georgiana, Alabama. Appears present sick on a company muster roll for September and October 1864, with pay due from time of enlistment. Captured at Blakeley, Alabama, on April 9, 1865. Appears on a roll of POW's received at Ship Island, Mississippi, on April 15, 1865. Transferred from Ship Island to Vicksburg, Mississippi, on May 1, 1865. Appears on a roll of POW's of Company F, 63rd Alabama Infantry commanded by Captain R. T. Simpson that were surrendered by Lt. General Richard Taylor at Citronelle, Alabama, on May 4, 1865, and paroled at Meridian, Mississippi, on May 11, 1865. Residence—Coosa County, Alabama.

Sample, Felix, Pvt. Co. B.
Enlisted on March 23, 1864, at Montgomery, Alabama, by Captain Zimmerman for the war. Appears on a company muster-in roll for March 23, 1864, at Montgomery, Alabama. Age—17. Drew clothing on July 8 and August 12, 1864. Appears present on a company muster roll for September and October 1864, with pay due from time of enlistment. Appears on a roll of nurses and patients of Moore Hospital CSA commanded by Surgeon W. C. Cavanaugh that were surrendered by Lt. General Richard Taylor at Citronelle, Alabama, on May 4, 1865, and paroled at Meridian, Mississippi, on May 16, 1865. Residence—Coosa County, Alabama.

Sanders, Charles, Pvt. Co. G.
Enlisted on May 16, 1864, at Troy, Alabama, by Captain Wilkerson for the war. Age—16, eyes—blue, hair—light, complexion—fair, 5 foot 8 inches, residence—Pike County, Alabama. Appears on a company muster-in roll for September 7, 1864, at Blakeley, Alabama. Drew clothing on September 11, 1864. Appears absent on a company muster roll for September and October 1864. Absent on 10 day

furlough from September 10, 1864. Captured at Blakeley, Alabama, on April 9, 1865. Appears on a roll of POW's received at Ship Island, Mississippi, on April 15, 1865. Transferred from Ship Island to Vicksburg, Mississippi, on May 1, 1865. Appears on a roll of POW's of Cos. E and G, 63rd Alabama Infantry commanded by Captain A. V. Lee that were surrendered by Lt. General Richard Taylor at Citronelle, Alabama, on May 4, 1865, and paroled at Meridian, Mississippi, on May 13, 1865. Residence—Pike County, Alabama.

Sanford, Samuel G., Pvt. Co. B.
Enlisted on July 20, 1864, at Montgomery, Alabama, by Lieutenant Calhoun for the war. Appears present on a company muster roll for September and October 1864, with pay due from time of enlistment. Captured at Blakeley, Alabama, on April 9, 1865. Appears on a roll of POW's received at Ship Island, Mississippi, on April 15, 1865. Transferred from Ship Island to Vicksburg, Mississippi, on May 1, 1865. Appears on a roll of POW's of Company B, 63rd Alabama Infantry commanded by 1st Lieutenant Thomas J. Calhoun that were surrendered by Lt. General Richard Taylor at Citronelle, Alabama, on May 4, 1865, and paroled at Meridian, Mississippi, on May 11, 1865. His residence is shown as Coosa County, Alabama.

Sawyer, Thomas, Pvt. Co. A.
Enlisted on July 10, 1864, at Lowndes County, Alabama, by Captain Echols for the war. Appears present on a company muster roll for September and October 1864, with pay due from time of enlistment. Captured at Blakeley, Alabama, on April 9, 1865. Here he is shown as Sergeant. Appears on a roll of POW's received at Ship Island, Mississippi, on April 15, 1865. Transferred from Ship Island to Vicksburg, Mississippi, on May 1, 1865. Appears on a roll of POW's of Company A, 63rd Alabama Infantry commanded by Lieutenant W. D. Kyle that were surrendered by Lt. General Richard Taylor at Citronelle, Alabama, on May 4, 1865, and paroled at Meridian, Mississippi, on May 13, 1865. Residence—Lowndes County, Alabama. There was an inquiry as to his file from the State of Texas in 1915.

Scott, R. S., Pvt. Co. K.
Enlisted on September 10, 1864, at Prattville, Alabama, by Captain Moore for the war. Appears absent on a company muster roll for September and October 1864. Absent detached to work in factory on October 25, 1864, by General Withers. Signed a parole at the headquarters of the 16th US Army Corps at Montgomery, Alabama, on May 26, 1865. Hair—light, eyes—grey, complexion—fair, 5 foot 6 inches. He signed by his mark "X."

Scott, W. T., Pvt. Co. E.
Enlisted on August 8, 1864, at Pollard, Alabama, by Captain A. V. Lee for the war. Age—17, eyes—blue, hair—light, complexion—fair. Drew clothing on September 11, 1864. Appears absent on a company muster roll for September and October 1864. Absent in hospital since September 17, 1864. Captured at Blakeley, Alabama, on April 9, 1865. Appears on a roll of POW's received at Ship Island, Mississippi, on April 15, 1865. Transferred from Ship Island to Vicksburg, Mississippi, on May 1, 1865. Appears on a roll of POW's of Cos. E and G, 63rd Alabama Infantry commanded by Captain A. V. Lee that were surrendered by Lt. General Richard Taylor at Citronelle, Alabama, on May 4, 1865, and paroled at Meridian, Mississippi, on May 13, 1865. Residence—Henry County, Alabama.

Scott, W. W., Sergeant Co. D.
Enlisted on September 15, 1864, at Blakeley, Alabama, by Captain Zorn for the war. Appears absent on a company muster roll for August 30 to October 30,

1864. Absent on sick furlough at Eufaula, Alabama. He was appointed 2 Sergeant on September 15, 1864. Sergeant Scott was furloughed by the Medical Examining Board for 60 days from October 2, 1864. Captured at Blakeley, Alabama, on April 9, 1865. Appears on a roll of POW's received at Ship Island, Mississippi, on April 15, 1865. Transferred from Ship Island to Vicksburg, Mississippi, on May 1, 1865. Appears on a roll of POW's of Company D, 63rd Alabama Infantry commanded by Captain Robert H. Pearson that were surrendered by Lt. General Richard Taylor at Citronelle, Alabama, on May 4, 1865, and paroled at Meridian, Mississippi, on May 13, 1865. Residence—Barbour County, Alabama.

Seagrist, Louis, Pvt. Co. D.
Enlisted on August 1, 1864, at Macon County, Alabama, by Major Ready for the war. Age—17, eyes—dark, hair—dark, complexion—dark, 5 foot 4 inches, residence—Tuskegee, Macon County, Alabama. Appears on a company muster-in roll for July 30, 1864, at Camp Watts near Notasulga, Alabama. Drew clothing on August 7, 1864. Appears absent on a company muster roll for August 30 to October 30, 1864, with pay due from time of enlistment. Absent sick at Greenville Hospital since August 10. Discharged by Surgeon's Certificate of Disability on September 1, 1864, due to epilepsy. The surgeon states that he has witnessed two of his fits. Signed by Surgeon Clark of Madison Hospital, Montgomery, Alabama. Born—Macon County, age—17, eyes—brown, complexion—dark, hair—dark, 5 foot 2 inches, a farmer by occupation. His discharge is in his file as well as a letter forwarding it to Richmond.

Sealy, J. H., Pvt. Co. I.
Enlisted on April 15, 1864, at Wedowee, Alabama, by Captain Robinson for the war. Appears absent on a company muster roll for September and October 1864. Absent on 30 day furlough from September 27, 1864.

Seet, Green M., Pvt. Co. B.
Enlisted on April 8, 1864, at Montgomery County, Alabama, by Captain Zimmerman for the war. Age—15. Appears on a company muster roll for March 23, 1864, at Montgomery. Drew clothing on July 8, 1864.

Sellers, J. J., Pvt. Co. E.
Enlisted on August 8, 1864, at Pollard, Alabama, by Captain A. V. Lee for the war. Age—17, eyes—blue, hair—light, complexion—fair. Drew clothing on September 11, 1864. Signed by his mark. Appears absent on a company muster roll for September and October 1864. Absent in hospital since September 30, 1864. Admitted to Ross Hospital, Mobile, Alabama, on September 20, 1864, with rubeola. Sent to General Hospital in Greenville, Alabama, on September 26. He signed a parole at the headquarters of the 16th US Army Corps in Montgomery, Alabama, on June 20, 1865. Signed by his mark "X." He was descrbed as: hair—light, eyes—blue, complexion—fair, 5 foot 5 inches. His parole is in his file.

Sewell, Wade, L., Pvt. Co. B.
Enlisted on August 15, 1864, at Pollard, Alabama, by Lieutenant Townsend for the war. Appears absent on a company muster roll for September and October 1864, with pay due from time of enlistment. Absent sick since October 10, 1864. See also W. L. Lervell.

Shamberger, J., Pvt. Co. I.
Enlisted on September 23, 1864, at Mobile, Alabama, by Captain Fulton for the war. Appears absent on a company muster roll for September and October 1864. Absent sick in Hospital Moore since October 20.

Sheffield, W. E., Pvt. Co. F.

Enlisted on August 1, 1864, at Georgiana, Alabama, by Captain Brown for the war. Appears absent on a company muster roll for September and October 1864. Absent in hospital at Mobile, Alabama, since September 20. Admitted to Ross Hospital, Mobile on September 20, 1864, with rubeola. Furloughed for 30 days on October 1, 1864. He signed a parole as a POW at Marion, Alabama, on May 16, 1864.

Shelby, Thomas, M., Pvt. Co. A.

Enlisted on April 25, 1864, at Montgomery, Alabama, by Captain Echols for the war. Drew clothing in 2nd quarter, August 12 and September 11, 1864. Appears present sick in quarters on a company muster roll for September and October 1864. Admitted to Ross Hospital, Mobile, Alabama, on September 2, 1864, with febris remittens. Returned to duty on September 7, 1864. Captured at Blakeley, Alabama, on April 9, 1865. Appears on a roll of POW's received at Ship Island, Mississippi, on April 15, 1865. Transferred from Ship Island to Vicksburg, Mississippi, on May 1, 1865. Appears on a roll of POW's of Company A, 63rd Alabama Infantry commanded by Lieutenant W. D. Kyle that were surrendered by Lt. General Richard Taylor at Citronelle, Alabama, on May 4, 1865, and paroled at Meridian, Mississippi, on May 13, 1865. Residence—Montgomery County, Alabama.

Shell, C. D., Sergeant Co. F.

Enlisted on March 9, 1864, as 5th Sergeant at Greenville, Alabama, by Captain Brown for the war. Age—17, eyes—grey, hair—dark, complexion—sallow, 5 foot 7 inches, residence—Butler County, Alabama. Appears absent sick on a company muster-in roll for July 25, 1864, at Georgiana, Alabama. Drew clothing on September 11, 1864. Appears present on a company muster roll for August 31 to October 31, 1864, with pay due from time of enlistment. Captured at Blakeley, Alabama, on April 9, 1865. Appears on a roll of POW's received at Ship Island, Mississippi, on April 15, 1865. Transferred from Ship Island to Vicksburg, Mississippi, on May 1, 1865. Appears on a roll of POW's of Company F, 63rd Alabama Infantry commanded by Captain R. T. Simpson that were surrendered by Lt. General Richard Taylor at Citronelle, Alabama, on May 4, 1865, and paroled at Meridian, Mississippi, on May 11, 1865. Residence—Butler County, Alabama. Here he is shown as 2nd Sergeant.

Shepherd, J. A., Pvt. Co. F.

Enlisted on March 9, 1864, at Greenville, Alabama, by Captain Brown for the war. Age—17, eyes—blue, hair—light, complexion—fair, 5 foot 8 inches, residence—Butler County, Alabama. Appears present on a company muster-in roll for July 25, 1864, at Georgiana, Alabama. Drew clothing on September 11, 1864. Appears present on a company muster roll for August 31 to October 31, 1864, with pay due from time of enlistment. Captured at Blakeley, Alabama, on April 9, 1865. Appears on a roll of POW's received at Ship Island, Mississippi, on April 15, 1865. Transferred from Ship Island to Vicksburg, Mississippi, on May 1, 1865. Appears on a roll of POW's of Company F, 63rd Alabama Infantry commanded by Captain R. T. Simpson that were surrendered by Lt. General Richard Taylor at Citronelle, Alabama, on May 4, 1865, and paroled at Meridian, Mississippi, on May 11, 1865. Residence—Butler County, Alabama.

Shirah, John N., Pvt. Co. D.

Enlisted on July 30, 1864, at Macon County, Alabama, by Major Ready for the war. Age—17, eyes—grey, hair—dark, complexion—fair, 5 foot 5 inches, residence—Adkinsons, Barbour County, Alabama. Appears on a company muster-in roll for July 30, 1864, at Camp Watts near Notasulga, Alabama. Drew clothing on August 7, 1864. Signed by his mark. Appears present on a company muster roll for August 30 to October 30, 1864, with pay due from time of enlistment. Here he is shown as having enlisted on March 2, 1864, at Clayton, Alabama, by D. M. Seales.

Sikes, J. A., Pvt. Co. F.
Enlisted on March 9, 1864, at Greenville, Alabama, by Captain Brown for the war. Age—17, eyes—blue, hair—light, complexion—fair, 5 foot 3 inches, residence—Butler County, Alabama. Appears on a company muster-in roll for July 25, 1864, at Georgiana, Alabama. Appears absent on a company muster roll for August 31 to October 31, 1864, with pay due from time of enlistment. Absent on furlough since October 27. Signed a parole on May 16, 1865, at Marion, Alabama.

Simmerly, T. D., Pvt. Co. F.
Enlisted on May 30, 1864, at Montgomery, Alabama, by Captain Jackson for the war. Age—17, eyes—grey, hair—dark, complexion—ruddy, 5 foot 6 inches, residence—Butler County, Alabama. Appears absent without leave on a company muster-in roll for July 23, 1864, at Georgiana, Alabama. Drew clothing on September 11, 1864. Appears present on a company muster roll for August 31 to October 31, 1864, with pay due from time of enlistment. Captured at Blakeley, Alabama, on April 9, 1865. Appears on a roll of POW's received at Ship Island, Mississippi, on April 15, 1865. Transferred from Ship Island to Vicksburg, Mississippi, on May 1, 1865. Appears on a roll of POW's of Company F, 63rd Alabama Infantry commanded by Captain R. T. Simpson that were surrendered by Lt. General Richard Taylor at Citronelle, Alabama, on May 4, 1865, and paroled at Meridian, Mississippi, on May 11, 1865. Residence—Butler County, Alabama. He also appears on a roll of POW of Quintard Hospital CSA commanded by Surgeon S. V. D. Hill that were surrendered by Lt. General Richard Taylor at Citronelle, Alabama, on May 10, 1865, and paroled at Meridian, Mississippi, on May 10, 1865. Residence shown as Honorville, Alabama.

Simmons, Andrew J., Pvt. Co. A.
Enlisted on January 1, 1864, at Tallapoosa County, Alabama, by Captain John Echols for the war. Age—16. Appears on a company muster-in roll for January 1, 1864, at Montgomery, Alabama. Appears present on a company muster roll for January and February 1864, with pay due from time of enlistment. Drew clothing in 2nd quarter, August 12 and September 11, 1864. He signed by his mark. Appears present on a company muster roll for September and October 1864. He is shown as having been last paid on February 29, 1864. Captured at Blakeley, Alabama, on April 9, 1865. Appears on a roll of POW's received at Ship Island, Mississippi, on April 15, 1865. Transferred from Ship Island to Vicksburg, Mississippi, on May 1, 1865. Appears on a roll of POW's of Company A, 63rd Alabama Infantry commanded by Lieutenant W. D. Kyle that were surrendered by Lt. General Richard Taylor at Citronelle, Alabama, on May 4, 1865, and paroled at Meridian, Mississippi, on May 13, 1865. Residence—Tallapoosa County, Alabama.

Simmons, James R., Pvt. Co. A.
Enlisted on March 1, 1864, at Macon County, Alabama, by Captain Echols, for the war. Drew clothing in 2nd quarter 1864. Appears present on a company muster roll of September and October 1864, with pay due from time of enlistment. Captured at Blakeley, Alabama, on April 9, 1865. Appears on a roll of POW's received at Ship Island, Mississippi, on April 15, 1865. Transferred from Ship Island to Vicksburg, Mississippi, on May 1, 1865. Appears on a roll of POW's of Company A, 63rd Alabama Infantry commanded by Lieutenant W. D. Kyle that were surrendered by Lt. General Richard Taylor at Citronelle, Alabama, on May 4, 1865, and paroled at Meridian, Mississippi, on May 13, 1865.

Residence—Macon County, Alabama. Signed a parole at the headquarters of the 16th US Army Corps at Montgomery, Alabama, on June 17, 1865. Hair—light, eyes—blue, complexion—fair, 5 foot 8 inches. His parole is in his file.

Simmons, Tillman S., Pvt. Co. A.
Enlisted on March 1, 1864, at Macon County, Alabama, by Captain Echols, for the war. Age—17. Appears on a company muster-in roll for January 1, 1864, at Montgomery, Alabama. Appears present on a company muster roll for January and February 1864, with pay due from time of enlistment. Drew clothing in 2nd quarter 1864. Appears present sick in quarters on a company muster roll of September and October 1864, with pay due from time of enlistment.

Simpson, Alford B., Pvt. Co. C.
Enlisted on May 11, 1864, at Russell County, Alabama, by Lieutenant Carnes for the war. Age—17, eyes—blue, hair—light, complexion—fair, 5 foot 10 ½ inches, residence—Seals Station, Russell County, Alabama. Drew clothing on August 6, 1864. Appears absent on a company muster roll for September and October 1864. Absent in hospital in Mobile, Alabama, since October 26, 1864.

Simpson, R. T., Captain Co. F.
Elected Captain on November 28, 1864. Appears on a roster of the 2nd Regiment Alabama Reserves, Fuller's Brigade, Maury's Corps, District of the Gulf. POW captured at Blakeley, Alabama, on April 9, 1865. Confined near Spanish Fort, Alabama, for one day. Appears on a roll of POW's received at Ship Island, Mississippi, on April 16, 1865. Transferred from Ship Island to Vicksburg, Mississippi, on April 28, 1865. Appears on a register of POW's received from Ship Island that were confined at New Orleans, Louisiana, on April 30, 1865. Exchanged on May 1, 1865. Signed a Parole of Honor at Meridian, Mississippi, on May 10, 1864. His parole is in his file.

Sims, J. W., Pvt. Co. H.
Enlisted on March 15, 1864, at Centerville, Alabama, by Captain Suttle for the war. Age—17, eyes—blue, hair—dark, complexion—fair. Died in hospital at Mobile, Alabama, on October 10, 1864.

Sims, Warren, Pvt. Co. D.
Enlisted on August 28, 1864, at Pollard, Alabama, by Captain Zorn for the war. Drew clothing on September 12, 1864. Signed by mark W. J. Sims. Appears present on a company muster roll for September and October 1864, with pay due from time of enlistment.

Sims, William, Pvt. Co. K.
Pvt. W. H. Sims, drew clothing on September 11, 1864. Pvt. W. J. Sims was admitted to Ross Hospital, Mobile, Alabama, on September 2, 1864, with febris remittens. Returned to duty on September 9, 1864. Private William Sims was admitted to Ross Hospital on September 16, 1864, with rubeola, plumonalis congestis. Died on September 21, 1864. Left $2.50. All the above are shown as having served in Company K of the 2nd Regiment Alabama Reserves.

Sistrunk, Herbert F., Pvt. Co. A.
Enlisted on May 10, 1864, at Macon County, Alabama, by Captain Echols for the war. Drew clothing in 2nd quarter of 1864. He appears absent on a company muster roll for September and October 1864. Absent sick at Tuskegee, Alabama, since August 9, 1864.

Skeen, J. M., Pvt. Co. E.
Enlisted on August 9, 1864, at Pollard, Alabama, by Captain A. V. Lee for the

war. Drew clothing on September 11, 1864. He appears absent on a company muster roll for September and October 1864. Absent in hospital since September 25, 1864. Captured at Blakeley, Alabama, on April 9, 1865. Appears on a roll of POW's received at Ship Island, Mississippi, on April 15, 1865. Transferred from Ship Island to Vicksburg, Mississippi, on May 1, 1865. Appears on a roll of sick and wounded Confederate POW's at USA General Hospital No. 2, Vicksburg. Admitted on May 3, 1865, from steamer with acute diarrhoea. Age—17. Returned to duty on May 10, 1865.

Skinner, J. P., Pvt. Co. F.
Enlisted on March 9, 1864, at Greenville, Alabama, by Captain Brown for the war. Age—17, eyes—blue, hair—dark, complexion—fair, 5 foot 8 ½ inches, residence—Butler County, Alabama. Appears on a company muster-in roll for July 25, 1864. Drew clothing on September 11, 1864. Appears present on a company muster roll for September and October 1864, with pay due from time of enlistment.

Skinner, W. A., 2nd Lieutenant Co. K.
Enlisted on October 1, 1864, at Blakeley, Alabama, by Captain May for the war. Appears absent on a company muster roll for September and October 1864. Absent, home on sick furlough, till November 12, 1864. Elected 2nd Lieutenant on October 1, 1864. POW captured at Blakeley, Alabama, on April 9, 1865. Appears on a report of prisoners confined by the Provost Marshal of the 2nd Division, 16th US Army Corps near Spanish Fort, Alabama for one day. Appears on a roll of POW's received at Ship Island, Mississippi, on April 16, 1865. Transferred from Ship Island to Vicksburg, Mississippi, on April 28, 1865. Appears on a register of POW's received from Ship Island that were confined at New Orleans, Louisiana, on April 30, 1865. Exchanged on May 1, 1865. Signed a Parole of Honor at Meridian, Mississippi, on May 11, 1865. His parole is in his file.

Skirlock, Daniel, N., Pvt. Co. A.
Enlisted on January 1, 1864, at Tallapoosa County, Alabama, for the war. Appears on a company muster-in roll for January 1, 1864, at Montgomery, Alabama. Age—17. Appears present on a company muster roll for January and February 1864, with pay due from time of enlistment. Drew clothing in the 2nd quarter of 1864. Signed by his mark. Appears present sick in quarters on a company muster roll for September and October 1864. Here he is shown as having been last paid on February 29, 1864. Captured at Blakeley, Alabama, on April 9, 1865. Appears on a roll of POW's received at Ship Island, Mississippi, on April 15, 1865. Transferred from Ship Island to Vicksburg, Mississippi, on May 1, 1865. Appears on a roll of POW's of divers companies and regiments of CSA Army commanded by Captain D. H. Todd that were surrendered by Lt. General Richard Taylor at Citronelle, Alabama, on May 4, 1865, and paroled at Meridian, Mississippi, on May 15, 1865. Residence—Tallapoosa County, Alabama.

Slaughter, Richard R., Sergeant/Pvt. Co. A.
Enlisted as 5th Sergeant on January 1, 1864, at Tallapoosa County, Alabama, by Captain John Echols for the war. Appears on a company muster-in roll for January 1, 1864, at Montgomery, Alabama. Age—17. Appears present on a company muster roll for January and February 1864, with pay due from time of enlistment. Drew clothing in the 2nd quarter of 1864. Appears as 1st Sergeant and present on a company muster roll for September and October 1864. Here he is shown as having been last paid on February 29, 1864. Signed a parole as Private in Company A, at the headquarters of the 16th US Army Corps in Montgomery, Alabama, on May 20, 1865. Hair—black, complexion—fair, eyes—blue, 6 foot 1 inch. His parole is in his file.

Smallwood, Z. T., Pvt. Co. F.
Enlisted on March 9, 1864, at Greenville, Alabama, by Captain Brown for the war. Age—17, eyes—blue, hair—light, complexion—sallow, 5 foot, residence— Butler County, Alabama. Appears absent sick on a company muster-in roll for July 25, 1864. Appears as having been discharged on a company muster roll for August 31 to October 31, 1864, and never paid. Discharged on October 12, 1864, at Mobile, Alabama, due to health and physical deformity. Stationed at Saluda Hill near Blakeley, Alabama. Age—17, eyes—blue, 4 foot 4 inches, hair—light, complexion—sallow. Born in Butler County, Alabama. Not shown as having an occupation. His discharge is in his file.

Smith, Alonzo, Pvt. Co. F.
Captured and wounded in the thigh at Blakeley, Alabama, on April 9, 1865. Appears on a list of hospital attendants and sick and wounded that were sent to Vicksburg, Mississippi, via New Orleans, Louisiana, from Spanish Fort, Alabama, on April 8, 1865. Appears on a list of wounded POW's to be transferred to hospital at New Orleans from Blakeley. List is dated April 13, 1865. Admitted to USA Hospital Steamer D. A. January on April 17, 1865, with gunshot wound to the right thigh. He was transferred to the US Hospital Steamer Elanore Carrell on April 25, 1865 [at New Orleans]. He was transferred to USA General Hospital No. 3 (Colored) at Vicksburg on April 28, 1865. Appears on a roll of POW's at USA General Hospital No. 3, Vicksburg that were transferred to USA General Hospital No. 2, Vicksburg on May 4. Appears on a list of sick and wounded Confederate POW's at USA General Hospital No. 2, Vicksburg. Admitted on May 4, 1865, with severe gunshot wound right thigh. Age—17. Returned to duty on May 8, 1865.

Smith, Andrew J., 1st Sergeant/1st Lieutenant Co. I.
Enlisted on October 1, 1864, at Blakeley, Alabama, by Captain Fulton, for the war. Appears as 1st Sergeant and present on a company muster roll for September and October 1864. He was elected 1st Lieutenant on November 24, 1864.

Smith, C., Pvt. Co. H.
Enlisted on March 15, 1864, at Montevallo, Alabama, by Captain Suttle for the war. Age—17, eyes—dark, hair—dark, complexion—dark. Appears absent on a company muster roll for September and October 1864. This muster roll reports him absent on sick furlough since September 23. Drew clothing on September 11, 1864.

Smith, J. D., Pvt. Co. A.
Captured at Blakeley, Alabama, on April 9, 1865. Appears on a roll of POW's received at Ship Island, Mississippi, on April 15, 1865. Transferred from Ship Island to Vicksburg, Mississippi, on May 1, 1865. Appears on a roll of POW's of Company A, 63rd Alabama Infantry commanded by Lieutenant W. D. Kyle that were surrendered by Lt. General Richard Taylor at Citronelle, Alabama, on May 4, 1865, and paroled at Meridian, Mississippi, on May 13, 1865. Residence—Macon County, Alabama.

Smith, John E., Pvt. Co. A.
Enlisted at Chambers County, Alabama, by Captain Echols for the war. Drew clothing in 2nd quarter of 1864. Appears present on a company muster roll for September and October 1864, with pay due from time of enlistment. Captured at Blakeley, Alabama, on April 9, 1865. Appears on a roll of POW's received at Ship Island, Mississippi, on April 15, 1865. Transferred from Ship Island to Vicksburg, Mississippi, on May 1, 1865. Appears on a roll of POW's of Company A, 63rd Alabama Infantry commanded by Lieutenant W. D. Kyle that were

surrendered by Lt. General Richard Taylor at Citronelle, Alabama, on May 4, 1865, and paroled at Meridian, Mississippi, on May 13, 1865. His residence is shown as Chambers County, Alabama.

Smith, Neil, Pvt. Co. G.
Enlisted on May 16, 1864, at Troy, Alabama, by Captain Wilkerson for the war. Age—17, eyes—blue, hair—dark, complexion—dark, 5 foot 10 inches, residence—Pike County, Alabama. Appears on a company muster-in roll for September 7, 1864, at Blakeley, Alabama. Drew clothing on September 11, 1864. Signed by his mark. Appears present on a company muster roll for September and October 1864. Captured at Blakeley, Alabama, on April 9, 1865. Appears on a roll of POW's received at Ship Island, Mississippi, on April 15, 1865. Transferred from Ship Island to Vicksburg, Mississippi, on May 1, 1865. Appears on a roll of POW's of Cos. E and G, 63rd Alabama Infantry commanded by Captain A. V. Lee that were surrendered by Lt. General Richard Taylor at Citronelle, Alabama, on May 4, 1865, and paroled at Meridian, Mississippi, on May 13, 1865. His residence is shown as Pike County, Alabama.

Smith, Seaborn S., Pvt./Corporal Co. G.
Enlisted on May 16, 1864, at Troy, Alabama, by Captain Wilkerson for the war. Age—17, eyes—blue, hair—light, complexion—fair, 5 foot 10 inches, residence—Montgomery County, Alabama. Appears on a company muster-in roll for September 7, 1864, at Blakeley, Alabama. Drew clothing on September 11, 1864. Appears present on a company muster roll for September and October 1864. Appointed 2nd Corporal vice Curtis [?] reduced by Regimental Court Marshal on October 19, 1864. Captured at Blakeley, Alabama, on April 9, 1865. Appears on a roll of POW's received at Ship Island, Mississippi, on April 15, 1865. Transferred from Ship Island to Vicksburg, Mississippi, on May 1, 1865. Appears on a roll of POW's of Cos. E and G, 63rd Alabama Infantry commanded by Captain A. V. Lee that were surrendered by Lt. General Richard Taylor at Citronelle, Alabama, on May 4, 1865, and paroled at Meridian, Mississippi, on May 13, 1865. Residence—Montgomery County, Alabama.

Smith, W. D., Pvt. Co. I.
Enlisted on April 15, 1864, at Wedowee, Alabama, by Captain Robinson for the war. Appears absent on a company muster roll for September and October 1864. Absent without leave from September 18, 1864.

Smith, W. H., Pvt. Co. H.
Enlisted on March 15, 1864, at Randolph County, Alabama, by Lieutenant Johnson for the war. Age—17, eyes—dark, hair—dark, complexion—dark. Drew clothing on September 11, 1864. Appears absent on a company muster roll for September and October 1864. Absent at hospital in Mobile, Alabama, since October 8. Appears on a roll of POW stragglers that were paroled by Colonel William R. Marshall, 7th Minn. Volunteers at Selma, Alabama, during June 1865. Residence was Bibb County, Alabama.

Smith, William M., Pvt. Co. B.
Enlisted on July 17, 1864, at Montgomery, Alabama, by Lieutenant Calhoun for the war. Appears absent on a company muster roll for September and October 1864, with pay due from time of enlistment. Absent sick since August 26, 1864. There is a hand written letter by W. M. Smith at Montgomery, Alabama, written on December 30, 1864. He requested permission to appear before a Medical Examining Board as he broke his leg on August 24, 1864. He reports his injury in the line of duty occurred while carrying mail for the Regiment. Discharged on January 20, 1865, by Medical Examining Board in Montgomery, Alabama, due to fractured leg. His leg was run over by a wagon wheel just above the ankle

joint. Born in Georgia, age—16, 5 foot 1 inch, eyes—blue, hair—light, complexion—fair. His occupation is shown as a student. His discharge with endorsements and his letter are in his file.

Smith, W. P., Pvt. Co. I.
Enlisted on April 15, 1864, at Wedowee, Alabama, by Captain Robinson for the war. Appears absent on a company muster roll for September and October 1864. Absent without leave from September 18, 1864.

Smith, Z. T., Pvt. Co. I.
Enlisted on April 16, 1864, at Talladega, Alabama, by Captain Parks for the war. Appears absent on a company muster roll for September and October 1864. Absent furloughed for 30 days from September 29, 1864. Captured at Blakeley, Alabama, on April 9, 1865. Here he is shown in Company G. Appears on a roll of POW's received at Ship Island, Mississippi, on April 15, 1865. Transferred from Ship Island to Vicksburg, Mississippi, on May 1, 1865. Appears on a roll of POW's of Cos. I and K, 63rd Alabama Infantry commanded by Lieutenant W. A. Skinner that were surrendered by Lt. General Richard Taylor at Citronelle, Alabama, on May 4, 1865, and paroled at Meridian, Mississippi, May 13, 1865. Residence—Randolph County, Alabama.

Smoke, L. K. [L. R., Lewis Robert], Pvt. Co. E.
Enlisted on July 26, 1864, at Montgomery, Alabama, by Captain A. V. Lee for the war. Age—17, eyes—blue, hair—light, complexion—fair. Appears absent on a company muster roll for September and October 1864. Absent in hospital since September 26, 1864. Appears as signature on a parole to a POW at Marion, Alabama, on May 16, 1864. [This man was a resident of Tyler, Dallas County, Alabama, and is buried at Sister Springs Baptist Church of that place. He is great grandfather of the transcriber of this roll.]

Smoot, Marcelius, Pvt. Co. D.
Enlisted on July 12, 1864, at Russell County, Alabama, by Lieutenant Carnes for the war. Age—17, eyes—blue, hair—dark, complexion—sallow, 5 foot 5 inches, residence—Uchee, Russell County, Alabama. Appears on a company muster-in roll for July 30, 1864, at Camp Watts near Notasulga, Alabama. Drew clothing on August 7, 1864. Signed by his mark. Appears as having died on a company muster roll for August 30 to October 30, 1864, with pay due from time of enlistment. Died at Division Hospital in October. Here he is shown as having enlisted at Notasulga on July 12, 1864, by Major Ready. Admitted to Ross Hospital, Mobile, Alabama, on October 1, 1864, with febris typhoides pneumonia. Died on October 5, 1864.

Snell, William E., Pvt. Co. B.
Enlisted on October 8, 1864, at Blakeley, Alabama, by Captain Zimmerman for the war. Appears present on a company muster roll for September and October 1864, with pay due from time of enlistment. Admitted to Ross Hospital, Mobile, Alabama, on November 17, 1864, with febris intermittens tert. Returned to duty on November 27.

Snider, Francis M., Pvt. Co. G.
Enlisted on May 18, 1864, at Troy, Alabama, by Captain Wilkerson for the war. Age—17, eyes—grey, hair—dark, complexion—florid, 5 foot 0 inch, residence—Pike County, Alabama. Appears on a company muster-in roll for September 7, 1864, at Blakeley, Alabama. Appears present on a company muster roll for September and October 1864. Captured at Blakeley, Alabama, on April 9, 1865. Appears on a roll of POW's received at Ship Island, Mississippi, on April 15, 1865. Transferred from Ship Island to Vicksburg, Mississippi, on May 1, 1865.

Appears on a roll of POW's of Cos. E and G, 63rd Alabama Infantry commanded by Captain A. V. Lee that were surrendered by Lt. General Richard Taylor at Citronelle, Alabama, on May 4, 1865, and paroled at Meridian, Mississippi, on May 13, 1865. Residence—Pike County, Alabama.

Sorrel, Green B. W., Pvt. Co. A.
Enlisted on April 8, 1864, at Chambers County, Alabama, by Captain Echols for the war. Drew clothing in 2nd quarter and August 12, 1864. Appears present sick in quarters on a company muster roll for September and October 1864, with pay due from time of enlistment. Admitted to Ross Hospital, Mobile, Alabama, on September 2, 1864, with febris remittens. Returned to duty on September 8, 1864. Captured at Blakeley, Alabama, on April 9, 1865. Appears on a roll of POW's received at Ship Island, Mississippi, on April 15, 1865. Transferred from Ship Island to Vicksburg, Mississippi, on May 1, 1865. Appears on a roll of POW's of Company A, 63rd Alabama Infantry commanded by Lieutenant W. D. Kyle that were surrendered by Lt. General Richard Taylor at Citronelle, Alabama, on May 4, 1865, and paroled at Meridian, Mississippi, on May 13, 1865. Residence—Chambers County, Alabama. This file contains the names Green B. W. Sorrel, G. B. Sorrel, G. W. Sorrel and E. W. Sorrel.

Sparks, S. C., Pvt. Co. E.
Enlisted on March 15, 1864, at Clayton, Alabama, by Captain A. V. Lee for the war. Age—17, eyes—blue, hair—light, complexion—fair. Appears as having been discharged on a company muster roll for September and October 1864. Discharged on September 14, 1864, by Medical Examining Board and Surgeon General CSA, due to feeble physical development and general bad health. Resident of Eufaula, Alabama, born in Muscogee County, Georgia, eyes—hazel, 5 foot 2 inches, complexion—sallow, hair—dark, by occupation a farmer. "Pvt. Sam C. Sparks is a miserable looking, sallow, feeble, abortion of a boy, who never should have been enrolled." Signed on August 17, 1864, by Captain C. J. Clark, Surgeon in charge, Madison Hospital, Montgomery, Alabama. His discharge is in his file.

Sparks, William J., Pvt. Co. E.
Enlisted on March 15, 1864, at Clayton, Alabama, by Captain A. V. Lee for the war. Age—17, eyes—blue, hair—light, complexion—fair. Appears as having been discharged on a company muster roll for September and October 1864. Discharged on September 14, 1864, by Medical Examining Board and Surgeon General CSA, due to feeble physical development and general bad health. Resident of Eufaula, Alabama, born in Muscogee County, Georgia, eyes—blue, 5 foot 2 inches, complexion—sallow, hair—light, by occupation a farmer. "Pvt. Sam C. Sparks is a small, sallow, feeble boy, who looks like he might have been addicted to dirt eating from childhood." Signed on August 17, 1864 by Captain C. J. Clark, Surgeon in charge, Madison Hospital, Montgomery, Alabama. His discharge is in his file. [Some confusion here by the Surgeon]

Spears, Lawrence, Pvt. Co. B.
Enlisted on April 14, 1864, at Montgomery County, Alabama, by Captain Zimmerman for the war. Appears on a company muster-in roll for March 23, 1864, at Montgomery, Alabama. Age—15. Drew clothing on July 8 and September 11, 1864. Signed by his mark. Appears as having been discharged on a company muster roll for September and October 1864, with pay due from time of enlistment. Discharged per Civil Authority on September 28, 1864.

Spencer, Julius P., Pvt. Co. D.
Enlisted on July 30, 1864, at Macon County, Alabama, by Major Ready for the war. Age—17, eyes—grey, hair—light, complexion—fair, 4 foot 6 inches,

residence—Clayton, Alabama. Appears on a company muster-in roll for July 30, 1864, at Camp Watts near Notasulga, Alabama. Drew clothing on August 7, 1864. Signed by his mark. Appears absent on a company muster roll for August 30 to October 30, 1864, with pay due from time of enlistment. Absent on 60 day sick furlough by Medical Examining Board since September 20, 1864. Here he is shown as having enlisted on April 20, 1864, at Eufaula, Alabama, by Captain Zorn. Captured at Blakeley, Alabama, on April 9, 1865. Appears on a roll of POW's received at Ship Island, Mississippi, on April 15, 1865. Transferred from Ship Island to Vicksburg, Mississippi, on May 1, 1865. Appears on a roll of POW's of Company D, 63rd Alabama Infantry commanded by Captain Robert H. Pearson that were surrendered by Lt. General Richard Taylor at Citronelle, Alabama, on May 4, 1865, and paroled at Meridian, Mississippi, on May 13, 1865. Residence—Barbour County, Alabama.

Spencer, John B., Pvt. Co. D.
Enlisted on March 10, 1864, at Eufaula, Alabama, by Captain Zorn for the war. Appears as a patient on a hospital muster roll for July and August 1864, and never been paid. Card dated September 1, 1864. His file is with Julius P. Spencer.

Spivey, Marion, P., Pvt. Co. G.
Enlisted on May 16, 1864, at Troy, Alabama, by Captain Wilkerson for the war. Age—17, eyes—grey, hair—light, complexion—fair, 5 foot 9 inches, residence—Pike County, Alabama. Appears on a company muster-in roll for September 7, 1864, at Blakeley, Alabama. Appears as having died on a company muster roll for September and October 1864. Died in hospital at Greenville, Alabama, on September 25, 1864.

Spragins, Benjamin, F., Pvt. Co. C.
Enlisted on May 12, 1864, at Tallapoosa County, Alabama, by Captain Brown for the war. Age—17, eyes—blue, hair—light, complexion—fair, 5 foot 7 inches, residence—Dudleyville, Tallapoosa County, Alabama. Appears on a company muster-in roll for June 24, 1864, at Camp Watts near Notasulga, Alabama. Drew clothing on August 6, 1864. Signed by his mark. Appears present on a company muster roll for September and October 1864.

Spurlock, S. M., Pvt. Co. E.
Enlisted on August 8, 1864, at Pollard, Alabama, by Captain A. V. Lee for the war. Age—17, eyes—blue, hair—light, complexion—fair. Drew clothing on September 11, 1864. Signed by his mark. Appears absent on a company muster roll for September and October 1864. Absent furloughed for 60 days from October 11, 1864.

Stanley, J. A., Pvt. Co. G.
Captured at Blakeley, Alabama, on April 9, 1865. Appears on a roll of POW's received at Ship Island, Mississippi, on April 15, 1865. Transferred from Ship Island to Vicksburg, Mississippi, on May 1, 1865. Appears on a roll of POW's of Cos. E and G, 63rd Alabama Infantry commanded by Captain A. V. Lee that were surrendered by Lt. General Richard Taylor at Citronelle, Alabama, on May 4, 1865, and paroled at Meridian, Mississippi, on May 13, 1865. Residence—Pike County, Alabama.

Stanly, A. T., Pvt. Co. F.
Enlisted on May 30, 1864, at Montgomery, Alabama, by Captain Jackson for the war. Age—17, eyes—blue, hair—light, complexion—fair, 5 foot 7 inches, residence—Coosa County, Alabama. Appears on a company muster-in roll for July 25, 1864. Drew clothing on September 11, 1864. Appears present sick on

a company muster roll for September and October 1864, with pay due from time of enlistment. Here his name appears as A. T. Stanley. Captured at Blakeley, Alabama, on April 9, 1865. Appears on a roll of POW's received at Ship Island, Mississippi, on April 15, 1865. Transferred from Ship Island to Vicksburg, Mississippi, on May 1, 1865. Appears on a roll of POW's of Company F, 63rd Alabama Infantry commanded by Captain R. T. Simpson that were surrendered by Lt. General Richard Taylor at Citronelle, Alabama, May 4, 1865, and paroled at Meridian, Mississippi, on May 11, 1865. Residence—Coosa County, Alabama.

Stanly, G. W., Pvt. Co. F.
Enlisted on August 3, 1864, at Auburn, Alabama, by Lieutenant Calhoun for the war. Drew clothing on September 11, 1864. Appears absent on a company muster roll for August 31 to October 31, 1864. Absent in hospital at Mobile, Alabama, since October 30, 1864. Admitted to Ross Hospital, Mobile, Alabama, on October 30, 1864, with febris intermittens tert. Returned to duty on November 29, 1864.

Stephens, George W., Pvt. Co. G.
Enlisted on July 1, 1864, at Troy, Alabama, by Captain Padgett for the war. Age—17, eyes—grey, hair—dark, complexion—fair, 5 foot 7 inches, residence—PIke County, Alabama. Appears on a company muster-in roll for September 7, 1864, at Blakeley, Alabama. Appears present on a company muster roll for September and October 1864. Drew clothing in the 3rd quarter of 1864.

Stephens, J., Pvt. Co. E.
Enlisted on July 17, 1864, at Montgomery, Alabama, by Major Thompson for the war. Age—17, eyes—dark, hair—dark, complexion—dark. Drew clothing September 11, 1864. Appears present on a company muster roll for September and October 1864.

Stephens, J. L., Pvt. Co. I.
Enlisted on April 15, 1864, at Wedowee, Alabama, by Captain Robinson for the war. Appears absent on a company muster roll for September and October 1864. Absent furloughed for 30 days from September 27.

Stephens, J. T., Pvt. Co. E.
Enlisted on July 14, 1864, at Montgomery, Alabama, by Major Thompson for the war. Age—17, eyes—dark, hair—dark, complexion—dark. Appears absent on a company muster roll for September and October 1864. Absent in hospital since August 17, 1864. Admitted to Ross Hospital, Mobile, Alabama, on August 26, 1864, with debilitas. Furloughed for 60 days on September 9, 1864.

Stephens, L., Pvt. Co. E.
Enlisted on March 8, 1864, at Clayton, Alabama, by Captain A. V. Lee for the war. Age—17, eyes—dark, hair—dark, complexion—dark. Appears present on a company muster roll for September and October 1864. Captured at Blakeley, Alabama, on April 9, 1865. Appears on a roll of POW's received at Ship Island, Mississippi, on April 15, 1865. Transferred from Ship Island to Vicksburg, Mississippi, on May 1, 1865. His name appears on a roll of POW's of Cos. E and G, 63rd Alabama Infantry commanded by Captain A. V. Lee that were surrendered by Lt. General Richard Taylor at Citronelle, Alabama, on May 4, 1865, and paroled at Meridian, Mississippi, on May 13, 1865. Residence—Barbour County, Alabama.

Stephens, R. W., Pvt. Co. A.
Captured at Blakeley, Alabama, on April 9, 1865. Appears on a roll of POW's received at Ship Island, Mississippi, on April 15, 1865. Transferred from Ship

Island to Vicksburg, Mississippi, on May 1, 1865. Appears on a roll of POW's of Company A, 63rd Alabama Infantry commanded by Lieutenant W. D. Kyle that were surrendered by Lt. General Richard Taylor at Citronelle, Alabama, on May 4, 1865, and paroled at Meridian, Mississippi, on May 13, 1865. Residence—Macon County, Alabama.

Stevens, H., Pvt. Co. K.
Enlisted on September 10, 1864, at Perry County, Alabama, by Captain Powers for the war. Appears present on a company muster roll for September and October 1864. Captured at Blakeley, Alabama, on April 9, 1865. Appears on a roll of POW's received at Ship Island, Mississippi, on April 15, 1865. Transferred from Ship Island to Vicksburg, Mississippi, on May 1, 1865. Appears on a roll of POW's of Cos. I and K, 63rd Alabama Infantry commanded by Lieutenant W. A. Skinner that were surrendered by Lt. General Richard Taylor at Citronelle, Alabama, on May 4, 1865, and paroled at Meridian, Mississippi, May 13, 1865. He residence was reported to be in Pickens County, Alabama.

Stevens, W. M., Pvt. Co. K.
Enlisted on September 19, 1864, at Montgomery, Alabama, by Lieutenant Brooks for the war. Appears absent on a company muster roll for September and October 1864. Absent without leave since October 18, 1864.

Stewart, A., Pvt. Co. F.
Enlisted on March 9, 1864, at Greenville, Alabama, by Captain Brown for the war. Age—17, eyes—blue, hair—light, complexion—fair, 5 foot 7 inches, residence—Butler County, Alabama. Appears on a company muster-in roll for July 25, 1864. Drew clothing on September 11, 1864. Appears present on a company muster roll for August 31 to October 31, 1864, with pay due from time of enlistment. A. O. Stewart was admitted on January 10, 1865, to Way Hospital, Meridian, Mississippi, with wound. Admitted to 1st Mississippi CSA Hospital, Jackson, Mississippi, on March 3, 1865, with chronic diarrhoea. Died on March 27, 1865. Here he is shown as A. O. Stewart.

Stewart, A. L., Pvt. 2nd Alabama Reserves
Admitted to Way Hospital, Meridian, Mississippi, on January 9, 1865. Returned to duty. This record is filed with Pvt. A. Stewart above.

Stewart, J. M., Pvt. Co. H.
He is reported to have been admitted to Ross Hospital, Mobile, Alabama, on September 19, 1864, with chronic bronchitis. Sent to General Hospital in Selma on September 21, 1864.

Stewart, L., Pvt. Co. I.
Enlisted on April 15, 1864, at Wedowee, Alabama, by Captain Robinson for the war. Appears absent on a company muster roll for September and October 1864. Absent sick in Hospital Moore since October 15.

Stewart, William B., Pvt. Co. G.
Enlisted on June 1, 1864, at Troy, Alabama, by Captain Wilkerson for the war. Age—17, eyes—hazel, hair—light, complexion—florid, 5 foot 7 inches, residence—Covington County, Alabama. Appears on a company muster-in roll for September 7, 1864, at Blakeley, Alabama. Drew clothing on September 11, 1864. Signed a parole at headquarters of the 16th US Army Corps in Montgomery, Alabama, on June 3, 1864. He is described as: hair—light, eyes—grey, complexion—dark, 5 foot 5 inches.

Stillwell, G. W., Pvt. Co. K.
Enlisted on August 12, 1864, at Columbus, Georgia, by Lieutenant Carnes for the war. Appears present on a company muster roll for September and October 1864. Captured at Blakeley, Alabama, on April 9, 1865. Appears on a roll of POW's received at Ship Island, Mississippi, on April 15, 1865. Transferred from Ship Island to Vicksburg, Mississippi, on May 1, 1865. Appears on a roll of POW's of Cos. I and K, 63rd Alabama Infantry commanded by Lieutenant W. A. Skinner that were surrendered by Lt. General Richard Taylor at Citronelle, Alabama, on May 4, 1865, and paroled at Meridian, Mississippi, May 13, 1865. Residence—Russell County, Alabama.

Stockman, W. V., Pvt. Co. F.
Enlisted on March 9, 1864, at Greenville, Alabama, by Captain Brown for the war. Age—17, eyes—hazel, hair—dark, complexion—fair, 5 foot 9 inches, residence—Butler County, Alabama. Appears on a company muster-in roll for July 25, 1865, at Georgiana, Alabama. Appears as having died on a company muster roll for September and October 1864, with pay due from time of enlistment. Died on October 23, 1864.

Stoddart, A. A., Pvt. Co. F.
Enlisted on May 30, 1864, at Montgomery, Alabama, by Captain Jackson for the war. Age—17, eyes—dark, hair—dark, complexion—dark, 5 foot, residence—Dale County, Alabama. He is reported absent sick on a company muster-in roll for July 25, 1864.

Stokes, Charner, Pvt. Co. B.
Enlisted on March 23, 1864, at Montgomery County, Alabama, by Captain Zimmerman for the war. Age—47. Appears on a company muster-in roll for March 23, 1864, at Montgomery, Alabama. Drew clothing on July 8, 1864. Appears absent on a company muster roll for September and October 1864, with pay due from time of enlistment. Absent with leave since October 18, 1864. Signed a parole at headquarters of the 16th US Army Corps in Montgomery, Alabama, on May 22, 1864. Hair—light, eyes—blue, complexion—fair, 5 foot 6 inches.

Stokes, W. W., Pvt. Co. E.
Enlisted on August 8, 1864, at Pollard, Alabama, by Captain A. V. Lee for the war. Age—17, eyes—dark, hair—dark, complexion—dark. Drew clothing on September 11, 1864. Signed by his mark. Appears absent on a company muster roll for September and October 1864. Absent in hospital since October 7, 1864. Captured at Blakeley, Alabama, on April 9, 1865. Appears on a roll of POW's received at Ship Island, Mississippi, on April 15, 1865. Transferred from Ship Island to Vicksburg, Mississippi, on May 1, 1865. Appears on a roll of POW's of Cos. E and G, 63rd Alabama Infantry commanded by Captain A. V. Lee that were surrendered by Lt. General Richard Taylor at Citronelle, Alabama, on May 4, 1865, and paroled at Meridian, Mississippi, on May 13, 1865. His residence is shown as Henry County, Alabama.

Stone, T. W., Pvt. Co. I.
Enlisted on April 15, 1864, at Columbiana, Alabama, by Lieutenant Bulger for the war. Appears absent on a company muster roll for September and October 1864. Absent on 30 day furlough from September 27, 1864.

Stoudermire, L. D., Pvt. Co. F.
Enlisted on May 30, 1864, at Montgomery, Alabama, by Captain Moore for the war. Age—17, eyes—grey, hair—light, complexion—fair, 5 foot 4 inches, residence—Autauga, County, Alabama. Drew clothing on September 11, 1864.

Appears on a company muster-in roll for July 25, 1864, at Georgiana, Alabama. Appears present on a company muster roll for August 31 to October 31, 1864, with pay due from time of enlistment.

Stowe, Leroy, Pvt. Co. A.
Enlisted on January 1, 1864, at Montgomery County, Alabama, by Captain Echols for the war. Age—16. Appears on a company muster-in roll for January 1, 1864, at Montgomery, Alabama. Appears present on a company muster roll for January and February 1864, with pay due from time of enlistment. Drew clothing in 2nd quarter of 1864. Appears present on a company muster roll for September and October 1864. Here he is shown as having been last paid on February 29, 1864. Captured at Blakeley, Alabama, on April 9, 1865. Appears on a roll of POW's received at Ship Island, Mississippi, on April 15, 1865. Transferred from Ship Island to Vicksburg, Mississippi, on May 1, 1865. Appears on a roll of POW's of Company A, 63rd Alabama Infantry commanded by Lieutenant W. D. Kyle that were surrendered by Lt. General Richard Taylor at Citronelle, Alabama, on May 4, 1865, and paroled at Meridian, Mississippi, on May 13, 1865. Residence—Montgomery, Alabama.

Strather, John M., Pvt. Co. A.
Enlisted on April 8, 1864, at Chambers [County], Alabama, by Captain Echols for the war. Drew clothing in 2nd quarter of 1864. Appears present on a company muster roll for September and October 1864, with pay due from time of enlistment. Admitted to Ross Hospital, Mobile, Alabama, on November 11, 1864, with febris intermittens quot. Sent to General Hospital Nidelet on November 20, 1864. Captured at Blakeley, Alabama, on April 9, 1865. Appears on a roll of POW's received at Ship Island, Mississippi, on April 15, 1865. Transferred from Ship Island to Vicksburg, Mississippi, on May 1, 1865. Appears on a roll of POW's of Company A, 63rd Alabama Infantry commanded by Lieutenant W. D. Kyle that were surrendered by Lt. General Richard Taylor at Citronelle, Alabama, on May 4, 1865, and paroled at Meridian, Mississippi, on May 13, 1865. Residence—Chambers [County], Alabama. There was a request for information on his file in 1911 from Louisiana.

Strickland, H., Pvt. Co. E.
Enlisted on August 8, 1864, at Pollard, Alabama, by Captain A. V. Lee for the war. Age—17, eyes—dark, hair—dark, complexion—dark. Appears present on a company muster roll for September and October 1864. Captured at Blakeley, Alabama, on April 9, 1865. Appears on a roll of POW's received at Ship Island, Mississippi, on April 15, 1865. Transferred from Ship Island to Vicksburg, Mississippi, on May 1, 1865. Appears on a roll of POW's of Cos. E and G, 63rd Alabama Infantry commanded by Captain A. V. Lee that were surrendered by Lt. General Richard Taylor at Citronelle, Alabama, on May 4, 1865, and paroled at Meridian, Mississippi, on May 13, 1865. Residence—Henry County, Alabama.

Stringer, John E., Pvt. Co. E.
Enlisted on June 18, 1864, at Clayton, Alabama, by Captain A. V. Lee for the war. Age—17, eyes—blue, hair—light, complexion—fair. Drew clothing on September 11, 1864. Signed by his mark. Appears present on a company muster roll for September and October 1864. Admitted to Ross Hospital, Mobile, Alabama, on October 4, 1864, with febris congestiva. Returned to duty on October 9, 1864.

Stringfellow, D., Pvt. Co. D.
Enlisted on August 25, 1864, at Greene County, Alabama, by Lieutenant Jones for the war. Appears present on a company muster roll for September and October 1864. Captured at Blakeley, Alabama, on April 9, 1865. Appears on a

roll of POW's received at Ship Island, Mississippi, on April 15, 1865. Transferred from Ship Island to Vicksburg, Mississippi, on May 1, 1865. Appears on a roll of POW's of Cos. I and K, 63rd Alabama Infantry commanded by Lieutenant W. A. Skinner that were surrendered by Lt. General Richard Taylor at Citronelle, Alabama, on May 4, 1865, and paroled at Meridian, Mississippi, May 13, 1865. Residence—Greene County, Alabama.

Sturkie, Calvin J., Pvt. Co. C.
Enlisted on June 20, 1864, at Macon County, Alabama, by Major Ready for the war. Age—17, eyes—blue, hair—light, complexion—fair, 5 foot 7 inches, residence—Salem, Russell County, Alabama. Appears on a company muster-in roll for June 24, 1864, at Camp Watts near Notasulga, Alabama. Drew clothing in August 1864. Appears absent on a company muster roll for September and October 1864. Absent in hospital at Mobile, Alabama, since October 28, 1864.

Summerlin, B. J., Pvt. Co. F.
Enlisted on May 30, 1864, at Montgomery, Alabama, by Captain Jackson for the war. Age—17, eyes—dark, hair—dark, complexion—dark, 5 foot 8 inches. Appears on a company muster-in roll for July 25, 1864, at Georgiana, Alabama. Drew clothing on September 11, 1864. Appears present on a company muster roll for September and October 1864, with pay due from time of enlistment. Wounded in action and captured at Blakeley, Alabama, on April 9, 1865. Admitted to US 2nd Division 16th Army Corps Hospital, on April 9, 1865, here his name appears as Bryant Summerland. Admitted to US Hospital Steamer D. A. January on April 17, 1865, with a bullet wound to the forearm with fracture. Transferred to the US Hospital Steamer Elanora Carrel at New Orleans, Louisiana, on April 25, 1865. Here he is shown as having Gunshot wound amputation and being sent to Hospital No. 3, on April 28, 1865. Appears on a roll of POW's at US General Hospital No. 3, Vicksburg, Mississippi. Transferred to General Hospital No. 2 on May 4, 1865. Admitted to US Hospital No. 2, Vicksburg, on May 4, 1865, with gunshot wound left forearm, flesh. Age—18. Returned to duty on May 8, 1865.

Summerlin, Columbus, Pvt. Co. D.
Enlisted on July 30, 1864, at Macon County, Alabama, by Major Ready for the war. Age—17, eyes—dark, hair—light, complexion—florid, 5 foot 9 inches, residence—Eufaula, Barbour County, Alabama. Appears on a company muster-in roll for July 30, 1864, at Camp Watts near Notasulga, Alabama. Appears absent on a company muster roll for August 30 to October 30, 1864. Absent at Greenville Hospital since September 10. Here he is shown as having enlisted on June 15, 1864, at Eufaula, by Lieutenant Walker. Captured at Blakeley, Alabama, on April 9, 1865. Appears on a roll of POW's received at Ship Island, Mississippi, on April 15, 1865. Transferred from Ship Island to Vicksburg, Mississippi, on May 1, 1865. Appears on a roll of POW's of Company D, 63rd Alabama Infantry commanded by Captain Robert H. Pearson that were surrendered by Lt. General Richard Taylor at Citronelle, Alabama, on May 4, 1865, and paroled at Meridian, Mississippi, on May 13, 1865. Residence—Barbour County, Alabama.

Summerlin, T. S., Pvt. Co. F.
Enlisted on May 30, 1864, at Montgomery, Alabama, by Captain Jackson for the war. Age—17, eyes—dark, hair—dark, complexion—dark, 5 foot 7 inches, residence—Butler County, Alabama. Appears on a company muster-in roll for July 25, 1864, at Georgiana, Alabama. Drew clothing on September 11, 1864. Appears present on a company muster roll for August 31 to October 31, 1864, with pay due from time of enlistment. Captured at Blakeley, Alabama, on April 9, 1865. Appears on a roll of POW's received at Ship Island, Mississippi, on April 15, 1865. Transferred from Ship Island to Vicksburg, Mississippi, on May

1, 1865. Appears on a roll of POW's of Company F, 63rd Alabama Infantry commanded by Captain R. T. Simpson that were surrendered by Lt. General Richard Taylor at Citronelle, Alabama, on May 4, 1865, and paroled at Meridian, Mississippi, on May 11, 1865. Residence—Butler County, Alabama.

Summers, James, Pvt. Co. B.
Enlisted on April 8, 1864, at Montgomery County, Alabama, by Captain Zimmerman for the war. Age—17. Drew clothing on July 8, August 12 and September 11, 1864. Signed by his mark. Appears present on a company muster roll for September and October 1864, with pay due from time of enlistment.

Suttle, James N., Captain Co. H/Major Field and Staff.
Enlisted on March 15, 1864. Appears present on a company muster roll for September and October 1864. Age—21, eyes—blue, hair—light, complexion—fair. Elected Captain on March 15, 1864. In the 3rd quarter of 1864, he requisitioned for Company H: 17 jackets, 20 pair pants, 26 pair of drawers, 20 pair of shoes, 2 pair of sheets, after being in Selma several months and not having drawn. On a separate requisition he drew: 3 skillets and lids, 2 ovens and lids, 4 mess pans, camp kettles, 39 tin cups, with the same notation of having been in Selma for some time. Signed a Parole of Honor at Selma, Alabama, on May 14, 1865. Here he signs as Major 2nd Alabama Regiment Infantry. His Parole of Honor and requisitions are in his file.

Swope, W., Pvt. Co. K.
Enlisted on October 5, 1864, at Talladega, Alabama, by Captain Ramius for the war. Appears present on a company muster roll for September and October 1864. Admitted to Ross Hospital, Mobile, Alabama, on November 5, 1864, with rubeola. Returned to duty on November 14, 1864. Captured at Blakeley, Alabama, on April 9, 1865. Appears on a roll of POW's received at Ship Island, Mississippi, on April 15, 1865. Transferred from Ship Island to Vicksburg, Mississippi, on May 1, 1865. Appears on a roll of POW's of Cos. I and K, 63rd Alabama Infantry commanded by Lieutenant W. A. Skinner that were surrendered by Lt. General Richard Taylor at Citronelle, Alabama, on May 4, 1865, and paroled at Meridian, Mississippi, May 13, 1865. Residence—Talladega County, Alabama.

Sylvester, W. O., Corporal/Sergeant Co. E.
Enlisted on March 18, 1864, at Clayton, Alabama, by Captain A. V. Lee for the war. Age—17, eyes—dark, hair—dark, complexion—dark. Drew clothing on September 11, 1864. Admitted to Ross Hospital, Mobile, Alabama, on September 18, 1864, with febris intermittens tert. Returned to duty on September 26, 1864. Appears present on a company muster roll for September and October 1864. Captured at Blakeley, Alabama, on April 9, 1865. Appears on a roll of POW's received at Ship Island, Mississippi, on April 15, 1865. Transferred from Ship Island to Vicksburg, Mississippi, on May 1, 1865. Appears on a roll of POW's of Cos. E and G, 63rd Alabama Infantry commanded by Captain A. V. Lee that were surrendered by Lt. General Richard Taylor at Citronelle, Alabama, on May 4, 1865, and paroled at Meridian, Mississippi, on May 13, 1865. Residence—Eufaula, Alabama.

Tate, Solon R., Corporal Co. A.
Enlisted on January 1, 1864, at Macon County, Alabama, by Captain John Echols for the war. Age—16. Appears on a company muster-in roll for January 1, 1864. Appears present on a company muster roll for January and February 1864, with pay due from time of enlistment. Appears present on a company muster roll for September and October 1864. Here he is shown as having been paid on February 29, 1864. Drew clothing in 2nd quarter of 1864.

Taunton, Temley, Pvt. Co. C.
 Enlisted on May 18, 1864, at Tallapoosa County, Alabama, by Captain Brown for the war. Age—17, eyes—blue, hair—light, complexion—fair, 5 foot 2 ½ inches, residence—Chonahatchie, Tallapoosa County, Alabama. Appears on a company muster-in roll for July 24, 1864, at Camp Watts near Notasulga, Alabama. He is reportted to be present on a company muster roll for September and October 1864.

Taylor, E. H. L., Pvt. Co. D.
 Admitted to Way Hospital, Meridian, Mississippi, on January 9, 1865, with a wound. Furloughed.

Taylor, H. H., Pvt. Co. F.
 Captured at Blakeley, Alabama, on April 9, 1865. Appears on a roll of POW's received at Ship Island, Mississippi, on April 15, 1865. Transferred from Ship Island to Vicksburg, Mississippi, on May 1, 1865. Appears on a roll of POW's of Company F, 63rd Alabama Infantry commanded by Captain R. T. Simpson that were surrendered by Lt. General Richard Taylor at Citronelle, Alabama, on May 4, 1865, and paroled at Meridian, Mississippi, on May 11, 1865. Residence—Butler County, Alabama.

Taylor, James M., Pvt. Co. B.
 Enlisted on August 15, 1864, at Pollard, Alabama, by Lieutenant Townsend for the war. Drew clothing on September 11, 1864. Appears present on a company muster roll for September and October 1864, with pay due from time of enlistment. Captured at Blakeley, Alabama, on April 9, 1865. Appears on a roll of POW's received at Ship Island, Mississippi, on April 15, 1865. Transferred from Ship Island to Vicksburg, Mississippi, on May 1, 1865. Appears on a roll of POW's of Company B, 63rd Alabama Infantry commanded by 1st Lieutenant Thomas J. Calhoun that were surrendered by Lt. General Richard Taylor at Citronelle, Alabama, on May 4, 1865, and paroled at Meridian, Mississippi, on May 11, 1865. Residence—Dale County, Alabama.

Teague, Harris, Pvt. Co. A.
 Appears present on a company muster roll for January and February 1864, with pay due from time of enlistment.

Terry, Henry C., Pvt. Co. D.
 Enlisted on July 6, 1864, at Chambers County, Alabama, by Captain Walker for the war. Age—17, eyes—hazel, hair—dark, complexion—dark, 5 foot 8 inches, residence—West Point, Georgia. His file also shows residence at Chambers County, Alabama. Appears on a company muster-in roll for July 30, 1864. Appears absent on a company muster roll for August 30 to October 30, 1864, with pay due from time of enlistment. Absent sick at Notasulga Hospital. Wounded at Chehaw on July 18 and has not returned.

Thigpen, J. E., Pvt. Co. F.
 Enlisted on May 30, 1864, at Montgomery, Alabama, by Captain Jackson for the war. Age—17, eyes—dark, hair—dark, complexion—dark, 5 foot 7 inches, residence—Butler County, Alabama. Appears on a company muster-in roll for July 25, 1864, at Georgiana, Alabama. Drew clothing on September 11, 1864. Appears present on a company muster roll for August 31 to October 31, 1864, with pay due from time of enlistment. Captured at Blakeley, Alabama, on April 9, 1865. Appears on a roll of POW's received at Ship Island, Mississippi, on April 15, 1865. Transferred from Ship Island to Vicksburg, Mississippi, on May 1, 1865. Appears on a roll of POW's of Company F, 63rd Alabama Infantry commanded by Captain R. T. Simpson that were surrendered by Lt. General

Richard Taylor at Citronelle, Alabama, on May 4, 1865, and paroled at Meridian, Mississippi, on May 11, 1865. Residence—Butler County, Alabama.

Thomas, John L., Pvt. Co. A.
Enlisted on April 13, 1864, at Butler [County], Alabama, by Captain Echols for the war. Drew clothing in 2nd quarter and September 11, 1864. Appears present sick in quarters on a company muster roll for September and October 1864, with pay due from time of enlistment. Captured at Blakeley, Alabama, on April 9, 1865. Appears on a roll of POW's received at Ship Island, Mississippi, on April 15, 1865. Transferred from Ship Island to Vicksburg, Mississippi, on May 1, 1865. Appears on a roll of POW's of Company A, 63rd Alabama Infantry commanded by Lieutenant W. D. Kyle that were surrendered by Lt. General Richard Taylor at Citronelle, Alabama, on May 4, 1865, and paroled at Meridian, Mississippi, on May 13, 1865. Residence—Butler County, Alabama.

Thomas, Jonathan, C., Pvt. Co. B.
Enlisted on July 30, 1864, at Macon County, Alabama, by Major Ready for the war. Age—17, eyes—grey, hair—dark, complexion—florid, 5 foot 7 inches, residence—Buford, Barbour County, Alabama. Appears on a company muster-in roll for July 30, 1864, at Camp Watts near Notasulga, Alabama. Drew clothing on August 7, 1864. Appears present on a company muster roll for August 30 to October 30, 1864, with pay due from time of enlistment. Here he is shown as having enlisted on March 2, 1864, at Clayton, Alabama, by D. M. Seals. POW captured on April 9, 1865, at Blakeley, Alabama. Appears on a list of wounded Confederates in the hospital of 1st Division, 13, US Army Corps at the battle of Fort Blakeley, Alabama, on April 9, 1865, with penetrating wound of the pelvis. Admitted to St. Louis USA General Hospital, New Orleans, Louisiana, from US Hospital Steamer D. A. January on April 15, 1865. Age—18. Shown to be suffering from gunshot wound of the abdominal wall (non. penet.) Transferred to Marine General Hospital on May 16, 1865. POW confined at New Orleans on May 1, 1865 at New Orleans. Released on May 16, 1865, on parole.

Thomas, M., Pvt. Co. E.
Enlisted on August 8, 1864, at Pollard, Alabama, by Captain A. V. Lee for the war. Age—17, eyes—dark, hair—dark, complexion—dark. Drew clothing on September 11, 1864. Appears absent on a company muster roll for September and October 1864. Absent in hospital since September 24, 1864. Captured at Blakeley, Alabama, on April 9, 1865. Appears on a roll of POW's received at Ship Island, Mississippi, on April 15, 1865. Transferred from Ship Island to Vicksburg, Mississippi, on May 1, 1865. Appears on a roll of POW's of Cos. E and G, 63rd Alabama Infantry commanded by Captain A. V. Lee that were surrendered by Lt. General Richard Taylor at Citronelle, Alabama, on May 4, 1865, and paroled at Meridian, Mississippi, on May 13, 1865. Residence—Henry County, Alabama.

Thomas, M. J., Pvt. Co. E.
Enlisted on September 12, 1864, at Camp Hood by Captain A. V. Lee for the war. Age—17, eyes—dark, hair—dark, complexion—dark. Drew clothing on September 11, 1864. He appears absent on a company muster roll for September and October 1864. Absent in hospital since September 18, 1864. Reported to have been admitted to Ross Hospital, Mobile, Alabama, on September 27, 1864, with febris remittens, acuta diarrhoea. Furloughed for 30 days from October 13, 1864.

Thomas, Zachariah T., Sergeant/Pvt. Co. D.
Enlisted as 2nd Sergeant on July 30, 1864, at Macon County, Alabama, by Major Ready for the war. Age—17, eyes—dark, hair—dark, complexion—dark, 5 foot 5

inches, residence—Buford, Barbour County, Alabama. Appears on a company muster-in roll for July 30, 1864, at Camp Watts near Notasulga, Alabama. Drew clothing on August 7 and September 12, 1864. Appears present on a company muster roll for August 30 to October 30, 1864, with pay due from time of enlistment. Here he is shown as having enlisted on March 2, 1864, at Clayton, Alabama, by D. M. Seals. He was reduced from 2nd Sergeant to ranks on September 15.

Thompkins, James M., Pvt. Co. G.
Enlisted on May 8, 1864, at Andalusia, Alabama, by Lieutenant Wiley for the war. Age—17, eyes—black, hair—dark, complexion—dark, 5 foot 0 inches, residence—Covington, County, Alabama. Appears on a company muster-in roll for September 7, 1864. Drew clothing on September 11, 1864. Signed by his mark. Appears absent on a company muster roll for September and October 1864. Absent in hospital at Mobile, Alabama, since October 12, 1864. Admitted to 1st Mississippi, CSA Hospital, Jackson, Mississippi, on November 10, 1864, with debilitas. Died on January 26, 1865.

Thompson, Andrew J., Pvt. Co. C.
Enlisted on May 12, 1864, at Macon County, Alabama, by Major Ready for the war. Age—17, eyes—black, hair—dark, complexion—dark, 5 foot 6 inches, residence—Society Hill, Macon County, Alabama. Appears on a company muster-in roll for June 24, 1864, at Camp Watts near Notasulga, Alabama. Drew clothing on August 6, 1864. Signed by his mark. Appears present on a company muster roll for September and October 1864. Captured at Blakeley, Alabama, on April 9, 1865. Appears on a roll of POW's received at Ship Island, Mississippi, on April 15, 1865. Transferred from Ship Island to Vicksburg, Mississippi, on May 1, 1865. Appears on a roll of POW's of Cos. C and H, 63rd Alabama Infantry commanded by Captain C. W. Martin that were surrendered by Lt. General Richard Taylor at Citronelle, Alabama, on May 4, 1865, and paroled at Meridian, Mississippi, on May 11, 1865. Residence—Macon County, Alabama.

Thompson, B., Pvt. Co. B.
Captured at Blakeley, Alabama, on April 9, 1865. Appears on a roll of POW's received at Ship Island, Mississippi, on April 15, 1865. Transferred from Ship Island to Vicksburg, Mississippi, on May 1, 1865.

Thompson, James Z., Pvt. Co. C.
Enlisted on May 9, 1864, at Macon County, Alabama, by Major Ready for the war. Age—17, eyes—blue, hair—light, complexion—fair, 5 foot 10 inches, residence—Society Hill, Macon County, Alabama. Appears on a company muster roll for June 24, 1864, at Camp Watts near Notasulga, Alabama. Drew clothing on August 6, 1864. Appears present on a company muster roll for September and October 1864.

Thompson, J. H., Pvt./Sergeant Co. B.
Appears on a list of prisoners in camp near Spanish Fort, Alabama, that require hospital treatment. List is dated April 12, 1865, Headquarters 23rd Iowa, Volunteers. Disease is shown as debility. Appears on a roll of POW's received at Ship Island, Mississippi, on April 15, 1865. Transferred from Ship Island to Vicksburg, Mississippi, on May 1, 1865. Admitted to USA Hospital No. 2, Vicksburg on May 4, 1865, from steamer with acute diarrhoea. Returned to duty on May 8, 1865. He is shown as both Private and a Sergeant in various reports.

Thompson, John, Pvt. Co. B.
Enlisted on March 23, 1864, at Montgomery County, Alabama, by Captain

Zimmerman for the war. Age—17. Appears on a company muster-in roll for March 23, 1864, at Montgomery, Alabama. Drew clothing on July 8 and August 12, 1864.

Thompson, P. M., Pvt. Co. F.
Enlisted on March 9, 1864, at Greenville, Alabama, by Captain Brown for the war. Age—17, eyes—dark, hair—dark, complexion—dark, 5 foot 6 inches, residence—Butler County, Alabama. Appears on a company muster-in roll for July 25, 1864, at Georgiana, Alabama. Appears present on a company muster roll for August 31 to October 31, 1864, with pay due from enlistment. Captured at Blakeley, Alabama, April 9, 1865. His name appears on a roll of POW's received at Ship Island, Mississippi, on April 15, 1865. He was among those men transferred from Ship Island to Vicksburg, Mississippi, May 1, 1865. Appears on a roll of POW's of Company F, 63rd Alabama Infantry commanded by Captain R. T. Simpson that were surrendered by Lt. General Richard Taylor at Citronelle, Alabama, May 4, 1865, and paroled at Meridian, Mississippi, on May 11, 1865. Residence—Butler County, Alabama. In his file is a parole for P. M. Thompson A. Q. M. Dept. issued on May 30, 1865, at Charlotte, North Carolina. This is likely filed here in error.

Thompson, R. T., Pvt. Co. E.
Enlisted on August 5, 1864, at Montgomery, Alabama, by Captain A. V. Lee for the war. Age—17, eyes—dark, hair—dark, complexion—dark. Appears absent on a company muster roll for September and October 1864. Absent furloughed for 60 days from September 27, 1864.

Thompson, W. L., 1st Sergeant Co. H.
Enlisted on March 15, 1864, at Centerville, Alabama, by Captain Suttle for the war. Age—17, eyes—gray, hair—light, complexion—fair. Appears present on a company muster roll for September and October 1864.

Thomley, J. M., Pvt. Co. E.
Enlisted on August 8, 1864, at Pollard, Alabama, by Captain A. V. Lee for the war. He is described as: age—17, eyes—blue, hair—light, complexion—fair. Drew clothing on September 11, 1864. Signed by his mark. Appears absent on a company muster roll for September and October 1864. Absent in hospital since October 17, 1864.

Thornton, Albert J., Lieutenant Co. B.
Appears as 3rd Lieutenant on a company muster-in roll for March 23, 1864, at Montgomery, Alabama. Elected 2nd Lieutenant on March 23, 1864. Appears absent sick on a company muster roll for September and October 1864. Absent sick since September 9, 1864. Signed a parole at Headquarters of US Forces of Northern Alabama, at Montgomery, Alabama, on May 8, 1864. Hair—black, eyes—blue, complexion—fair, 6 foot 3 ½ inches. Appears on a Medical Certificate at Demopolis, Alabama, on April 15, 1865. Unfit for duty for 30 days due to chronic bronchitis of fourteen months and convalescent of pneumonia. Furloughed to his place of residence at Montgomery, Alabama. His furlough is in his file.

Thornton, James T., Pvt. Co. G.
Enlisted October 11, 1864, at Blakeley, Alabama, by Captain Garland. Drew clothing on September 11, 1864. Appears present on a company muster roll for September and October 1864. Captured at Blakeley, Alabama, on April 9, 1865. Appears on a roll of POW's received at Ship Island, Mississippi, on April 15, 1865. Transferred from Ship Island to Vicksburg, Mississippi, on May 1, 1865. Appears on a roll of POW's of Cos. E and G, 63rd Alabama Infantry commanded

by Captain A. V. Lee that were surrendered by Lt. General Richard Taylor at Citronelle, Alabama, on May 4, 1865, and paroled at Meridian, Mississippi, on May 13, 1865. Residence—Pike County, Alabama. There is an inquiry about his service with his file from the State of Georgia, dated 1915.

Thornton, S. S., Corporal Co. K.
Enlisted on May 23, 1864, at Greene County, Alabama, by Lieutenant Jones for the war. Appears present on company muster roll for September and October 1864. Captured at Blakeley, Alabama, on April 9, 1865. His name appears on a roll of POW's received at Ship Island, Mississippi, on April 15, 1865. Transferred from Ship Island to Vicksburg, Mississippi, on May 1, 1865. Appears on a roll of POW's of Cos. I and K, 63rd Alabama Infantry commanded by Lieutenant W. A. Skinner that were surrendered by Lt. General Richard Taylor at Citronelle, Alabama, on May 4, 1865, and paroled at Meridian, Mississippi, May 13, 1865. Residence—Greene County, Alabama. There is an inquiry about his service with his file from the State of Alabama, dated in 1920.

Thrash, W. V., Pvt. Co. K.
Enlisted on October 14, 1864, at Coosa County, Alabama, by Captain Hancock for the war. Appears present on a company muster roll for September and October 1864. Discharged by Medical Examining Board on December 9, 1864, at Mobile, Alabama. Atrophy of the whole left lower extremity caused possibly by an injury to the hip joint. Born in Coosa County, Alabama, Age—17, eyes—grey, hair—dark, complexion—fair, 5 foot 8 inches. A farmer by occupation. His certificate of disability for discharge is in his file.

Thrower, T. J., Pvt. Co. F.
Enlisted on July 12, 1864, at Lowndes County, Alabama, by Captain Buell for the war. Age—17, eyes—dark, hair—dark, complexion—fair, 5 foot 9 inches, residence—Lowndes County, Alabama. Appears present on a company muster-in roll for July 25, 1864. Drew clothing on September 11, 1864. Appears present on a company muster roll for August 31 to October 31, 1864, with pay due from time of enlistment. Captured at Blakeley, Alabama, on April 9, 1865. Appears on a roll of POW's received at Ship Island, Mississippi, on April 15, 1865. Transferred from Ship Island to Vicksburg, Mississippi, on May 1, 1865. Appears on a roll of POW's of Company F, 63rd Alabama Infantry commanded by Captain R. T. Simpson that were surrendered by Lt. General Richard Taylor at Citronelle, Alabama, on May 4, 1865, and paroled at Meridian, Mississippi, on May 11, 1865. Residence—Lowndes County, Alabama.

Thurmond, D., Pvt./Corporal Co. E.
Enlisted on August 8, 1864, at Pollard, Alabama, by Captain A. V. Lee for the war. Age—17, eyes—blue, hair—light, complexion—fair. Drew clothing on September 11, 1864. Appears present on a company muster roll for September and October 1864. Captured at Blakeley, Alabama, on April 9, 1865. Here he is shown as 1st Corporal. Appears on a roll of POW's received at Ship Island, Mississippi, on April 15, 1865. Transferred from Ship Island to Vicksburg, Mississippi, on May 1, 1865. His name appears on a roll of POW's of Cos. E and G, 63rd Alabama Infantry commanded by Captain A. V. Lee that were surrendered by Lt. General Richard Taylor at Citronelle, Alabama, on May 4, 1865, and paroled at Meridian, Mississippi, on May 13, 1865. Residence—Dale County, Alabama.

Tinsley, C., Pvt. Co. E.
Enlisted on September 12, 1864, at Camp Hood by Captain A. V. Lee for the war. Age—17, eyes—blue, hair—light, complexion—fair. Drew clothing on

September 11, 1864. Signed by his mark. Appears present on a company muster roll for September and October 1864.

Tolbert, Charles L., Sergeant Co. C.
Enlisted as 2nd Sergeant on June 9, 1864, at Macon County, Alabama, by Major Ready for the war. Age—17, eyes—hazel, hair—light, complexion—fair, 5 foot 7 inches, residence—Society Hill, Macon County, Alabama. Appears on a company muster-in roll for June 24, 1864, at Camp Watts near Notasulga, Alabama. Drew clothing on August 6, 1864. Appears present on a company muster roll for September and October 1864, with pay due from time of enlistment. His name appears on a list of wounded Confederates in the hospital of the 1st Division 13th Corps of US Army at the battle of Blakeley Fort on April 9, 1865. POW captured at Fort Blakeley, Alabama, on April 9, 1865. He was admitted to St Louis USA General Hospital, New Orleans, Louisiana, on April 15, 1865, with gunshot wound to left arm, flesh. "Minnie entered two inches above internal condyle of humerus passing over joint emerging three inches below joint on inside of forearm. Bones not injured." Shown as POW confined at New Orleans on May 1, 1865. He was paroled at New Orleans on May 16, 1865. Transferred to Marine General Hospital on May 22, 1865. Age—18. Returned to duty on June 2, 1865.

Townsend, Phillip A., 2nd Lieutenant Co. B.
Appears on a company muster-in roll for March 23, 1864, at Montgomery, Alabama. Elected 2nd Lieutenant on March 23, 1864. Drew clothing on July 8, 1864. Requisitioned for Co. B, 21 pair of shoes on August 11, 1864. Appears present on a company muster roll for September and October 1864. Appears on a roster of 2nd Regiment Alabama Reserves, Fuller's Brigade, Maury's Corps CSA in January 1865. POW captured on April 9, 1865, by 2nd Division, 16th US Army Corps at Blakeley, Alabama. Confined one day near Spanish Fort, Alabama. Appears on a roll of POW's received at Ship Island, Mississippi, on April 16, 1865. Appears on a roll of POW's transferred from Ship Island to Vicksburg, Mississippi, on April 28, 1865. He was actually transferred to New Orleans, Louisiana, April 28, 1865. Confined at New Orleans on April 30, 1865. Exchanged on May 1, 1865. Signed a parole of honor on May 11, 1865, at Meridian, Mississippi. Montgomery, Alabama, [residence?] is noted on his parole which is in his file.

Trammell, David, Pvt. Co. A.
Enlisted on January 1, 1864, at Tallapoosa County, Alabama, by Captain John Echols for the war. Appears on a company muster-in roll for January 1, 1864. Age—16. Appears present on a company muster roll for January and February 1864, with pay due from time of enlistment. Drew clothing in 2nd quarter and September 11, 1864. Appears present on a company muster roll for September and October 1864. Here he is shown as having been last paid on February 29, 1864. Captured at Blakeley, Alabama, on April 9, 1865. Appears on a roll of POW's received at Ship Island, Mississippi, on April 15, 1865. Transferred from Ship Island to Vicksburg, Mississippi, on May 1, 1865. Appears on a roll of POW's of Company A, 63rd Alabama Infantry commanded by Lieutenant W. D. Kyle that were surrendered by Lt. General Richard Taylor at Citronelle, Alabama, on May 4, 1865, and paroled at Meridian, Mississippi, on May 13, 1865. Residence—Tallapoosa County, Alabama.

Traywick, Harrison, Pvt. Co. A.
Enlisted on January 1, 1864, at Macon County, Alabama, by Captain Echols for the war. Appears on a company muster-in roll for January 1, 1864, at Montgomery, Alabama. Age—16. Appears present on a company muster roll for January and February 1864, with pay due from time of enlistment. Drew

clothing in 2nd quarter of 1864. Appears present sick in quarters on a company muster roll for September and October 1864. Here he is shown as having been last paid on February 29, 1864. Captured at Blakeley, Alabama, on April 9, 1865. Appears on a roll of POW's received at Ship Island, Mississippi, on April 15, 1865. Transferred from Ship Island to Vicksburg, Mississippi, on May 1, 1865. Appears on a roll of POW's of Company A, 63rd Alabama Infantry commanded by Lieutenant W. D. Kyle that were surrendered by Lt. General Richard Taylor at Citronelle, Alabama, on May 4, 1865, and paroled at Meridian, Mississippi, on May 13, 1865. Residence—Macon County, Alabama.

Tucker, George W., Corporal Co. C.
Enlisted as 4th Corporal on May 27, 1864, at Russell County, Alabama, by Lieutenant Morton. Age—17, eyes—grey, hair—dark, complexion—fair, 5 foot 6 ½ inches, residence—Opelika, Macon County, Alabama [note Opelika is in Russell County]. Appears on a company muster-in roll for June 24, 1864, at Camp Watts near Notasulga, Alabama. Drew clothing on August 6, 1864. Signed by his mark. Appears on a company muster roll for September and October 1864, with pay due from time of enlistment. Captured at Blakeley, Alabama, on April 9, 1865. Appears on a roll of POW's received at Ship Island, Mississippi, on April 15, 1865. Transferred from Ship Island to Vicksburg, Mississippi, on May 1, 1865. Appears on a roll of POW's of Cos. C and H, 63rd Alabama Infantry commanded by Captain C. W. Martin that were surrendered by Lt. General Richard Taylor at Citronelle, Alabama, on May 4, 1865, and paroled at Meridian, Mississippi, on May 11, 1865. Residence—Russell County, Alabama. His name also appears as a POW of Quintard Hospital, CSA commanded by Surgeon S. V. D. Hill that were surrendered by Lt. General Richard Taylor at Citronelle, Alabama, on May 4, 1865, and paroled at Meridian, Mississippi, on May 10, 1865. His residence is shown as Opelika, Alabama.

Tucker, N. H., Pvt. Co. E.
Appears as a POW of Moore Hospital, CSA commanded by Surgeon W. C. Cavenaugh that were surrendered by Lt. General Richard Taylor at Citronelle, Alabama, on May 4, 1865, and paroled at Meridian, Mississippi, on May 16, 1865. Residence—Lowndes County, Alabama.

Tucker, William, Pvt. Co. C.
Enlisted on May 3, 1864, at Russell County, Alabama, by Lieutenant Carnes for the war. Age—17, eyes—grey, hair—light, complexion—fair, 5 foot 7 ¼ inches, residence—Osichee, Russell County, Alabama. Appears on a company muster-in roll for June 24, 1864, at Camp Watts near Notasulga, Alabama. Drew clothing on August 6, 1864. Appears present on a company muster roll for September and October 1864. Captured at Blakeley, Alabama, on April 9, 1865. Appears on a roll of POW's received at Ship Island, Mississippi, on April 15, 1865. Transferred from Ship Island to Vicksburg, Mississippi, on May 1, 1865. Appears on a roll of POW's of Cos. C and H, 63rd Alabama Infantry commanded by Captain C. W. Martin that were surrendered by Lt. General Richard Taylor at Citronelle, Alabama, on May 4, 1865, and paroled at Meridian, Mississippi, on May 11, 1865. Residence—Russell County, Alabama.

Turk, Charles T., Pvt. Co. C.
Enlisted on June 13, 1864, at Russell County, Alabama, by Lieutenant Carnes for the war. Age—17, eyes—17, hair—dark, complexion—dark, 5 foot 4 ¼ inch, residence—Vilulah, Russell County, Alabama. Appears on a company muster-in roll for June 24, 1864, at Camp Watts near Notasulga, Alabama. Appears present on a company muster roll for September and October 1864. Here his enlistment date is shown as June 15, 1864.

Turner, E. L., Pvt. Co. K.

Enlisted on September 12, 1864, at Talladega, Alabama, by Captain Ramises for the war. Appears present on a company muster roll for September and October 1864. Captured at Blakeley, Alabama, on April 9, 1865. Appears on a roll of POW's received at Ship Island, Mississippi, on April 15, 1865. Transferred from Ship Island to Vicksburg, Mississippi, on May 1, 1865. Appears on a roll of POW's of Cos. I and K, 63rd Alabama Infantry commanded by Lieutenant W. A. Skinner that were surrendered by Lt. General Richard Taylor at Citronelle, Alabama, on May 4, 1865, and paroled at Meridian, Mississippi, May 13, 1865. Residence—Tuscaloosa County, Alabama.

Turner, John W., Pvt. Co. D.

Enlisted on July 10, 1864, at Tallapoosa [County], Alabama, by Captain Brown for the war. Age—17, eyes—grey, hair—dark, complexion—florid, 5 foot 3 inches, residence—Barnesville, Alabama. Appears on a company muster-in roll for July 30, 1864, at Camp Watts near Notasulga, Alabama. Drew clothing on August 7, 1864. Appears present on a company muster roll for August 30 to October 30, 1864, with pay due from time of enlistment. Captured at Blakeley, Alabama, on April 9, 1865. Appears on a roll of POW's received at Ship Island, Mississippi, on April 15, 1865. Transferred from Ship Island to Vicksburg, Mississippi, on May 1, 1865. Appears on a roll of POW's of Company D, 63rd Alabama Infantry commanded by Captain Robert H. Pearson that were surrendered by Lt. General Richard Taylor at Citronelle, Alabama, on May 4, 1865, and paroled at Meridian, Mississippi, on May 13, 1865. Residence—Tallapoosa County, Alabama.

Turner, L. W., 2nd Lieutenant Co. E.

Appears on a roster for January 1865, of the 2nd Regiment Alabama, Reserves, Fuller's Brigade, Maury's Corps, CSA which was organized on August 16, 1865. Elected 2nd Lieutenant on August 10, 1864. Drew clothing on August 11, 1864. Resigned on September 16, 1864. There was an inquiry as to his service from the State of Texas in 1916.

Turner, Mark, A., Pvt. Co. D.

Enlisted on July 10, 1864, at Tallapoosa [County], Alabama, by Captain Brown for the war. Age—17, eyes—grey, hair—dark, complexion—florid, 5 foot 2 inches, residence—Barnesville, Alabama. Appears on a company muster-in roll for July 30, 1864, at Camp Watts near Notasulga, Alabama. Drew clothing on August 7, 1864. Appears absent on a company muster roll for August 30 to October 30, 1864, with pay due from time of enlistment. Absent sick at Mobile hospital since October 27. Captured at Blakeley, Alabama, on April 9, 1865. Appears on a roll of POW's received at Ship Island, Mississippi, on April 15, 1865. Transferred from Ship Island to Vicksburg, Mississippi, on May 1, 1865. Appears on a roll of POW's of Company D, 63rd Alabama Infantry commanded by Captain Robert H. Pearson that were surrendered by Lt. General Richard Taylor at Citronelle, Alabama, on May 4, 1865, and paroled at Meridian, Mississippi, on May 13, 1865. Residence—Tallapoosa County, Alabama.

Twiford, D., Corporal/Pvt. Co. K.

Enlisted on September 14, 1864, at Bibb County, Alabama, by Captain Hughes for the war. Appears as 2nd Corporal and absent on a company muster roll for September and October 1864. Absent in hospital at Mobile, Alabama, since October 20, 1864. Captured at Blakeley, Alabama, on April 9, 1865. Here and hereafter he is shows as a Private. Appears on a roll of POW's received at Ship Island, Mississippi, on April 15, 1865. Transferred from Ship Island to Vicksburg, Mississippi, on May 1, 1865. Appears on a roll of POW's of Cos. I and K, 63rd Alabama Infantry commanded by Lieutenant W. A. Skinner that were surrendered by Lt. General Richard Taylor at Citronelle, Alabama, on May

4, 1865, and paroled at Meridian, Mississippi, May 13, 1865. Residence—Bibb County, Alabama.

Tyler, John, Pvt. Co. D.
Captured at Blakeley, Alabama, on April 9, 1865. Appears on a roll of POW's received at Ship Island, Mississippi, on April 15, 1865. Transferred from Ship Island to Vicksburg, Mississippi, on May 1, 1865. Appears on a roll of POW's of Company D, 63rd Alabama Infantry commanded by Captain Robert H. Pearson that were surrendered by Lt. General Richard Taylor at Citronelle, Alabama, on May 4, 1865, and paroled at Meridian, Mississippi, on May 13, 1865. Residence—Henry County, Alabama.

Usery, A., Pvt. Co. I.
Enlisted on April 15, 1864, at Wedowee, Alabama, by Captain Robinson for the war. He appears absent on detail on a company muster roll for September and October 1864. A reference card in his file: Special Order no 81, October 4, 1864. Subject: Report to Surgeon Potts. Pvt. Captain Fulton's Company.

Van, L. E., Pvt. Co. F.
Enlisted on March 9, 1864, at Greenville, Alabama, by Captain Brown for the war. He is described as: age—17, eyes—hazel, hair—dark, complexion—fair, 5 foot 11 inches, residence—Butler County, Alabama. Appears on a company muster-in roll for July 25, 1864, at Georgiana, Alabama. Appears absent on a company muster roll for August 31 to October 31, 1864. This muster roll reports him absent on 60 day sick leave since September 27, 1864. He had never been paid at this point.

Van Curn, J. M., Pvt. Co. I.
Enlisted on April 15, 1864, at Wedowee, Alabama, by Captain Robinson for the war. Appears present on a company muster roll for September and October 1864. He was discharged on January 21, 1865, at Mobile, Alabama, by a Medical Examining Board due to phthisis and general debility. Born—Randolph County, Alabama, age—17, 5 foot 8 inches, hair—light, eyes—blue, complexion—fair, by occupation a farmer. His Certificate of Disability is in his file.

Vaughan, William, Pvt. Co. K.
Appears on a roll of POW's of nurses and patients of CSA Moore Hospital commanded by Surgeon W. G. Cavanaugh, that were surrendered by Lt. General Richard Taylor at Citronelle, Alabama, on May 4, 1865, and paroled at Meridian, Mississippi, on May 13, 1865. His residence was reported to be Calhoun County, Alabama.

Veasey, Simon C., Pvt. Co. A.
Enlisted on January 1, 1864, at Tallapoosa County, Alabama, by Captain Echols for the war. Age—16. Appears on a company muster-in roll for January 1, 1864, at Montgomery, Alabama. Appears present on a company muster roll for January and February 1864, with pay due from time of enlistment. Drew clothing in 2nd quarter of 1864. Appears present on a company muster roll for September and October 1864. He is shown as having last been paid on February 29, 1864. Captured at Blakeley, Alabama, on April 9, 1865. Appears on a roll of POW's received at Ship Island, Mississippi, on April 15, 1865. Transferred from Ship Island to Vicksburg, Mississippi, on May 1, 1865. Appears on a roll of POW's of Company A, 63rd Alabama Infantry commanded by Lieutenant W. D. Kyle that were surrendered by Lt. General Richard Taylor at Citronelle, Alabama, on May 4, 1865, and paroled at Meridian, Mississippi, on May 13, 1865. Residence—Tallapoosa County, Alabama.

Vernon, E. W., Pvt. Co. C.
Captured at Blakeley, Alabama, on April 9, 1865. Appears on a roll of POW's received at Ship Island, Mississippi, on April 15, 1865. Transferred from Ship Island to Vicksburg, Mississippi, on May 1, 1865. Appears on a roll of POW's of Cos. C and H, 63rd Alabama Infantry commanded by Captain C. W. Martin that were surrendered by Lt. General Richard Taylor at Citronelle, Alabama, on May 4, 1865, and paroled at Meridian, Mississippi, on May 11, 1865. Residence—Chambers County, Alabama.

Vincent, E. M., Pvt. Co. A/C.
Appears on a register of paroled Confederate soldiers that were paroled on June 7, 1864, by Provost Marshal of the 16th US Army Corps. He is shown here as being from Company C. Signed, by his mark "X", a parole at Montgomery, Alabama, at the headquarter of the 16th US Army corps on June 7, 1864. Hair—grey, eyes—blue, complexion—fair, 5 foot 11 inches.

Vines, G. B., Pvt. Co. H.
Enlisted on July 29, 1864, at Selma, Alabama, by Captain Suttle for the war. Age—17, eyes—blue, hair—light, complexion—dark. Drew clothing on September 11, 1864. Appears absent on a company muster roll for September and October 1864. Absent without leave since October 15.

Vines, J., Pvt. Co. H.
Enlisted on July 29, 1864, at Selma, Alabama, by Captain Suttle for the war. Age—17, eyes—dark, hair—dark, complexion—dark. Appears absent on a company muster roll for September and October 1864. Absent in Camp of Correction since August 14. Captured at Blakeley, Alabama, on April 9, 1865. Appears on a roll of POW's received at Ship Island, Mississippi, on April 15, 1865. Transferred from Ship Island to Vicksburg, Mississippi, on May 1, 1865. Appears on a roll of POW's of Cos. C and H, 63rd Alabama Infantry commanded by Captain C. W. Martin that were surrendered by Lt. General Richard Taylor at Citronelle, Alabama, on May 4, 1865, and paroled at Meridian, Mississippi, on May 11, 1865. Residence—Jefferson County, Alabama.

Vines, W. B., Pvt. Co. H/I.
Enlisted on July 29, 1864, at Selma, Alabama, by Captain Suttle for the war. Age—17, eyes—blue, hair—light, complexion—fair. Appears absent on a company muster roll for September and October 1864. Absent on sick furlough since October 10. Appears on a roll of POW's paroled by Brevet Brigadier General M. H. Chrysler commanding Forces at Talladega, Alabama. Paroled on June 24, 1865, at Talladega. Here he is shown as being from Company I.

Vinson, Robert, Pvt. Co. B.
Enlisted on March 23, 1864, at Montgomery, Alabama. Age—16. Appears on a company muster-in roll for March 23, 1864, at Montgomery, Alabama. Drew clothing on July 8, August 12 and September 11, 1864. Signed by his mark. Appears present on a company muster roll for September and October 1864, with pay due from time of enlistment. Captured at Blakeley, Alabama, on April 9, 1865. Appears on a roll of POW's received at Ship Island, Mississippi, on April 15, 1865. Transferred from Ship Island to Vicksburg, Mississippi, on May 1, 1865. Appears on a roll of POW's of Company B, 63rd Alabama Infantry commanded by 1st Lieutenant Thomas J. Calhoun that were surrendered by Lt. General Richard Taylor at Citronelle, Alabama, on May 4, 1865, and paroled at Meridian, Mississippi, on May 11, 1865. Residence—Coosa County, Alabama.

Vinson, Sanford F., Corporal/Pvt. Co. D.
Enlisted as 3rd Corporal on July 30, 1864, at Macon County, Alabama, by Major

Ready for the war. Age—17, eyes—grey, hair—light, complexion—fair, 5 foot 10 inches, residence—Buford, Barbour County, Alabama. Appears on a company muster-in roll for July 30, 1864, at Camp Watts near Notasulga, Alabama. Drew clothing on August 7, 1864. Appears sick at Mobile hospital on a company muster roll for August 30 to October 30, 1864, with pay due from time of enlistment. Here he is shown as having enlisted on March 2, 1864, at Clayton, Alabama, by D. M. Seales. Appears as a Private on a roll of POW's of Company D, 63rd Alabama Infantry commanded by Captain Robert H. Pearson that were surrendered by Lt. General Richard Taylor at Citronelle, Alabama, on May 4, 1865, and paroled at Meridian, Mississippi, on May 13, 1865. Residence—Barbour County, Alabama.

Wade, Charles B., Pvt. Co. C.
Enlisted on April 24, 1864, at Russell County, Alabama, by Lieutenant Carnes for the war. Age—17, eyes—grey, hair—dark, complexion—dark, 5 foot 7 ¼ inches, residence—Dove, Russell County, Alabama. Appears on a company muster-in roll for June 24, 1864, at Camp Watts near Notasulga, Alabama. Appears present on a company muster roll for September and October 1864. Captured at Blakeley, Alabama, on April 9, 1865. Appears on a roll of POW's received at Ship Island, Mississippi, on April 15, 1865. Transferred from Ship Island to Vicksburg, Mississippi, on May 1, 1865.

Wade, John P., Pvt. Co. A.
Enlisted on January 1, 1864, at Coosa County, Alabama, by Captain John Echols for the war. Age—16. Appears on a company muster-in roll for January 1, 1864, at Montgomery, Alabama. Appears present on a company muster roll for January and February 1864, with pay due from time of enlistment.

Wadsworth, J. P., Pvt. Co. F/H.
Enlisted on May 30, 1864, at Montgomery, Alabama, by Captain Moore for the war. Age—17, eyes—grey, hair—light, complexion—fair, 5 foot 4 inches, residence—Autauga County, Alabama. Appears on a company muster-in roll for July 25, 1864, at Georgiana, Alabama. Drew clothing on September 14, 1864. Appears present sick on a company muster roll for August 31, to October 31, 1864, with pay due from time of enlistment. Captured at Blakeley, Alabama, on April 9, 1865. Appears on a roll of POW's received at Ship Island, Mississippi, on April 15, 1865. Transferred from Ship Island to Vicksburg, Mississippi, on May 1, 1865. On these two entries he is shown as being from Company H. Appears on a register of sick and wounded Confederate POW's at USA General Hospital No. 2, Vicksburg. Age—17. Admitted from steamer on May 3, 1865, with acute diarrhoea. Returned to duty on May 8, 1865.

Waldron, M. T., Pvt. Co. F.
Appears on a roll of POW's of Lee Hospital, Lauderdale, Mississippi, CSA commanded by Surgeon Henry Yandell that were surrendered by Lt. General Richard Taylor at Citronelle, Alabama, on May 4, 1865, and paroled at Meridian, Mississippi, on May 13, 1865. Residence—Lime Creek, Montgomery County, Alabama.

Walker, David L., Pvt. Co. D.
Enlisted on July 30, 1864, at Macon County, Alabama, by Major Ready for the war. Age—17, eyes—dark, hair—dark, complexion—dark, 6 foot 3 inches, residence—Buford, Barbour County, Alabama. Appears on a company muster-in roll for July 30, 1864, at Camp Watts near Notasulga, Alabama. Drew clothing on August 7, 1864. Appears present on a company muster roll for August 30 to October 30, 1864, with pay due from the time of enlistment. Here he is shown as having enlisted on April 12, 1864, at Clayton, Alabama, by Captain

Zorn. Captured at Blakeley, Alabama, on April 9, 1865. Appears on a roll of POW's received at Ship Island, Mississippi, on April 15, 1865. Transferred from Ship Island to Vicksburg, Mississippi, on May 1, 1865. Appears on a roll of POW's of Company D, 63rd Alabama Infantry commanded by Captain Robert H. Pearson that were surrendered by Lt. General Richard Taylor at Citronelle, Alabama, on May 4, 1865, and paroled at Meridian, Mississippi, on May 13, 1865. Residence—Barbour County, Alabama.

Walker, James J., Pvt. Co. G.
Enlisted on May 16, 1864, at Troy, Alabama, by Captain Wilkerson for the war. Age—17, eyes—grey, hair—light, complexion—florid, 5 foot 8 inches, residence—Pike County, Alabama. Appears on a company muster-in roll for September and October 1864. Drew clothing on September 11, 1864. Appears present on a company muster roll for September and October 1864. Here he is shown as having enlisted on August 1, 1864, at Pollard, Alabama by Captain Padgett. Appears on a roll of POW's of the 30th Regiment Louisiana Volunteer Infantry commanded by Captain T. O. Trepagnico that were surrendered by Lt. General Richard Taylor at Citronelle, Alabama, on May 4, 1865, and paroled at Meridian, Mississippi, on May 4, 1865. Residence—Pike County, Alabama. [This is an unusual entry and we may never know why he is listed with the 30th Louisiana Infantry.]

Walker, J. F., Pvt. Co. F/H.
Enlisted on May 30, 1864, at Montgomery, Alabama, by Captain Jackson for the war. Age—17, eyes—blue, hair—light, complexion—fair, 5 foot 8 inches, residence—Butler County, Alabama. Appears on a company muster-in roll for July 25, 1864, at Georgiana, Alabama. Appears present on a company muster roll for August 31 to October 31, 1864, with pay due from time of enlistment. Captured at Blakeley, Alabama, on April 9, 1865. Appears on a roll of POW's received at Ship Island, Mississippi, on April 15, 1865. Transferred from Ship Island to Vicksburg, Mississippi, on May 1, 1865. He is shown here as being from Company H. His name appears on a roll of POW's of Company F, 63rd Alabama Infantry commanded by Captain R. T. Simpson that were surrendered by Lt. General Richard Taylor at Citronelle, Alabama, on May 4, 1865, and paroled at Meridian, Mississippi, on May 11, 1865. Residence—Butler County, Alabama.

Walker, J. W., Pvt. Co. F/H.
Enlisted on July 12, 1864, at Lowndes County, Alabama, by Captain Buell for the war. Age—17, eyes—blue, hair—dark, complexion—dark, 5 foot 8 inches, residence—Lowndes County, Alabama. Appears on a company muster-in roll for July 25, 1864, at Georgiana, Alabama. Drew clothing on September 11, 1864. Appears present sick on a company muster roll for August 31 to October 31, 1864, with pay due from time of enlistment. Captured at Blakeley, Alabama, on April 9, 1865. Appears on a roll of POW's received at Ship Island, Mississippi, on April 15, 1865. Transferred from Ship Island to Vicksburg, Mississippi, on May 1, 1865. He is shown here as being from Company H. Appears on a roll of POW's of Company F, 63rd Alabama Infantry commanded by Captain R. T. Simpson that were surrendered by Lt. General Richard Taylor at Citronelle, Alabama, on May 4, 1865, and paroled at Meridian, Mississippi, on May 11, 1865. Residence—Lowndes County, Alabama.

Walker, J. W., Pvt. Co. G.
Appears on a roll of POW's of Cos. E and G, 63rd Alabama Infantry commanded by Captain A. V. Lee that were surrendered by Lt. General Richard Taylor at Citronelle, Alabama, on May 4, 1865, and paroled at Meridian, Mississippi, on May 13, 1865. Residence—Pike County, Alabama.

Walker, Mark, Pvt. Co. C.
Enlisted on June 11, 1864, at Henry [County], Alabama, by Major Hunt for the war. Age—17, eyes—grey, hair—light, complexion—dark, 5 foot 5 ½ inches, residence—Russell County, Alabama, Post Office—Columbus, Georgia. Appears on a company muster-in roll for June 24, 1864, at Camp Watts near Notasulga, Alabama. Appears on a company muster roll for September and October 1864. Here he is shown as having deserted on or about June 15, 1864, from Camp Watts, Alabama.

Walker, Thomas J., Pvt. Co. G.
Enlisted on May 16, 1864, at Troy, Alabama by Captain Wilkerson for the war. Age—17, eyes—grey, hair—dark, complexion—florid, 5 foot 6 inches, residence—Coffee County, Alabama. Appears on a company muster-in roll for September 7, 1864, at Blakeley, Alabama. Appears present on a company muster roll for September and October 1864. There was an inquiry from Oklahoma as to his service in 1917.

Walkley, Bryant S., Corporal/Pvt. Co. B.
Enlisted as 2nd Corporal on March 23, 1864, at Montgomery, Alabama, by Captain Zimmerman for the war. Age—17. Appears on a company muster roll for March 23, 1864, at Montgomery, Alabama. Drew clothing on July 8, 1864. Appears absent on a company muster roll for September and October 1864, with pay due from time of enlistment. Absent sick since October 28, 1864. Captured at Blakeley, Alabama, on April 9, 1865. He is shown here and hereafter as a Private. Appears on a roll of POW's received at Ship Island, Mississippi, on April 15, 1865. Transferred from Ship Island to Vicksburg, Mississippi, on May 1, 1865. Appears on a roll of POW's of Company B, 63rd Alabama Infantry commanded by 1st Lieutenant Thomas J. Calhoun that were surrendered by Lt. General Richard Taylor at Citronelle, Alabama, on May 4, 1865, and paroled at Meridian, Mississippi, on May 11, 1865. Residence—Coosa County, Alabama.

Waller, J., Pvt. Co. E.
Enlisted on April 13, 1864, at Clayton, Alabama, by Captain A. V. Lee for the war. Age—17, eyes—blue, hair—light, complexion—fair. Appears on a company muster roll for September and October 1864. Drew clothing on September 11, 1864. Signed by his mark. Died on September 12, 1864. Appears on a register of solders of the Army of the Confederate States who were killed in Battle or who died of wounds or disease. Effects No. 6908, of $35.25 turned over to the Quartermaster.

Ward, W. T., Pvt. Co. B.
He was admitted to 1st Mississippi CSA Hospital, Jackson, Mississippi, on March 3, 1865, with febris intermittens tert. It was reported that he returned to duty on April 14, 1865.

Warren, R., Pvt. Co. I.
Enlisted on April 15, 1864, at Wedowee, Alabama, by Captain Robinson. Appears absent on a company muster roll for September and October 1864. Absent without leave from September 18, 1864.

Warren, James P., Pvt. Co. B.
Enlisted on March 23, 1864, at Montgomery County, Alabama, by Captain Zimmerman for the war. Age—17. Appears on a company muster-in roll for March 23, 1864. Reference card is in his file - See manuscript No. 1645 Coffin & hearse & burying. Date - August 30, 1864. Died on May 23, 1864, at Montgomery, Alabama. Appears on a register of solders of the Army of the Confederate States who were killed in battle or who died of wounds or disease.

Effects No. 6599, of $15.50 turned over to the Quartermaster. Reference card in his file to see personal papers of R. H. Ewart, Co. G/K, 51st Tennessee Infantry. Provost Guard.

Waterson, James, Pvt. Co. C.
Enlisted on June 4, 1864, at Russell [County], Alabama, by Lieutenant Carnes for the war. Age—17, eyes—grey, hair—dark, complexion—dark, 5 foot 9 inches, residence—Hurtsville [Hurtsboro?], Russell County, Alabama. Appears on a company muster-in roll for June 24, 1864, at Camp Watts near Notasulga, Alabama. Drew clothing on August 6, 1864. Signed by his mark. Appears present on a company muster roll for September and October 1864. Captured at Macon, Georgia, on April 20, 1865, by the 1st Brigade, 2nd US Cavalry Division.

Watkins, James, Pvt. Co. K.
Enlisted on September 12, 1864, at Tallapoosa [County?], Alabama by Major Ready for the war. Appears absent on a company muster roll for September and October 1864. Absent without leave September 12, 1864.

Watkins, Micajah L., Pvt. Co. D.
Enlisted on July 30, 1864, at Macon County, Alabama, by Major Ready for the war. Age—17, eyes—grey, hair—auburn, complexion—fair, 5 foot 7 inches, residence—Kings, Barbour County, Alabama. Appears on a company muster-in roll for July 30, 1864, at Camp Watts near Notasulga, Alabama. Drew clothing on August 7, 1864. Appears present on a company muster roll for August 30 to October 30, 1864, with pay due from time of enlistment. Here he is shown as having enlisted on March 2, 1864, at Clayton, Alabama, by Captain Zorn. Captured at Blakeley, Alabama, on April 9, 1865. Appears on a roll of POW's received at Ship Island, Mississippi, on April 15, 1865. Transferred from Ship Island to Vicksburg, Mississippi, on May 1, 1865. Appears on a roll of POW's of Company D, 63rd Alabama Infantry commanded by Captain Robert H. Pearson that were surrendered by Lt. General Richard Taylor at Citronelle, Alabama, on May 4, 1865, and paroled at Meridian, Mississippi, on May 13, 1865. Residence—Barbour County, Alabama.

Watson, A. M., Pvt. Co. F/H.
Enlisted on March 9, 1864, at Greenville, Alabama, by Captain Brown for the war. Age—17, eyes—grey, hair—brown, complexion—fair, 5 foot 4 inches, residence—Butler County, Alabama. Appears on a company muster-in roll for July 25, 1864, at Georgiana, Alabama. Drew clothing on September 11, 1864. Appears present on a company muster roll for August 31 to October 31, 1864, with pay due from time of enlistment. Captured at Blakeley, Alabama, on April 9, 1865. Appears on a roll of POW's received at Ship Island, Mississippi, on April 15, 1865. Transferred from Ship Island to Vicksburg, Mississippi, on May 1, 1865. He is shown here as being from Company H. Appears on a roll of POW's of Company F, 63rd Alabama Infantry commanded by Captain R. T. Simpson that were surrendered by Lt. General Richard Taylor at Citronelle, Alabama, on May 4, 1865, and paroled at Meridian, Mississippi, on May 11, 1865. Residence—Butler County, Alabama.

Weatherhead, B. B., Pvt. Co. K.
Drew clothing on September 11, 1864. Admitted to Ross Hospital, Mobile, Alabama, on September 26, 1864, with rubeola. Returned to duty on October 28, 1864.

Weaver, W. R., Pvt. Co. I.
Enlisted on April 15, 1864, at Wedowee, Alabama, by Captain Robinson for the

war. Appears absent on a company muster roll for September and October 1864. Absent without leave from September 18, 1864.

Webb, William T., Pvt. Co. A.
Enlisted on January 1, 1864, at Macon County, Alabama, by Captain Echols for the war. Age—16. Appears on a company muster-in roll for January 1, 1864, at Montgomery, Alabama. Drew clothing in 2nd quarter and September 11, 1864. Appears present on a company muster roll for January and February 1864, with pay due from time of enlistment. Appears present sick in quarters on a company muster roll for September and October 1864. Here he is shown as having been last paid on February 29, 1864. POW captured at Blakeley, Alabama, on April 9, 1865. Appears on a roll of POW's received at Ship Island, Mississippi, on April 15, 1865. Transferred from Ship Island to Vicksburg, Mississippi, on May 1, 1865. Appears on a roll of POW's of Company A, 63rd Alabama Infantry commanded by Lieutenant W. D. Kyle that were surrendered by Lt. General Richard Taylor at Citronelle, Alabama, on May 4, 1865, and paroled at Meridian, Mississippi, on May 13, 1865. Residence—Macon County, Alabama.

Weldon, J. A., Pvt. Co. K.
Enlisted on September 17, 1864, at Tallapoosa [County?], Alabama, by Lieutenant Walker for the war. He appears absent on a company muster roll for September and October 1864. This muster roll reports him absent in hospital at Mobile, Alabama, from October 26, 1864.

Wells, James M., Pvt. Co. A.
Enlisted on January 1, 1864, at Coosa County, Alabama, by Captain Echols for the war. Age—16. Appears on a company muster-in roll for January 1, 1864, at Montgomery, Alabama. Appears absent on a company muster roll for January and February 1864, with pay due from time of enlistment. Absent sick in Stonewall Hospital. Drew clothing in 2nd quarter and September 11, 1864. Appears present sick in quarters on a company muster roll for September and October 1864, with pay due from time of enlistment. Captured at Blakeley, Alabama, on April 9, 1865. Appears on a roll of POW's received at Ship Island, Mississippi, on April 15, 1865. Transferred from Ship Island to Vicksburg, Mississippi, on May 1, 1865. Appears on a roll of POW's of Company A, 63rd Alabama Infantry commanded by Lieutenant W. D. Kyle that were surrendered by Lt. General Richard Taylor at Citronelle, Alabama, on May 4, 1865, and paroled at Meridian, Mississippi, on May 13, 1865. His residence is shown as Coosa County, Alabama.

West, Amos, Pvt. Co. D.
Enlisted on July 30, 1864, at Macon County, Alabama, by Major Ready for the war. Age—17, eyes—blue, hair—dark, complexion—fair, 5 foot 6 inches, residence—Kings, Barbour County, Alabama. Appears on a company muster-in roll for July 30, 1864, at Camp Watts near Notasulga, Alabama. Drew clothing on August 8, 1864. Signed by his mark. Appears present on a company muster roll for September and October 1864, with pay due from time of enlistment. Here he is shown as having enlisted on May 25, 1864, at Eufaula, Alabama, by Captain Zorn. Captured at Blakeley, Alabama, on April 9, 1865. Appears on a roll of POW's received at Ship Island, Mississippi, on April 15, 1865. Transferred from Ship Island to Vicksburg, Mississippi, on May 1, 1865. Appears on a roll of POW's of Company D, 63rd Alabama Infantry commanded by Captain Robert H. Pearson that were surrendered by Lt. General Richard Taylor at Citronelle, Alabama, on May 4, 1865, and paroled at Meridian, Mississippi, on May 13, 1865. His residence is shown as Barbour County, Alabama.

West, H. F., Corporal/Sergeant Co. I.
    Enlisted on April 15, 1864, at Columbiana, Alabama, by Lieutenant Bulger for the war. Appears as 1st Corporal and absent on a company muster roll for September and October 1864. Absent sick in Hospital Moore since October 28, 1864. Captured at Blakeley, Alabama, on April 9, 1865. Here and hereafter he is shown as Sergeant. Appears on a roll of POW's received at Ship Island, Mississippi, on April 15, 1865. Transferred from Ship Island to Vicksburg, Mississippi, on May 1, 1865. Appears as 5th Sergeant on a roll of POW's of Cos. I and K, 63rd Alabama Infantry commanded by Lieutenant W. A. Skinner that were surrendered by Lt. General Richard Taylor at Citronelle, Alabama, on May 4, 1865, and paroled at Meridian, Mississippi, May 13, 1865. Residence—Shelby County, Alabama.

Weatherly, P. M., Pvt. Co. K.
    Enlisted on September 22, 1864, at Prattville, Alabama, by Captain Moore for the war. Appears absent on a company muster roll for September and October 1864. Reported absent detailed to work in factory by General Withers on October 25.

Whatley, H. A., Pvt. Co. E.
    Enlisted on September 12, 1864, at Camp Hood by Captain Lee for the war. Age—17, eyes—blue, hair—light, complexion—fair. Appears present on a company muster roll for September and October 1864. Reported as a POW and that he signed a parole on May 16, 1864, at Marion, Alabama.

Whatley, S. J., Pvt. Co. K.
    Enlisted on August 8, 1864, at Montgomery, Alabama, by Lieutenant Brooks for the war. Appears absent on a company muster roll for September and October 1864. Absent in hospital at Mobile, Alabama, since October 26, 1864. Captured at Blakeley, Alabama, on April 9, 1865. Appears on a roll of POW's received at Ship Island, Mississippi, on April 15, 1865. Transferred from Ship Island to Vicksburg, Mississippi, on May 1, 1865. Appears on a roll of POW's of Cos. I and K, 63rd Alabama Infantry commanded by Lieutenant W. A. Skinner that were surrendered by Lt. General Richard Taylor at Citronelle, Alabama, on May 4, 1865, and paroled at Meridian, Mississippi, May 13, 1865. Residence—Montgomery County, Alabama.

Whatley, W. H., Sergeant Co. H/D.
    Enlisted on March 15, 1864, at Centerville, Alabama, by Captain Suttle for the war. Age—17, eyes—blue, hair—dark, complexion—fair. Drew clothing on September 11, 1864. Appears as 2nd Sergeant and present on a company muster roll for September and October 1864. Captured at Blakeley, Alabama, on April 9, 1865. Here he is shown as being in Company D. Appears on a roll of POW's received at Ship Island, Mississippi, on April 15, 1865. Transferred from Ship Island to Vicksburg, Mississippi, on May 1, 1865. Appears on a roll of POW's of Cos. C and H, 63rd Alabama Infantry commanded by Captain C. W. Martin that were surrendered by Lt. General Richard Taylor at Citronelle, Alabama, on May 4, 1865, and paroled at Meridian, Mississippi, on May 11, 1865. Residence—Bibb County, Alabama.

Wheat, William L., Pvt. Co. A.
    Enlisted on January 1, 1864, at Macon County, Alabama, by Captain John Echols for the war. Appears on a company muster roll for January 1, 1864, at Montgomery, Alabama. Age—15. Appears present on a company muster roll for January and February 1864, with pay due from time of enlistment. Drew clothing in 2nd quarter and September 11, 1864. Appears present on a company muster roll for September and October 1864. Here he is shown as having been

last paid on February 29, 1864. Captured at Blakeley, Alabama, on April 9, 1865. Appears on a roll of POW's received at Ship Island, Mississippi, on April 15, 1865. Transferred from Ship Island to Vicksburg, Mississippi, on May 1, 1865. Appears on a roll of POW's of Company A, 63rd Alabama Infantry commanded by Lieutenant W. D. Kyle that were surrendered by Lt. General Richard Taylor at Citronelle, Alabama, on May 4, 1865, and paroled at Meridian, Mississippi, on May 13, 1865. Residence—Macon County, Alabama.

Wheeler, H. S., Pvt. Co. K.
Enlisted on August 18, 1864, at Sumpter County, Alabama, by Lieutenant Kendrick for the war. Appears absent on a company muster roll for September and October 1864. Absent in hospital in Mobile, Alabama, since October 10, 1864.

Wheeles, Edward J., Pvt. Co. A.
Enlisted on January 1, 1864, at Macon County, Alabama, by Captain John Echols for the war. Age—17. Appears on a company muster-in roll for January 1, 1864, at Montgomery, Alabama. Appears present on a company muster roll for January and February 1864, with pay due from time of enlistment. Here he is shown as having enlisted in Tallapoosa by Captain Echols on January 1. Drew clothing in 2nd quarter of 1864. Appears present on a company muster roll for September and October 1864. Here he is shown as having been last paid on February 29, 1864. Captured at Blakeley, Alabama, on April 9, 1865. Appears on a roll of POW's received at Ship Island, Mississippi, on April 15, 1865. Transferred from Ship Island to Vicksburg, Mississippi, on May 1, 1865. Appears on a roll of POW's of Company A, 63rd Alabama Infantry commanded by Lieutenant W. D. Kyle that were surrendered by Lt. General Richard Taylor at Citronelle, Alabama, on May 4, 1865, and paroled at Meridian, Mississippi, on May 13, 1865. Residence—Macon County, Alabama.

Whidby, Thomas., Pvt. Co. H.
Enlisted on March 15, 1864, at Randolph County, Alabama, by Lieutenant Johnson for the war. Age—17, eyes—blue, hair—dark, complexion—dark. Appears present on a company muster roll for September and October 1864. Captured at Blakeley, Alabama, on April 9, 1865. Appears on a roll of POW's received at Ship Island, Mississippi, on April 15, 1865. Transferred from Ship Island to Vicksburg, Mississippi, on May 1, 1865. Appears on a roll of POW's of Cos. C and H, 63rd Alabama Infantry commanded by Captain C. W. Martin that were surrendered by Lt. General Richard Taylor at Citronelle, Alabama, on May 4, 1865, and paroled at Meridian, Mississippi, on May 11, 1865. Residence—Bibb County, Alabama.

Whitaker, Daniel, Pvt. Co. C.
Enlisted on May 9, 1864, at Henry County, Alabama, by Captain Burdett for the war. Residence—Woodville, Henry County, Alabama, age—17, eyes—dark, hair—dark, complexion—dark, 5 foot 5 inches. Appears on a company muster-in roll for June 24, 1864, at Camp Watts near Notasulga, Alabama. Appears as having died on a company muster roll for September and October 1864. Reference card in his file to see the personal papers of James M. Alexander - Alabama.

White, M. J., Pvt. Co. E.
POW paroled on June 23, 1865, at Talladega, Alabama, by Brevet Brigadier General Chrysler commanding US forces there.

White, S. M. P., Pvt. Co. I.
Enlisted on April 15, 1864, at Wedowee, Alabama, by Captain Robinson for the war. Appears absent on a company muster roll for September and October 1864. Absent sick in Hospital Moore since October 18, 1864.

White, W., Pvt. Co. E.
Enlisted on August 8, 1864, at Pollard, Alabama, by Captain A. V. Lee for the war. Age—17, eyes—dark, hair—dark, complexion—dark. Appears absent on a company muster roll for September and October 1864. Admitted to 1st Mississippi CSA Hospital, Jackson, Mississippi, on September 25, 1864, with chronic diarrhoea. Appears on a roll of POW's of Cos. E and G, 63rd Alabama Infantry commanded by Captain A. V. Lee that were surrendered by Lt. General Richard Taylor at Citronelle, Alabama, on May 4, 1865, and paroled at Meridian, Mississippi, on May 13, 1865. Residence—Tallapoosa County, Alabama.

Whitman, James, Pvt. Co. E.
Captured at Blakeley, Alabama, on April 9, 1865. Appears on a roll of POW's received at Ship Island, Mississippi, on April 15, 1865. Transferred from Ship Island to Vicksburg, Mississippi, on May 1, 1865. Appears on a roll of POW's of Cos. E and G, 63rd Alabama Infantry commanded by Captain A. V. Lee that were surrendered by Lt. General Richard Taylor at Citronelle, Alabama, on May 4, 1865, and paroled at Meridian, Mississippi, on May 13, 1865. His residence is shown as Russell County, Alabama.

Whittle, Elisha, Pvt. Co. G.
Enlisted on May 16, 1864, at Troy, Alabama, by Captain Wilkerson for the war. Age—17, eyes—black, hair—black, complexion—fair, 5 foot 7 inches, residence—Pike County, Alabama. Appears on a company muster-in roll for September 7, 1864, at Blakeley, Alabama. Drew clothing on September 11, 1864. Appears present on a company muster roll for September and October 1864. Captured at Blakeley, Alabama, on April 9, 1865. Appears on a roll of POW's received at Ship Island, Mississippi, on April 15, 1865. Transferred from Ship Island to Vicksburg, Mississippi, on May 1, 1865. Appears on a roll of POW's of Cos. E and G, 63rd Alabama Infantry commanded by Captain A. V. Lee that were surrendered by Lt. General Richard Taylor at Citronelle, Alabama, on May 4, 1865, and paroled at Meridian, Mississippi, on May 13, 1865. Residence—Pike County, Alabama.

Wiggins, Jasper W., Pvt. Co. B.
Enlisted on August 15, 1864, at Pollard, Alabama, by Lieutenant Townsend for the war. Appears present on a company muster roll for September and October 1864, with pay due from time of enlistment. Captured at Blakeley, Alabama, on April 9, 1865. Appears on a roll of POW's received at Ship Island, Mississippi, on April 15, 1865. Transferred from Ship Island to Vicksburg, Mississippi, on May 1, 1865. Appears on a roll of POW's of Company B, 63rd Alabama Infantry commanded by 1st Lieutenant Thomas J. Calhoun that were surrendered by Lt. General Richard Taylor at Citronelle, Alabama, on May 4, 1865, and paroled at Meridian, Mississippi, on May 11, 1865. Residence—Dale County, Alabama. He is sometimes shown as W. J. Wiggins.

Wiggins, W. A., Pvt. Co. F.
Enlisted on August 1, 1864, at Georgiana, Alabama, by Captain Brown for the war. Drew clothing on September 11, 1864. Signed by his mark. Appears absent on a company muster roll for August 31 to October 31, 1864, with pay due from time of enlistment. Absent in hospital at Greenville, Alabama, since September 6, 1864. Signed a paroled by his mark "X' on June 7, 1865, at headquarters of the US 16th Army Corps in Montgomery, Alabama. Hair—black, eyes—black, complexion—fair, 5 foot 3 inches.

Wilder, Anderson A., Pvt./Sergeant Co. A.
Enlisted on January 1, 1864, at Montgomery, Alabama, by Captain John Echols for the war. Age—17. Appears on a company muster-in roll for January 1, 1864, at Montgomery, Alabama. Appears present on a company muster roll for

January and February 1864, with pay due from time of enlistment. Drew clothing in 2nd quarter and August 12, 1864. Appears present on a company muster roll for September and October 1864. Here he is shown as last having been paid on February 29, 1864. POW captured and wounded at Blakeley, Alabama, on April 9, 1865. Here he is shown as serving with C. A. Thomas' Brigade in the 2nd Regiment Alabama. Admitted aboard the US Hospital Steamer D. A. January on April 17, 1865, with gunshot wound to the right side of face. Transferred to USA Hospital Steamer Elanora Carrel on April 25, 1865, at New Orleans, Louisiana. Admitted to No. 3 (Colored) USA General Hospital, Vicksburg, Mississippi, on April 28, 1865. Transferred to Hospital No. 2 at Vicksburg on May 4, 1865, as a POW. Appears on a register as admitted to USA General Hospital No. 2, Vicksburg on May 4, 1865. Age—18. Wounded by conical ball in his face (severe). Returned to duty on May 8, 1865. There was an inquiry as to his service from the State of Texas in 1915. His name was shown as Andrew Alexas Wilder.

Wilkerson, D. P., Pvt. Co. F/H.
Enlisted on March 9, 1864, at Greenville, Alabama, by Captain Brown for the war. Age—17, eyes—grey, hair—brown, complexion—fair, 5 foot 8 inches, residence—Butler County, Alabama. Appears on a company muster-in roll for July 25, 1864, at Georgiana, Alabama. Drew clothing on September 11, 1864. Appears present sick on a company muster roll for August 31 to October 31, 1864, with pay due from time of enlistment. Captured at Blakeley, Alabama, on April 9, 1865. He is shown here as being from Company H. Appears on a roll of POW's received at Ship Island, Mississippi, on April 15, 1865. Transferred from Ship Island to Vicksburg, Mississippi, on May 1, 1865. Appears on a register of sick and wounded Confederate POW's admitted on May 3, 1865, to USA General Hospital No. 2, Vicksburg, Mississippi, from steamer, with intermitten fever. Age—17. Returned to duty on May 10, 1865. Appears on a roll of POW's of Company B, 63rd Alabama Infantry that were surrendered by Lt. General Richard Taylor at Citronelle, Alabama, in May 1865, and paroled at Selma, Alabama, on May 25, 1865. Residence shown here is Russell County, Alabama.

Wilkerson, Samuel, Pvt. Co. D.
Enlisted on July 30, 1864, at Macon County, Alabama, by Major Ready for the war. Age—17, eyes—dark, hair—dark, complexion—dark, 5 foot 6 inches, residence—Clopton [Clayton?], Barbour County, Alabama. Appears on a company muster-in roll for July 30, 1864, at Camp Watts near Notasulga, Alabama. Drew clothing on August 7, 1864. Appears present on a company muster roll for August 30 to October 30, 1864, with pay due from time of enlistment. Here he is shown as having enlisted on June 30, 1864, at Eufaula, Alabama, by Captain Zorn. His name appears on a roll of POW's of Company D, 63rd Alabama Infantry commanded by Captain Robert H. Pearson that were surrendered by Lt. General Richard Taylor at Citronelle, Alabama, on May 4, 1865, and paroled at Meridian, Mississippi, on May 13, 1865. His residence is shown as Dale County, Alabama.

Wilkey, S. F., Pvt. Co. H.
Enlisted on July 29, 1864, at Selma, Alabama, by Captain Suttle for the war. Age—17, eyes—blue, hair—light, complexion—fair. Drew clothing on September 11, 1864. Appears absent on a company muster roll for September and October 1864. Absent sick at hospital in Mobile, Alabama, since October 12. Admitted to Ross Hospital, Mobile, Alabama, on October 14, 1864, with febris typhoides. Furloughed for 30 days on November 17, 1864. Appears on a roll of POW's paroled at Talladega, Alabama, on June 19, 1865, by Brevet Brigadier General Chrysler in command of US forces there.

Williams, Charles, J. F., Pvt. Co. B.
Enlisted on April 14, 1864, at Montgomery County, Alabama, by Captain Zimmerman for the war. Age—17. Appears on a company muster-in roll for March 23, 1864, at Montgomery, Alabama.

Williams, H. H., Pvt. Co. F.
Enlisted on March 9, 1864, at Greenville, Alabama, by Captain Brown for the war. Age—17, eyes—blue, hair—light, complexion—fair, 5 foot 5 inches, residence—Butler County, Alabama. Appears on a company muster-in roll for July 25, 1864, at Georgiana, Alabama. Drew clothing on September 11, 1864. Appears present on a company muster roll for August 31 to October 31, 1864, with pay due from time of enlistment. Captured at Blakeley, Alabama, on April 9, 1865. Appears on a roll of POW's received at Ship Island, Mississippi, on April 15, 1865. Transferred from Ship Island to Vicksburg, Mississippi, on May 1, 1865. Appears on a roll of POW's of Company F, 63rd Alabama Infantry commanded by Captain R. T. Simpson that were surrendered by Lt. General Richard Taylor at Citronelle, Alabama, on May 4, 1865, and paroled at Meridian, Mississippi, on May 11, 1865. Residence—Butler County, Alabama.

Williams, James, Pvt. Co. A.
Enlisted on February 1, 1864, at Montgomery, Alabama, by Captain John Echols for the war. Appears present on a company muster roll for January and February 1864, with pay due from time of enlistment.

Williams, Lon, S., Corporal/Pvt. Co. B.
Enlisted on April 18, 1864, at Montgomery County, Alabama, by Captain Zimmerman. Age—17. Appears as 1st Corporal on a company muster-in roll for March 23, 1864, at Montgomery, Alabama. Drew clothing on July 8, 1864. Here and hereafter he is shown as a Private. Appears absent on a company muster roll for September and October 1864, with pay due from time of enlistment. Absent sick since October 28, 1864. There is a reference card in his file to see the personal papers of Amzi J. Blair, Rice's Tennessee Battery.

Williams W. N. L., Pvt. Co. G.
Enlisted on May 16, 1864, at Troy, Alabama, by Captain Wilkerson for the war. Age—17, eyes—grey, hair—dark, complexion—florid, 5 foot 8 inches, residence—Pike County, Alabama. Appears on a company muster-in roll for September 7, 1864, at Blakeley, Alabama. Drew clothing on September 11, 1864. Appears present on a company muster roll for September and October 1864. Captured at Blakeley, Alabama, on April 9, 1865. His name appears on a roll of POW's received at Ship Island, Mississippi, on April 15, 1865. Transferred from Ship Island to Vicksburg, Mississippi, on May 1, 1865. Appears on a roll of POW's of Cos. E and G, 63rd Alabama Infantry commanded by Captain A. V. Lee that were surrendered by Lt. General Richard Taylor at Citronelle, Alabama, on May 4, 1865, and paroled at Meridian, Mississippi, on May 13, 1865. Residence—Pike County, Alabama. There is an 1915 inquiry in his file from the State of Florida.

Williamson, Monroe, Pvt. Co. G.
Enlisted on August 1, 1864, at Pollard, Alabama, by Captain Padgett. Appears on a company muster-in roll for September 7, 1864, at Blakeley, Alabama. Age—17, eyes—grey, hair—light, complexion—florid, 5 foot 8 inches. Appears present on a company muster roll for September and October 1864. Captured at Blakeley, Alabama, on April 9, 1865. Appears on a roll of POW's received at Ship Island, Mississippi, on April 15, 1865. Transferred from Ship Island to Vicksburg, Mississippi, on May 1, 1865. Appears on a roll of sick and wounded Confederate POW's at USA General Hospital, No. 2, Vicksburg, Mississippi.

Admitted on May 3, 1865, from steamer with acute diarrhoea. Returned to duty on May 8, 1865. Age—17.

Williamson, N., Pvt. Co. I.
Enlisted on April 15, 1864, at Wedowee, Alabama, by Captain Robinson for the war. Appears absent on a company muster roll for September and October 1864. Absent furloughed for 30 days from September 27.

Willingham, C., Pvt. Co. I.
Enlisted on April 15, 1864, at Wedowee, Alabama, by Captain Robinson for the war. He appears present on a muster roll for September and October 1864.

Willingham, Jacob L., Pvt. Co. G.
Enlisted on May 16, 1864, at Troy, Alabama, by Lieutenant Murphy for the war. Age—17, eyes—grey, hair—sandy, complexion—fair, 5 foot 9 inches, residence—Pike County, Alabama. Appears on a company muster-in roll for September 7, 1864, at Blakeley, Alabama. Drew clothing on September 11, 1864. Signed by his mark. Appears present on a company muster roll for September and October 1864.

Willis, F. M., Pvt. Co. I.
Enlisted in April 1864, at Columbiana, Alabama, by Lieutenant Bulger for the war. Appears present on a muster roll for September and October 1864.

Willis, F. M., Corporal Co. I.
Enlisted on July 20, 1864, at Selma, Alabama, by Major Haskell for the war. Appears as 3rd Corporal and present on a company muster roll for September and October 1864. Captured at Blakeley, Alabama, on April 9, 1865. Appears on a roll of POW's received at Ship Island, Mississippi, on April 15, 1865. Transferred from Ship Island to Vicksburg, Mississippi, on May 1, 1865. Appears on a roll of POW's of Cos. I and K, 63rd Alabama Infantry commanded by Lieutenant W. A. Skinner that were surrendered by Lt. General Richard Taylor at Citronelle, Alabama, on May 4, 1865, and paroled at Meridian, Mississippi, May 13, 1865. Residence—Shelby County, Alabama. Here he is shown with the rank of 4th Corporal.

Willis, George W., Pvt. Co. A.
Enlisted on May 25, 1864, at Chambers [County], Alabama, by Captain Echols for the war. Appears absent on a company muster roll for September and October 1864, with pay due from time of enlistment. Absent sick at Opelika, Alabama, since August 6, 1864. Drew clothing in 2nd quarter of 1864. Appears on a roll of POW's paroled at Talladega, Alabama, on June 19, 1865, by Brevet Brigadier General Chrysler in command of US forces there.

Wilson, J. D., Pvt. Co. H.
Enlisted on March 15, 1864, at Montevallo, Alabama, by Captain Suttle for the war. Age—16, eyes—dark, hair—dark, complexion—fair. Appears absent on a company muster roll for September and October 1864. Absent sick in hospital at Mobile, Alabama, since August 11. Appears on a roll or POW's at Tuscaloosa, Alabama, captured by 2nd Regiment of Illinois Cavalry and paroled in May 1865. Captured on May 22, 1865.

Wilson, J. H., Pvt. Co. I.
Enlisted on August 1, 1864, at Selma, Alabama, by Lieutenant Eckford for the war. Appears present on a company muster roll for September and October 1864. Captured at Blakeley, Alabama, on April 9, 1865. Appears on a roll of POW's received at Ship Island, Mississippi, on April 15, 1865. Transferred from Ship Island to Vicksburg, Mississippi, on May 1, 1865. Appears on a roll of

POW's of Cos. I and K, 63rd Alabama Infantry commanded by Lieutenant W. A. Skinner that were surrendered by Lt. General Richard Taylor at Citronelle, Alabama, on May 4, 1865, and paroled at Meridian, Mississippi, May 13, 1865. Residence—Sumpter County, Alabama.

Wilson, John T., Pvt. Co. G.
Enlisted on May 16, 1864, at Troy, Alabama, by Captain Wilkerson for the war. Age—17, eyes—dark, hair—dark, complexion—dark, 5 foot 6 inches, residence—Pike County, Alabama. Appears on a company muster-in roll for September 7, 1864. Appears present on a company muster roll for September and October 1864. Captured at Blakeley, Alabama, on April 9, 1865. Appears on a roll of POW's received at Ship Island, Mississippi, on April 15, 1865. Transferred from Ship Island to Vicksburg, Mississippi, on May 1, 1865. Appears on a roll of POW's of Cos. E and G, 63rd Alabama Infantry commanded by Captain A. V. Lee that were surrendered by Lt. General Richard Taylor at Citronelle, Alabama, on May 4, 1865, and paroled at Meridian, Mississippi, on May 13, 1865. Residence—Pike County, Alabama.

Wilson, V. A., Pvt. Co. H.
Enlisted on March 15, 1864, at Elyton, Alabama, by Lieutenant Killough for the war. Age—16, eyes—dark, hair—dark, complexion—dark. Drew clothing on September 11, 1864. Appears present on a company muster roll for September and October 1864. Captured at Blakeley, Alabama, on April 9, 1865. Appears on a roll of POW's received at Ship Island, Mississippi, on April 15, 1865. Transferred from Ship Island to Vicksburg, Mississippi, on May 1, 1865. Appears on a roll of POW's of Cos. C and H, 63rd Alabama Infantry commanded by Captain C. W. Martin that were surrendered by Lt. General Richard Taylor at Citronelle, Alabama, on May 4, 1865, and paroled at Meridian, Mississippi, on May 11, 1865. Residence—Jefferson County, Alabama.

Wims, T. J., Pvt. Co. E.
Enlisted on August 8, 1864, at Pollard, Alabama, by Captain A. V. Lee for the war. Age—17, eyes—dark, hair—dark, complexion—florid. Appears present on a company muster roll for September and October 1864. Captured at Blakeley, Alabama, on April 9, 1865. Appears on a roll of POW's received at Ship Island, Mississippi, on April 15, 1865. Transferred from Ship Island to Vicksburg, Mississippi, on May 1, 1865. Appears on a roll of sick and wounded Confederate POW's at USA General Hospital, No. 2, Vicksburg, Mississippi. Admitted on May 3, 1865, from steamer with remittent fever. Returned to duty on May 10, 1865. Age—18.

Winn, Edward, T., Pvt. Co. A.
Enlisted on January 1, 1864, at Chambers County, Alabama, by Captain John Echols for the war. Appears on a company muster-in roll for January 1, 1864. Age—15. Appears present on a company muster roll for January and February 1864, with pay due from time of enlistment. Drew clothing 2nd quarter, August 12 and September 11, 1864. Appears present on a company muster roll for September and October 1864. Here he is shown as having been last paid on February 29, 1864.

Winslet, A. W., Sergeant/Pvt. Co. G.
Enlisted on May 16, 1864, at Troy, Alabama, by Captain Wilkerson for the war. Age—16, eyes—blue, hair—light, complexion—fair, 5 foot 10 inches, residence—Covington County, Alabama. Appears as 5th Sergeant on a company muster-in roll for September 7, 1864, at Blakeley, Alabama. Drew clothing on September 11, 1864. Signed by his mark. Appears as a Private and present on a company muster roll for September and October 1864. Captured at Blakeley,

Alabama, on April 9, 1865. Appears on a roll of POW's received at Ship Island, Mississippi, on April 15, 1865. Transferred from Ship Island to Vicksburg, Mississippi, on May 1, 1865. Appears on a roll of POW's of Cos. E and G, 63rd Alabama Infantry commanded by Captain A. V. Lee that were surrendered by Lt. General Richard Taylor at Citronelle, Alabama, on May 4, 1865, and paroled at Meridian, Mississippi, on May 13, 1865. Residence—Pike County, Alabama. There is a reference card in his file to see the personal papers of James M. Alexander - Alabama.

Winslett, David B., Pvt. Co. C.
Enlisted on May 9, 1864, at Macon County, Alabama, by Major Ready for the war. Age—17, eyes—hazel, hair—dark, complexion—dark, 5 foot 5 inches, residence—Monticello, Pike County, Alabama. Drew clothing on August 6, 1864. Signed by his mark. Appears on a company muster-in roll for June 24, 1864, at Camp Watts near Notasulga, Alabama. Appears as having died on a company muster roll for September and October 1864.

Winslett, James A., Pvt. Co. G.
Enlisted on April 27, 1864, at Troy, Alabama, by Captain Wilkerson for the war. Age—17, eyes—grey, hair—dark, complexion—dark, 5 foot 9 inches, residence—Covington County, Alabama. Appears on a company muster-in roll for September 7, 1864, at Blakeley, Alabama. Drew clothing on September 11, 1864. Appears present on a company muster roll for September and October 1864. Appears on a roll of Hospital Attendants and Patients at Hinkley Hospital, Demopolis, Alabama of the CSA commanded by Surgeon H. Hinkley that were surrendered by Lt. General Richard Taylor at Citronelle, Alabama, on May 4, 1865, and paroled at Meridian, Mississippi, on May 14, 1865. Residence—New Providence, Covington County, Alabama.

Winslett, Thomas J., Pvt. Co. C.
Enlisted on May 19, 1864, at Macon County, Alabama, by Major Ready for the war. Age—17, eyes—blue, hair—dark, complexion—dark, 5 foot 5 inches, residence—Monticello, Pike County, Alabama. Appears on a company muster-in roll for June 24, 1864, at Camp Watts near Notasulga, Alabama. Drew clothing on August 6, 1864. Signed by his mark. Appears absent on a company muster roll for September and October 1864. Absent in hospital in Mobile, Alabama, since October 28, 1864. Signed a parole with his mark "X" at headquarters of the 16th US Army Corps at Montgomery, Alabama, on May 27, 1864. Hair—light, eyes—blue, complexion—fair, 5 foot 5 inches. His parole is in his file.

Winslett, B. B., Pvt. Co. H.
Enlisted on July 29, 1864, at Selma, Alabama, by Lieutenant Killough for the war. Age—17, eyes—blue, hair—dark, complexion—fair. Appears present on a company muster roll for September and October 1864.

Woodam, James W., Pvt. Co. B.
Enlisted on August 15, 1864, at Pollard, Alabama, by Lieutenant Townsend for the war. Drew clothing on September 11, 1864. Signed by his mark. Appears present on a company muster roll for September and October 1864, with pay due from time of enlistment. Died on November 17, 1864, at Mobile, Alabama. Left $7.50. Effects turned over to Quartermaster CSA was $32.

Woodham, John, Pvt. Co. C.
Enlisted on June 3, 1864, at Macon County, Alabama, by Captain Hughes for the war. Age—17, eyes—grey, hair—dark, complexion—fair, 5 foot 5 ½ inches, residence—Golin, Dale County, Alabama. Appears on a company muster roll for June 24, 1864, at Camp Watts near Notasulga, Alabama. Appears as deserted on

a company muster roll for September and October 1864. Deserted on July 7, 1864, from Camp Watts, Alabama.

Woodruff, Pvt. Co. I.
Enlisted on April 15, 1864, at Wedowee, Alabama, by Captain Robinson for the war. Appears absent on a company muster roll for September and October 1864. Absent furloughed for 30 days from September 27, 1864.

Woods, John G., Pvt. Co. B.
Enlisted on August 15, 1864, at Pollard, Alabama, by Lieutenant Townsend for the war. Drew clothing on September 11, 1864. Appears present on a company muster roll for September and October 1864, with pay due from time of enlistment. Appears on a roll of POW's of Company B, 63rd Alabama Infantry commanded by 1st Lieutenant Thomas J. Calhoun that were surrendered by Lt. General Richard Taylor at Citronelle, Alabama, on May 4, 1865, and paroled at Meridian, Mississippi, on May 11, 1865. Residence—Dale County, Alabama.

Woods, Thomas H., Pvt. Co. B.
Enlisted on October 2, 1864, at Blakeley, Alabama, by Captain Zimmerman for the war. Appears present on a company muster roll for September and October 1864, with pay due from time of enlistment.

Wooten, Edward L., Pvt. Co. A.
Enlisted on March 7, 1864, at Macon County, Alabama, by Captain Echols for the war. Drew clothing in 2nd quarter and September 11, 1864. He appears present sick in quarters on a company muster roll for September and October 1864, with pay due from time of enlistment. He is reported to have been admitted to Ross Hospital on April 6, 1865. Returned to duty on April 23, 1865. He signed a parole at headquarters of 16th US Army Corps in Montgomery, Alabama, on May 16, 1865. Hair—dark, eyes—blue, complexion—fair, 5 foot 8 inches. His parole is in his file.

Wright, George W., Pvt. Co. A.
Enlisted on January 1, 1864, at Coosa, County, Alabama, by Captain Echols for the war. Age—16. Appears on a company muster roll for January 1, 1864. Appears present on a company muster-in roll for January and February 1864, with pay due from time of enlistment. Admitted to Ross Hospital, Mobile, Alabama, on September 12, 1864, with febris intermittens. Returned to duty on September 18, 1864. Admitted to Ross Hospital at Mobile on September 28, 1864, with febris intermittens quot. Returned to duty on October 10, 1864.

Wright, J. H., Pvt. Co. K/G.
Enlisted on October 13, 1864, at Sumpter County, Alabama, by Lieutenant Kendrick for the war. Appears present on a company muster roll for September and October 1864. Captured at Blakeley, Alabama, on April 9, 1865. Here he is shown in Company G elsewhere he is shown in Company K. Appears on a roll of POW's received at Ship Island, Mississippi, on April 15, 1865. Transferred from Ship Island to Vicksburg, Mississippi, on May 1, 1865. Appears on a roll of POW's of Cos. I and K, 63rd Alabama Infantry commanded by Lieutenant W. A. Skinner that were surrendered by Lt. General Richard Taylor at Citronelle, Alabama, on May 4, 1865, and paroled at Meridian, Mississippi, May 13, 1865. Residence—Shelby County, Alabama.

Wright, Joseph A., Pvt. Co. A.
Enlisted on January 1, 1864, at Macon County, Alabama, by Captain John Echols for the war. Appears on a muster-in roll for January 1, 1864, at Montgomery, Alabama. Age—16. Appears present on a company muster roll for January and

February 1864, with pay due from time of enlistment. Drew clothing in 2nd quarter of 1864. He appears present on a company muster roll for September and October 1864. Here he is shown as having been last paid on February 29, 1864.

Wyatte, Silas, M., Pvt. Co. C.
Enlisted on May 11, 1864, at Macon County, Alabama, by Major Ready for the war. Age—17, eyes—blue, hair—dark, complexion—fair, 5 foot 1 ¼ inches, residence—Lafayette, Chambers County, Alabama. Appears on a company muster-in roll for June 24, 1864, at Camp Watts near Notasulga, Alabama. Drew clothing on August 6, 1864. Appears present on a company muster roll for September and October 1864. Captured at Blakeley, Alabama, on April 9, 1865. Appears on a roll of POW's received at Ship Island, Mississippi, on April 15, 1865. Transferred from Ship Island to Vicksburg, Mississippi, on May 1, 1865. Appears on a roll of POW's of Quintard Hospital, CSA commanded by Surgeon S. V. D. Hill that were surrendered by Lt. General Richard Taylor at Citronelle, Alabama, on May 4, 1865, and paroled at Meridian, Mississippi, on May 10, 1865. Residence—Fayette, Alabama. Also appears on a roll of POW's of Cos. C and H, 63rd Alabama Infantry commanded by Captain C. W. Martin that were surrendered by Lt. General Richard Taylor at Citronelle, Alabama, on May 4, 1865, and paroled at Meridian, Mississippi, on May 11, 1865. His residence is shown as Chambers County, Alabama.

Yarbrough, Nimrod P., Pvt./Corporal Co. A.
Enlisted on January 1, 1864, at Coosa County, Alabama, by Captain John Echols for the war. Age—16. Appears present on a company muster roll for January 1, 1864, with pay due from enlistment. Drew clothing in 2nd quarter and August 12, 1864. Appears present on a company muster roll for September and October 1864. Here he is shown as having been last paid on February 29, 1864. Appears on a roll of POW's of nurses and patients of CSA Moore Hospital commanded by Surgeon W. G. Cavanaugh, that were surrendered by Lt. General Richard Taylor at Citronelle, Alabama, on May 4, 1865, and paroled at Meridian, Mississippi, on May 16, 1865. Residence—Coosa County, Alabama. Here he is shown as a Corporal.

Youngblood, Wyth C., Pvt. Co. A.
Enlisted on January 1, 1864, at Tallapoosa County, Alabama, by Captain John Echols for the war. Appears on a company muster-in roll for January 1, 1864, at Montgomery, Alabama. Age—17. Appears present on a company muster roll for January 1, 1864, with pay due from enlistment.

Zimmerman, Eugene, Pvt./Ensign Co. A/F & S.
Enlisted on January 1, 1864, at Montgomery County, Alabama, by Captain John Echols for the war. Age—17. Appears on a company muster-in roll for January 1, 1864. Appears present on a company muster roll for January and February 1864, with pay due from time of enlistment. Drew clothing in 2nd quarter and on September 11, 1864. Appears on a company muster roll for September and October 1864. Here he is shown as having been last paid on February 29, 1864. Transferred on September 11, 1864, to Company B, 2nd Alabama Reserves per Special Order. Appears as Ensign and present on a Field and Staff muster roll for September and October 1864. Appointed Ensign by Colonel Rice on September 21, 1864, near Mobile, Alabama. Captured on April 9, 1865, by the 2nd Division 16th US Army Corps. Confined one day near Spanish Fort, Alabama. Appears on a roll of POW's received at Ship Island, Mississippi, on April 16, 1865. Transferred from Ship Island to Vicksburg, Mississippi, on April 28, 1865. Appears on a roll of POW's at New Orleans, Louisiana from Ship Island and exchanged on May 1, 1865. Signed a Parole of Honor at Meridian,

Mississippi, on May 11, 1865. Residence shown is Montgomery, Alabama. His parole is in his file.

Zimmerman, W. Connoway, 2nd Lieutenant/Captain Co. A/B.
Appears as 2nd Lieutenant and present on a company muster roll for January and February 1864. Elected 2nd Lieutenant on January 1, 1864. Promoted to Captain of Company B on March 23, 1864. Appears as Captain on a company muster-in roll for March 23, 1864. Requisitioned in the 3rd quarter of 1864: 31 jackets, 40 trowsers, 18 shirts, 15 shoes, 24 drawers. Appears present on a Company B muster roll for September and October 1864. Appears on a roster of Company B, 2nd Regiment, Alabama Reserves, Fuller's Brigade, Maury's Corps. District of the Gulf CSA, for January 1865. Appears on a signature to a Parole of POW's sworn and subscribed to May 15, 1865, at Marion, Alabama.

Zorn, Dennis, H., Captain Co. D.
Enlisted on August 3, 1864, at Macon County, Alabama, by Major Ready for the war. Age—21, eyes—grey, hair—auburn, complexion—fair, 6 foot 1 inch, residence—Buford, Barbour County, Alabama. Lost his left arm at Battle of Gaines Mill. Appears on a company muster-in roll for July 30, 1864, at Camp Watts near Notasulga, Alabama. Elected Captain on March 2, 1864, of Company D, 2nd Regiment, Alabama Reserves, Fuller's Brigade, Maury's Corps., District of the Gulf, CSA. Requisitioned in the 3rd quarter of 1864: 56 caps, 56 jackets, 56 pants, 56 drawers, 56 shoes, 56 socks, 56 shirts. Appears absent on a company muster roll for August 30 to October 30, 1864. Absent on 30 day furlough since October 25, 1864. Here he is shown as having enlisted on March 2, 1864, at Clayton, Alabama, by D. M. Seals. Tendered his resignation at Camp of Company D, 2nd Alabama Regiment Reserves, at Battery H Mobile, Alabama, December 13, 1864, for the reason stated in the Surgeon's Certificate attached. Assistant Surgeon McFarin certifies that Zorn is unfit to preform the duties of a soldier due to his left arm being amputated at the middle third of the humerus. His wound was received at the Battle of Gaines Mill on June 27, 1862. This resignation and attached Surgeon's Certificate are in his file. The following letter is also found in his file.

Letters Received
A & I G O

Camp McNab near Eufaula, Alabama
June 6, 1864

To his excellency
James A. Seddon
Sir

I have a company composed of boys between the ages of 17 & 18 and men between 45 and 52 old. The company was organized on the 2nd day of March 1864, and assigned to Provost duty at the above named place by authority of Lt. Col. C. C. Lockhart chief enrolling officer of the Conscript Bureau of Alabama. I received an order from Col. Thomas M. Jack, A. A. G. of Lt. Gen. Polk stating the no companies would be received unless they were raised by authority from Gen. Polk or from the war Department. I am perplexed about the authority. Col. Lockhart received the Company and placed it on duty at this place. I have sent my muster rolls and descriptive list on through the Conscript Bureau. The Company has been doing duty here ever since its organization. We are also doing duty here for the Enrolling Officer of this Post. We have sent off several deserters and men subject to conscription since we came here. The company has drawn all the necessary camp equipments from the Government and the men being disciplined and prepared for

Regular Service very fast. The Company now numbers (90) men rank and file. Since I received the order from Col. Jack I have been informed that no man would be allowed the opportunity of holding commissions in State Companies who was between the ages of 18 & 45 years unless he had a certificate of physical disability approved by a Board of Army Surgeons.

I am the only officer in the Company that is 18 years old, I am twenty one, though I have a certificate of disability. I lost my left arm in the series of battles around Richmond. I have been retired from Service since I lost my arm but I am disposed to aid my county and my government still if there is any thing that I could do. I went off in the beginning of the war and I remained there as a Private until I lost my arm. Now I am not able to take my musket and go to the field or I would willingly do so. If I succeed in retaining my company I can fill the position of some athletic man and put him the ranks where he will be able to do duty. If the authority that I have organized the company upon was not compatible with law and the good of Services and County I respectfully ask you to give me the proper instructions as how to proceed with the company. I have been wrongly informed so often by men in authority who profess to be conversant with the law until I do not know when I get the proper instructions. I do not know that the authority that I got has been annulled. I wish to get the proper authority and the proper instructions and I resort to you to as I think you are the proper one to give all necessary instructions in such cases as this. I hope to hear a reply from you so soon as circumstances will permit and honestly hope that the above request may be granted.
   I have the honor to be your most Obt. Svt.
   D. H. Zorn Capt. Commanding Co. D
   of State Reserves

[This document is two pages and was stamped Rebel Archives]

Zorn, N., Pvt. Co. D.
   Appears as a POW of Moore Hospital, CSA commanded by Surgeon W. C. Cavenaugh that were surrendered by Lt. General Richard Taylor at Citronelle, Alabama, on May 4, 1865, and paroled at Meridian, Mississippi, on May 16, 1865. Residence—Henry County, Alabama.

Zuber, C. W. F., Pvt. Co. C/H.
   Enlisted on July 25, 1864, at Macon County, Alabama, by Major Ready for the war. Drew clothing on August 6, 1864. Appears present on a company muster roll for September and October 1864. Captured at Blakeley, Alabama, on April 9, 1865. Appears on a roll of POW's received at Ship Island, Mississippi, on April 15, 1865. Transferred from Ship Island to Vicksburg, Mississippi, on May 1, 1865. Appears on a roll of POW's of Cos. C and H, 63rd Alabama Infantry commanded by Captain C. W. Martin that were surrendered by Lt. General Richard Taylor at Citronelle, Alabama, on May 4, 1865, and paroled at Meridian, Mississippi, on May 11, 1865. Residence—Macon County, Alabama.

89th Alabama Militia

Company C in service March 28 to April 14

Fitz, Newton - Captain
Wilkins, Chas. - 1st Lt.

No other Company of this regiment has been identified. Regimental Commander is not identified. [Note a Major and several Captains appear on this roster.]

Roll for pay March 28 to April 14, 1862

Alvinge, J. F., 1st Corp. Co. D.
   Appears on a pay roll for March to April 16, 186_, 18 days.

Andrews, Daniel, Pvt. Co. D.
   Appears on a pay roll from April 9 to April 16, 186_, 7 days.

Andrews, John, Pvt. Co. B.
   Appears on a pay roll from March 28 to April 14, 186_, 17 days.

Badami, P. T., Pvt. Co. B.
   Appears on a pay roll from March 28 to April 14, 186_, 17 days. signed P. T. Badami.

Battemmy, Joseph, Pvt. Co. B.
   Cards filed with P. T. Badami.

Baxter, William, Pvt. Co. B.
   Appears on a pay roll from March 28 to April 14, 186_, 17 days. signed W. Baxter.

Beckman, Thomas, Pvt. Co. C.
   Appears on a pay roll from March 28 to April 14, 1862, 17 days.

Boone, George F., Adjutant
   Paid $60 on July 10, 1862, for service March 28 to April 14, 1862, 18 days at $100 per month. Received pay from G. W. Holt A. Q. M. at Mobile County, Alabama.

Bostwick, O., 2nd Lt. Co. C.
   Appears on a pay roll from March 28 to April 14, 1862, 17 days. Paid $45.33 on July 17, 1862, for service from March 28 to April 14, 1862, by Major G. W. Holt Quarter Master at Mobile County, Alabama.

Boyce, W. H., Pvt. Co. D.
   Appears on a pay roll from April 9 to April 16, 186_, 7 days.

Brown, Franklin, Pvt. Co. B.
   Appears on a pay roll from March 28 to April 14, 186_, 17 days.

Calhoun, James C., Captain
   His name appears on a pay roll from March 28 to April 14, 1862, 17 days. Paid $70.66 on July 15, 1862, for service March 28 to April 14, 1862, 17 days at $130 per month by Major G. W. Holt at Mobile County, Alabama.

Calhoun, W. T., 2nd Sergeant
   Appears on a pay roll from March 28 to April 14, 1862, 17 days.

Crabtree, L. Sr., Pvt. Co. B.
>His name appears on a pay roll from March 28 to April 14, 186_, 17 days.

Crabtree, Samuel, Pvt. Co. G.
>Appears on a pay roll from March 28 to April 14, 186_, 17 days, signed Saml. Crabtree.

Dabney, J. M., 1st Lt. Co. D.
>Appears on a pay roll from March 28 to April 16, 186_, 18 days.

Dickens, J. W., Pvt. Co. D.
>Appears on a pay roll from March 28 to April 16, 186_, 18 days.

Dunn, J. M., Pvt. Co. D.
>Appears on a pay roll from April 9 to April 16, 186_, 7 days.

Duval, Joseph T., Pvt. Co. D.
>Appears on a pay roll from March 28 to April 16, 186_, 18 days.

Eckert, A., Pvt. Co. E.
>Appears on a pay roll from March 28 to April 14, 1862, 17 days at $11 per month, signed A. Ecbert.

Ennis, Michael, Pvt. Co. C.
>Appears on a pay roll from March 28 to April 14, 1862, 17 days.

Finch, Thomas, Pvt. Co. G.
>Appears on a pay roll from March 28 to April 14, 186_, 17 days, signed Thomas Finch.

Fitz, Newton, Captain Co. G.
>His name appears on a pay roll from March 28 to April 14, 186_, 17 days. Paid $78 on July 8, 1862, for service March 28 to April 14, 1862. and 18 days at $130 per month by Major George W. Holt, Chief Paymaster at Mobile County, Alabama.

Foster, George, Pvt. Co. C.
>Appears on a pay roll from March 28 to April 14, 1862, 17 days.

Foster, Jacob M., 1st Sgt. Co. B.
>Appears on a pay roll from March 28 to April 14, 186_, 17 days, signed Jacob M. Foster.

Foster, John, Pvt. Co. C.
>Appears on a pay roll from March 28 to April 14, 1862, 17 days.

Foster, J. S., Pvt. Co. B.
>Appears on a pay roll from March 28 to April 14, 186_, 17 days.

George, W. M., Pvt. Co. E.
>Appears on a pay roll from March 28 to April 14, 1862, 17 days.

Grayson, A. L., Surgeon
>He was paid $66 on July 25, 1862, for service from March 28 to April 14, 1862, 18 days at $110 per month at the rank of Sugeon by Major G. W. Holt, at Mobile, County, Alabama.

Green, Dennis, Pvt. Co. G.
　　Appears on a pay roll from March 28 to April 14, 1862, 17 days. Furloughed to receive proper pay.

Greer, J. H., Pvt. Co. D.
　　Appears on a pay roll from March 28 to April 16, 1862, 18 days.

Hall, George, Pvt. Co. D.
　　Appears on a pay roll from April 9 to April 16, 1862, 7 days.

Hand, Patrick, Corporal Co. G.
　　Appears on a pay roll from March 28 to April 14, 186_, 17 days.

Harryman, J. R., Pvt. Co. D.
　　Appears on a pay roll from March 28 to April 16, 186_, 18 days.

Hayte, George F., Pvt. Co. D.
　　Appears on a pay roll from April 9 to April 16, 186_, 7 days.

Hicks, A. L., Pvt. Co. D.
　　Appears on a pay roll from March 28 to April 16, 186_, 18 days.

Howard, Emanuel, Pvt. Co. E.
　　Appears on a pay roll from March 28 to April 14, 186_, 17 days.

Howard, James, Pvt. Co. E.
　　Appears on a pay roll from March 28 to April 14, 1862, 17 days.

Jackson, Andrew, 1st Lt. Co. B.
　　Appears on a pay roll from March 28 to April 14, 1862, 17 days. Paid $51 for service March 28 to April 14, 1862, on August 4, 1862, by G. W. Holt AGQG at Mobile County, Alabama. Signs as Andrew Jackson.

Johnson, J. S., 1st Sgt. Co. D.
　　Appears on a pay roll from March 28 to April 16, 186_, 18 days.

Kelly, George, Pvt. Co. D.
　　Appears on a pay roll from April 9 to April 16, 186_, 7 days.

Kennedy, A. B. W., Pvt. Co. E.
　　Appears on a pay roll from March 28 to April 14, 1862, 17 days. Rate of pay $11 per month.

Kidd, Oliver J., Pvt. Co. E.
　　Appears on a pay roll from March 28 to April 14, 1862, 17 days. Rate of pay $11 per month.

King, W. T., Pvt. Co. E.
　　Appears on a pay roll from March 28 to April 14, 1862, 17 days.

Ladd, J. M., Captain Co. D.
　　Appears on a pay roll from March 28 to April 16, 1862, 18 days. Paid $73.66 for service March 28 to April 14th, 1862, 17 days at $130 per month. Paid on July 25, 1862, by Major G. W. Holt Paymaster.

Lott, William, 2nd Lt. Co. E.
　　Appears on a pay roll from March 28 to April 14, 1862, 17 days.

Lyon, James F., Captain and A. Q. M.
    Appears on a pay roll from March 28 to April 3, 1862, 7 days. Paid $32.66 on August 25, 1862, for service March 28 to April 3, 1862, 7 days at $140 per month at the rank of Captain. Paid by Major G. W. Holt. G. Q. M. at Mobile, County, Alabama.

Lyons, Sewell, Sergeant Co. G.
    Appears on a pay roll from March 28 to April 14, 186_, 17 days.

Malone, James, 1st Lt. Co. E.
    His name appears on a pay roll from March 28 to April 14, 1862, 17 days. Paid $51 on July 15, for service March 28 to April 3, 1862, 17 days by Major G. W. Holt.

Martin, F. A., Pvt. Co. D.
    Appears on a pay roll for April 9 to April 16, 186_, 7 days.

Mason, John, 1st Sergeant Co. E.
    Appears on a pay roll from March 28 to April 14, 1862, 17 days.

McCary, J. A., Pvt. Co. D.
    Appears on a pay roll for April 9 to April 16, 186_, 7 days.

McCoy, A. L., 1st Lt. Co. B.
    Paid $51.60 on September 6, 1862, for service March 28 to April 14, 1862, 17 days at $90 per month by G. W. Holt, Major. There is a affidavit in his file attesting to his service and payment by a Justice of the Peace, M. W. Handa, from Greene County.

McDonald, Patrick, Pvt. Co. G.
    Appears on a pay roll from March 28 to April 14, 1862, 17 days.

McGrath, William, Corporal Co. G.
    Appears on a pay roll from March 28 to April 7, 1862, 10 days.

McMillan, W. Y., Pvt. Co. E.
    Appears on a pay roll from March 28 to April 14, 1862, 17 days at $11 per month.

Monk, R. T., Pvt. Co. E.
    Appears on a pay roll from March 28 to April 14, 1862, 17 days at $11 per month.

Moore, James A., Colonel
    Paid $117 at Mobile, Alabama, on July 10, 1862, for service March 28th to April 14, 1862, by Major G. H. Holt A. Q. M.

Neill, Pvt. Co. C.
    Appears on a pay roll from March 28 to April 14, 1862, 17 days at $11 per month.

Nelson, P. W., Pvt. Co. D
    Appears on a pay roll from April 9 to April 16, 186_, 7 days.

Overstreet, Stephen, Corporal Co. G
    Appears on a pay roll from March 28 to April 14, 1862, 17 days.

Pearson, D. J., Pvt. Co. E.
    Appears on a pay roll from March 28 to April 14, 1862, 17 days.

Pitman, John, Pvt. Co. B.
    Appears on a pay roll from March 28 to April 14, 1862, 17 days.

Powell, Hiram, Pvt. Co. E.
    Appears on a pay roll from March 28 to April 14, 1862, 17 days.

Rabman, Michael, Pvt. Co. C.
    Appears on a pay roll from March 28 to April 14, 1862, 17 days.

Rane, E., Pvt. Co. G.
    Appears on a pay roll from March 28 to April 14, 1862, 17 days. Signed E. Rane. Furloughed to receive proper pay.

Richardson, H. B., Pvt. Co. E.
    Appears on a pay roll from March 28 to April 14, 1862, 17 days.

Robinson, M. A., 3rd Corporal Co. D.
    Appears on a pay roll from March 28 to April 16, 1862, 18 days.

Ross, D. M. N., Captain Co. B.
    Appears on a pay roll from March 28 to April 14, 1862, 17 days. Paid $73.66 on July 28, 1862, at Mobile for service March 28 to April 14, 1862. Paid by G. W. Holt, Major.

Sanford, Rob., Pvt. Co. B.
    Appears on a pay roll from March 28 to April 14, 186_, 17 days.

Shepard, R. B., 2nd Lt. Co. D.
    Appears on a pay roll from March 28 to April 16, 1862, 18 days. Paid $ 42.66 on November 1, 1862, for service from March 28 to April 16, 1862, at $80 per month. Paid at Mobile by G. W. Holt Major and Q. M.

Stewart, G. N., Sgt. Co. C.
    Appears on a pay roll from March 28 to April 14, 1862, 17 days at $17 per month.

Summers, George, Sgt. Co. C.
    Appears on a pay roll from March 28 to April 14, 1862, 17 days at $17 per month. Signed George Summers.

Taylor, David, Pvt. Co. D.
    Appears on a pay roll from April 9 to April 16, 186_, 7 days.

Toomer, Benjamin, Lt. Colonel
    Paid $102 on July 10, 1862, for service March 28 to April 14, 1862, at $170 per month. Paid at Mobile by Major G. W. Holt A. Q. M.

Toomer, William H., Captain
    Appears on a pay roll from March 28 to April 14, 1862, 17 days. Paid $73.66 on July 19, 1862, at Mobile for service from March 28 to April 14, 1862, at $130 per month. Paid by Major G. W. Holt Q. M.

Volcan, George, Pvt. Co. G.
    Appears on a pay roll from April 3 to April 14, 186_, 10 days.

Walker, R. P., Pvt. Co. E.
　　Appears on a pay roll from March 28 to April 14, 1862, 17 days at $11 per month.

Ward, Elijah C., Pvt. Co. E.
　　Appears on a pay roll from March 28 to April 14, 1862, 17 days at $11 per month. Signed by mark X.

Warner, A. P., Captain
　　Paid $73.66 on August 23, 1862, for service from March 28 to April 14, 1862, at $130 per month. Paid at Mobile by Major G. W. Holt Q. M.

Waters, Joshua, Pvt. Co. B.
　　Appears on a pay roll from March 28 to April 14, 186_, 17 days.

Whitaker, William, H. Jr., 1st Lt. Co. C.
　　Appears on a pay roll from March 28 to April 14, 1862, 17 days. Paid $51 on July 16, 1862, at Mobile, Alabama for service March 28 to April 14, 1862, 17 days at $90 per month. Paid by Major G. W. Holt, Quarter Master.

Wilkins, Charles, 1st Lt. Co. G.
　　Appears on a pay roll from March 28 to April 16, 186_, 17 days. Paid $54 on July 14, 1862, at Mobile, Alabama, for service March 28 to April 16, 1862, 28 days at $90 per month. Paid by Major G. W. Holt.

Williams, N. W., Pvt. Co. D.
　　Appears on a pay roll from March 28 to April 16, 186_, 18 days.

Williamson, W., 2nd Corp. Co. D.
　　Appears on a pay roll from March 28 to April 16, 186_, 18 days.

Worley, J. J., Pvt. Co. C.
　　Appears on a pay roll from March 28 to April 14, 1862, 17 days.

94th Regiment Alabama Militia
Company A in service March 26 to April 19.

Wilikins, H. G. - Captain
Tew, Thomas R. - Lieutenant
English, T. M., - 2 Lt.
Scheuerman, F., - Ensign
No other Company of this Regiment has been identified.
Regimental Commander not identified.

Acorn, F., Pvt. Co. A.
Appears on a pay roll for March 26 to April 19, 186_, 25 days. Signed F. Accorn.

Agen, M., Pvt. Co. A.
Appears on a pay roll for March 26 to April 19, 186_, 25 days duration. Signed with an "X".

Anderson, C., Pvt. Co. A.
Appears on a pay roll for April 3 to April 19, 186_, 17 days. Signed C. Anderson.

Bateman, J., Pvt. Co. A.
Appears on a pay roll for March 26 to April 19, 186_, 25 days.

Bernstein, J., 4th Corporal Co. A.
Appears on a pay roll for March 26 to April 19, 186_, 25 days.
Signed J. Bernstein.

Bernstein, L., Pvt. Co. A.
Appears on a pay roll for March 26 to April 19, 186_, 25 days.

Bitzen, F., Pvt. Co. A.
Appears on a pay roll for March 26 to April 19, 186_, 25 days.

Bogle, J. C., Pvt. Co. A.
Appears on a pay roll for March 26 to April 19, 186_, 25 days. Furloughed by General Beall.

Bresnehan, James, Pvt. Co. A.
Appears on a pay roll for March 26 to April 19, 186_, 25 days. Signed James Bresnehan.

Bromberg, C., 3rd Corporal Co. A.
Appears on a pay roll for March 26 to April 19, 186_, 25 days.
Signed C. Bromberg.

Brown, Charles, Pvt. Co. A.
Appears on a pay roll for March 26 to April 19, 186_, 25 days.
Signed Charles Brown.

Burger, J., Pvt. Co. A.
Appears on a pay roll for March 26 to April 19, 186_, 25 days duration. Signed by mark "X".

Casper, F., Pvt. Co. A.
Appears on a pay roll for March 26 to April 19, 186_, 25 days.

Cass, J., Pvt. Co. A.
    Appears on a pay roll for March 26 to April 19, 186_, 25 days duration. Signed by mark "X".

Classen, H., Pvt. Co. A.
    Appears on a pay roll for March 26 to April 19, 186_, 25 days duration. Signed by mark "X".

Clifford, J. B., Pvt. Co. A.
    Appears on a pay roll for April 3 to April 19, 186_, 17 days.

Donovan, J., Pvt. Co. A.
    Appears on a pay roll for March 26 to April 19, 186_, 25 days. Signed J. Donovan.

Eberline, George, Pvt. Co. A.
    Appears on a pay roll for March 26 to April 19, 186_, 25 days. Signed George Eberline.

Elsaser, J. G., Pvt. Co. A.
    Appears on a pay roll for March 26 to April 19, 186_, 25 days.

Emerson, George, Pvt. Co. A.
    Appears on a pay roll for March 26 to April 19, 186_, 25 days. Signed G. Emerson.

English, T. M., 2nd Lt. Co. A.
    Appears on a pay roll for March 26 to April 19, 186_, 25 days. Signed at T. M. English. Paid $66.66 on July 9, 1862, for service March 26 to April 19, 1862. Paid at Mobile by G. W. Holt, Major A. Q. M.

Finegan, Michael, Pvt. Co. A.
    Appears on a pay roll for March 26 to April 19, 186_, 25 days. Signed Michael Finegan.

Fink, George, Corp. Co. A.
    Appears on a pay roll for March 26 to April 19, 186_, 25 days. Signed George Fink.

Flinn, J., Pvt. Co. A.
    Appears on a pay roll for March 26 to April 19, 186_, 25 days. Signed J. Flinn.

Foote, M. S., 1st Lt. Adjutant
    Paid $83.33 on August 30, 1862, at Mobile for service March 26 to April 19, 1862. Paid by Major G. W. Holt, A. Qr. Mr.

Frolickstein, H. Pvt. Co. A.
    Appears on a pay roll for March 26 to April 19, 186_, 25 days.

Geary, D., Pvt. Co. A.
    Appears on a pay roll for March 26 to April 19, 186_, 25 days. Signed D. Geary.

Geftner, G., Pvt. Co. A.
    Appears on a pay roll for March 26 to April 19, 186_, 25 days. Signed G. Geftner.

Gessler, A., Pvt. Co. A.
   Appears on a pay roll for March 26 to April 19, 186_, 25 days. Signed A. Gessler.

Goldthwaite, John, Major
   Paid $120 at Mobile on July 11, 1862, for service March 26 to April 19, 1862, at $180 per month. Paid by Major G. W. Holt A. Q. M.

Goodman, John H., Pay Master
   Paid $112 at Mobile on August 5, 1862, for service March 26, to April 19, 1862, 25 days at $140 per month. Paid by Major G. W. Holt. Q. M.

Green, C., 2nd Sergeant Co. A.
   Appears on a pay roll for March 26 to April 19, 186_, 25 days. Signed C. Green.

Grotz, A., 4th Sergeant Co. A.
   Appears on a pay roll for March 26 to April 19, 186_, 25 days. Signed A. Grotz.

Hanna, C. F., Pvt. Co. A.
   Appears on a pay roll for March 26 to April 19, 186_, 25 days. Signed C. F. Hanna.

Hartmann, C., Pvt. Co. A.
   Appears on a pay roll for March 26 to April 19, 186_, 25 days. Signed C. Hartmann.

Hegemeister, M., Pvt. Co. A.
   Appears on a pay roll for March 30 to April 19, 186_, 21 days. Signed M. Hegemeister.

Hellers, E., Pvt. Co. A.
   Appears on a pay roll for March 26 to April 19, 186_, 25 days. Signed E. Hellers.

Hendrix, P. H., Pvt. Co. A.
   Appears on a pay roll for March 26 to April 19, 1862, 25 days. Detached Gov'mt. Express.

Herbert. J., Pvt. Co. A.
   Appears on a pay roll for March 26 to April 19, 1862, 25 days.

Hoffmann, Fried, Corporal Co. A.
   Appears on a pay roll for March 26 to April 19, 186_, 25 days. Signed Fried Hoffmann.

Johnston, W. F., Orderly Co. A.
   Appears on a pay roll for March 26 to April 19, 186_, 25 days. Signed W. F. Johnston.

Keplin, G., Pvt. Co. A.
   Appears on a pay roll for March 26 to April 19, 186_, 25 days. Signed G. Keplin.

Leary, C., Pvt. Co. A.
   Appears on a pay roll for March 26 to April 19, 186_, 25 days. Signed C. Leary.

Lipps, Jacob, Sergeant Co. A.
    Appears on a pay roll for March 26 to April 19, 186_, 25 days. Signed Jacob Lipps. Cards in his file indicate some confusion as to Jake Lipse of Anderson's Battery, Virginia Lt. Arty. Records do not indicate a J. Lipse in the Virginia Regiment. This correspondence was generated by a request from the Texas Pension Commissioner of Austin, Texas, May of 1915.

Mallin, F., Pvt. Co. A.
    Appears on a pay roll for March 26 to April 19, 186_, 25 days. Signed F. Mallin.

McCann, P., Pvt. Co. A.
    Appears on a pay roll for March 26 to April 19, 186_, 25 days. Signed P. McCann.

McCleskey, L. A., Surgeon
    Paid $135 on August 1, 1862, for service March 26 to April 19, 1862, at $135 per month. Paid at Mobile, Alabama, by Major G. W. Holt.

McGuire, W., Pvt. Co. A.
    Appears on a pay roll from March 30 to April 19, 186_, 21 days. Signed W. McGuire.

McNeil, P., Pvt. Co. A.
    Appears on a pay roll for March 26 to April 19, 186_, 25 days. Signed P. McNeil.

Nelson, F. D., Pvt. Co. A.
    Appears on a pay roll for March 26 to April 19, 186_, 25 days. Signed F. D. Nelson.

O'Donnell, P., Pvt. Co. A.
    Appears on a pay roll for March 26 to April 19, 186_, 25 days duration. Signed by mark "X".

O'Grady, S. T., Sergeant Co. A.
    Appears on a pay roll for March 26 to April 19, 186_, 25 days.

Pepper, P. H., Pvt. Co. A.
    Appears on a pay roll for March 26 to April 19, 186_, 25 days.

Purdy, G., Pvt. Co. A.
    Appears on a pay roll for March 26 to April 19, 186_, 25 days. Signed G. Purdy.

Raue, T. A., Pvt. Co. A.
    Appears on a pay roll for March 26 to April 19, 186_, 25 days. Signed T. A. Raue.

Ross, George, Pvt. Co. A.
    Appears on a pay roll for March 26 to April 19, 186_, 25 days. Signed Geo Ross.

Rutledge, Charles, Pvt. Co. A.
    Appears on a pay roll for March 26 to April 19, 186_, 25 days. Signed Chas Rutledge.

Schenerman, F., Ensign Co. A.
Appears on a pay roll for March 26 to April 19, 186_, 25 days. Signed as F. Schenerman, Ensign.

Seamon, J., Pvt. Co. A.
Appears on a pay roll for March 26 to April 19, 186_, 25 days duration. Signed by mark "X".

Sheehan, J., Pvt. Co. A.
Appears on a pay roll for March 26 to April 19, 186_, 25 days. Signed J. Sheehan.

Sherbaith, J., Pvt. Co. A.
Appears on a pay roll for March 26 to April 19, 186_, 25 days.

Siegert, George, Pvt. Co. A.
Appears on a pay roll for March 26 to April 19, 186_, 25 days. Signed G. Siegert.

Simon, S., Pvt. Co. A.
Appears on a pay roll for March 26 to April 19, 186_, 25 days.

Slayman, M., Pvt. Co. A.
Appears on a pay roll for March 26 to April 19, 186_, 25 days. Signed M. Slayman.

Sullivan, John, Pvt. Co. A.
Appears on a pay roll for March 26 to April 19, 186_, 25 days. Signed John Sullivan.

Tew, Thomas R., 1st Lt. Co. A.
Appears on a pay roll for March 26 to April 19, 186_, 25 days. Paid $75 on July 9, 1862 for service March 26 to April 19, 1862, at $90 per month. Paid at Mobile, Alabama by G. W. Holt, Major A. Q. M.

Whitfield, L. J., Pvt. Co. A.
Appears on a pay roll for March 26 to April 19, 186_, 25 days. Detailed to Express.

Whiting, James, Pvt. Co. A.
Appears on a pay roll for March 26 to April 19, 186_, 25 days. Signed Jas Whiting.

Wilkins, H. G., Captain Co. A.
Appears on a pay roll for March 26 to April 19, 186_, 25 days. Signed as H. G. Watkins. Paid $108.33 on July 9, 1862, for service March 26 to April 19, 1862. Paid at Mobile, Alabama by G. W. Holt, Major P. M.

Wing, William, Pvt. Co. A.
Appears on a pay roll for March 26 to April 19, 186_, 25 days. Signed William Wing.

95th Alabama Militia, Company D
Pay roll for March 25 to April 20, 1862 or 1863?

Albert, Prince, Pvt. Co. D.
Appears on a pay roll from March 25 to April 20, 186_, 4 days.

Anthony, John, Pvt. Co. D.
Appears on a pay roll from March 25 to April 20, 186_, 4 days.

Anthony, Joseph, Pvt. Co. D.
Appears on a pay roll from March 25 to April 20, 186_, 1 days.

Bencento, Augustin, Pvt. Co. D.
Appears on a pay roll from March 25 to April 20, 186_, 4 days.

Bentie, Domenic, Pvt. Co. D.
Appears on a pay roll from March 25 to April 20, 186_, 4 days.

Bowen, E., Pvt. Co. C.
Appears on a pay roll, not dated, for 2 days.

Bowmann, F. J., 4th Corporal Co. C.
His name appears on a pay roll, not dated, for 13 days. He signed F. J. Bowmann.

Brenardo, John, Pvt. Co. D.
Appears on a pay roll, not dated, for 5 days.

Campintich, Vincent, Pvt. Co. D.
Appears on a pay roll from March 25 to April 20, 186_, 3 days.

Carrican, Patrick, Pvt. Co. D.
Appears on a pay roll from March 25 to April 20, 186_, 4 days.

Cars, Michal, Pvt. Co. C.
Appears on a pay roll, not dated, for 1 day.

Chamberlain, Jacob, 2nd Sgt. Co. D.
Appears on a pay roll from March 25 to April 20, 186_, 25 days. Signed by mark.

Chaudron, E. T., Pvt. Co. C.
Appears on a pay roll, not dated, for 5 days.

Clemings, Joseph, Pvt. Co. D.
Appears on a pay roll from March 25 to April 20, 186_, 1 day.

Conon, Francisco, 3rd Corp. Co. D.
Appears on a pay roll from March 25 to April 20, 186_, 10 days. Signed by mark.

Conway, J. S., 3rd Corporal Co. C
Appears on a pay roll, not dated, for 23 days. Signed J. S. Conway.

Cord, Charles W., Captain Co. D.
Appears on a pay roll from March 25 to April 20, 186_, 25 days.

Corry, John, 1st Corporal Co. D.
Appears on a pay roll, not dated, for 10 days.

Cosgrove, Thomas, Pvt. Co. C.
Appears on a pay roll, not dated, for 10 days.

Curran, John E., Major
Paid $125 on June 13, 1862, for service from March 26 to April 19, 1862, at $150 per month. Paid at Mobile, Alabama, by Major G. W. Holt.

Covas, Raphail, Pvt. Co. D.
Appears on a pay roll, not dated, for 1 day.

Domingo, John, Pvt. Co. D.
Appears on a pay roll from March 25 to April 20, 186_, 6 days.

Dragas, Peter, (Dreyer, Petter), Pvt. Co. D.
Appears on a pay roll from March 25 to April 20, 186_, 25 days. Signed Petter Dreyer.

Ebeltoft, G. W., 2nd Lt. Co. C.
Appears on a pay roll, not dated, for 25 days. Paid $66 on June 17, 1862 for service from March 26 to April 20, 1862, at $80 per month. Paid at Mobile, Alabama, Major G. W. Holt. Signed E. W. Ebeltoft.

Francansisco. Gloria, Pvt. Co. D.
Appears on a pay roll from March 25 to April 20, 186_, 4 days.

Francheschi, M., 2nd Lt. Co. B
Paid $66.70 on June 18, 1862, for service from March 25 to April 19, 1862, at $80 per month. Paid at Mobile, Alabama, by Quarter Master G. W. Holt P. M. Signed M. Francheschi.

Fuller, Robert, 4th Sgt. Co. C.
Appears on a pay roll, not dated, for 7 days. Signed Robert Fuller.

Glass, Daniel, 1st Sgt. Co. C.
Appears on a pay roll, not dated, for 3 days.

Glazes, Francis, Pvt. Co. D.
Appears on a pay roll, not dated, for 1 day.

Green, Andrew, 1st Lt. Co. C.
Appears on a pay roll, not dated, for 25 days. Paid $75 on July 3, 1862, for service from March 26 to April 20, 1862, at $90 per month. Paid at Mobile, Alabama, by G. W. Holt A. Q. M.

Gregory, J. H., Captain Co. C.
Appears on a pay roll from March 25 to April 20, 186_, 25 days. Paid $ 108.33 for service from March 26 to April 20, 1862, at $130 per month. Paid at Mobile, Alabama, by Major G. W. Holt. Signed J. H. Gregory.

Gueringer, A. F., Capt. Co. A.
Paid $108.33 on June 18, 1862, for service from March 25 to April 20, 1862, at $130 per month. Paid at Mobile, Alabama, by Major G. W. Holt P. M. Signed A. F. Gueringer Capt.

Gueringer, Oct., 1st Lt. Co. A.
   Paid $75 on July 1, 1862, for service March 25 to April 20, 1862, at $90 per month. Paid at Mobile, Alabama, by Geo. W. Holt, Major and P. M. Signed Oct. Gueringer.

Helmetag, F. W., 2nd Corp. Co. C.
   Appears on a pay roll, not dated for 14 days. Signed F. W. Helmetag.

Jackson, John, Pvt. Co. D.
   Appears on a pay roll from March 25 to April 20, 186_, 4 days.

Johnston, Hord, Pvt. Co. D.
   Appears on a pay roll from March 25 to April 20, 186_, 1 day.

Kearns, Joseph, Pvt. Co. C.
   Appears on a pay roll, not dated for 1 day.

Kennedy, Furgus, Pvt. Co. D.
   Appears on a pay roll from March 25 to April 20, 186_, 10 days.

Kennedy, John P., 2nd Lt. Co. A.
   Paid $66.67 on July 15, 1862, for service March 25 to April 20, 1862, at $80 per month. Paid at Mobile, Alabama, by Major G. W. Holt, P. M. Signed John P. Kennedy.

Laps, (Lapo) Ballentine, Pvt. Co. D.
   Appears on a pay roll from March 25 to April 20, 186_, 4 days.

Lawrence, Francis, Pvt. Co. D.
   Appears on a pay roll from March 25 to April 20, 186_, 1 day.

Loughren, John, Pvt. Co. D.
   Appears on a pay roll from March 25 to April 20, 186_, 3 days.

Lucendo, Francis, Pvt. Co. D.
   Appears on a pay roll from March 25 to April 20, 186_, 4 days.

Mangren, Josheph, Pvt. Co. D.
   Appears on a pay roll from March 25 to April 20, 186_, 4 days.

Manning, Antony, 4th Sgt. Co. D.
   Appears on a pay roll from March 25 to April 20, 186_, 13 days.

McCord, Charles, Captain Co. D.
   Paid $108 on July 5, 1862, for service March 25 to April 20, 1862, at $130 per month. Paid at Mobile, Alabama, by Major G. W. Holt A. Q. M. Signed Charles McCord.

McDonald, William, Pvt. Co. C.
   Appears on a pay roll, not dated, for 5 days.

McGonegal, James, 2nd Lt. Co. D.
   His name appears on a pay roll from March 25 to April 20, 186_,14 days. Paid $37.33 on July 7, 1862, for service from April 6 to April 20, 1862, at $180 per month. Paid at Mobile, Alabama, by W. G. Holt, Major and Q. M. Signed James McGonegal.

McMahan, Thomas, Pvt. Co. C.
    Appears on a pay roll, not dated, for 5 days.

Nason, Reuben, 2nd Sgt. Co. C.
    Appears on a pay roll, not dated, for 15 days. Signed Reuben Nason.

Neal, William, Pvt. Co. D.
    Appears on a pay roll, not dated, for 2 days.

Noah, M., Pvt. Co. C.
    "Reported himself sick during the whole time the company was in service."

Occillas, Droado, Pvt. Co. D.
    Appears on a pay roll from March 25 to April 20, 186_, 4 days.

O'Donall, Dan, Pvt. Co. D.
    Appears on a pay roll from March 25 to April 20, 186_, 4 days.

Parker, Charles, Pvt. Co. D.
    Appears on a pay roll from March 25 to April 20, 186_, 25 days.

Payson, Lewis, 3rd Sgt. Co. C.
    Appears on a pay roll, not dated, for 12 days. Signed L. Payson.

Phillips, Rod., 2nd Corporal Co. D.
    Appears on a pay roll from March 25 to April 20, 186_, 10 days. Signed by mark.

Pouchele, Vincent, Pvt. Co. D.
    Appears on a pay roll from March 25 to April 20, 186_, 5 days.

Reid, David, 1st Sgt. Co. D.
    Appears on a pay roll from March 25 to April 20, 186_, 25 days. Paid $75 on July 5, 1862, for service from March 25 to April 19, 1862, at $90 per month. Paid at Mobile, Alabama, by G. W. Holt A. Q. M. Signed David Reid.

Ritto, John, 3rd Sgt. Co. D.
    Appears on a pay roll from March 25 to April 20, 186_, 12 days.

Rose, John, Pvt. Co. C.
    Appears on a pay roll, not dated, for 2 days.

Ruban, Thomas, Pvt. Co. D.
    Appears on a pay roll from March 25 to April 20, 186_, 4 days.

Sanders, John, Pvt. Co. D.
    Appears on a pay roll from March 25 to April 20, 186_, 1 day.

Sandy, Thomas, Pvt. Co. D.
    Appears on a pay roll from March 25 to April 20, 186_, 4 days.

Sherry, Lewis, Pvt. Co. D.
    Appears on a pay roll from March 25 to April 20, 186_, 2 days.

Stoll, Fred, 1st Corporal Co. C.
    His name appears on a pay roll, not dated, for 9 days. Signed Fred Stoll.

Terridoes, Joseph, Pvt. Co. D.
    Appears on a pay roll from March 25 to April 20, 186_, 4 days.

Thompson, James, Pvt. Co. D.
    Appears on a pay roll from March 25 to April 20, 186_, 15 days. Signed James Thompson.

Tudor, Lord, Pvt. Co. D.
    Appears on a pay roll from March 25 to April 20, 186_, 4 days.

Valorse, Joseph, Pvt. Co. D.
    Appears on a pay roll from March 25 to April 20, 186_, 5 days.

Vincent, Carlo, Pvt. Co. D.
    Appears on a pay roll from March 25 to April 20, 186_, 4 days.

Winstock, Charles, Pvt. Co. D.
    Appears on a pay roll from March 25 to April 20, 186_, 25 days.

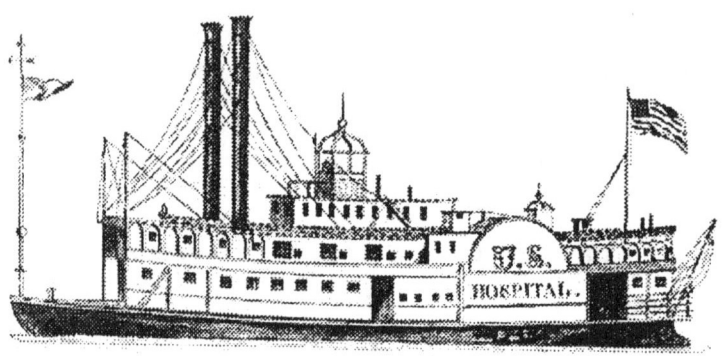

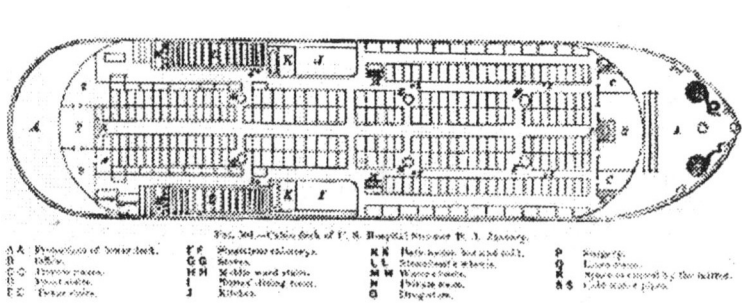

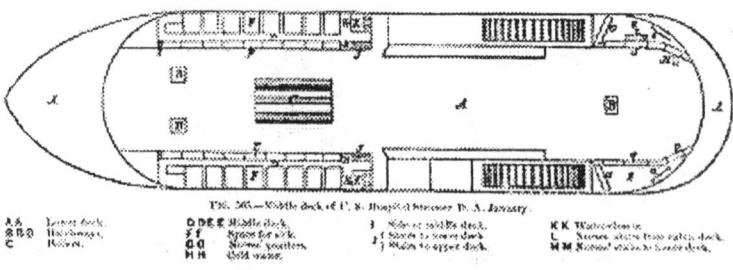

US Hospital Steamer D. A. January
From *Medical and Surgical History of the War of the Rebellion*

Flag of the 2nd Alabama Reserves/63rd Alabama Infantry CSA
Alabama Department of Archives and History

The 2nd Alabama flag is in the collection of Alabama Department of Archives and History, Montgomery, Alabama. Their records report that it was manufactured in Mobile, Alabama, by either Jackson O. Belknap or James A. Cameron sometime before the regiment changed it's designation to the 63rd Alabama Infantry. The Department records indicate that the flag was captured at Blakeley on April 9, 1865, by **Sgt. George F. Rebman** of Co. B, 119 Illinois Infantry. He received the Congressional Medal of Honor for his part in the Battle of Blakeley.